THE JOHN BIRCH SOCIETY

Its History Recounted By Someone Who Was There

© Copyright 2018 John F. McManus; Overview Productions
All rights reserved

Published by Overview Productions
in Association With The John Birch Society

P.O. Box 3076
Wakefield, MA 01880

Cover Design by Joseph W. Kelly

Library of Congress Catalog Card Number: 2018946413

Hard Cover:
ISBN 978-0-692-13296-8

Printed and Manufactured in the United States of America

THE
JOHN BIRCH
SOCIETY

Its History Recounted By Someone Who Was There

By
John F. McManus

Dedication

• To the memory of Robert Welch who never held back from championing the country into which he was born, or from baring the truths about America's foreign and domestic enemies.

• To the many, many thousands of John Birch Society members whom I met over past decades while traveling into all fifty states during my years of service to the organization.

• To several proofreaders whose sharp eyes and knowledge of the English language improved the readability of this book.

• And to Mary, my wonderful wife of more than sixty years, and to our four children and their spouses, all of whom always understood and accepted my frequent absences from home as I sought to preserve freedom and defeat a well-entrenched conspiracy seeking totalitarian rule over all of mankind.

Table of Contents

Prologue 1
Preface. 3
A Chapter Before the First: Robert Welch's Creation. 11
Chapter 1: Welch's Ambitious Undertaking 19
Chapter 2: Making Candy and Spreading Patriotism 23
Chapter 3: Political Loss Teaches a Hard Lesson 27
Chapter 4: Plans To Launch JBS Crusade 31
Chapter 5: "Something Worthwhile To Say" 35
Chapter 6: Society Launched, December 1958 39
Chapter 7: Education Combined With Action 45
Chapter 8: Combating the Nation's Problems 49
Chapter 9: Gaining Members and Forming Chapters. 53
Chapter 10: An Eventful First Year. 57
Chapter 11: 1960: Gaining Strength 65
Chapter 12: Welch's Long Letter About Eisenhower 71
Chapter 13: JBS and Welch Targeted 75
Chapter 14: The Politician Published and Boycotted 79
Chapter 15: Attacks Stimulate Growth .85
Chapter 16: Impeach the Chief Justice? .93
Chapter 17: Pleading To Be Investigated 97
Chapter 18: Smears From Many; Plaudits From Some 103
Chapter 19: American Opinion Helps the Cause 109
Chapter 20: "One Dozen Candles" Published 113
Chapter 21: Stepped Up Attacks Spur More Growth 117
Chapter 22: 1963: Plenty of Activity 125
Chapter 23: 1964: "None Care Call It Treason" 145
Chapter 24: 1964 Cont'd: The Goldwater Year 151
Chapter 25: 1965: Civil Rights Revolution 159
Chapter 26: 1965 Cont'd: Buckley's Dishonesty 165
Chapter 27: 1966: Chief Victory – Staying Alive. 171
Chapter 28: 1967: Conspiracy Above Communism 179
Chapter 29: 1968: Vietnam War; Council Defection 189
Chapter 30: 1989: MOTOREDE and Culture War 197

Chapter 31: 1970: JBS Members Win Elections. 205
Chapter 32: 1971: Overview Of Our World Filmstrip 213
Chapter 33: 1972: None Dare Call It Conspiracy 217
Chapter 34: 1973: Birch Log and Alan Stang Report 221
Chapter 35: 1974: McDonald Wins Election 225
Chapter 36: 1975: Ford Foundation's Subversion 231
Chapter 37: 1976: TRIM Shakes Up Congress .237
Chapter 38: 1977: Prof. Quigley's Revelations .241
Chapter 39: 1978: Exposing SIECUS and Sex-Ed 247
Chapter 40: 1979: The Insiders Filmstrip 251
Chapter 41: 1980: Left-wing Senators Exposed .267
Chapter 42: 1981: Reagan Doesn't Deliver 273
Chapter 43: 1982: ERA Suffers Deserved Defeat 277
Chapter 44: 1983: Frail Welch Steps Aside 283
Chapter 45: 1983 Continued: McDonald Aboard KAL007 289
Chapter 46: 1984: Barker Named CEO 295
Chapter 47: 1985-86: Financial Woes; Armour CEO 301
Chapter 48: 1987-88: Protecting the Constitution 307
Chapter 49: 1989: Move To Appleton; Bubolz CEO 313
Chapter 50: 1990: Bogus Environmentalism 317
Chapter 51: 1991: New Leadership Team 321
Chapter 52: 1992: Saying No To UN Army 327
Chapter 53: 1993: C-SPAN Helps JBS Cause 331
Chapter 54: 1994: Countering Wild Rumors 335
Chapter 55: 1995: Gingrich Exposed; New Books 339
Chapter 56: 1996: "Conspiracy" Targeted In TNA 345
Chapter 57: 1997: Clinton Impeached But Survives 349
Chapter 58: 1998: Open House at Headquarters 357
Chapter 59: 1999: "Get US Out" Campaign Grows 361
Chapter 60: 2000: JBS Never Worried About Y2K 365
Chapter 61: 2001: Twentieth Century Heroes Published 371
Chapter 62: 2002: New Book Exposes Buckley 375
Chapter 63: 2003: Gay Marriage Opposed 379
Chapter 64: 2004: Saying Loud NO to FTAA 383
Chapter 65: 2005: Change in JBS Leadership 387

Chapter 66: 2006: CFR Leader Trashes Sovereignty 393
Chapter 67: 2007: Neoconservatism Exposed 399
Chapter 68: 2008: EU Wants a New Tower of Babel 403
Chapter 69: 2009: Obama Adds Revolutionary To Court. 411
Chapter 70: 2010: Fidel Praises Obamacare. 419
Chapter 71: 2011: JBS Exhibits at CPAC. 427
Chapter 72: 2012: Exposing the SPLC. 433
Chapter 73: 2013: Internet Traffic Soars. 441
Chapter 74: 2014: Beware Entangling Alliances 449
Chapter 75: 2015: Overview In Spanish. 455
Afterword: Becoming President Emeritus 459
Appendix: Who Was John Birch?. 463
Index 467
Books 471

About the Author

John F. McManus was born in Brooklyn, New York, on January 24, 1935. He attended Catholic grade and high schools in Brooklyn before the family relocated elsewhere in 1956. Awarded an NROTC scholarship to attend college, he chose Holy Cross College in Worcester, Massachusetts, for continuing his studies. During the second half of his four years at Holy Cross, he chose the option of earning a commission in the U.S. Marine Corps rather than in the U.S. Navy.

He graduated from Holy Cross in 1957 with a B.S. degree in physics and a commission as a lieutenant in the USMC. He married Mary Helen O'Reilly of Boston in the fall of 1957 and they raised four children. In 1958, his Marine detachment aboard a navy vessel in the Mediterranean Sea was sent into Lebanon to support the Lebanese government in the midst of that nation's leftist-created civil turmoil.

In 1960, he parted honorably as an active duty officer in the USMC and accepted a position as an electronics engineer with a Massachusetts firm producing transistors. This was the era when the manufacture of "silicon chips" began its eventual dominance in the field of electronics.

His constant study of history and current events led him to investigate The John Birch Society in the early 1960s. After satisfying himself that the Society's was a complete opposite of the image created by prominent Americans and the mass media, he joined the organization as a local member in 1964. The Society hired him in 1966 as its field Coordinator for five New England states. He earned promotion in 1968 to the Society's staff at its Belmont, Massachusetts, headquarters. In this post, he helped to manage the Society's Speakers Bureau and ad hoc committee programs.

His steady work as a writer and speaker led JBS Founder Robert Welch to appoint him the organization's National Public Relations Director in 1973. He immediately began writing a weekly Birch Log column that soon appeared in over 100 small U.S. newspapers and also served as a popular handout among members. In 1991, he was named the Society's President while continuing as its Public Relations Director.

The author of six books (noted elsewhere) and dozens of filmstrip and video programs, his versatility always proved a great asset to the Society's efforts. In 2016, after serving as a member of the organization's staff for 50 years, he accepted a diminished role and became President Emeritus. He continues contributing to the Society's work by writing, speaking and submitting to interviews.

Prologue

The original plan for this book was to present a history of The John Birch Society. But as is well known by most readers of history books, such a volume customarily makes for dull reading. What I experienced during my 50-plus years with the Society, much of the time at its very core, turned out to be anything but dull.

Therefore, instead of only listing events and dates, I decided (with promptings from a select few who had read my initial manuscript) to convert what I had already written into a chronicle featuring my own personal involvement and experiences. Many one-on-one exchanges with Robert Welch, the man who launched the Society, will now appear. He became almost a second father to me – supplying counsel, directing me to books I should read, encouraging, explaining, and certainly correcting me when the need arose. The years I spent as one of his trusted aides within the Society's inner circle turned out to be an unusual honor and also a source of real satisfaction. I knew I was making a contribution in the battle for freedom. Having altered the original approach to telling this story, I decided to discard the phrase "this writer" and use first person pronouns "I" and "me."

My involvement with the Society began in the early 1960s with my downright skepticism about the organization. Far from becoming a member, I had been persuaded by others – William F. Buckley, Jr. in particular – that the John Birch Society was more of a problem than a solution to America's woes. How that changed is discussed in these pages. By late 1964, I had completely shed my skepticism and joined the organization as a local member. One year later, I became a chapter leader and then a section leader overseeing the efforts of several chapters. In 1966, I left a promising career as an electronics engineer and accepted a full-time staff position with the organization. My first assignment saw me as the Society's field coordinator for five New England states.

After two years helping members build chapters in New England, I was surprised when I was assigned to a staff position at JBS headquarters. My new role had me working alongside Wallis W. "Chip" Wood in the management of the increasingly successful ad hoc committee programs and speakers bureau. Then, in 1973 when a vacancy arose, Robert Welch named me the Society's National Director of Public Relations. I was now the organization's chief spokesman with the mass media and the go-to man for the general public. In that post, I soon became known nationally as the public face of the Society, so recognized by numerous mass media personalities and by the organization's members. It was while serving in this post that I spent many hours with Mr. Welch until he passed away in 1985.

Named President in 1991 (there was always a CEO above me), I had already helped to guide three of Welch's successors who readily accepted my input about the Society's needs. I had already found that many field staff individuals, headquarters personnel, and members from coast to coast were coming to me both for guidance about Society positions and about national and international matters. I made a practice of spending time with all in the course of sharing perspective about the deeply entrenched enemies of freedom we were seeking to expose.

But I'm getting ahead of the inside look promised in this book's title. So let me back up and begin to relate how The John Birch Society came to be, what it seeks to accomplish, its numerous successes and setbacks and, after a reversal of my personal attitude about Robert Welch's creation, the part that I have played during five decades of my involvement before I stepped aside and became President Emeritus on January 1, 2016.

PREFACE

The Society's earliest years were marked by Robert Welch's dramatically successful speaking events throughout the nation. Most of the early members resulted from his laying out America's problems and suggesting the Society as the way to deal with them. Many thousands heard him and significant numbers signed up on the spot. But he couldn't be everywhere. Soon films of his talks were being shown to smaller groups. They produced a further swelling of the ranks.

Over several later decades, postal workers will confirm that The John Birch Society always received a great deal of mail. The daily deliveries included reports from staff and members, orders for materials, news items telling of local activity, clippings rife with assorted attacks on the organization, inquiries about the Society's stance on issues, and more. In recent years however, email has replaced postal mail and the regular piles arriving from postal workers became smaller in size.

The most gratifying mail received during the early years came from individuals who had somehow "discovered" the Society and wanted further information. Many expressed genuine surprise at finding themselves in agreement with stances taken by the organization that was being trashed by much of the nation's media. Having been led to believe that the Society was extreme, or that it justly deserved being labeled racist, anti-Semitic, or loony, these concerned Americans had decided to find out for themselves. They soon learned that the Society had been targeted over several decades by a wave of unjust smearing. Others were delighted to learn there was an organization taking stands they believed needed support. Over many years, floods of letters arrived in the wake of appearances by Society officials on radio or television.

In 1983, for example, I represented the Society in a pair of PBS and C-SPAN interviews. These resulted in 1,600 requests for further information. Later that year, I jousted for three hours with Larry King on his late-night radio program. Over 500 letters arrived at Society headquarters, each seeking more information. Then the December 13, 1983, issue of *USA Today* published a lengthy interview in which I answered questions and explained JBS positions on a number of issues. This kind of exposure led many to become more familiar with the Society, even enlist as members.

In 1993, C-SPAN broadcast one of my speeches in which I focused on President Bill

Clinton's plans to use his office to aid in creation of a "new world order." Part of the annual Griffith Lecture Series at American University, the entire speech and its 30-minute Q&A session aired nationwide several times during the following week. It resulted in more than 1,100 inquiries.

Not all who received the requested introductory information became active members. But, after being contacted by one of the Society's area representatives, or by a local member, many did join. These experiences, and many more just like them, demonstrated that the continuous stream of negativity about the Society issued via various means had never achieved the goal of its purveyors. They hoped that their negative portrayal of the Society and its efforts would destroy the organization. That surely didn't happen.

In early 1991, while still serving as the Society's Public relations director, I submitted to an interview on a Florida radio station. I vividly recall what occurred. The main topic on the mind of most Americans at the time happened to be the recently conducted war in Iraq known as Desert Storm. President George H.W. Bush and practically all media commentators termed the exercise a great victory. But I explained over the airwaves that U.S. forces shouldn't have been called on to defend the America-hating dictator in Kuwait whose small country had just been seized by Saddam Hussein's Iraqi army. Instead, I offered that our nation's military isn't supposed to be the policeman of the world and should be employed only to defend the lives and property of the American people. America wasn't threatened when Iraq invaded Kuwait, I insisted, and I additionally disagreed with President Bush's securing "authorization" from the United Nations to proceed with the U.S. military action. Further, I condemned Mr. Bush's repeated assurances that the operation would contribute significantly to building a UN-led "new world order."

After discussing the matter more thoroughly with the radio show's host, it was time for listeners to call in. The very first caller led off his participation with "I'm angry," and I expected to be given a verbal thrashing, even a condemnation of the Society. But the caller continued,

> I have listened intently to everything this man from the John Birch Society has said and I'm angry because he's the only one saying it and his view makes this whole business understandable for the first time. I'm angry because no one else is saying it and it's extremely important.

Many of the listeners who followed this man obviously agreed and several hundred contacted the Society seeking additional information.

In May 2001, the mailman's daily delivery brought a remarkable communication to the Society's headquarters (now in Wisconsin). It was unusual not only in what it stated, but because of where it had come from – Ireland. Much of its content was later transcribed and placed in the Society's June *Bulletin* for members to savor. In part, the letter from the Irish citizen stated:

> To the *bienpensants* [a European term for politically correct individuals] everywhere, the name of the John Birch Society not improbably conjures up images of died-in-the-wool obscurantists, a danger to themselves and, more importantly, a danger to society.
>
> I have beside me as I write a book review entitled "On America's Protest Fringe" which was published in the *Sunday Times* [London] on May 2, 1968. The book reviewer, a Mr. Walter Allen, proclaimed the John Birch Society to be "more sinister and more mysterious, because of being less obviously motivated [than the Ku Klux Klan]." That, in sum, was the impression that I, too, received in the 1960s and it seemed to me to be so obviously true that I did not bother to question it until very recently.
>
> However, last December, a friend in the United States sent me a copy of a magazine which I did not recall ever having heard of before. The magazine was *The New American* for November 20, 2000. I found it most bracing, eminently sane, and anything but obscurantist, even if its line of thought might not be in accordance with that of the *bienpensants*.
>
> I resolved then to find out more about the magazine and, to that end, frequently consulted its website on the Internet during the course of the subsequent month or so. Everything I found there confirmed the one good opinion I had formed of it from the only copy of it that had ever come into my hands. Moreover, in browsing through that website, I found *The New American* and the John Birch Society belonged to the same "school of thought," the former actually being an associate enterprise of the latter. All of which completely banished – overnight – the impression of the John Birch Society that I had had for over thirty years.
>
> In conclusion, I might suitably summarize the view I have now formed of the John Birch Society by repeating what I have recently written with regard to what I now think of the "American national school thought," that the most authentic – and most intellectually comprehensive and most intellectually profound – expression of the mind of that school most probably is the John Birch

Society and the enterprises associated with it such as *The New American*.

The Society sent this Irish correspondent a letter expressing gratitude for his most welcome thoughts and a package of JBS printed materials.

Experiences such as these have occurred repeatedly throughout the decades. They have frequently led many individuals to abandon the negativity planted in them by the mass media and others. Also, some of the Society's most determined foes have become active members. Gary Allen, a prolific writer for Society publications for many years, wrote a compelling piece about his turnabout from JBS scoffer to JBS member and highly regarded scribe. Earlier, I began my own association with JBS by publicly agreeing with an attack on the Society appearing in a national magazine. (Details about my own reversal from skepticism to activism appear in Chapter 14.) Numerous other Society activists rose from being scoffers, even enemies, to becoming ardent champions of the organization and its message.

But here we are in the second decade of the 21st Century. Mention the John Birch Society to a person not yet 50 years old and the reaction you receive might be a quizzical, "What's that?" Some older Americans will respond with welcome praise for the organization but still not commit to helping in the educational struggle. Others might flinch and ask disdainfully, "Is that still around?" Most, no matter what response they offer, will demonstrate a superficial knowledge of current events, a deficient awareness of the history of their nation, and even an attitude holding that "nothing can be done about anything anyway." Yet, across the land, a growing number of Americans has concluded that things haven't been going very well for their country, or for themselves and their families.

The Society has always pointed to a powerfully situated group of highly educated individuals who do know a great deal about what The John Birch Society says and does. They are seekers of change who want our nation to abandon its remarkable underpinnings, and they are also the Society's foes. And because they know what the Society stands for, what its goals are, and how it operates, these movers and shakers fear its potential to awaken America and steer the nation back on to the course that made it the envy of the world. These are the powerful few who make up what has come to be known as the "Establishment," the perennial wielders of control over our nation's affairs and its mores. From their mighty perches in numerous fields, they have spread an attitude claiming that The John Birch Society possesses extreme views, holds positions outside the realm of reasonableness in a changing world, and even poses a danger to the nation. In short, Establishment luminaries believe The John Birch Society is at least something to avoid –

better still, even to be driven out of existence.

This book has been written to provide an inside look at the Society, a report about the nearly 60-year-old organization formed to protect and preserve the system of limited government and unqualified independence given us by our nation's founders. The Society has accomplished much, and it continues to warn fellow Americans about the enemies of freedom, both external and internal. Along the way, I shall introduce the Society's founder, lay out what he intended for our nation and the world, discuss the many stands the Society has taken, list its accomplishments, hopes and desires, note where it has yet to reach its long-range goals, and discuss why it is feared by some and championed by a growing number. Even more, what follows in these pages shall address the need for some plan, some path the American people can take in order to reverse our country's numerous – and growing – problems. The something so sorely needed happens to be The John Birch Society. And the man who founded it is the someone who chose to do something rather than just grouse about problems.

The Establishment

But who and what is the "Establishment" mentioned above? What are its goals? Who are its members? Does it really shape our nation's policies? Years ago, nationally syndicated columnist Edith Kermit Roosevelt provided an answer to these questions. Referring to the Establishment as a "legitimate Mafia," the granddaughter of President Theodore Roosevelt wrote in December 1961:

> The word "Establishment" is a general term for the power elite in international finance, business, the professions and government, largely from the northeast, who wield most of the power, regardless of who is in the White House…. Yet the power of the Establishment makes itself felt from the professor who seeks a foundation grant, to the candidate for a Cabinet post or a State Department job. It affects the nation's policy in almost every area.
>
> What is the Establishment's viewpoint? Through the Roosevelt, Truman, Eisenhower and Kennedy administrations, its ideology is constant: That the best way to fight Communism is by a One World Socialist state governed by "experts" like themselves. The result has been policies which favor the growth of the superstate, gradual surrender of United States sovereignty to the United Nations, and a steady retreat….

Five years later, famed Georgetown University Professor Carroll Quigley supplied alarming details about this force in his monumental *Tragedy and Hope: The History of the World In Our Time*. His 1,348-page tome told of a secret society begun in 19th Century England whose stated goal sought to "create a world system of financial control in private hands able to dominate the political system of each country and the economy of the world as a whole." Never employing the word "conspiracy" Professor Quigley believed instead that what he described was beneficial for mankind. He explained that this extremely ambitious organization planned to create "Institutes of International Affairs" in various countries. In the United States, wrote Quigley, the main branch of this secret society "is known as the Council on Foreign Relations."

Then in 1993, *Washington Post* columnist Richard Harwood stated his opinion about this same upper-level force and concluded that it amounted to "the nearest thing we have to a ruling establishment in the United States." Pointing almost exclusively to the New York City based Council on Foreign Relations (CFR), Harwood named numerous members who have been presidents, cabinet secretaries, members of Congress, media moguls, and holders of other influential posts. All out of proportion to the organization's small size, it is they, wrote Harwood, who constitute our nation's power base. He summarized their on-going accomplishment: "They do not merely analyze and interpret foreign policy for the United States; they help make it."

This Establishment, led by members of the Council on Foreign Relations, is indeed a group of power-wielding individuals who seek to convert our nation into a mere single branch of a United Nations-led superstate. If this group succeeds in reaching its goal, an array of socialistic agencies and bureaus will govern mankind with unchallenged power. Members of this cabal have long been well aware that The John Birch Society is the leading foe of what they intend. Hence, many smears, distortions, and a host of misinformation have been aimed at it.

In its earliest years, the Society was widely known as a leading foe of communism. Founder Robert Welch gradually introduced information about something above communism, and this "something" is the Establishment. Welch labeled its activists "Insiders." Society members quickly grasped the significance of this force and, helped by an array of pamphlets and books explaining the existence of a "conspiracy above Communism," they began to shower attention on the sophisticated "Insiders" who were using Communism to frighten mankind into accepting their rule over the planet. These same Insiders were busily undermining Welch and his creation, or stimulating others to do so.

Beyond the several tens of thousands who have held membership in The John Birch Society, countless Americans have read a Society pamphlet, viewed Society videos and

DVDs, attended speeches given by the organization's speakers, or tuned into one of its officials during a radio or television interview. If more of these individuals had decided to devote some of their time, talent and energy to combating the threats facing our nation and themselves, our country would be far better off. But the alternative most have chosen amounts to taking the wonders of our nation for granted – and letting someone else deal with problems.

A Chapter Before the First

Robert Welch's Creation

For a beginning, we turn to a long ago warning issued by an American who is known, at least to a small degree, by virtually every one in this nation. This man looked into the future and saw a need for determined watchfulness lest a calamity overwhelm the country.

In 1838, more than two decades before 28-year-old Abraham Lincoln climbed to national prominence and electoral success, he delivered a memorable speech at the Lyceum in Springfield, Illinois. In it, he claimed that an obviously strong and vibrant America should live for many years. Realist that he was, he nevertheless insisted that the United States was a nation that could indeed be destroyed, but only by treachery from within. His thoughts about self-inflicted harm and its potential to bring about our nation's demise hit home with his listeners in the still very young nation. What he said remains worthy of consideration today. The future that seemed full of promise to the man who became America's 16th president twenty-two years later was a bright one indeed. Here is what Abraham Lincoln stated at that long ago gathering in Springfield, Illinois:

> *Shall we expect some transatlantic military giant to step across the ocean and crush us at a blow? Never! All the armies of Europe, Asia and Africa combined, with all the treasure of the earth (our own excepted) in their military chest, with a Bonaparte for a commander, could not by force take a drink from the Ohio or make a track on the Blue Ridge in a trial of a thousand years. At what point then is the approach of danger to be expected? I answer. If it ever reach us, it must spring up among us; it cannot come from abroad. If destruction be our lot, we must ourselves be its author and finisher. As a nation of freemen, we must live through all time or die by suicide.*
> — A. Lincoln, January 27, 1838

Die by suicide? Is that even a remote possibility? If it is, who might be the author of America's destruction? Even more, is America actually on a path leading to its demise? Who is responsible? What can be done to reverse the slide? Where is the United States in the 21st Century?

Even a partially aware American knows our nation is struggling. What most don't know is that America has been victimized, not by any "transatlantic military giant" or some other outside force, but by activists from within who have captured many seats of power and are using their influence to undo the great enterprise begun in Philadelphia in the late 18th Century. These individuals are the "Establishment" noted by Edith Kermit Roosevelt, pointed to by Carroll Quigley, acknowledged by Richard Harwood, and opposed by The John Birch Society. Their aim? Overturn the Declaration of Independence and cast the U.S. Constitution aside. Into that vacuum, they intend to create an all-powerful world government run by them and like-minded allies. In short, as some of the haughty world planners occasionally refer to their nefarious goal: Create a United Nations-led "New World Order."

Calling attention to these individuals and their deeds has set The John Birch Society apart. The Society's constant raising of alarms about numerous issues, and its continuing claim that sinister design exists behind an array of damaging policies and programs, has earned it a flood of slanderous attacks and frequent ridicule. Yet, while many Americans sense that the Society's warnings are on target, most continue to remain uninvolved. That decision amounts to a form of suicide, just as Abraham Lincoln suggested in 1828.

What has gone wrong in America? Consider: One of the chief "self-evident" truths proclaimed in the Declaration of Independence asserts with appropriate boldness: "Men … are endowed by their Creator with certain unalienable Rights." Yet this clearly stated belief that basic rights are God-given has been largely driven from public consciousness. The predictable result? Many now believe government grants rights. What follows that fundamental error is the logical conclusion that rights can therefore be limited or suppressed by government because what government gives, it logically has power to take away. With vital assistance supplied by the nation's academia, mass media, and throngs of left-leaning partisans, government has supplanted God to the degree that the Almighty's very existence can no longer be affirmed in the nation's public schools. Nor can God be mentioned during many public events.

If downgrading the Almighty had been attempted or suggested during the period known as Colonial America, by which we mean the decades leading up to our separation from Great Britain, there would have been instant reprisals. Those who risked everything to form our independent nation would also have taken up arms to put down any downgrading of the place of God in their laws and their culture. Sadly, such a spirit exists in fewer Americans year after year.

A brief survey of current realities follows. Any of these problems, if not dealt with competently, could lead to overturning America's remarkable experiment in liberty. As disturbing as all of these threats truly are, however, each would be a greater problem, and any one of them might well have already become the fatal "destroyer" feared by Lincoln, had there never been a John Birch Society.

After looking at America in the early years of the 21st Century, we present only ten of the many menacing clouds threatening to undo the American dream. Each has become a more ominous threat with each passing year.

1. **Enormous Indebtedness**: The admitted national debt has reached $20 trillion and borrowing from other nations continues. This figure does not include scores of trillions more in unfunded future obligations. U.S. indebtedness, the greatest for any nation in world history, has resulted in heavy borrowing from China whose leaders have never renounced their intention to defeat the United States.

2. **Shrinking Manufacturing Base**: From 20 million manufacturing jobs in the 1980s to 12 million in 2017, the effects of NAFTA and other trade pacts have taken a huge toll. Yet, proposals have been floated to further entangle the U.S. in a number of similar pacts.

3. **Porous Borders**: Somewhere between 10 and 20 million non-citizens have entered the nation illegally and the federal government's constitutional duty to protect the states from invasion has for too long been ignored.

4. **Declining Educational Quality**: Outcome Based Education, Goals 2000, No Child Left Behind, and Race To the Top constitute a parade of failing programs that have succeeded in bringing the world rankings of America's teens to 31st in math, 24th in science, and 21st in reading. (See the 2014 report issued by the Program for International Student Assessment.) Federally imposed Common Core promises to make matters worse.

5. **Misuse of the Military**: U.S. military forces are posted in 130 different nations. For decades, prominent deployments have received authorization for their action from the United Nations or its NATO subsidiary. The constitutional requirement for a congressional declaration of war before sending troops into war has been ignored since 1941. That the U.S. has not won a war since WWII should surprise no realist.

6. **Federal Reserve**: During its full century of existence, the Fed has presided over a shrinking of the dollar's worth from 100 cents to two cents. As the leading producer of inflation, the Fed has long engineered theft of the value of money and should be abolished.

There has never been any constitutional authorization for the Federal Reserve to wield its power over our nation's economic life. Not a government-run body, the Fed has never been audited.

7. **United Nations**: The UN Charter requires all member nations to "accept and carry out" decisions of the Security Council. During the early days of the George W. Bush administration in 2001, Secretary of State Colin Powell obediently announced, "When it comes to our role as a member of the Security Council, we are obviously bound by UN resolutions and we're not trying to modify that." That attitude blows away the restraints contained in the U.S. Constitution. Also, the UN Charter's explicit prohibition against intervention in any nation's domestic affairs is regularly ignored.

8. **Executive Orders**: Thousands of mandates have been created via the stroke of a presidential pen, an obvious violation of the Constitution's very first article granting "all" law-making power solely to Congress. Federal departments, agencies, and bureaus have been given, or have assumed, vast powers that trample on the liberties of every citizen.

9. **Huge Numbers Receiving Government Handouts**: Approximately 47 million individuals receive food stamps (many of these are illegal entrants). Several other welfare programs dole out more billions. When a majority receives government handouts, the noble experiment known as Americanism will become a bygone dream.

10. **Ignoring the Solemn Oath**: If federal officials would honor their oath to abide by the limitations on government power set forth in the U.S. Constitution, the federal government would shrink to 20 percent its size and 20 percent its cost.

Yes, there are problems. Some have received noisy but ineffective attention. None has been dealt with to the degree that it can be described as "solved." The destructiveness lurking in each remains and steadily grows despite the determined efforts of The John Birch Society and other true patriots. But it isn't too late for an alarmed and organized populace to force U.S. leaders to reverse our nation's downward spiral and restore adherence to the principles that made America such an enviable success.

Part of the process of reversing should begin with a comment about America's foundation offered by John Adams, our nation's second president. He stated:

> Our Constitution was made only for a moral and religious people. It is wholly inadequate to the government of any other.

Getting back to America's fundamentals is what a man named Robert Welch sought to accomplish when he launched The John Birch Society in 1958.

The Welch Plan

Imagine, as Robert Welch did, the effectiveness of small but determined groups of citizens armed with indisputable facts who are busily spreading those facts and principle-based perspective within their own communities. These people would share the many lessons of history, the worth of limited government, the importance of morality, and more. Such groups would constitute something new: **an alternative medium of information**. They would break the numbing control possessed by the well entrenched Establishment dominated mainstream media, and by left wing professors, self-serving politicians, liberal clergymen, and others. Their efforts would bring about real change when new candidates – or incumbents who fear being ousted by a better informed populace – ask voters to choose them on Election Day. Almost without exception, candidates have as their main goal simply getting reelected. Awareness of that truism should be a prime motivator for any concerned American.

Obviously, an organized corps such as Welch envisioned would possess great **potential** to have our nation honor its remarkable roots, champion its real heroes, overcome widespread falsehoods, and solve its problems. Many who affiliate with such a movement would happily find themselves part of an effort designed to stop the erosion of liberty. These determined citizens could, indeed, alter the course of history for our nation, even for the world.

As we shall show in the following pages, The John Birch Society was created with such a goal in mind. A little more than a single year after its 1958 formation, well-placed foes discovered its remarkable **potential**. They knew there had never been anything like it. Yes, there had been valiant attempts by newsletter and magazine dispensers, and by orators, book publishers, and single-issue partisans, all of whom were doing their best to spread awareness and ring alarm bells. But there was no well-organized national effort whose adherents were working on a coordinated program, and whose leaders sought only to preserve all that made America great.

When thousands across the nation decided to commit their energy, resources and influence to the Society's program, opponents knew it had to be slowed down, even destroyed. Hence, a withering smear campaign ensued. It wasn't bad judgment, erroneous information, or bumbling leaders that brought on the attacks. It was the Society's **potential** that had to be combated, a potential that has been realized in several campaigns over the years. But, as Society leaders freely admit, there is still plenty of work yet to be done.

When concluding his remarks at the 1958 founding of The John Birch Society, Robert Welch insisted that the nation's downward course could be reversed. "All we must find and build and use to win," he insisted, "is sufficient understanding. Let's create that understanding and build that resistance with everything mortal men can put into the effort." Would creation of understanding do the job? History says yes, and Robert Welch knew history.

The formula he devised has hindered or destroyed various harmful programs intended to serve as building blocks for the "new world order." But the drive toward canceling freedom and destroying our nation's hard-won independence continues.

Countless legitimately frustrated Americans have suffered through truly irritating experiences with elected and appointed leaders. While seeking answers about a government program, or suggesting cancellation of a meddlesome portion of the gigantic bureaucracy, they have been given a well-practiced runaround. Their pleas have been met with empty promises, form letters, and additional frustration. Especially is this true in forums large and small, or in sessions where a high-ranking office holder or government functionary has presided.

Repeatedly, anxious citizens are informed that competent authorities are capably dealing with the nation's latest crisis. Rarely satisfied after being taken on a well-rehearsed waltz around a pressing matter, or when the opportunity arises for a citizen to aim his inquiry straight at the individual at the podium, good people ask: "Look, our country is in trouble. What are you doing about it?" What they usually get in return is more dancing and no satisfaction.

Consider the following largely forgotten summation of what made America such a great country, a thought I have shared with many: "America became great, not because of what government did, but because of what government was prevented from doing by the Constitution." Say that to many of today's Americans, especially the young, and be prepared for glazed-over eyes, haughty objection, or both. Worse still, it's sadly true that most current Americans, even people who are quite proud of having acquired degrees from some prestigious educational institution, have never heard anything like it.

Everyone who has benefited from our nation's remarkable foundations should be working to safeguard or restore what made America so different, so full of freedom and prosperity. But most wouldn't know how or where to begin. How does one repair a structure without awareness of the blueprint that built it? America's blueprint is the U.S. Constitution. Knowledge of its contents is rare. Some Americans even fear retaliation directed at them if they aim serious questions at entrenched holders of power. And millions have been convinced that government alone is equipped to deal with any problem, even if government has been its cause.

In short, "the land of the free and the home of the brave" faces being transformed into a bastion of do-nothing docility. The certain end result is a loss of freedom for the people and the termination of independence for our nation. Activists are indeed working to change America by repeating the follies of history. Most fellow citizens who want only the best for America suffer from abysmal ignorance of basic principles. They have even become tolerant of ever-expanding government power as if there were nothing they could do to stop it or to roll it back. Others have adopted the siren songs of socialists and big government promoters. Some whose awareness hasn't been completely dulled have become afraid, numbed by worry that outspokenness might cost a job, a loss of social standing, even a visit from the Internal Revenue Service. Nevertheless, there are still enough Americans who want to take action to right the ship of state. These are the good citizens who can be heard shouting, "Somebody ought to do something!" Happily, **somebody did do something**, and that's the subject of this book.

I have written what follows with hope for the future. My hope is based on the certainty that there are many more good people than bad, and that a sizable number of today's Americans do want to get involved in reversing the downward course on which the U.S. has been proceeding. Many are primed to participate in a nationwide crusade that champions the uniqueness of our nation, wants its principles back on the pedestal, and sees a need to persuade current leaders, or find new ones, to rebuild what has been torn down. If these would-be activists knew where to turn, where to become effective, and where to commit some of their time, energy and resources, prospects for the future would surely become brighter.

The good news, as stated above, is that somebody did take action. The John Birch Society does exist. That it has been tar-brushed to keep good people away should surprise no one. As noted earlier, some of its very best members rose over time from being misinformed detractors to become proud and active JBS members. These Americans learned that the Society's undeserved negative reputation hadn't been earned because its leaders were knaves or incompetents. They also found that unfair blackening of reputations has been the fate of numerous others throughout history. But no group in America, they further discovered, has experienced the ongoing assault the Society has been forced to withstand.

Consequently, many who really want to take part in rebuilding and preserving what was created in years past have remained on the sidelines. They may have spent some time and effort with one or more of the quick-fix groups or the big-promise-but-never-deliver organizations that regularly arise and accomplish little. They may have placed great hope while working in one or more of the big-promising but non-delivering blind alleys that, in all likelihood, were deliberately created by our nation's domestic and foreign enemies. Or, they may have been among the many good Americans who listened to appealing rhetoric from office holders or aspiring political newcomers and thought well enough of their many promises to believe that positive change would indeed occur. But failure to follow up in order to ensure that subsequent performance matched appealing rhetoric has far too often seen promises never kept, expectations never realized, and frustration taking over.

Our book is an attempt to familiarize Americans with a man named Robert Welch and The John Birch Society he founded. The solidly built and highly experienced Society is an enterprise that could, with sufficient numbers and the added strength they would bring, put America back on the track that earned it more respect and generated more prosperity than any other nation in history.

Who was Robert Welch? What led him to form the Society? What success has it achieved? How did it become controversial? What solutions does the organization offer to counter real problems? These and other questions are answered and the Society's remarkable history is recounted in the pages ahead. (A brief history of the man named John Birch, the individual whose exemplary life and heroic deeds were chosen as the symbol for the organization, appears in the Appendix.)

Chapter 1
Welch's Ambitious Undertaking

Until Robert Welch is fully known, he may well be the Unknown Soldier of our time. But in the time to come, if there is to be a future and a history for the United States of America, Robert Welch will be revered, as the Unknown Soldier should be, with a shrine and an undying flame.
— G. Edward Griffin, 1975

A book about the John Birch Society certainly has to focus attention on the man who founded it and guided it until he passed into eternity on January 6, 1985. Those who knew Welch – through business contacts, shared concerns about America, voluminous correspondence, or membership in the Society he formed – knew well that he possessed a formidable intellect, had a prodigious knowledge of history, maintained a great love for his country, and brought an unfailing determination to deal with causes he felt were important.

In 1975, veteran Society staff official G. Edward Griffin authored the only biography of the Birch Society's Founder. *The Life and Words of Robert Welch* tells more about the man than we intend here. But we gratefully draw from its pages some interesting and revealing facts while adding some of what we learned through our own years of working alongside the man.

Born on December 1, 1899 in a small farming community in North Carolina's Perquimans County, Robert Henry Winborne Welch, Junior, gave early indication of unique ability. When only two, he learned to read and, before his third birthday, he was devouring children's books entirely on his own. Griffin tells of his rapid progression into other fields:

He knew his multiplication tables by the time he was four. He had become proficient in elementary algebra at the age of six. At seven, he began the study of Latin…. During the summer when he was seven years old, he had read on his own initiative (although undoubtedly with encouragement from his mother) all nine volumes of Ridpath's History of the World.

Carefully and capably guided by his mother, a college graduate and former teacher, young Robert soon gave evidence of a need for formal schooling. But the closest high school happened to be in Elizabeth City, ten miles from the Welch farm and home. Sending him there required convincing the school's principal that enrolling a ten-year-old in secondary education would be a wise move – both for the boy and his schoolmates. So the school principal tested young Robert and discovered not only that the aspiring entrant possessed extraordinary knowledge in the fields of math, history, Latin and English, but also that he belonged in the school's junior year! For the next two academic years, therefore, Robert Welch became the remarkably young high school student who stayed four nights each week at a hotel only blocks away from the school. Every Monday morning, the family transported their prodigy to Elizabeth City by horse and buggy, and then retrieved him every Friday afternoon.

At the ripe old age of 12, Welch graduated from that high school with numerous honors and moved on to the University of North Carolina. There he developed a great love of chess, even frequently challenging and defeating faculty members while still being dutifully attentive to his studies. The four years at UNC flew by and he graduated with honors. Next, he won appointment to the U.S. Naval Academy, arriving there in 1917 just as the U.S. deepened its involvement in Europe's "Great War." At the Academy, he earned the nickname "Savvy" which was a complimentary moniker given by grateful classmates whom he tutored even though each was several years his senior. It was their way of saying thanks for the help that enabled them to gain passing grades in mathematics and language courses.

After two very successful years at Annapolis, and with the European War mercifully over, Welch resigned honorably from the Academy. Then 19 years old and having already decided to enter the business world, he felt the need for some additional schooling and sought entrance to Harvard University's law school. After all, he reasoned, much of the business world could expect to become embroiled in legal matters and he wanted to be prepared. Which law school? Everyone knew that Harvard University had the best reputation, so that's where he wanted to be. His acceptance won, he hurried off to Massachusetts in the Fall of 1919 for the three-year course.

Needing some income while attending law school, he spent many hours composing light-hearted poetry that earned him a few dollars each time something he wrote appeared in one of the area's publications. He added more to his personal coffers by tutoring undergraduates during evenings and weekends. On a memorable visit to nearby Wellesley College, he met and soon fell in love with one of its students, Ohio native Marian Probert. They would marry in 1922 as soon as she had earned her degree.

In 1921, during his third year at Harvard, Welch found himself repeatedly arguing with Professor Felix Frankfurter, the instructor of a course in labor law. The eventual Supreme Court Justice repeatedly insisted that management and labor were – and always would be – fundamental enemies, a concept Welch found completely intolerable. He believed, and frequently interrupted class to tell his professor and 300 classmates, that labor and management were two arms of the same productive body and were certainly not foes. When he concluded that his frequent challenges were getting him nowhere, Welch, who never intended to practice law anyway but wanted to learn its intricacies, walked out of Harvard in the middle of his third year and turned his attention to earning a living.

Having already decided to be a manufacturer, he now had to decide what to make. After much study, he concluded it should be something that would be consumed almost immediately with such satisfaction that the user would return to purchase more. Plenty of thought went into discovering what that product might be. It certainly couldn't be anything requiring much start-up money because he had next to none. After considering and quickly discarding numerous possibilities, he settled on candy. Robert Welch then began a near lifetime of making and marketing candy. Eventually teaming up with younger brother James, the two built the very successful James O. Welch Company candy manufacturing enterprise based in Cambridge, Massachusetts.

Chapter 2
Making Candy and Spreading Patriotism

The 1930s found Welch deeply immersed in business as the sales and advertising manager of the James O. Welch Candy Company, now a nationwide success. And he was also raising a family with his loving wife and two sons. But he never ignored the responsibilities of citizenship. Soon after President Franklin Delano Roosevelt launched the New Deal with its dramatic increases in the size and power of government, Welch composed a short essay entitled "A Weight on My Shoulders." In it, he expressed sharp disagreement with the way the nation was being led even while indicating his intense admiration for his beloved country. The excerpt given below amounts to a glimpse of the kind of thinking that would lead him down a path toward creation of The John Birch Society. He wrote in 1934:

> The glory that is passing in the America that I was born in; that was given to me by courageous and far-seeing men, many of whom died for that purpose; that I grew up in, went to school in, and loved more every year as I came to understand what a miraculous achievement it was as compared with any other social group at any place or any time in the history of the world; … my America is being made over into a carbon copy of thousands of despotisms that have gone before.

From those early days when he was marketing candy, to his years at the helm of the Society, he would repeat that assessment on many occasions. He loved his country and greatly admired its creators. But he surely didn't like what was being done to it.

In 1940, he wrote a satirical book entitled *Lost Island*. It told of a colony of industrious ants that managed to take control of the world about them – including some humans. He likened the dominating grip achieved by the ants to the determined efforts of the

Roosevelt led bureaucracy to have government gain similar control over the American people. *Lost Island* was about to be published as a small counterweight to the Roosevelt New Deal just as America found itself in World War II. Sensing that it would have been wrong to criticize the President while the nation was at war, he placed the manuscript on a shelf where it proceeded to gather dust. It has never been published.

In 1941, his small *The Road To Salesmanship* book did see publication. Having already visited and traveled with each of the Welch company's hundreds of salesmen in their respective territories, he wanted to leave something permanent for them, something that might assist them in their profession but also help them understand the philosophical underpinnings of the free enterprise system. A portion of that understanding pointed to the contrast between America's "million salesmen moving the too much" and the certain consequence of socialism where "a million ration clerks and bureaucrats were apportioning the too little."

Welch also became a leader of the National Confectioners Association, later earning the group's coveted "Kettle Award" at one of its annual national conventions. He likewise affiliated with and took a leadership role in the larger and more prestigious National Association of Manufacturers (NAM). Numerous men he met within the NAM during his seven years as a board member became close friends and regular correspondents. During those years, he undertook the task of persuading NAM's leaders that parents, not the government, possessed the ultimate authority over the education of their children. He then supervised publication of an NAM study pointing out the important role of parents – and their duty to their offspring. Later, several top leaders of the NAM would be among the first members of The John Birch Society.

Never content with involvement only in business-related endeavors, he became a member of the school committee in his home community of Belmont, Massachusetts, a director of a local bank, a member of the Chamber of Commerce in both Boston and Cambridge, a national councilor of the U.S. Chamber of Commerce, and a board member of the charitable United Prison Association of Massachusetts. In addition to all this extra effort, he always found time for extensive correspondence.

During the World War II years, he also wrote *The Romance of Education*, a 290-page book extolling the wisdom of continuing to learn for the sheer joy of doing so. In manuscript form, it too remained forgotten on a dusty shelf for almost three decades. In the early 1970s, while we two were discussing something of then-current importance, I summarized something Welch had just said with, "Of course, knowledge is the discovery of ignorance." He immediately asked me to repeat that small sentence, wrote its six words on the pad he always kept within easy reach, and responded with a smile. "I wrote an entire book about education some years ago," he remarked, "and it took you only six words to say what took me hundreds of pages to write." At which point, I asked the "boss" if I might borrow the manuscript. Borrow it I did and, after reading it and sharing it with my wife, I pleaded that it be published for others to enjoy and reap the benefit of its valuable message.

That plea led to the 1973 publication of *The Romance of Education* containing Welch's thoughts about the joy of appreciating language, history, poetry, mathematics, and education itself. The very thought I so casually uttered many months before could be found in Welch's summation: "In simple truth, education is merely a process of finding out, ever more clearly and intelligently, how little we know."

But we have jumped ahead and must return to the World War II years when the Welch brothers managed to keep their company humming even though chocolate and sugar, the two main ingredients in their products, became scarce – and even though Robert ventured into politics.

Chapter 3
Political Loss Teaches a Hard Lesson

The war years (1941-1945) found James and Robert feverishly scouring the earth for their company's needs. Still, Robert's concern about the downward path on which he saw the country traveling accelerated. He would often note that the two most certain consequences of war befalling any nation were more government and moral decline. He believed that minimizing those consequences was essential.

More government was indeed being fastened on America. But Welch knew that a similar scourge had grown even more oppressive in England. In 1946, only a year after the final shots in World War II had been fired and some amount of normalcy had returned, he availed himself of a two-week vacation to England in order to see firsthand what the ruling socialist Labor Party had done to America's chief ally. With help from some English friends, he discovered that government had not only increased, but that its growth greatly exceeded what might have been expected even as a consequence of being at war. Much of the ballooning, he found, resulted from deliberate actions traceable to the efforts of a powerful few. In other words, he began to suspect the presence of hidden efforts driving Great Britain toward totalitarianism. It was the work of a conspiracy, he concluded, adding that a well-situated clique had gained a strong toehold in the country.

After returning to America, he saw evidence at home that similar wartime growth of government hadn't all been canceled even though most of it could no longer be remotely justified. For instance, diminished personal freedoms such as rationing of consumer goods should have been abolished but were kept in place – at least for a time. Some government agencies built during the war years weren't closed down as they should have been. And the beginning of a reliance on the United Nations (launched in mid-1945) had given evidence that it intended to erode our nation's hard-won independence. His concerns about where America was being taken escalated. A return to England two years later supplied confirmation of his earlier assessment. And visits to Paris and Brussels on that trip showed similar growth of government in France and Belgium. Ed Griffin relates that in 1949, Welch embarked on a lengthy fact-finding trip that took him completely around the world. Stops in a chronological order included Turkey, Lebanon, Syria, Iraq, India, Thailand, and the Philippines before returning to the U.S.

To inject a bit of levity into his serious discussions and speeches – something he often did – Welch frequently referred to an incident he termed "The Perfect Squelch" aimed at him during his 1949 stop in the Philippines. He even retold the story in a footnote found in the Society's *Blue Book*. In his words, here is what occurred:

> In Manila, in 1949, I had to spend a whole day getting a certificate from some government bureau, showing that I did not owe the Republic of the Philippines any income taxes before I would be allowed to board my plane for departure. When I got back to the Manila Hotel I was mad and went up to the Pan American Airlines counter to have somebody on whom to let off steam.
>
> "It just doesn't make sense," I said to the very clean-cut, well-groomed, friendly – and smart – young Filipino behind the counter. "I have been in the Philippines only a few days, strictly as a tourist, personally paying all of my expenses. I haven't engaged in any business, and there is no way I could possibly owe the government of the Philippines any income tax, if I had tried. The regulation is idiotic.
>
> "Yes, sir," he said with a smile. "I thoroughly agree with you, sir. That's one regulation of the United States government which I don't think we should have copied when we went into the government business ourselves."

The immediate post-war years also saw Welch seizing opportunities to provide his thoughts to audiences large and small. In January 1946, the League of Women Voters in nearby Brookline, Massachusetts, gave him precisely what he wished for. For that group, he eagerly targeted the folly and destructiveness of government-imposed price controls. Any Libertarian of that era, and certainly any one holding its views today, would delight in perusing Welch's condemnation of the horrors of "collectivism" (another name for socialism). Other opportunities to speak followed and, in each of his talks during the next few years, he made no reference to any conspiratorial design behind policies and programs that were harming the nation and impacting the American people.

However, as Griffin explained, Welch began gradually to point out one of history's sure lessons – that nations and civilizations rise from infancy to vibrancy and then gradually disintegrate over a span of many hundreds of years. But he would insist that America was still very young, and our nation possessed great promise that would surely blossom far more beneficially as it reached adulthood. The United States, he contended, should have many more centuries of prosperity and overall success. But, he lamented, it was already beginning to fade because an internal enemy was undermining it. These thoughts became a major part of the presentation he gave to the 11 friends who joined him at the founding of the Society a few years later.

In September 1949, he ventured into the political world by announcing his candidacy for the Republican nomination for the admittedly minor post of Lieutenant Governor of Massachusetts. His hope that it might be a springboard for higher political office was no secret. A primary election to select the GOP's candidate wouldn't take place for a full year and, soon, there were five other candidates competing for the same nomination. When the votes were finally counted in the fall of 1950, Welch came in second. It was a respectable showing for a political novice, but it was still a defeat.

While campaigning throughout the state, he won many new friends but he also made an important discovery. He learned to his dismay that awareness among the general public about the fundamentals of good government and the marvelous system created by our nation's founders was almost non-existent. As much as he had initially thought that gaining even the secondary political office of lieutenant governor would be a good start to begin stemming the rising tide of government growth, he sensed that a broad-based educational campaign reaching many — and not just during political races — was sorely needed before political victories could be achieved.

Griffin noted that, in a July 1950 letter analyzing the tactics of his political foes, Welch concluded that the way they had been conducting their campaigns against him suggested some sort of conspiracy. Welch's biographer quoted his subject's attitude: "The forces on the socialist side amount to a vast conspiracy to change our political and economic system," said Welch. He had seen his adversaries employing a host of reprehensible tactics such as calling businessmen crooks, bribing farmers with their own money, infiltrating labor unions, discrediting the medical profession, and attacking virtually every segment of the population with smear and innuendo. And they were doing so, he claimed, in a well-organized manner. His inescapable conclusion was that he had faced a conspiracy, something that couldn't be fought with mere ideological arguments. Although he hadn't yet abandoned all hopes for political office and for politics in general, he started moving away from traditional political endeavors as evidenced in the post-campaign thank you letter he sent to his many supporters. It emphatically stated: "So far as I am concerned, this crusade has just started."

Chapter 4
Plans To Launch JBS Crusade

Early in 1951, Welch started local educational committees in several Massachusetts communities. These were actually forerunners of what would become chapters of The John Birch Society. He also found time to serve diligently as a member of the Belmont School Committee. And he was still working full-time as the vice president at the increasingly successful Welch Candy Company. Serious fatigue finally caught up with him and forced him to back away from the network of local committees he so dearly wanted to build. The dawn of 1952 then found him running, not for a political post, but for a place as a delegate supporting the presidential candidacy of Ohio Senator Robert Taft at the forthcoming Republican National Convention.

He had been delivering a speech entitled "Acheson and MacArthur" when President Truman fired General MacArthur on April 11, 1951. The general had led the U.S. forces to victory in Korea, freeing both South and North Korea of totalitarian (communist) rule. But huge numbers of Chinese Communist forces then stormed into North Korea from Manchuria, and MacArthur learned that his plan to repel them was denied by superiors in Washington. Because he responded to an inquiry about the situation from Speaker of the House Joseph Martin (R-Mass.), President Truman deemed him untrustworthy and relieved him of command. He returned home where he was greeted by huge ticker tape parades and deep gratitude.

The president's action regarding MacArthur increased Welch's suspicions about our own government's leaders. He gathered evidence to support his claim that Washington was overrun by disloyal Communist infiltrators, many of whom he had already named in the aforementioned speech. His presentation startled an audience in Portland, Maine, and had a similar effect on listeners in New Bedford, Massachusetts. Many who heard him immediately wanted to share Welch's thoughts with others. Their pleas led to completion of a manuscript that became his 1952 book *May God Forgive Us*.

Forgive us for what? Welch answered: For delivering China into the hands of Communist Mao Tse-tung; for betraying America's real ally, the Nationalist Chinese and their leader Chiang Kai-shek; for firing General MacArthur whose only real "crime" was his desire to end the war in Korea by winning it; and for allowing a swarm of Communists to be serving in important government posts where they formulated U.S. policy. Communists he named were Alger Hiss, Maxwell Stewart, Lauchlin Currie, Owen Lattimore, Agnes Smedley, John Carter Vincent, and Frederick Vanderbilt Field. Subsequent investigations conducted by appropriate congressional panels confirmed the Communist label Welch attached to these and numerous other individuals. The book sold 200,000 copies in 1952 alone and was later republished with additional information in 1972 under the newer title *Again, May God Forgive Us*.

While assembling facts and perspective for his speeches and books, Welch became more solidly convinced that the United States was the most important target of a worldwide conspiracy. During the summer of 1955, he ventured forth on more fact-finding trips, first to Korea, Japan, Taiwan and Hong Kong, and later to Portugal, France, Germany, England and Greece. In the aforementioned Welch biography, Griffin pointed out that, although Welch was exposing Communists, he knew their ultimate goal was socialism, something all Americans should have figured out by simply realizing that the full name of the USSR was always the Union of Soviet **Socialist** Republics.

After several days in Japan, he was warmly welcomed in South Korea where he began a long-standing friendship with South Korea's President Syngman Rhee. The war that had engulfed Korea had by 1953 been downgraded to a shaky armistice that could collapse at any time. But President Rhee related to Welch that his nation was threatened by a far different enemy, a horde of Communist diplomats from Eastern Europe and elsewhere. He wanted to expel these troublemakers but found himself unable to do so because, as he claimed, U.S. military personnel acting under directives from Washington were protecting them.

Back in Tokyo, Welch gathered more evidence of Communist designs, and moved on to Taiwan where he spent a great deal of time with Chiang Kai-shek and Madame Chiang. Nationalist Chinese forces had been given back-of-the hand treatment by Washington and eventually fled the mainland for Taiwan (then widely known as Formosa). The exceedingly gracious Madame Chiang was thoroughly familiar with the English language, having earned her college degree in America. She was well able to pass along to her husband what she learned from their American visitor. After hearing the Welch analysis of Communist efforts, including his thoughts about China that confirmed the Generalissimo's own views about subversion emanating from within the United States, the Chinese leader wanted Welch to extend his visit for several more days. But flight arrangements could not be altered. The Free Chinese leader let it be known, however, that he was most pleased to learn that at least some Americans were aware of how the U.S. government was favoring the Communist cause.

Welch took advantage of the time he spent with various world leaders and their aides to inform them of his plans to create an educational organization designed to provide Americans with solid information along with action programs that could combat the steady drift of the United States into communist/socialist hands. After having bared his thoughts in Japan and Taiwan, he met and shared the same perspective with senior members of the Franco government in Spain and then with similarly high placed individuals in Salazar's Portugal. He also spent time with government officials and other prominent individuals in England and France. After he shared his plans for America, all of his listeners encouraged him to proceed. When he visited with Germany's Chancellor Konrad Adenauer, however, Welch received some cautionary advice that became foundational in the formation of The John Birch Society.

Adenauer, known affectionately throughout Germany as "Der Alte," said a citizen-led educational army, unconnected to government and formed to spread reliable information about what government was doing and what was occurring worldwide, would benefit any country. He even lamented that his own nation needed something like it. But he also expressed concern about the religious differences of the American people. These, he felt, could in time fracture any such effort, diminish its effectiveness, or even lead to its destruction. Urging Welch to proceed, he suggested that such a potential roadblock ought to be addressed from the outset in hopes of avoiding its damaging consequences. The German statesman hoped that religious differences of the American people would never become serious enough to keep the American people from working together. Welch agreed and included mention of Adenauer's concern in his eventual construction of the Society. The time for launching the Society grew nearer.

Chapter 5
"Something Worthwhile To Say"

In 1956, Welch began publishing *One Man's Opinion*, a small magazine written almost entirely by him. Its initial issue in February 1956 greeted "Dear Reader" with an explanatory declaration: "Because I believe I have something worthwhile to say, now and then, about what is going on in the world, I am starting a one-man now-and-again magazine in which to say it." The cost for a subscription was set at $5.00, which would get any subscriber six issues. But there wasn't any schedule stating when they might arrive. Readers were advised that a new issue of the magazine would be sent when he found time to produce it. He produced six issues in 1956, and six again in 1957.

Each 32-page issue of *One Man's Opinion* featured Welch's biographical sketch of a political figure he admired, an article written by someone Welch knew and trusted, or a Welch discourse on a topic he considered important. The magazine was spiced with bits of humor and poetry, both of which he loved dearly. Its serious content consisted of laudatory portrayals of such Welch favorites as China's Chiang Kai-shek, California's Republican Senator William Knowland, Ohio's Democrat Governor Frank Lausche, South Korea's Syngman Rhee, and Germany's Konrad Adenauer.

One Man's Opinion also published serialized portions of his lengthy "Appeal to the Liberals." These thoughts constituted Welch's attempt at persuading liberals and others that government action wasn't the best way to deal with every problem. He then requested and published feature articles written by others: former Polish Premier Stanislaw Mikolajczyk, U.S. General Albert C. Wedemeyer, and Medford Evans, PhD. The Evans piece provided a stern warning about the scourge of an escalating national debt at a time when its total was less than $300 billion, not the many trillions currently hanging around the necks of Americans and threatening our nation's very existence.

Addressing an assortment of current issues, *One Man's Opinion* carried Welch's thoughts about the mid-1956 Hungarian Revolt and his claim that Communists had actually stimulated the failed uprising in order to lure anti-Communist opponents into the open where they could be rounded up and dealt with. He supplied commentary about the 1956 closing of the Suez Canal. And he wrote "A Letter To the South" predicting that "formal segregation" would happily be abandoned in time because of the "pressures of enlightened opinion." He counseled that men of good will should be watchful to assure that race-baiting agitators weren't successful in reversing some helpful developments in that area.

In the very first issue of *One Man's Opinion*, Welch addressed the fundamental need for morality as the guide for any personal or governmental action. This was always one of his pet topics. From obscure poet J.A. Froude, he borrowed a line that became one of his favorite watchwords: "Morality sees farther than intellect." He condemned the growing number of fellow Americans who, instead of relying on immutable moral principles, opted for the "smart" thing to do, or the "expedient" path to follow, or the "realistic" course to take instead of the morally sound alternative. Throughout his life, he championed "honor and morality" in government, business, organizations and individuals while also suggesting that readers be on guard against being corrupted by prosperity. To the very best of his ability, Welch always avoided what wasn't morally correct while urging similar conduct among all he was able to reach.

In 1957, Welch resigned his position with the Welch Candy Company in order to spend full time planning the venture that became The John Birch Society. He continued to gather information about what to do and how best to do it by studying other organizations, even some that had recently been created and were either floundering or had already folded. There were lessons gained from the experiences of these groups, one of which showed him that trying to combat government wrongs while accepting any form of government oversight or financial aid was suicidal. He contended that once any organization or person had benefited from government and achieved some goal, or even become a minor nuisance to government or its media allies, restrictions would be created, charges of misconduct would be leveled, nasty adjectives would be attached, and other steps would be taken to put an end to such opposition. He even warned against dreaded intervention by the Internal Revenue Service.

Having gained an appreciation of the troubles experienced by other groups and individuals, he launched The John Birch Society and never sought tax-exempt status. Begun legally as an educational corporation complying with all the laws of Massachusetts, the Society could easily have obtained IRS tax-exempt status. But Welch had already learned that being dependent on favorable IRS status had cost other groups at a critical point when their tax-exempt status was arbitrarily removed. He never wanted the Society to be in that position. Consequently, fund-raising for the organization has always been more difficult than most might have expected.

Even before launching the Society, Welch expanded *One Man's Opinion* and gave it the new name, *American Opinion*. He started inviting others to contribute their thoughts for publication. The February 1958 edition (the first under the new name) contained an amazingly prescient article detailing the untrustworthiness of Vietnam's President Ngo dinh Diem. Its author, America's Hilaire du Berrier, had spent many years in the Far East and knew the area and its prominent citizens as well as any man alive. America's costly efforts during the Vietnam War hadn't begun in earnest but it was safe to say that had du Berrier's background knowledge become the basis of our nation's policy, the eventual costly war in Southeast Asia might have been avoided. In addition, the tremendous loss of American life and treasure in that struggle would never have occurred.

The April issue contained Welch's "Open Letter to Nikita Khrushchev" which informed the Soviet leader that there were, indeed, some in America who understood Moscow's reliance on American material and diplomatic aid, both of which were sustaining the Kremlin and threatening the West. Subsequent issues provided incisive looks at other world leaders and some of their organizations. But what Welch had to say about Fidel Castro in September 1958 should have elevated him to national prominence as a man whose facts and opinions were worthy of consideration by everyone, even those only slightly concerned about Communism.

During the decade leading up to the final months of 1958, the menace of Communism concerned every thinking American. Easter Europe had already fallen to the Soviet Union. And Mao Tse-tung's forces had seized the vast nation of China. The *Guinness Book of Records* would name Mao as history's greatest mass murderer, a deserved assessment. Congressional investigations had unearthed conclusive evidence that the U.S. government had been penetrated by individuals whose loyalty was not to America but to Communism. (See the reports of the House Committee on Un-American Activities and the Senate Internal Security Subcommittee. These two congressional watchdog agencies were abolished in subsequent years.)

Adding to each of these concerns was an ongoing revolution in nearby Cuba. But only *American Opinion* magazine, with its truly small circulation, told its readers that a lifelong Communist named Fidel Castro was seizing this country, only 90 miles from Florida. America's government and mass media were busily presenting Castro as a glorious revolutionary seeking to oppose a corrupt dictator named Fulgencio Batista. But Robert Welch knew better, and he stated clearly and forcefully months before the bearded revolutionary seized control of Cuba: "Now the evidence from Castro's whole past, that he is a Communist carrying out Communist orders and plans, is overwhelming. The evidence from his method of operation is even more so." If Welch, a mere private citizen, knew the truth about Castro, key government personnel favoring the Cuban revolutionary surely knew it as well.

Castro accomplished his takeover of Cuba on January 1, 1959. *American Opinion* immediately published additional hard truths about the Cuban revolutionary's lifetime of efforts on behalf of Communism. Its February 1959 edition informed readers that, when he was a mere 21-year-old, Castro had played a key role in the bloody 1948 Communist uprising in Bogata, Colombia. In the mid-1950s, he had spent time in New York where he received millions to finance his efforts. A few years later, he went to Mexico and consorted with Reds there, then moved back into Cuba in 1956 with fewer than 100 followers. He received a strategically important boost when the U.S. State Department, in March 1958, imposed an embargo on all shipments of arms to the Batista government. Taking control of Cuba then became a simple task with all of the assistance and favorable publicity being supplied by America.

Nowhere else in the United States was the truth about Fidel Castro being published. The Cuban dictator became glorified by the U.S. media as the "George Washington of Cuba" or the "Robin Hood of the Sierra Maestra Mountains." More than two years later, after he had wiped out resistance and solidified control of the island nation, Castro freely admitted that he'd been a Communist during his entire adult life – just as Robert Welch had claimed. *American Opinion's* few readers wondered: If Welch knew about Castro's history, and if government officials were aware of the Cuban revolutionary's Communist career but still helped him to succeed, what else might the publisher of that small-circulation publication know?

Chapter 6
Society Launched, December 1958

In summary, Gentlemen, we are losing, rapidly losing, a cold war in which our freedom, our country, and our very existence are at stake.
- Robert Welch, December 1958

Created in 1958 at the close of Welch's two-day speech in Indianapolis, The John Birch Society would soon spread to all parts of the nation. Indiana's capital city had been Welch's choice for the launching because of its central location for the men who had agreed to hear a "very important message," which was just about all the invitees were told to expect.

The men who committed their time to listen to Welch weren't strangers, either to him or, in most cases, to each other. Each had an awareness of Welch's thinking because of speeches they had heard him deliver, books he had written, correspondence they had shared, and the small *One Man's Opinion* magazine he started in 1956. Nor was the two-day event held over a weekend. The dates chosen by Welch were a Monday and Tuesday, which meant each attendee had to commit valuable working days away from customary pursuits. The 11 who did accept were:

Wm. J. Grede, founder and president of Milwaukee-based Grede Foundries; a former NAM president.

Laurence E. Bunker, (Colonel, U.S. Army, Ret.), a Boston-based attorney who served for six years as an aide to General Douglas MacArthur before returning home to Wellesley, Massachusetts.

T. Coleman Andrews, a Virginian who had served as Commissioner of the Internal Revenue Service before resigning over opposition to the federal income tax.

Ernest G. Swigert, the founder of heavy-equipment manufacturer Hyster Corporation of Portland, Oregon; a former NAM president.

W.B. McMillan, President of Hussmann Refrigerator Company, St. Louis, Missouri;

active member of the NAM.

Fred C. Koch, Founder and President of Rock Island Oil and Refining Company that later became Koch Industries; he would later author the small but popular book *A Businessman Looks at Communism*; active within the NAM.

Revilo P. Oliver, PhD. Professor of Classical Languages and Literature at the University of Illinois.

Louis Ruthenburg, former Chairman of the Board of Servel Corporation of Evansville, Indiana; active member of the NAM.

William R. Kent, a businessman from Milwaukee who was unable to stay for the entire two days. He retained his friendship with Welch and never expressed any differences about the Society's efforts.

Fitzhugh Scott, President of Fitzhugh Scott Architects and Planners, Milwaukee, Wisconsin.

Robert Stoddard, President of Wyman-Gordon Company, Worcester, Massachusetts; Chairman of the Worcester *Telegram & Gazette* newspaper company; board member of the NAM.

In 1957 during the spring of my senior year at Holy Cross College in Worcester, Massachusetts, I received an award during the annual military review. The event featured recognition of several students and a closing parade when all members of the Navy and Air Force ROTC units showed pride in their relationship with our nation's military. At this particular review, I was fortunate to receive the annual Wyman-Gordon Company Award given to the top NROTC graduating senior who had chosen to accept a commission as a lieutenant in the U.S. Marine Corps rather than as an ensign in the U.S. Navy. The award consisted of a Marine Corps officer's ceremonial sword suitably marked with my name and the name of the presenting company.

As was his annual custom, Wyman-Gordon Company President Robert Stoddard made the presentation. Little did Mr. Stoddard or I know that we would meet many times in future years at John Birch Society gatherings. He was one of the eleven at the Society's founding meeting and I became a member and an eventual top official of the organization. I even had the sword at my side when, in full USMC uniform, I married Mary Helen O'Reilly of Boston in October 1957.

Mr. Stoddard's presentation to me was photographed and shown in the Worcester newspaper the next day. The man who took the picture was kind enough to send me a copy in the mail. For many years, the framed photo and the crossed sword and scabbard hung in my office at JBS headquarters in Belmont, Massachusetts. Robert Welch was delighted to learn of the connection between his good friend, Robert Stoddard, and his assistant, then his Public Relations Director. I was further honored when Mr. Stoddard brought his wife from their home in Worcester to see the sword and the photo hanging in a prominent bit of wall space in my office.

What America Faced in the 1950s

Communist activity in America during the 1950s was extensive. Country after country in eastern and central Europe had fallen under Communist control. The 1950-1953 Korean War had wound down to a nerve-wracking 1953 ceasefire, not a victory. More than 30,000 American families were still grieving over the loss of loved ones in that struggle. The Senate Internal Security Subcommittee reported with absolute certainty in its July 30, 1953 report entitled *Interlocking Subversion in Government Departments* that four huge Soviet espionage rings were operating within our country and only two had been exposed. The McCarthy era had many Americans rightly worried about Communist agents and sympathizers within government.

In 1957, the USSR launched a man-made satellite that circled the Earth, a feat sparking genuine concern that the Soviets had surpassed our own nation's technological and military skills. And government's steady growth added to the uneasiness of some while its waste and mismanagement continued to worsen. It was a worrisome time, and even a short look ahead sparked reasons for alarm.

During his 17-hour presentation over December 8-9, 1958, Welch offered ten disconcerting predictions about what the future would hold for the United States and the American people. He ended his look ahead with a well-considered conclusion that "we are losing" both the Cold War and our country. He then proposed "something new," something different yet apt for the times in which he spoke, and something that could indeed restore "sanity to a world gone crazy." He was determined to convert impending defeat into victory.

As anyone who has ever been associated with the Society knew, Welch never did anything in a cursory manner. Hence, he took two full days to present his "Look at the Score" of Communist takeovers of many nations, his plan for the future, some historical lessons, even his glimpse into the future. For his look ahead, we present in condensed form the ten Welch predictions. While each of these forecasts has been shown to be an accurate assessment of what soon did occur, the matters he addressed would likely have led to unchallengeable finalities had there never been the counterforce Welch was launching. In 1958, he predicted:

1. Greatly expanded government spending ... for foreign aid, for every conceivable means of getting rid of ever larger sums of American money – as wastefully as possible.

2. Higher and much higher taxes.

3. An increasingly unbalanced budget, despite the higher taxes.

4. Wild inflation of our currency, leading rapidly toward its complete repudiation.

5. Government control of prices, wages and materials, supposedly to combat inflation.

6. Greatly increased socialistic controls over every operation of our economy and every activity of our daily lives. This is to be accompanied ... by a correspondingly huge increase in the size of our bureaucracy....

7. Far more centralization of power in Washington....

8. The steady advance of federal aid to and control over our educational system....

9. A constant hammering into the American consciousness of the horror of modern warfare, the beauties and absolute necessity of "peace" – peace always on Communist terms....

10. The consequent willingness of the American people to allow the steps of appeasement by our government which amount to piecemeal surrender of the rest of the free world and of the United States itself to the Kremlin-ruled tyranny.

Today, few are aware that President Nixon did impose wage and price controls. These were soon canceled after a storm of protest, much of it generated by future Society members. And while a "Kremlin-ruled tyranny" is no longer a likely development, a tyranny with its headquarters located in the West at the United Nations is steadily being erected. Each of the Welch forecasts was fully or partially on target. Over succeeding years, many who came to know what he stated in 1958 have commented: "He said all of that in 1958? Amazing!" Which is precisely the comment uttered by then-Congressman Ron Paul after he watched an old and grainy film of Welch listing his ten 1958 predictions that was shown during the Society's 50th Anniversary celebration in 2008.

When a friendly columnist writing in the Berkeley (Cal.) *Daily Gazette* learned of the Welch forecast, he wrote to debunk the many widespread and frequently nasty slurs aimed at the JBS Founder. Then, in his August 26, 1971 column headlined "Whatever

Else, Call Him Correct," columnist Mike Culbert presented the ten 1958 Welch predictions and concluded: "Whether he is correct by mistake, correct by coincidence, correct because his monster conspiracy theory is on target, or correct because all that has happened is simply the result of the natural flow of events, this is all of secondary importance to the reality that he is correct." Members of the Society happily copied the Culbert article and distributed it by the thousands across the nation.

However, all who chose to follow Welch and join the Society knew that while information was important, action based on that information was essential. What to do and how to do it had to be accompanied by solid guidance from a trusted leader.

Chapter 7
Education Combined With Action

I know of no safe depository of the ultimate powers of the society but the people themselves; and if we think them not enlightened enough to exercise their control with a wholesome discretion, the remedy is not to take it from them but to inform their discretion by education. This is the true corrective of abuses of constitutional power.

- Thomas Jefferson

A unique undertaking like The John Birch Society didn't come about suddenly. As we have indicated, far from a single middle-of-the-night inspiration, it arose as the culmination of years of hard-earned experience and a diligent study of history. The Society would be a new and more reliable source of what people ought to know, in reality a new medium of information. But it would also produce an action program implemented by the people who possess what can be labeled the potential possessed by a determined few. Not a copy of anything that had gone before, the Society filled a void many knew existed although no one had yet taken the initiative to fill it. Our nation's third President addressed this very problem when he recommended an action program that would enable the people "to exercise their control" over leaders. Any success enjoyed by the new organization would come by supplying needed information to the people with a program designed to have them use what they had learned to effect change. The Welch creation was right in line with the "true corrective" pointed to by Thomas Jefferson.

Welch's citizen-based educational program to bring about an era of "less government, more responsibility, and a better world" (the Society's initial motto) came to life after his several decades of intense thought and study. It became a reality when he delivered his monologue to those friends in Indianapolis. The entire text of his presentation, known as *The Blue Book of The John Birch* Society, is still available for purchase by anyone who wants to know what he proposed.

Welch began his lengthy oration by tracing the considerable progress already achieved by three enemies of both the United States and the rest of mankind. These foes were Communism, collectivism, and loss of faith. His discussion of the Communist threat centered on Soviet dictator Vladimir Lenin's three-step strategy to conquer the world paraphrased and summarized as: first, take Eastern Europe; second, gain control of the masses of Asia; and third, encircle the last bastion of capitalism, the United States, which would not have to be attacked because, as Lenin expected, it would "fall like overripe fruit into our hands."

By 1958 when Welch painted his grim picture of Communist advances, the Moscow-centered scourge had already taken control of Eastern Europe and seized China, Tibet, North Korea, and North Vietnam. Regarding Lenin's claims that there would be no need to attack the U.S. because it would simply fall into communist hands, Welch pointed to the experiences of some who had tried unsuccessfully to spread an alarm. One individual he featured was former U.S. Ambassador to Poland Arthur Bliss Lane who had written of the "deliberate and treasonous betrayal of Poland, by our government, into Soviet hands." In his 1948 book *I Saw Poland Betrayed*, Lane provided irrefutable evidence that supporters of Communism within the U.S. government had gained such tight control over America's diplomatic machinery that they could deliver an entire nation and its people to Soviet dominance. But the book was almost completely ignored by both the press and the nation's intelligentsia. Finding a second-hand copy a few years later had become impossible. Lane, who had sacrificed his entire career by publishing the names, dates, places and events leading to the Soviet conquest of Poland, was himself betrayed when he and his work weren't even challenged. Robert Welch befriended this former diplomat but Lane concluded that his effort had failed, that he and his book had almost never existed. He died broken-hearted before Welch launched The John Birch Society.

Another example of communist power within the U.S. offered by Welch was the saga of Dr. Medford Evans who told of his experiences in his 1953 book *The Secret War for the A-Bomb*. A Yale Ph.D., he had accepted responsibility for security at atomic energy installations. In the course of his work, he discovered that Soviet scientists and technicians hadn't created their own nuclear weapons. Instead, their agents within the U.S. had stolen (or been given) the plans and parts for such a weapon to be reassembled in Russia two years before they were able to construct one themselves. Like the startling truth issued by Ambassador Lane, the Evans book sold only a few copies and was itself ignored. It caused no change in the treasonous activity being conducted within our nation.

Welch presented a list of hideous crimes committed by Communists during the 1936-

1939 Spanish Civil War, and the brutality of communist forces in Algeria, Indonesia and China. He pointed to the savagery of Klimenti Voroshilov, Nikita Khrushchev, Nikolai Bulganin, and other USSR mass murderers. Having already published proof of Fidel Castro's Communist background in his small magazine that each of the men at this founding meeting had seen, Welch merely reminded them that Cuba, where Castro-imposed atrocities were now being perpetrated on innocent people, was only 90 miles from the United States. As he wound up the first part of his presentation, he concluded that "our side" in the war for freedom was losing – not because the Communists were so able and so powerful – but because they were receiving help from their agents and supporters within our own country. A conspiracy, said Welch, was steadily carrying out its evil plans, and it had already piled up numerous successes.

Over the years, many have erroneously characterized The John Birch Society as a one-issue crusade against Communism. But, the Society has always opposed all forms of totalitarianism no matter what name it was using (communism, socialism, Nazism, fascism, tyrannical dictatorship, etc.). All of these were polar opposites of "the humane civilization" Welch knew had been created in America, something he wanted to protect and strengthen.

Shifting gears from the subject of worldwide advances of Communism, Welch's discourse then dwelled on what he termed "the cancer of collectivism," the growth of government that leads to its collapse and invites tyrannical rule. He claimed that ancient Greece and Rome had each fallen because of too much government, but in those cases it took hundreds of years for each to collapse. He insisted that a still vibrant and youthful United States was being prematurely strangled by homegrown socialism and the misguided belief that government alone could – and should – solve all problems and control all activity. Welch claimed that the induced cancer of collectivism had already eaten away at America's vitality and he wanted to reverse the progress it had made.

The third significant problem Welch pointed to was a widespread "loss of faith," not only in God but also with man. He discussed the spread into many churches of a social gospel that was "indistinguishable from advocacy of the welfare state." It was a deliberately manufactured development, he stressed, a scourge that had previously undermined many of history's nations and civilizations. While never promoting any particular religion, he targeted as the most identifiable result of man's dwindling faith "the rise of the amoral man," a creature personified by all Communists who care not a whit for right and wrong but only for self and the cause that could benefit them. He then offered a distinction between the immoral man who might be a worrisome arch criminal yet still had not totally discarded the influence of his conscience and might possibly be steered away from his crimes. The opposite, Welch claimed, was the amoral individual who "has simply wiped out his conscience" and was now motivated solely by unbridled self-promotion. It is the amoral man, he insisted, who "is one of the greatest causes of our constant retreat, and one of the greatest dangers to our survival." Yes, we must stop the Communist advance, he stated, but "we have the equally important longer-range job of ending this mass psychological flight towards amorality; and of restoring convincing reasons for men once again to strive to live up to moral and humanitarian ideals."

    A huge mountain to climb! Yes indeed. And there were other mountains that lay ahead. How to climb them and get others to participate was next.

Chapter 8
Combating the Nation's Problems

The picture Welch had painted in Day 1 of his presentation contained mostly bad news. No one knew that better than he, but he certainly believed it all needed a thorough airing. In *The Blue Book,* or in the many speeches Welch would give over the years, thousands upon thousands would be introduced to his concerns. But what to do about all of this was always presented as well. Having provided a frightening summary of existing reality, Welch turned to the more positive portion of his message on Day 2 when he offered a plan to have the nation reverse course. As part of the solution, he shared numerous insights about what constituted truly good government, the importance of religious faith, and an appreciation of the need for solid organization.

Listing the many tactics he planned to have members of his new organization employ, Welch stressed that all were perfectly legal and unquestionably honorable. Some may indeed have been adopted by Communist organizations that employed fair as well as foul means to achieve their goals. There would be letter-writing campaigns, petitions, book and pamphlet publishing, a magazine, a chain of bookstores functioning also as "reading rooms," a speakers bureau, ad hoc committees, campaigns to accurately expose known Communists and phony allies, and more – all completely open and above board. Community leaders and average citizens would use these methods as ways to create awareness. He would stimulate members to support worthy publications produced by others, patronize the dwindling number of patriotic book publishers, and rejoice that there still were a few radio/television programs dispensing solid information and perspective.

The organization he proposed would be based on religious ideals with no particular religion favored. And, while the Society itself would never nominate, finance or support political candidates at any level, members would be encouraged to get involved in the political process by personally backing their choices of candidates at all levels. Welch had little worry that those he helped to greater awareness would make bad decisions when casting a vote.

Those who joined his organization would function in organized units called chapters located in their communities. He would raise funds to hire a field staff tasked to enlist new members and guide those already enrolled. There would be a headquarters staff to carry out a variety of administrative duties, and a separate group to aid in formulating the JBS agenda. But Welch also insisted on the need for monolithic leadership. Having studied many well-intentioned organizations, most of which had already failed completely or were beset with internal dissension, he saw the need for "dynamic personal leadership." Then he summarized the power of well-entrenched enemies of freedom as follows: "At present we are in the position of trying to defeat a disciplined, well-armed and expertly commandeered army with a collection of debating societies. And it can't be done."

During Welch's study of other organizations, he had learned of infiltration into promising groups by deliberate wreckers such as Klansmen, anti-Semites or other undesirables who caused no end of trouble while blackening the name of the organization. Over the years, there developed a need to dismiss some, but such a step was always taken after careful deliberation and as a last resort. Many who exhibited a leaning toward unsavory attitudes were persuaded away from them, and the Society should be credited for such an accomplishment. Being able to terminate the membership of someone deemed undesirable has always saved the Society from a host of problems including member embarrassment. It also saved the organization from time-consuming and expensive court battles that might have been generated by disgruntled ex-members.

The John Birch Society would not be another well-intentioned group bogged down with internal dissensions. There would be no parliamentary proceedings, debates or reliance on Robert's Rules of Order. Anyone who joined and found himself in serious disagreement with anything the Society was doing or with anything Welch had recommended would be free to refrain from participating in those projects with which they disagreed. Those who chose to leave the organization would be given a refund of any dues paid in advance. The application blank signed by every member noted that membership could be revoked at any time "without the reason being stated" and with an appropriate refund of already paid dues. Welch would set the Society's agenda and there would be no tolerance for anyone using the Society's structure for other ideas or projects.

Suggestions would always be welcome and they eventually came, as he stated, "by the ton." Everyone was expected to be aware that not all ideas, however grandiose and deeply felt, would be adopted. Finally, Welch stated that he expected some criticism because of his insistence on being its sole leader, but he added, "with all of my shortcomings, there wasn't anybody else on the horizon willing to give the whole of their lives to the job with the determination and dedication I would put into it."

Before winding up this portion of his lengthy proposal, Welch offered his thoughts about government. It is necessary, he conceded, though it is "frequently evil." It will always be an enemy of individual freedom, will keep mistakes in place longer than any other organization, will inevitably squeeze out the middle class, and its size is more to be feared than whatever form it takes. Finally, he said, "The increasing quantity of government, in all nations, has constituted the greatest tragedy of the twentieth century."

With this entire preparatory base having been laid, he insisted that an awakened and energized populace could indeed reverse the downward slide into totalitarianism and world government. At the very end of his presentation, he asked the small group before him for their assistance. He assured them that he would proceed even if none chose to be involved. Immediately, St. Louis industrialist W.B. McMillan handed Welch a check and said, "Bob, I guess we're in business." From that day forward, McMillan proudly claimed to be the Society's "first member." Most but not all who were there enthusiastically followed McMillan's lead. None disagreed with what Welch had presented.

So, on December 9, 1958, in the Indianapolis home of the gracious Marguerite Dice, The John Birch Society was born. Miss Dice and Robert Welch had never met before December 1958 but had come to know each other through correspondence. Weeks before the meeting as he was finalizing his presentation, deciding whom to invite, and choosing Indianapolis as the best location, he asked Miss Dice to suggest a suitable location in Indianapolis where the meeting could be held. She responded by offering her home where privacy would be assured and refreshments and luncheon could be served. Also, without making her intention known, she planned to sit outside her own living room and listen to the proceedings. Her offer was gratefully accepted.

After the meeting when each of the invitees had departed for home, Welch stayed over an extra day to gather his papers and to show appreciation to his hostess by taking her to a fine restaurant for dinner. The next day she rode with Welch to the airport. While highly complimentary about all of what she had heard, Miss Dice added her rather blunt conclusion that "it won't work." As recounted by Welch years later, the hostess for his inaugural meeting explained, "I'm sorry to say this but you're wasting your time. Nobody will pay attention. You go into things too deeply. The only way to reach the masses is like this." And she handed Welch a one-sheet flyer crammed with sensationalized information about a current government outrage. "Here is what I recommend," she said. He took the flyer (an eyesore to be sure), thanked her, and commented with brief and utmost politeness that he appreciated her idea but disagreed with it. The two continued their friendship.

As all members of the Society would eventually learn, Welch always abhorred the one-sheet flyer approach, especially if the single sheet contained underlinings, marginal comments, screaming headlines, etc. He was committed to thoroughness and he always insisted that any topic should be examined completely, and not presented in a slipshod and eye-irritating manner that would chase potential allies away. A rather sad commentary about current America is that too many Americans have gotten away from reading in-depth books and articles. They have been led to believe that brief messages – however factual and tastefully created – will suffice. The Society has attempted to counter that attitude in the midst of the electronic age that has become largely dominant. Important books and thoroughly incisive articles will always be recommended.

Marguerite Dice didn't join the Society in 1958. Several years later, however, after she had followed the Society's progress and read all the JBS materials sent to her as gifts from her appreciative friend, she forwarded a signed application for membership to Welch with a short note that said simply, "I guess you were right. Do you still have room for me?" Her application was promptly and joyfully accepted. She became a faithful member until she passed away in 1969. Over time, many members who initially thought Welch's insistence on thoroughness and tasteful visual appeal was overstressed were told of her eventual appreciation of the detailed explanations Welch always provided. And practically all learned to appreciate "the Welch way."

Chapter 9
Gaining Members and Forming Chapters

There were no media reports about the launching of The John Birch Society. Neither Welch nor anybody connected with its formation had informed *The New York Times*, or *Time* magazine, or any radio and television network about the creation of something new and its goal of preserving freedom. As planned by Welch, the Society would be its own medium of information, an alternative means of reaching the American people with needed facts and perspective they weren't getting from others considered to be reliable sources. The information would arrive from Welch to members via the mail and, from them, to other Americans by way of mouth-to-mouth and hand-to-hand transmission.

Because he had no illusions about the mass media helping his organization, Welch had concluded that obtaining their assistance would be an exercise in futility, possibly even a counterproductive move. Instead, he wanted the Society to rise from the grass-roots, built by people he could reach, enlist and trust. He based his attitude on an array of simple facts such as: If the mass media were universally telling the American people that Castro was a glorious revolutionary, or that various branches of the U.S. government were capably functioning within the restrictions contained in the Constitution, or that Communist infiltration of various sectors of our nation was nothing to fret over, then the newspapers, magazines, radio and television networks, and even many clergymen and educators could hardly be relied upon to portray with any kind of accuracy what he intended to build. Also, because it took him two full days to inform his friends about his plan and the reasons for it, it would hardly be possible to convey in a brief press release the goals he wanted the Society to accomplish.

Fresh from the launching pad in Indianapolis, Welch invited close to a hundred friends and supporters from the Greater Boston area to an early January 1959 repeat of his founding speech. Approximately 70 were able to attend and, after a follow-up dinner meeting, many joined and the Society's first six chapters were formed, all of them in Massachusetts. Those unable to attend regular Chapter meetings were encouraged to join the Home Chapter.

One of the first Chapter Leaders was Dr. N.E. Adamson, a promising young surgeon residing in Belmont, Massachusetts. A U.S. Navy medical officer during the late stages of World War II, Adamson found himself called back into service and assigned to the Marine Corps during the 1950-1953 Korean War, a conflict he and others later learned was directed by the United Nations. As he recalled years later, his status as the regimental surgeon enabled him to attend high-level meetings where he heard senior officers grumbling about the UN, even complaining about the UN flag flying alongside Old Glory. He especially recalled hearing complaints voiced by senior combat officers about the Communist enemy's awareness of U.S. activity, a development that made many of them extremely suspicious of the world body. Though he knew of those concerns, he had no deep feelings about the UN himself when he left active duty in 1954. He did remain attached to the Naval Reserve for many more years and earned promotion to the rank of Captain, U.S. Naval Reserve Medical Corps.

Adamson's wife Anne, a highly regarded nurse, regularly attended monthly professional meetings conducted by her peers. During one 1957 gathering, she heard a guest speaker deliver a truly alarming talk about Communist subversion occurring in the United States. That speaker was none other than Robert Welch. Startled by what he related about Communist progress in America, she recounted for her husband several portions of the Welch message. "And he lives right here in Belmont," she stated. "You've got to meet him." As he told me many years later during frequent meetings we two enjoyed, Adamson had been unnerved by the abrupt removal of General Douglas MacArthur from command during the Korean War, by the curtailment of the McCarthy investigations of subversives within the government, and why there were disturbing but unanswered questions about the UN. But he didn't know what he could do about any of these concerns. Nevertheless, he did exactly what his wife suggested and contacted Welch. The two men became close friends with the older man filling the role of teacher and the young doctor the eager student.

It so happened soon after these two men began cementing their relationship that Dr. Adamson incurred a personal medical problem from which he recovered but which left him in need of an extended recuperative period. Somewhat incapacitated but well able to read, he devoured numerous books, articles, and back issues of *One Man's Opinion,* all happily supplied by Welch. Unable to continue functioning as a surgeon, he obtained employment as a medical examiner at one of the nationwide insurance firms headquartered in Boston.

Both Adamsons were in the Massachusetts audience when Welch delivered his two-day speech early in January 1959. They later confessed not knowing anyone else at the meeting, but they soon had many good friends among the Society's newest members. And when Welch proceeded to enlist prominent individuals for the formation of his National Council, Dr. N.E. Adamson became the youngest man named to that prestigious body.

Welch then traveled to several states where friends assembled large audiences to hear his two-day speech. He actually delivered the two-day seminar approximately 80 times during the first three years of the Society's existence. In the organization's early months, chapters were begun in Michigan, Florida and Illinois. Then he headed out to California where audiences numbering as many as 2,000 both cheered him and filled him with hope. During 1959, he began sending the Society's monthly *Bulletin* to chapter leaders and then, after a few months, to all members.

Chapter 10
An Eventful First Year

During February 1959, chapter leaders received a box full of Society-recommended books along with the urging that all members read one each month. The first monthly *Bulletin* arrived in time for a March chapter meeting. Written entirely by Welch, these monthly messages consisted of five to twelve pages printed via the spirit-duplicator process (similar to mimeographing). That initial five-page March 1959 *Bulletin* asked the six Massachusetts chapter leaders to have their members join in a "Boston Tea Party" by tying a tea bag to the printed protest message Welch supplied about their state's high rate of taxation and sending it to their Governor. More than 50 years later, new organizations began under the name "Tea Party." But they surely were not the first to refer to the famous 1773 dumping of tea into Boston's harbor. The *Bulletin* also urged members to consider subscribing to one or more publications such as *American Opinion*, *Human Events*, *National Review* and *The Dan Smoot Report*. And, as was repeatedly stated in many *Bulletins*, Welch wanted all "to keep your eyes, ears and mind open for any good prospects" for membership.

In April, the *Bulletin* announced a new project, a postcard whose message protested the unconstitutionality and enormous cost of foreign aid. Each chapter received a supply of the cards and members were asked to send one to the President, and one to each of their congressman and two senators. In that month's *Bulletin*, Welch alerted members about a subversive plan, already well underway, to have department stores substitute United Nations paraphernalia for traditional Christmas decorations in the weeks prior to the great holiday. Reprints of an article from *American Opinion* entitled "There Goes Christmas" were offered to all for the asking, and members were encouraged to send a copy to their local department store officials. A few months later, Welch happily announced that several department store executives had indicated in letters that they would continue with Christmas decorations as in the past.

The announcement of an important national petition campaign entitled CASE (Committee Against Summit Entanglements) dominated the May *Bulletin*. It's "Please, President Eisenhower, Don't!" headline urged the President to cancel plans to hold meetings with Soviet dictator Nikita Khrushchev, the first to be held in the U.S. followed by another soon afterward in the Soviet Union. Among the reasons for protesting the planned Eisenhower-Khrushchev meetings, Welch listed brutal crimes committed by Khrushchev personally and by the Soviet regime he was leading. Mentioned specifically were the Soviet leader's role in the mass murder by starvation of seven million of Ukraine's people in the 1930s and the bloody suppression of Hungarian freedom fighters in 1956. Khrushchev himself had stated in a Moscow reception to Western diplomats on November 18, 1956: "We will bury you." The Welch document addressed to President Eisenhower concluded, "… nothing could be more disastrous to anti-Communist morale throughout the world, or more beneficial to the Communist tyranny, than the proposed exchange of visits between Khrushchev and yourself."

Welch then invited Massachusetts members and their prospects to attend a recorded presentation of his somewhat pared-down speech that explained the Society in a single day. All would be welcomed and encouraged to bring friends and, of course, prospects for membership. This version of his speech was played at private homes via a wire-recording machine, a cumbersome electronic process soon replaced by tapes and phonograph records. In June, Welch announced the formation of eight new chapters in New York City.

The July *Bulletin* told of the swelling membership resulting from Welch's speeches in various parts of the nation. Now sending the *Bulletin* to all members, not just to chapter leaders, he asked that letters of support be addressed to French anti-Communist stalwart Jacques Soustelle who was valiantly attempting to thwart a Communist-led uprising in the French province of Algeria. Then, Welch composed a statement dated July 4, 1959 in which he answered questions anyone might be asking of JBS members. It explained, "What is The John Birch Society?", "Who is John Birch?", "What is expected of members?", and more. He answered the question "Why haven't I heard more about The John Birch Society?" in three short sentences that answered the inquiry: "Partly because it is still so young. But mainly because we avoid all publicity as far as is practicable. It is our purpose to build strength and understanding, not to create noise."

The August *Bulletin* contained a photo-reproduced copy of a letter sent from France by Jacques Soustelle himself. It thanked Welch, the many members whose letters had been forwarded to him, and Hilaire du Berrier, the American journalist whose factual article about the crisis in Algeria and Soustelle's role in trying to combat it had appeared in *American Opinion*. In his brief letter, the French patriot stated openly that the subversion underway in Algeria was part of "Communist plans for world domination."

Welch then announced the publication of *The Blue Book of The John Birch Society,* the transcript of his two-day founding speech. Charge: $2.00 postpaid. He noted that new tape recordings of his presentation were already being employed, and a filmed version of portions of the founding speech would soon be available. He called on members to read more recommended books and develop greater determination to reach more Americans with the truth about what was happening and what could be done about it.

As he had mentioned in his founding presentation, Welch intended to hire field operatives called coordinators to build and lead Birch activity throughout the nation. These fully paid men would be assigned a specific geographical area where they would assist members, recruit more into the Society, build chapters, and tend to the many organizational duties that would arise. He named the men who had already been assigned in Illinois, Michigan, Texas, Massachusetts, Florida, Tennessee and New York. Of note among these initial hires was young Thomas N. Hill, a Massachusetts native who was finishing up studies at Southern Methodist University in Dallas. Through the generosity of a family friend, Tom had traveled to San Francisco to hear Robert Welch deliver one of his two-day presentations. Already quite aware of the Society's goals because of an astute parent who was already a member, Tom readily joined the Society and accepted employment as its Coordinator for Texas. He would soon be asked to return to Massachusetts and become Robert Welch's "right hand man," a post he capably held for the next 30 years. Of Tom Hill, Welch would frequently note that he had the good fortune to have an able assistant "who possessed a 60-year-old brain in his 30-year-old body."

Only several weeks after he became immersed in his coordinator duties, Hill found himself in need of a statement dealing with Welch's personal religious views. So he asked "the boss" to provide something that might be useful in addressing the matter with prospective members, many of whom had deep religious perspectives and wanted to know more about the Society's leader before committing to membership. As was his habit, Welch didn't dash off a quick note; he sent a three-page letter. A copy of what became known as "the Roemer Letter" (because it was sent to a pastor named Roemer) would then be supplied to anyone who wanted to know more about the thinking of the man whose organization they were being asked to join.

Welch's letter about his personal religious attitude contained four lengthy – and numbered – paragraphs. Portions of each in condensed version appear below (emphasis in the original):

1. I have tried all my life, in my weak and human way, to be a good Christian. But I am not a fundamentalist.

2. I do not intend nor attempt to be a leader in matters of doctrinal religion. I do not ask anybody to follow, nor even to accept, my specific religious views.

3. My concern is with morality and purpose, based on those eternal truths on which we <u>can</u> all agree. It is nobody else's business what my exact shades of religious belief may be, so long as I am giving my life to preserving <u>his</u> right to believe exactly what he wishes.

4. I am fully aware that even a slight modification of my non-conformity, a tiny pretense to more fundamentalism in the Christianity which I follow, would be of immense help in eliminating roadblocks to the growth of The John Birch Society in some areas of our country today. But I am not wiling to make the slightest concession in that direction, any more than I ask the most devout Catholic or fundamentalist Protestant to give up any iota of his fundamentalist faith in order to work with me in our common cause. For to make any such concession or pretense would be a deviation from the truth.

The letter, shared with those who indicated a need for it, did "calm the waters" while enabling individuals possessing strong religious views to realize that working together with other Americans as members of the Society would not compromise their beliefs. San Diego's prominent Pastor Tim LaHaye found the letter personally helpful. In a message he sent to the Society's San Diego Coordinator, LaHaye discussed some initial concerns he had about mixing his religious efforts and the anti-Communist work of the Society. Calling his decision an "exception" to his personal rule "not to join non-religious organizations," he then wrote, "I would consider it an honor to be a member" and he joined with enthusiasm. He later appeared in a Society film telling of his membership and giving the Society his enthusiastic endorsement.

In September, Welch proudly announced that the CASE petition imploring President Eisenhower to cancel plans for summit meetings with Khrushchev had been placed as a full-page advertisement in 48 newspapers throughout the nation. These included the *New York Times, Detroit Free Press, Indianapolis Star, Charlotte Observer, Oakland Tribune, Arizona Republic, Cincinnati Enquirer, Milwaukee Sentinel, Washington Star, Chicago Tribune, Wall Street Journal, Houston Chronicle*, and many more. In addition, the petition had been inserted by JBS members at their own expense as a full-page ad in over 100 more newspapers.

Welch had enlisted more than 50 prominent Americans from various parts of the nation as supporters of CASE. All agreed to have their names appear in the full-page spread. Twenty of these individuals would later become members of the Society's National Council. Well-known among CASE supporters who never became JBS members were Arizona Senator Barry Goldwater, New Hampshire Senator Styles Bridges, former Indiana Congressman Samuel Pettengill, and Retired U.S. Army General A.C. Wedemeyer. One noteworthy individual who participated as one of five CASE Vice Chairmen happened to be New York City resident and JBS member Alfred Kohlberg, a prominent Jewish American. His presence within the group dispelled any possible charge of anti-Semitism. In the project's early days when Welch was gathering names of prominent supporters, young William F. Buckley, Jr. contacted Welch with a plea that his name be added to the list. His request was granted.

The effort put forth by CASE succeeded only partially inasmuch as Khrushchev did come to the United States in September 1960. But the greeting he received as he traveled throughout the land wasn't what he or President Eisenhower and administration officials had hoped for. After a 21-gun salute and parade through Washington followed by two days of talks with the President, the Soviet Union's leader made an appearance at the headquarters of the United Nations where he addressed the General Assembly. He succeeded mostly in letting the world know how boorish and uncompromising he truly was. A visit to Southern California didn't include the trip to Disneyland he clearly wanted and, in San Francisco, the AFL-CIO's executive committee snubbed him during its convention. His reception at an Iowa farm was noteworthy because most Iowans chose to ignore him. Shown a steel mill in Pittsburgh and an atomic power plant in the East, the trip avoided Chicago and Detroit because, as *Business Week* magazine reported, those two cities were home to "volatile, anti-Communist groups."

In addition to the campaign inaugurated by CASE, Welch wrote a 50-page "Letter To Khrushchev" and had it printed in booklet format. He then sent it to the Soviet leader and shared copies with Society members. It capably detailed many reasons why the Soviet dictator should be shunned rather than welcomed in America. Welch buttressed his argument by sending members a copy of "The Killer in the Kremlin," an article about Khrushchev initially appearing in *Reader's Digest*. All recipients were urged to obtain additional copies of each of these revelations about the murderous history of the Soviet leader.

The September edition of the monthly *Bulletin* announced that copies of Eugene

Castle's book *The Great Giveaway* were in the mail for every member. Based on Castle having spent three years traveling and researching what Welch termed the "idiocy and worse" of the U.S. foreign aid program, the book added needed ammunition to the campaign against the totally unconstitutional distribution of the American peoples' hard-earned wealth.

In October, the *Bulletin* contained Welch's lament that the CASE effort hadn't succeeded in canceling the Khrushchev visit. But he insisted that the project had been hugely worthwhile because it informed many Americans about the truly murderous history of Communism's leader and why he never should have been accorded any dignity whatsoever. He then repeated his call for more members with the following assessment.

> Merely being anti-Communist is not a sufficient qualification for membership in The John Birch Society. We are far different from, and more than, a political action organization. Our ultimate objective is not only less government and more responsibility, but a better world in every moral and humane sense. We must have associated with us, therefore, only those who will join our own efforts to set an example, by dedication, integrity, and purpose, – in both word and deed – which men of good will, good conscience, and religious ideals may follow without hesitation.

In November, Welch happily reported that members had received more positive results from department store officials about the campaign to cease using Christmas decorations. Success regarding the planned change by some department stores led Welch to stress the importance of letter writing, an urging he never ceased to deliver. He then called for letters to be sent to the Editor of *Newsweek* magazine protesting the portraying of a German communist whose real name was Muller as a freedom fighter working to sever Algeria from France. For several succeeding months, *Newsweek* had repeatedly extolled the man portraying himself as an Arab named Si Mustapha but who was, in fact, the communist Muller. A few months later, Welch received a letter from *Newsweek* admitting that he was correct, that Si Mustapha was indeed Muller. But *Newsweek* never published any correction for its readers.

Welch added to the November *Bulletin* a copy of Tom Anderson's "Straight Talk" column addressed to Khrushchev. Known for his wit that frequently had a real bite, Anderson didn't find anything positive about the Khrushchev visit when he wrote: "But some reactionaries hope there's only one American you'll do business with: an undertaker." Soon to become a favorite as he traveled throughout the nation sponsored by the Society's Speakers Bureau, Anderson brought his often humorous but always incisive speeches to state after state. All of his talks remained a topic of conversation among veteran Society members for decades.

The final *Bulletin* of 1959 began by noting a number of suspicious deaths of anti-Communists such as Manning Johnson, the courageous Negro ex-Communist whose book "Color, Communism and Common Sense" was eventually published by the Society with great positive effect. Danish diplomat and United Nations official Povl Bang-Jensen also died mysteriously after he refused to give UN superiors the names of anti-Communist refugees from the failed 1956 Hungarian uprising. Those who had fled when Soviet tanks entered the fray supplied first-hand evidence of Communist atrocities. They rightly feared retaliation against family members still in Hungary if they provided information about Soviet crimes. In order to enable them to speak freely, Bang-Jensen solemnly promised that their names would never be made public. But when UN Secretary General Dag Hammarskjold demanded the names, Bang-Jensen publicly burned all his lists. His dead body was soon found in a New York City park and his passing was deemed a "suicide."

Five months later, the May 1960 issue of *American Opinion* magazine contained Julius Epstein's 46-page monograph entitled "The Bang-Jensen Tragedy." Distribution of this reprinted booklet constituted the Society's opening salvo in a campaign to have many more Americans understand the danger to freedom posed by the United Nations. Other deaths deemed suspicious by Welch were those of Ohio Senator Robert Taft, Wisconsin Senator Joseph McCarthy, and Secretary of Defense James Forrestal.

The *Bulletin's* agenda for December called for opposition to fluoridation of water supplies, a topic ably discussed by former FBI official Dan Smoot in his newsletter. Begun in 1956 and always highly recommended by Welch, *The Dan Smoot Report* for September 28, 1959 focused on keeping water supplies free of fluoridation. Copies were sent to members with an urging that they inform themselves about the matter and get others to do likewise. Welch claimed that adding such a substance to the water, while likely bad health policy itself, was more to be feared as a precedent leading to future insertions of other substances into the drinking water.

December, of course, marked the first anniversary of the Society and Welch noted that there were now "seven full-time paid Coordinators, and five volunteer Coordinators." While he delighted in reporting that chapters were already functioning in 15 states, and Home Chapter members could be counted in 25, he added, "We have barely scratched the surface in building The John Birch Society." And he was extremely pleased to note that a flood of letters, mainly initiated by Society members, had persuaded United Airlines officials to remove U.N. insignia from their planes. He then announced that the time had come for members to start thinking about "reading rooms" where interested citizens could find out about the Society and discover the existence of many good books. These storefront locations eventually became the chain of American Opinion Bookstores, all fully staffed and financed at the local level by members and friends.

Chapter 11
1960: Gaining Strength

As 1960 began, the monthly *Bulletin* arrived to all as a 28-page pamphlet. (In the months ahead, it would customarily fill 32 pages.) On the very first page of the January offering, Welch noted with delight that, less than a month ago, he had delivered a speech to an audience of 1,200 at the Freedom Club in Los Angeles. His talk entitled "A Look at the Score" (the initial chapter in his founding speech and the first chapter of the *Blue Book*) dwelled on Communist progress throughout the world but especially within the United States. As was always the case, his audience sat in rapt attention throughout the course of his disturbing message. His report about the event didn't mention how many new members were enlisted but several hundred did sign up. The following evening while still in California, he was pleasantly surprised when an invitation to a dinner meeting with a few friends turned out to be a gathering of approximately 100 who came to celebrate the Society's first anniversary.

Always encouraging all members to read important books, he filled two pages of the first 1960 *Bulletin* with titles of "Approved Books" and the cost of each. His stamp of approval meant only that such books contained no counterproductive propaganda and leftist slant. Other than several dozen marked "Out of Print," all could be purchased from **The Bookmailer,** a New York City firm marketing both old and new books. Many of the titles on Welch's list would later be republished by the Society in paperback format. Repeating his oft-stated assessment of the world conspiracy's goal, he emphasized that the continuing surrender of the West was leading to "a one-world socialist government."

In February, Welch announced that 25 prominent Americans had agreed to serve on the Society's newly formed National Council, and the entire group had already met in early January. Members of this prestigious group always paid their own way to attend any of its meetings – a policy that has never been altered.

The announcement about the Council told of the threefold purpose of the group: "1) To show the stature and standing of the leadership of the Society; 2) to give the Founder the benefit of the Council's advice and guidance, both in procedural or organizational matters, and in substantive matters of policy; and 3) to select, with absolute and final authority, a successor to myself as head of The John Birch Society, if and when any accident, 'suicide,' or anything sufficiently fatal is arranged for me by the Communists – or I simply die in bed of old age and a cantankerous disposition."

Nine who had attended the two-day founding session in Indianapolis formed the core of the 24-man Council. They were Messrs. Andrews, Bunker, Grede, Koch, McMillan, Oliver, Ruthenburg, Stoddard and Swigert. Backgrounds about each of these were previously noted in Chapter Six. The remaining 15 original Council members included Dr. N.E. Adamson, Tom Anderson, John Beatty, Spruille Braden, Ralph Davis, S.M. Draskovich, A.G. Heinsohn, Dr. Granville Knight, Alfred Kohlberg, Dean Clarence Manion, Frank Masland, Adolphe Menjou, Cola Parker, James Simpson, and Lt. Gen. Charles B. Stone.

The Council would meet "at fairly regular intervals" said Welch. And they did gather quarterly for years on Saturdays in one of four cities: Los Angeles, Chicago, Dallas, and New York. Soon, each daylong Council meeting would be followed by the Council Dinner to which area members and friends happily flocked. In later years, the quarterly meetings were held in several other cities where area members would have an opportunity to meet Welch and the Society's top leaders.

He then happily announced that copies of Senator Barry Goldwater's book, *The Conscience of a Conservative*, would soon be in the mail to each chapter leader. Welch said that his friend's book "pulls no punches and is a very forceful presentation of the Americanist point of view." The choice of "Americanist" instead of "Conservative" when referring to the attitude held by Goldwater and a few others was a deliberate move by Welch. He knew that the term "conservative" had already been adopted by several individuals who could never be rightly labeled "Americanists." Along with praise for Goldwater's new book came a request that members send written congratulations to the senator for his March 15 speech urging U.S. withdrawal of diplomatic recognition of the Soviet government.

This same April *Bulletin* urged Protestant members to talk to their ministers about the pro-Communist stances being taken by clergymen of a variety of Christian denominations, most of which were linked to the National Council of Churches. Welch cited the efforts of Herbert Philbrick who had infiltrated some Communist cells and for years reported to the FBI about the subversive activity carried out by various churches and organizations. He also noted the efforts of Dr. J.B. Matthews who had quit his affiliation with the Communist movement to spend ensuing years reporting to appropriate government agencies about his knowledge of Communist designs, especially within organized religion. Welch then mentioned that the Council had met again and since their initial meeting in January, "the Society had actually doubled in size."

The May *Bulletin* reproduced a four-page transcript of one of the weekly "Manion Forum" radio programs. This particular broadcast was filled with reasons why supplying additional dignity to the Soviet leader with the planned trip to Russia by the President was a grave mistake. The Manion presentation pointed to the U.S. State Department's plan to have President Eisenhower offer to disarm our military along with the thoroughly absurd expectation that the USSR would do likewise.

After the May *Bulletin* had been mailed to members, something completely unforeseen occurred. On May 1, 1960, the Soviets downed an American U-2 spy plane flying over Russia. Soviet officials expressed immediate outrage while the response from Washington insisted that the aircraft was simply monitoring weather patterns and had strayed off course. Soviet authorities countered by producing some of the plane's wreckage and its pilot, Gary Powers, who openly admitted that he had been conducting a CIA spy mission. When Khrushchev faced Eisenhower in Paris two weeks later, the Soviet leader launched into a diatribe against America, demanded the banning of any future flights of that type, insisted on punishment for U.S. perpetrators of the "deliberate violation" of Soviet airspace, and declared that President Eisenhower would not be welcome in Russia. Had the downing of the U.S. plane in Russia not occurred, would President Eisenhower have traveled to Moscow and offered the Soviet leader the actual disarmament scheme worked out by his State Department? Welch obviously believed that such a plan would not only have been offered, it would have been carried out in every detail.

The May 1960 *Bulletin* also contained information about the Senate Internal Security Subcommittee's recent questioning of former U.S. Communist Party leaders. Welch found the comments of ex-Communist Leonard Patterson so worthy of praise that he published an excerpt of what the compellingly contrite man had told the senators. A Black American, Patterson had joined the Party, spent two years being trained in Russia, and had returned to the U.S. where he became one of the Party's highest officials during the 1930s. During February 2-3, 1960 Senate session, the now apologetic Patterson told the panel:

> I have traveled in Russia. I have lived there almost two years. I went all over Russia, and I saw how the people live in Russia. I have traveled practically

all over this country of ours, both in the Communist Party and since I have been out of the Communist Party, and have had a chance to make up my mind which is the best system. I have seen how the so-called national minorities live in Russia, in the Crimea, Yalta, in the Ukraine, and different places. I was born in the South, in North Carolina, and I know how we live in this country, and I make this statement very brazenly as to the 'paradise' in Russia: With all the shortcomings that we have in the United States, if you want to put it on a racial basis, or a Negro basis, we American Negroes are better off, not only than minorities in Russia, but the so-called Great Russians themselves. I wouldn't say there wasn't room for improvement, but if you take it as a whole, we have the highest standard of living, we are better educated, we have more wealth distributed among us, and I defy anyone to deny it.

At the time, Leonard Patterson was earning his living as a taxi driver in New York City. He would then spend several years as a member of the Society's American Opinion Speakers Bureau during the rise of the Civil Rights Movement. His efforts telling what he knew about Communist plans to tear America apart over racial differences led to cancellation of many planned Communist-inspired uprisings. JBS veterans have always remembered his unique patriotism with appropriate gratitude.

The May 1960 *Bulletin* contained sad news of the passing of Council Member Alfred Kohlberg and the acceptance of a place on the Council by the Honorable M.T. Phelps, the Chief Justice of the Supreme Court of Arizona. The June *Bulletin* urged sending letters of support to Congressman Francis Walter (D-Pa.), Chairman of the House Committee on Un-American Activities, thanking him for his leadership in the work of exposing Communist activity within the U.S.

In July, Welch discussed finances and let members know that their dues alone didn't cover the cost of the field and office staffs. He inaugurated the system known as "Member's Monthly Messages" that provided a small envelope to accompany each *Bulletin*. Members were encouraged to use it to send a question or comment and a donation beyond dues. Late in July, Welch accepted an invitation to speak to a sizeable group of delegates and alternates to the Republican Convention as they gathered in Chicago. Most in that audience were supporters of Senator Barry Goldwater, as was Welch himself. Among them were many who wanted Goldwater to be the GOP nominee but who also believed that chances of that happening were virtually nil. So, they were seriously considering launching a third party, and they hoped to receive Welch's support for their plan.

With the title of his July 24 speech, "To Prevent a Third Party," he let that audience (and many others to whom he would send copies) know that he strongly disagreed with that plan. Much of what he said on that occasion heaped praise on the Arizona senator who, he hoped, would some day become the nation's president. But starting a new political party at that point in history, he said, was not a wise course to follow, and he knew that Goldwater agreed. He predicted that Richard Nixon would win the GOP's nomination and that John Kennedy would be the choice of Democrats. And he urged his listeners to write-in Goldwater's name, as he intended to do himself. Eight years later, he would change his mind about a third party and, while never formally announcing his support for George Wallace, let it be known in numerous ways that he had given up on both Democrats and Republicans and thought the nation should choose the Alabama Governor instead.

Welch then noted that The John Birch Society now had "several thousand members." Many he felt would vote for Nixon and not for Kennedy. Still, he expressed complete disdain for Richard Nixon claiming that, after watching his career as a senator and his eight years as vice president, he should be expected to follow the path taken by many others: Pose as a conservative but perform as a liberal once in office. The opposite never occurs, he insisted: "Nowhere in the pages of history have I discovered one conservative who built up his political following as a liberal, ran for office as a liberal and was elected by liberal support, and then proved, by inaugurating an era of conservatism in government, that he had been deceiving his followers." While recognizing that choices still had to be made among politicians, he suggested that disappointments were customarily inevitable, and he cited the conclusion of an unnamed individual who had stated, "the value of complete honesty in politics is utterly unknown because nobody has ever tried it."

Before the year ended, Welch addressed the "derogatory remarks" aimed at him and the Society by Dr. Fred Schwarz, the Australian physician who had come to America and founded the "Christian Anti-Communism Crusade." Schwarz sought to awaken Americans to the Communist threat with his lectures and publications. In a nine-page letter, Welch told his unexpected detractor that many in the Society had helped gather audiences for well-attended Schwarz seminars, and that there ought to be cooperation, not competition, between the Society and anyone who was alerting people to the Communist reality. Schwarz continued to conduct his seminars and even published a book entitled *You Can Trust the Communists To Be Communists* that Society members were encouraged to distribute. The Australian doctor capably targeted the false ideology promoted by Marx, Lenin, and Mao Tse-tung. But he always avoided the notion of conspiracy, urging instead that the way to combat Communist designs was to create small local groups here and there. This amounted to the main disagreement Welch had with Schwarz. Over the years, Schwarz published other books and authored a newsletter for 40 years. He returned to Australia in the 1990s and passed away in 2009.

Chapter 12
Welch's Long Letter About Eisenhower

We come now to the main matter seized upon by the Society's enemies as their weapon to blunt the organization's steady growth and rising effectiveness. How Welch's severe view of Dwight David Eisenhower developed, became known, and rose to become a prominent weapon against him and The John Birch Society, constitutes a significantly important development in the organization's history.

As far back as mid-1954, while riding with three friends in an automobile near New York City, one of Welch's companions asked for his opinion of President Eisenhower (who, after being elected in November 1952, had moved into the White House in January 1953). These friends had been wondering about promises made by the new president that had not been kept, how support for the President had continued to come from questionable sources, and why the former Army commander had actually harmed the congressional candidacies of some Republicans during the 1952 election year. Welch answered their questions frankly and with customary thoroughness. What he offered startled his companions and prompted further questions and more responses providing additional reasons for concern. Before these men separated and went their respective ways, one asked Welch to put what he had stated in writing. The other two immediately made the same request. He agreed to do so and, after returning to his home and his files, he added several more disturbing revelations before sending his thoughts to each of the three.

Once having digested what Welch had written, each of these men asked for additional copies to share with others. Assured that the individuals who would receive them were seeking information and not trying to cause him trouble, Welch responded in complete frankness and had more copies typed. (There were no photocopy machines at the time). He requested that each new recipient consider what he had written as strictly confidential, not to be shared with anyone. He obviously knew that what he had provided was explosive – and explosively frank. Still more requests came and each new typing of the document saw Welch adding more information about highly questionable moves taken by the new president. By 1958, well into Eisenhower's second four-year term, the Welch thesis had become a 300-page expose' printed in inexpensive booklet format. He indicated to some recipients his possible willingness to edit the entire manuscript at a later date when he would undertake softening the wording of some of his conclusions while making the whole presentation more suitable for general circulation.

Anyone who received a copy of this manuscript would immediately note a brief message pasted on an early blank page. It told the reader that the entire document started as a letter to a friend, and that its author does not "try to prove anything, nor to marshal evidence for either a court of law or the court of public opinion." Then followed two more pages addressed to "Dear Reader" which stated that the manuscript was "on loan" and should be returned, that its content was "strictly confidential," and that it may "at some future time become a book." Welch said he was "willing to guarantee" the accuracy of everything he had written and noted that practically all of what appeared in the manuscript "had already been widely published elsewhere." He also welcomed any corrections, criticisms, or additions of relevant facts that any reader might wish to send.

Obviously, a great deal of caution accompanied the sharing of the manuscript. But one copy fell into the hands of *Chicago Daily News* columnist Jack Mabley. How he obtained it – by chance, theft, or purchase – has never been discovered. Two articles by Mabley dealing with what Welch considered his private opinion appeared in the Chicago newspaper on July 25-26, 1960 under Mabley's byline. The first carried the headline, "Bares Secrets Of Red-Haters – They Think Ike is a Communist." The second saw publication under the headline, "Strange Threat To Democracy – Anti-Red Group Hits Leaders." The two articles were quickly followed by a front-page spread in a Sunday edition of the *Milwaukee Journal* under the headline "Group Brands Ike Red." Soon, a floodgate opened, and Welch's conclusion about President Eisenhower, never including why he had come to such an assessment, made its way throughout the nation.

Other than a few of his closest friends within the Society, all mid-1960 John Birch Society members had no awareness of the Welch thesis. While it would always be difficult to separate what he had written about Eisenhower from The John Birch Society itself, the repeated linking of all members to his charges made in a manuscript he'd written prior to founding the Society was unjust.

What Mabley wrote, and what he likely shared with friends at the *Milwaukee Journal* and elsewhere contained the following sentence that appeared in the manuscript after nearly 300 pages of damning information:

But my firm belief that Dwight Eisenhower is a dedicated, conscious agent of the Communist conspiracy is based on an accumulation of detailed evidence so extensive and so palpable that it seems to me to put this conviction beyond any reasonable doubt.

That conclusion, repeated nationwide in print and over the airwaves during subsequent years, is all that most Americans have ever heard or read about Welch and the Society. None of the facts noted in Eisenhower's career that prompted such an admittedly stark assessment were provided by Mabley, or by others. Nor was there any distinction made between the charge of being an "agent" of the conspiracy and being one of its actual members. Any "agent" of a group is never the equivalent of a member of the group. He or she could, as is customarily the case, be merely a collaborator or a spokesman for a particular cause. In a similar way, an agent for a movie actor or a sports figure is not the actor or the sportsman. But this distinction was never made, not even by Welch himself.

Forces who would defend Eisenhower and attack the Society in years to come didn't want people to know that Welch eventually published a 450-page book (300 pages text and 150 additional pages of documentation and footnotes) full of damning evidence that led to his conclusion. Welch had even suggested the possibility of attributing all of Eisenhower's deeds to political ambition or gross unawareness of the consequences of what he was doing. While certainly allowing any reader to arrive at his own conclusion after reading many facts, Welch summarized his own attitude when he published his thoughts in book form under the title *The Politician*. In that format, he stated:

> … the only serious alternative to the theme of *The Politician* is even more disturbing. It is the suggestion, which cannot be ignored, that Eisenhower's motivation has been more ideologically honest than shallowly opportunistic. Or, to put the matter bluntly, that he has been sympathetic to ultimate Communist aims, realistically and even mercilessly willing to help them achieve their goals, knowingly receiving and abiding by Communist orders, and consciously serving the Communist conspiracy, for all of his adult life.

Soon after Mabley's revelations, press reports about the Society began telling readers that Welch had labeled Dwight Eisenhower "a card-carrying member of the Communist Party." The Birch Society's leader swiftly denied that he had ever used such terminology. His denial was accurate because he never stated such a conclusion and never believed it. But he never backed away from the quote noted above.

CHAPTER 13
JBS AND WELCH TARGETED

No discussion of *The Politician* should omit or gloss over the facts leading to its startling conclusions. By means of the title Welch chose for the book, he suggested to others that the nation's 34th President might well be an intensely ambitious politician who was always committed to nothing but self. Knowing that he had arrived at this possible assessment shared by some of his close associates, he would later state in the final pages of the book, "And if this history contains facts that are unpleasant and disturbing to both the reader and myself, that is the fault of those who made the history, not of him who wrote it."

With these thoughts in mind, we offer a minuscule sampling of the book's facts and encourage readers of this book to obtain a copy of *The Politician* itself. As Society officials have always maintained, "No one should judge Welch's conclusions about our nation's 34th president without knowing at least some of the facts that led to the Society leader's admittedly stark conclusion." Here is a very brief look at only a few of the incidents related by Welch.

> 1. The manuscript's early pages dwell on an otherwise routine Seattle dinner party in 1940 where Lieutenant Colonel Eisenhower met Anna Roosevelt Boettiger, the daughter of President Franklin Roosevelt. The attention Eisenhower paid to this lady and the praise he heaped on her father throughout the evening impelled her to call her father the very next morning to tell him about the remarkable Army officer she had greatly enjoyed meeting. There began Eisenhower's meteoric rise from relative obscurity in 1940 to become, **in a mere two years**, a full colonel, a brigadier general, a major general, a lieutenant general, a four-star general and, finally, win appointment as Commander in Chief of all allied forces during the European phase of World War II. Such a meteoritic elevation to that exceedingly high post had never previously been accomplished by anyone, especially by a man who had never command-

ed any troops in combat and, therefore, had no battlefield experience.

2. Soon after World War II ended in 1945, while Eisenhower was still functioning as Supreme Allied Commander in Europe, he ordered the forced repatriation to Soviet tyranny of more than two million refugees from Communism. American troops – frequently wielding bayonets – forced hordes of unwilling civilians, war prisoners, and military defectors into railroad cars destined for the Soviet Union or nations under control of Soviet forces. Many of these hapless individuals committed suicide rather than meekly submitting to being transported to waiting gulags and worse. The situation was so unnerving to those ordered to carry out the directive that numerous American soldiers balked at performing their grisly task. When the U.S. Army's General Patch demanded assurance from Washington that Eisenhower's order had to be obeyed, he received confirmation of its legitimacy from the Joint Chiefs of Staff, one of whose most recent appointees happened to be Eisenhower himself who used his newly acquired position to persuade fellow JCS members to give the mandate an additional stamp of approval. The forced repatriation known revealingly as "Operation Keelhaul" continued.

3. In 1956, thousands of brave Hungarians rose up against Soviet domination of their country. They succeeded in gaining control of Budapest, the nation's capital city. Repeated promises that military aid would be supplied, if such an uprising had shown any potential for success, had been beamed into their country by America's Radio Free Europe. Once the revolt showed positive signs, anti-Communist leaders in Spain attempted to send weapons and supplies to the Hungarians. Needing a fuel stop on the way to Hungary, the Spaniards contacted German leaders and received their permission to refuel in Germany. But President Eisenhower and Secretary of State John Foster Dulles actively intervened and forced the German officials to withdraw their refueling offer. At the very same time, the State Department sent assurances to Moscow's allies in Yugoslavia that the U.S. did not favor the campaign of the anti-Communist Hungarians. Armed with that message given them by Yugoslav officials, Soviet forces sent their tanks and troops into Hungary where they overwhelmed the freedom fighters and regained control of Budapest. As many as 50,000 Hungarians were rounded up and killed for their effort. Hungary remained under tyrannical Soviet domination for three more decades.

4. Eisenhower's own widely heralded 1948 book, *Crusade in Europe*,

dealing with his management of the World War II effort, was actually ghost written for him by a known Communist named Joseph Fels Barnes. Its pages are replete with carefully doctored history about Eisenhower's life and military career.

There are, of course, many additional incidents in the life and career of Dwight Eisenhower contained in the book's 300 pages. What appears above is only a sample of information that has shocked most readers and caused them to begin questioning America's mass media that never reported what Welch, a private citizen acting alone, had compiled, and what no critic of Welch has ever claimed was false.

Three years after the Mabley attack, when a huge number of damaging articles had targeted not only Welch but the entire John Birch Society, and after the JBS founder and some aides had combed through a mountain of files to find and include documentation to support what he had written, Welch published *The Politician*. No error has ever been found in its 300 pages or in the 150 additional pages of footnotes and bibliography. There were, to be sure, many hours spent by numerous researchers examining the book to find mistakes, exaggerations, etc. Not one was ever found. But Welch's conclusion about Eisenhower received an enormous amount of attention. Any reader of *The Politician* will find plenty more about our nation's 34th president in this 300-page book – still available for anyone who cares to obtain a copy.

Chapter 14
The Politician Published and Boycotted

Attacks on Welch and the Society, almost all pointing to his conclusion about former President Eisenhower grew in number and intensity. Much of the May 1963 *Bulletin* dwelled on the availability of *The Politician*, issued by the Belmont Publishing Company, a separate firm created by Welch. With the additions of a prologue, introduction, epilogue, bibliography, footnotes, and index, the book now filled 448 pages. It was easily the most controversial book of recent decades.

In the book's Prologue, Welch declared that the flood of attacks he had been forced to endure left "no way I could defend myself or my statements without publishing the whole document." He added: "Any man, hounded long enough and mercilessly enough, for merely saying what he believes and doing what he thinks is right should be allowed to respond. That response included letting anyone who desired to do so read in its entirety what he had written about the former President." He stated his belief that "the lions of the left, including Mr. Eisenhower himself, knew all about this manuscript [and] they did not want it published because there was too much devastating evidence in it concerning matters which they preferred to have forgotten." And, in a surprising confession, he noted that even he didn't want it made available in its original format because it "had never been prepared or put in shape for publication." According to Welch, the book would lead readers "too rapidly into a realization of truths they were unwilling to accept." But the repeated attention given to the concluding sentences in the 300-page manuscript gave him no other choice.

At the very end of his presentation of details about Eisenhower's career, Welch answered reasonable questions anyone might have after they had gained awareness about the former President's deeds. One asked whether Eisenhower could have been "simply a smart politician, entirely without principle and hungry for glory, who is only a tool of the Communists." Welch responded: "The answer is yes." Next, he turned to a different possibility suggested by others that Dwight Eisenhower could have simply been "too dumb to understand" what he had been doing. But Welch, who was certainly aware that anyone had the right to arrive at this or any other conclusion, discounted it as a reasonable explanation for all the horrors he had presented.

Readers of this history of the Society might care to know of my own personal experiences dealing with the Welch book. Having in 1962 attended a JBS "Introductory Meeting" (where two friends and I purchased and shared a set of the 12 reprinted books entitled *One Dozen Candles*), I sought to learn from some members who were present why Welch had reached such a startling conclusion about Dwight Eisenhower. But no one at that meeting knew precisely what he had written and why he had issued such a startling conclusion. The JBS members I questioned might have been aware of some deeds of the former President, but all anyone could tell me was that the book had not been published. I did ask one Society member at that meeting how he could belong to an organization whose founder had made such stridently condemnatory statements about the former president without knowing why such a condemnation had been made. He responded somewhat matter-of-factly, "I know enough about Eisenhower to have made my own conclusions about him. I don't need Welch's information about him."

Somewhat taken aback by that very frank response because it failed to provide the more thorough kind of answer I was seeking, I pressed no further. But I was driven at that time to suspect that Welch likely didn't want to make his thoughts available because his case was weak and, even more, indefensible. Hence I decided the JBS was not for me. Eventually I concluded I was wrong about Welch's intention regarding the book. He did want people to read it. But before he made it available, he wanted to explain how it came to be and, even more, to document its contents, which he had not done in the version sent to friends during the late 1950s.

Some months later (now mid-1963), I received a phone call from a JBS member who told me that *The Politician* had been published and I could purchase a copy for $8.00. That was a lot of money in 1963, and my family had grown to include my good wife and three very young children. As much as I wanted to read the book, I honestly didn't have an extra $8.00, and that's what I told this caller. Then in early 1964, I met a member of the Society whom I had never previously known and he **gave** me a copy of *The Politician*. When I told him I didn't have the $8.00 to pay for it, he immediately informed me that he was giving me a new $2.00 paperback version. He even told of his expectation that I would read it.

Read it I did. I found its contents extremely distressing – but believable. Its many pages of documentation were most impressive. The book caused me numerous nights of tossing and turning. The evidence of serious wrongdoing on the part of Dwight Eisenhower, who had been president for eight recent years including the three years I served as an officer in the U.S. Marine Corps, was overwhelming. I looked at my three youngsters and their mother and said to myself, "I've got to get involved. My country is in danger." Then I re-read *The Blue Book* and joined the Society. A few months later, I gathered some friends who became members and I was now a JBS chapter leader. In 1966, I accepted an offer to become a full-time member of the Society's staff. After serving in several ascending roles, I was appointed President of the organization in 1991.

But there's so much more to relate about the saga surrounding the Welch book. Almost immediately after its publication, Welch took dramatic action. The Sunday, April 21, 1963, issue of *The New York Times* carried his full-page ad telling of the availability of *The Politician*. It urged, "Read it – and judge it for yourself!" A brief message toward the bottom of this expensive ad said simply, "Because this has been made by my critics into one of the most controversial books of the Twentieth Century, I have neither asked nor allowed anyone else to take responsibility for it except myself." The ad noted that the book could be purchased from any bookstore or directly through the mail at $8.00 per copy. He then sent a reproduction of that ad, again at his own expense, to 5,000 U.S. bookstores. Years later, he reported that 250,000 copies had already been sold and, of that total, fewer than 1,000 had been purchased via commercial bookstores. Somehow, practically all of the nation's commercial bookstores had been persuaded to ignore the book.

Once *The Politician* became available, Richard Ober, one of Welch's close assistants, took a copy to the famous bookstore in Harvard Square known as "The Coop." He showed the book to an employee and suggested that the store might want to purchase copies to sell. The eager but junior Coop employee recognized that there would indeed be substantial sales because of the enormous amount of publicity the book had already received. So he estimated that they should purchase six cases (24 books per case) but immediately confessed his inability to commit to so large a transaction. He told Welch's friend to return in several hours to pick up the order from his superior.

Welch's friend did return, met with a senior purchasing agent, and was rather brusquely told, "We'll take six." "Don't you mean six cases?" asked the JBS staffer. "No, I said six" came the reply, "and if you don't want an order for six, that would be fine." So the Harvard Coop purchased six copies, which were promptly delivered and duly paid for. But not one copy was ever put on the store's shelves for sale. Bookstores throughout the nation that could have sold many copies because of all the publicity about it refrained from ordering any. Welch never hesitated to speculate that refusals of bookstores to order the book had been engineered somehow by enemies of himself and The John Birch Society.

In less than two years, however, Society members led the way in purchasing and distributing so many copies that there were six separate printings, the largest numbering 100,000 in December 1964. Substantial though these sales were, they were certainly far short of what had been expected. A quiet but effective behind-the-scenes campaign to smother the book's availability through normal channels had succeeded. A great many individuals who finally obtained a copy and read it reacted as I did by joining the Society. Welch would later publish one letter he received while noting its similarity to "many hundreds" arriving at Society headquarters. Containing thoughts that I could easily have written, it stated:

> I would like to express my warmest congratulations to Mr. Welch on the publication of his excellent treatise on Mr. Eisenhower, *The Politician*. While I realize this book has nothing to do with our Society, I chose this medium to express my thanks. This should mean more to Mr. Welch, since it comes from one who nine months ago considered Mr. Welch a "crackpot" for attacking such a fine "patriot" as Mr. Eisenhower. My deepest and most sincere apologies.

Not every reaction was so friendly. The relatively few negative responses relied only on the passages extracted from the single copy of the manuscript obtained by the Chicago newspaperman. California Senator Thomas Kuchel delivered a speech to the Senate condemning Welch and JBS. Senators Mark Hatfield of Oregon, Jacob Javits of New York, Mike Mansfield of Montana, and Stephen Young of Ohio jumped on the anti-Welch and anti-Birch bandwagon. But once the book had been published and was now available, a curious change occurred. Rarely were there references to an actual book providing reasons why Welch had such an explosive view of Eisenhower's history. Only the Welch conclusion was cited, and quite frequently those citations were grossly distorted, even completely incorrect.

During this period, Massachusetts Republican Congressman Silvio Conte sought to elevate his own stature by attacking Welch and the controversial book in remarks he delivered from the floor of the House of Representatives. Holding high a copy of *The Politician* so television cameras and his colleagues before him could see it, he condemned "this horrible book." But he had seriously erred by supplying confirmation that Welch's indictment of Eisenhower was now in book form and was available for anyone to read. Quite likely, he was soon taken to the proverbial woodshed and told it was perfectly OK to condemn Welch and the Society on any occasion. But mentioning the availability of a book containing Welch's indictment of the former president was not the way to proceed.

The Politician was, and still is, a book that will upset a reader. As noted previously, Welch said the blame should be directed not at the writer who complied the information but at the individual "who made the history." Jack Mabley wasn't alone in never mentioning that rather important suggestion.

Chapter 15
Attacks Stimulate Growth

We back up a bit here to August 1960, when Welch told the Society's growing membership that his thoughts about Eisenhower were in an unpublished lengthy letter sent to some friends that fell into the hands of a newspaperman who wrote disparagingly about it. He added that virtually all reports about its existence assured Americans that the Society was something to avoid, even abhor. But, much of the notoriety given the matter worked in Welch's favor. As the Society's Founder explained, "If Jack Mabley expected to do serious damage to The John Birch Society, he must by now be badly disappointed." Welch estimated that approximately one thousand members had read the two Mabley columns and "not a single member resigned" as a result. He did suggest, however, that he may have "made a mistake by being so outspoken, even in a confidential statement of opinions." Friends of the Birch Founder agreed.

In September 1960, after publicity about Welch's opinion of the sitting president (Eisenhower's second term ended in January 1961) had been spread across the nation, the JBS leader commented further to members. Noting that mentions of him and the Society were rarely favorable, he nevertheless predicted "one to three thousand new members will be coming into the Society during September [1960]." That estimate proved to be correct. Many joined after hearing him deliver a speech and far more signed up after reading *The Blue Book*. Then, in somewhat somber tones, he warned, "We are heading into some very stormy weather." He was correct about that as well. Negative depiction of Welch and the Society mushroomed. Despite the unwanted publicity built around a sentence or two out of 300 pages of his yet unpublished critique of the President, Welch was still able in the November *Bulletin* to claim, "… we are currently gaining about two thousand new members per month."

Reporters insistently began asking for the names of the members. Because Welch steadfastly refused to supply any beyond those who had accepted Council membership, his stand led some media personnel to label the Society "a secret organization." His response: "We're as secret as the Boy Scouts and the League of Women Voters who, like numerous other organizations, don't publish a membership roster." Others portrayed the Welch creation as a fascist enterprise, even "like the Nazis" with Welch as its "Fuhrer." More charges followed claiming the Society was "un-American," or "like the communists," or "like the Ku Klux Klan." It seemed as though many in the media and political world would use any nasty adjective they could find to keep people away from the Society. But all of this negative attention worked in the Society's favor as many good people felt a duty to take a hard look at this supposedly evil group. Some actually sought information about the Society in order to be able to counter its efforts should JBS activity show up in their communities. Many who began as combatants of the caricature they were given ended up as members.

In late 1960, Communist Party leaders from more than 80 nations, including several high-ranking U.S. Communists, received orders to travel to Moscow. Once there, they were given official instructions about how to wage a "resolute struggle against anti-Communism" in their respective countries. Seven months later, the U.S. Senate Internal Security Subcommittee (SISS) conducted hearings about this high-level Communist gathering. Well-known authority on communist strategy and tactics Edward Hunter answered the committee's call to discuss the Communist activity. (Heralded also as a knowledgeable authority in the field of psychological warfare, Hunter is remembered for having coined the word "brainwashing" after studying the disappointing conduct of many of America's Korean War POWs.) His lengthy testimony published by SISS on July 11, 1961, appeared under the headline, "The New Drive Against the Anti-Communist Program." In that very informative study, Hunter referred to a growing number of "anti-anti-Communists." These were opponents of those who opposed Communism. Hunter offered his opinion that "Anti-Communism only became news when the pillorying of the Birch Society gave them [the Communists] the opportunity to refer to all opponents of Communism as the work of 'the Birchites,' and to smear all indiscriminately as 'right and extremist.'"

During these years, Communists from the West Coast published an official party newspaper known as *Peoples World*. (In January 2010, it became an online-only publication.) Acting on the December 1960 mandate given to the world's Communists, the February 25, 1961 issue of *Peoples World* targeted Robert Welch and the Society under a headline, "Enter (from stage right) the John Birch Society." Labeling Welch as the Society's "absolute boss," it claimed that he required members to demonstrate "complete obedience to the leader." It quoted Robert Welch's condemnation of democracy as "merely a deceptive phrase, a weapon of demagoguery, and a perennial fraud" with no hint about why he had said it or any mention of the views of numerous Founding Fathers who had pronounced their own harsh assessment of democracy. By pointing to Welch's concluding condemnation of democracy out of his lengthy essay on the topic, the Communist publication expected fellow Reds to rely on the American peoples' erroneous acceptance of democracy as our nation's form of government. Further, the Society had created "cells," said *Peoples World* and "is named for John Birch, a U.S. Army captain who is supposed to have died in China 10 days after VJ day." "Welch blames his death," said the Communist Party's newspaper, "on Chinese Communists."

Birch Society officials and members have always considered an attack by the communist press as something to be rather proud of. They found, however, that numerous elements of the mainstream press – at this particular time and then continuously – have followed the lead set by the Communists. No example of this pattern was more obvious than *Time* magazine's report about the Society a mere two weeks after the *Peoples World* article appeared.

On March 10, 1961, *Time* published its view under the heading "The Americanists." Where the Communist publication had labeled local JBS chapters "cells," so did *Time*. Where the Communist press had taken Welch's disapproval of democracy as an example of his extremism, so did *Time*. Where *Peoples World* had erroneously claimed that famed Hollywood actor Adolphe Menjou was a member of the Society's Council, so did *Time*. (Menjou, a well-known anti-Communist, had accepted a place on the Society's Council but had resigned in September 1960 for personal reasons without ever attending a Council meeting.)

What is extremely revealing, however, is that prior to *Time* publishing its diatribe against the Society, one of its reporters showed up at the Society's headquarters in Belmont, Massachusetts, where he was given three hours of Welch's time. All questions posed were answered forthrightly. The *Time* reporter received copies of every Society publication he asked for, plus others Welch felt he should have. He was shown the several errors of fact appearing in the *Peoples World* article. And he was taken on a tour of the Society's facilities where he chatted with numerous Society employees. Welch explained the differences between a democracy and a republic, even providing a copy of his recently printed speech on the topic in which any reader could find the strong condemnations of democracy issued by Washington, Franklin, Adams, Hamilton and other founders of our nation. The reporter was shown the Communist publication's reference to "cells" instead of chapters. But these and other errors and distortions still appeared in the *Time* article. It was obvious not only that *Time* had drawn its information from the Communist newspaper (without admitting so), but also that the information it published had most likely been written prior to sending its reporter to JBS headquarters.

Toward the end of 1961, *Time* featured JBS in a much longer and even more uncomplimentary article about anti-communist groups. Its December 8, 1961 issue labeled JBS "the most formidable of the extremist groups." The magazine insisted that the Welch-led organization believed that "internal Communism can best be fought by Communist tactics." Welch's response to that particular slur – repeated by numerous others over the years – has always pointed out that, while communists regularly employ both moral and immoral means to further their goals, JBS would never descend to using foul means for even the most worthy of ends.

On April 1, 1961, a JBS husband and wife team from California sent a telegram to FBI Director J. Edgar Hoover. Having that very day read in the *Los Angeles Examiner* that the Birch Society had been branded by the FBI leader as "anti-American, anti-Catholic and anti-Semitic" and, further, that Director Hoover had "a dim view of the Society and has it under surveillance," the couple asked the FBI's top official for a response. It came promptly via a Western Union telegram sent to Murray and Marion Beebe and signed by Director Hoover himself. It stated:

> *The FBI is an investigative agency of the federal government and does not make evaluations or draw any conclusions as to the character or integrity of any organization, publication or individual. Consequently, neither myself nor any representative of this bureau could have made the statement to which you referred.*

Mr. and Mrs. Beebe shared the Hoover response with Society officials and copies were immediately supplied to many members.

All the negative attention given the organization, combined with the public's widespread detestation of Communism, generated a reaction built partially on the American people's preference for fair play. A growing number began to examine the Society's literature and read one or more of the recommended books. Many asked for a sample of Welch's *American Opinion* magazine and even attended one of Welch's speeches. In numerous instances, what these people found out startled them. They discovered that the derogatory adjectives targeting Welch and the Society were baseless. A fairly common by-product of such discovery saw many wondering openly, or more often quietly to themselves: "What other falsehoods have the media and political leaders been sending to all of us?" Literally thousands found out that the Society was capably and honorably sounding a much needed alarm while also offering a realistic long-range plan to deal with the serious problem manifested by ascending Communist power. Membership continued to grow.

Early in 1961 when attacking the Society became widespread, Welch's position with the James O. Welch Candy Company became an issue. He had retired as the company's vice president at the end of 1956 after having built a nationwide network of 8,000 accounts reaching into all 50 states. In the course of his work, he developed a solid relationship with several thousand company employees and customers. Still a member of the firm's Executive Committee and always willing to find time for consultation with Welch Company officials, he realized after the Society had been discovered and he had become so "notorious" that the company might suffer retaliation of some kind.

The accuracy of that surmise became obvious when late-night television personality Jack Paar stated during his nationally televised program that the way to deal with Welch was to cease purchasing any products from the Welch Candy Company. Obvious pressures directed at others to follow such a plan soon reached down to some of the company's customers. Then during a chance meeting in the Chicago airport with three of the company's salesmen (each of whom he had hired and trained), Welch learned that all of the company's customers in a large mid-western city had just canceled their outstanding orders.

As soon as possible, therefore, older brother Robert sat down with younger brother James and, at Robert's insistence, their business relationship ended in every way. From that day forward, the company could say with complete candor that Robert Welch owned no stock in the company, was not connected with it in any way, and could neither gain any profit nor suffer any loss related to the company's operations. Then, the May 9, 1961 issue of the New York-based fortnightly *Candy Industry Journal* published an editorial written by one of its executives who claimed to have known and admired Welch "for over 25 years." Headlined "The Bob Welch story," it gave a brief and laudatory history of the now controversial Robert Welch and then told of his creation of The John Birch Society and his separation from the candy company. And, as had been worked out by the Welch brothers, James Welch supplied the following statement: "I know that there must be many of our customers who not only disagree with Bob Welch's viewpoints, but must be very much disturbed over his activities. Our company emphatically has nothing to do with the John Birch Society, and my brother has no connection with this company." He added that he "did not share his brother's view on all matters." The company very quickly regained lost business and continued to be a leader in the highly competitive candy industry. It was sold to the National Biscuit Company several years later.

Glad to get away from all the negativity sent his way, Welch journeyed to Chicago on September 17, 1961, where he had committed to be the featured speech at a luncheon arranged by the patriotic "We, the People" organization. Attendance was exceptionally high because advanced publicity had named the now controversial speaker. But those who expected the Society's leader to use the occasion to defend himself and the Society from the wave of negativity sent his way as a result of press coverage about his Eisenhower attitude received instead his remarkable history lesson entitled "Republics and Democracies." *American Opinion* had already published the speech in booklet form a month earlier but very few in that audience had seen a copy.

The date for this event happened to be "Constitution Day," and the Illinois crowd was delightedly commemorating the anniversary of the September 17, 1787 signing of the U.S. Constitution. Because the overwhelming majority in that audience (as well as throughout the nation) had been victimized by mis-education and the media/government never-ending insistence that our nation's governing system was and always had been democracy, Welch chose to speak about the Founders' success in creating a republic. Like other Americans, everyone at the gathering knew how to pledge allegiance to Old Glory and "to the **republic** for which it stands." But discussions about the actual distinctions between the meanings of republic and democracy would customarily inspire a mere shrug, possibly even an erroneous claim that the U.S. governmental system is "a democratic republic."

Welch proceeded to take that audience on a trip through ancient Greece and Rome to show the difference between the folly of rule by a majority (Greece's democracy) and the enduring wisdom of rule by fixed law (Rome's republic). Much of his speech focused on the thinking of America's Founders who knew the history of pre-Christian Greece and Rome and wanted nothing to do with either the Greek experiment in democracy or Rome's descent from a republic into majority rule and eventual despotism. Not only did Welch cite the wisdom inherent in a republic noted by Washington, Franklin, Adams, Hamilton, Madison and other early Americans, he discussed the deliberate propagation of its polar opposite, democracy, and its frequent promotion by Woodrow Wilson, Franklin Roosevelt, and others.

From the series of essays known as *The Federalist Papers*, Welch quoted the devastatingly accurate condemnation of democracy written by James Madison. Later dubbed the "Father of the Constitution" because of his valuable note-taking prowess during the 1787 convention, Madison was greatly respected by his peers. His perspective about the folly and danger inherent in any democracy was certainly shared by his colleagues. Ambitious political leaders and teachers at virtually all levels of academia regularly ignore his and other soundly based condemnations of the political movement that history has shown to be a path to ruin. For decades, certainly including current times, any condemnation of democracy has invited condemnation of oneself.

But that didn't bother Welch as he pointed to Madison's accurate conclusion about the absurdity of relying on what would always degenerate into rule by the mob. Madison's condemnation of democracy was aimed at the people of New York State in hopes that their state officials would ratify the just-completed Constitution. What Madison said appeared in Essay #10 in *The Federalist Papers*, the collection of essays explaining the Constitution to New York residents. The man who became the fourth president of our nation wrote:

> Hence it is that democracies have ever been spectacles of turbulence and contention; have ever been found incompatible with personal security or the rights of property; and have in general been as short in their lives as they have been violent in their deaths.

On this occasion, Welch introduced the slogan widely used by Society members over the years: "This is a Republic, not a Democracy. Let's keep it that way!" For most in that audience, and in other audiences who later heard him deliver that same speech, the information he provided was stunningly new and it left many of its listeners somewhat open-mouthed. Many decided they had found a man worthy of their time and their loyalty. As so often happened, these people also wondered, "What else have I been told that isn't true?" and "What else has Robert Welch stated?" The complete text of the speech entitled "Republics and Democracies" remains a sorely needed history lesson for Americans. One by-product of sharing this speech has always been an appreciation of the real Robert Welch, quite a departure from the caricature painting him as a daft or even dangerous lunatic.

Chapter 16
Impeach the Chief Justice?

As 1961 dawned, the Birch Society forged ahead with an entirely new project entitled "The Movement To Impeach Earl Warren." Those who considered the new campaign a mere publicity stunt didn't know Robert Welch. He was as serious about getting Warren removed as Chief Justice of the Supreme Court as he was about having our nation withdraw from the United Nations. In keeping with his disdain for the national media, he issued no press releases and called in no reporters to announce the new project.

JBS members immediately found that one of Welch's charges aimed at the Chief Justice centered on Warren's determination to "change our country from a republic, governed by laws, into a democracy governed by men unchecked by law and precedent." Furthermore, claimed Welch, Warren's attitude "epitomizes the newborn theory that our Constitution means absolutely nothing against the changing sociological views of the Supreme Court Justices … [and] that both our Constitution and our laws are simply whatever the Supreme Court says they are."

In what must have been a minor refresher course for some, Welch carefully pointed out that the power to impeach resides in the House of Representatives, that an affirmative vote regarding impeachment by that body does not constitute conviction and removal from office, and that any decision to impeach reached by the House must be followed by a Senate trial where two-thirds approval would be needed to accomplish the removal of the individual in question. For his main charge, Welch cited Article III, Section 1 of the Constitution stating "judges, both of the supreme and inferior Courts, shall hold their offices during good behavior…." And he insisted Earl Warren's performance in his high post should most emphatically be considered to be bad behavior.

According to Welch, the 1954 *Brown v. Board of Education* decision was the first of Warren's deeds meriting his removal. Never railing against the decision because of any considerations about race, the JBS leader insisted it had been based by the court not on American law and precedent but, as its partisans admitted, on "a set of psychological and sociological theories advanced by Swedish socialist Gunnar Myrdal and a group of American Communist-fronters with whom Myrdal had been associated." In other words, the nation's highest court completely avoided reliance on the Constitution of the United States and opted instead to base their ruling on a foreign "expert," on the court's unconstitutional involvement in education, and on its disdain for the rights of the states. Only the beginning of the Welch case against Warren, he then pointed to numerous decisions of the Court obliterating law and precedent in favor of Communist designs. For examples of the pro-Communist decisions rendered by the Warren-led court, he offered:

> In the Steve Nelson case, the Warren Court simply wiped out the anti-sedition laws of more than forty states and denied those states the right to protect themselves against treason.... In the Konigsberg case, the Warren Court canceled the right of any state to deny a license to practice law to a man after he wouldn't say whether he was or wasn't a Communist.... In the Sweezy case, the Warren Court revised a decision of the New Hampshire Supreme Court and held that the Attorney General of New Hampshire was without authority to question a lecturer at the State University concerning his reported subversive activities.

Welch then listed several dozen reports, books, newsletters and government publications showing a multiplicity of highly questionable decisions issued by the high court. One document he highly recommended was the December 1958 report issued by the American Bar Association's "Special Committee On Communist Tactics, Strategy, and Objectives." It presented a synopsis of 20 Warren Court decisions favoring Communism during the previous two years. Each of those rulings overturned one or more existing federal or state laws that had been created to protect America against communist subversion.

Welch also highly recommended Rosalie Gordon's small book, *Nine Men Against America*, in which the case against Warren and his leadership of the high court had been capably laid out for lawyers and non-lawyers alike in easily understood prose. Later republished by the Society on several occasions, this thin book (121 pages in the pocket-sized edition) provided a devastating summary of what the Supreme Court under Warren's leadership had been doing. Welch emphatically agreed with the book's conclusion that the Warren-led court "has been destroying every safeguard which might prevent the Communists from carrying out their plans."

The Gordon book also made note of the jubilation expressed by former Los Angeles Communist Party Chairman Dorothy Healey after the Warren Court had voided the Smith

Act. Citing provisions of that 1940 law, 11 leaders of the Communist Party USA had been convicted and sent to prison for seeking to overthrow the government of the United States. Healey rejoiced, "This is the greatest victory the Communist Party ever had." In New York, the Communist *Daily Worker* organized a huge rally "To pay honor to the U.S. Supreme Court and its recent decisions." At that well-attended event, thousands of Communists and fellow travelers saluted Warren and his court.

The Impeachment project resulted in a new round of scorn aimed at the Society. But it also earned praise from many while providing needed lessons about important portions of the U.S. Constitution and the damage already done to national security by the Court. Welch urged members to write letters to congressmen and newspapers, seek support for the Movement from other patriotic groups, form a local Impeach Warren Committee, and distribute copies of his "Republics and Democracies" speech along with other pertinent items. Soon, billboards blaring the headline "Impeach Earl Warren" began appearing in numerous parts of the nation and banners proclaiming the same message were strung high across the main streets of smaller communities.

Another weapon employed by the Movement was the conclusion reached at the August 1958 "Conference of Chief Justices of the States." Jurists from most of the states had met in California and, by a vote of 36 to 8, they strongly criticized the Supreme Court for its "lack of judicial restraint." Welch urged Society members to obtain copies of this report. Aiding the Impeach Warren campaign were recent issues of *The Dan Smoot Report* featuring the revealing opinions of other justices who, from their unique platforms, sharply disagreed with many of the stands taken by the Chief Justice and his allies. Smoot also supplied the critical comments of other renowned constitutional authorities. And Congressman Mendel Rivers (D-S.C.) inserted his own supporting comments as well as his defense of the Society's "Impeach" campaign in the March 22, 1961 issue of the *Congressional Record*. These were only some indications of support favoring the project Welch had initiated.

Welch repeatedly stressed that the case against Warren should focus simply on his "violation of the constitutional provision for good behavior in office." He wrote that the Chief Justice was "tearing down the Constitution which it is his sworn and official duty to uphold." He pointedly discounted the notion that Warren was himself a Communist. But that didn't keep liberals and leftists from mockingly claiming that the Society believed Warren to be an actual member of the Communist Party.

Because of the Impeach campaign, attacks aimed at the Society increased in number and intensity. It seemed as though the Society's focus on the Chief Justice had hit a nerve stimulating leftists and liberals to respond when they might have preferred to ignore the Society and its efforts. Welch noted, however, that the Society had enjoyed a "net gain in our membership right while the campaign against us has been at its peak." He reported that, because of the Impeach project, there had been losses adding up to "one-quarter of one percent" of the Society's total but the number of new members "every day" always exceeded those losses. Encouraged by continued growth, and by the agreement of others about having Warren removed, Welch created a "Petition to Congress" calling for all in that body to use its constitutional authority to impeach the Chief Justice. Society members were urged to reach out to others, not only to get their signatures on the petition, but also to have them gain an appreciation about the harm the Supreme Court was doing and what could be done about it.

The Warren-led court had also weakened the criminal justice system while crippling legal protections against internal subversion. In 1968, the Society's Western Islands publishing arm issued G. Edward Griffin's small book entitled *The Great Prison Break: The Supreme Court Leads the Way*. It summarized several Supreme Court decisions (almost all rendered by the Warren Court) that hampered law enforcement personnel, set known criminals free, eased distribution of pornography and harmful drugs, removed prayer and Bible reading from public schools, interfered with traditional religious practices, and propagated the false notion that the Constitution mandated separation of church and state – which attitude soon became separation of **God** and state.

Many thousands of signatures were gathered on the Impeach Warren petition. But Warren retired in 1969 and the Impeach Earl Warren campaign became a topic for history books. Welch declared the campaign a limited success in that many Americans had been made aware of the damage Warren and his fellow jurists had done, while great numbers of Americans had learned more about the U.S. Constitution and about many of its enemies.

Chapter 17
Pleading To Be Investigated

Responding eagerly to Welch's prompting, Society members throughout the nation earnestly began filling their living rooms or a nearby hired hall to show programs to audiences large and small. Accompanied by a voice recording, the filmstrip "Communism on the Map" proved to be a very effective tool in creating awareness and gaining new members. Produced by Harding College in Searcy, Arkansas, and narrated by the college's president Dr. George Benson, the program graphically traced Communism's successful implementation of Lenin's three-step plan for world conquest. Large portions of Asia were already under Communist control; Eastern Europe had been overrun; and Communist penetration of government and various sectors of life in the U.S. had become demonstrable.

Success in carrying out these three steps of the Lenin plan would essentially accomplish seizure of the planet. Critics of the Society had to admit that the information presented in this brief program couldn't be denied. It was no surprise to Society leaders that "Communism on the Map" adhered closely to what Welch had written in the first chapter of the Society's *Blue Book*.

The Harding College filmstrip gained enthusiastic plaudits from Birchers across the nation and from many who viewed it and joined the Society. But it also generated condemnation from several quarters. One blast came in a February 1961 newsletter published by an organization labeling itself "Protestant Social Action." A project of the Congregational Conference of Southern California and the Southwest, its main message targeted The John Birch Society even though the filmstrip had been produced and circulated by Harding College. Its vitriolic content condemned the Society for its "extreme right-wing social, economic and political point of view." The newsletter insisted that the filmstrip's message was "distorted," "full of smear and innuendo," and had sunk to such extremes as to name "Vice President Richard Nixon and Secretary of State Christian Herter as possible communist conspirators." Those two high government officials were indeed criticized but neither was labeled as the "Social Action" group suggested.

Sent to Protestant ministers for their use as a warning for their flocks, Protestant Social Action's newsletter pulled several quotations out of the *Blue Book* and claimed each to be totally indefensible. As had already become the custom in any disparagement of the Society, this warning for ministers and their congregations included mention of Welch's conclusion about Dwight Eisenhower. But, like so many who parroted what had been lifted from Welch's manuscript, the newsletter's authors had never seen a copy of *The Politician.*

Another highly recommended program put to use by JBS members depicted communist disruption of the work of the House Committee on Un-American Activities (HCUA) during that panel's investigation of Communist activity in the San Francisco Bay Area. Entitled "Operation Abolition," the 16mm film dramatically showed Communists using standard Red tactics to impede the committee's efforts while calling for total abolition of HCUA. It shocked viewers, especially individuals who had little or no awareness that well-organized Communist activity was actually occurring within the borders of our nation.

Welch proudly claimed that Birch Society members had shown one or both of these programs to audiences numbering more than the total viewers gathered by all other patriotic groups put together. The two films helped local members swell their chapter membership rolls, even leading to formation of new chapters.

But the controversy about *The Politician* and its conclusions about President Eisenhower continued to grow. Repeatedly hounded by members of the press and even questioned by loyal members who had never seen the manuscript, Welch distributed a three-page memorandum commenting on what he had written. Dated February 17, 1961, the memo said of the now-famous (infamous?) manuscript, "It was never intended or offered for publication." And, in a somewhat remarkable *mea culpa*, the increasingly badgered Society leader wrote, "It contained personal and offhand opinions, such as anybody might express in a letter, which I would not have been willing to express for publication."

It would be unfair, Welch insisted, to hold members of the Society responsible for what he had written in a private letter before the Society had been formed, or to insist that what was stated there should be considered as the hard and fast beliefs of the Society. He suggested that whenever JBS members received questions about the matter, their response should indicate that the manuscript is in no way "part of the materials or beliefs of The John Birch Society." Two years later, however, driven both by a need for self-defense and a rising number of requests for an explanation, he did publish it with the addition of

122 pages of supporting footnotes to demonstrate that the history he related about Dwight Eisenhower was indeed available from other sources.

In March, an obviously irritated member sent a lengthy letter to all members of the Society's National Council. In it, he questioned Welch, the Society, its funding, and more. Council member N. E. Adamson, M.D., capably and frankly answered the letter for Welch while sending copies to each Council member. One matter addressed by Dr. Adamson in that response, stated, "… as I happen to know, Mr. Welch has never drawn one penny of salary or wages or pay of any kind from either the magazine or The John Birch Society for his services." Also stated Adamson, "The Society's books, though not made available publicly but to Council members, had been competently audited by a respected area firm, a policy that has continued throughout the years." The irritated member ceased being irritated.

When the media storm began, two Society members, both from California, were serving as elected members of the U.S. House of Representatives. Neither escaped attention as reporters started asking questions about the Society. Congressman John Rousselot carefully explained his reasons for joining the Society in a three-page statement issued in 1961. He declared that the "Society is dedicated to the preservation of our American heritage." As a way of putting down the notion that members had to agree with everything Robert Welch ever said, he mentioned his own disagreements with the Society's founder about President Eisenhower, Chief Justice Warren, and others. He said there was a need for people "dedicated to fighting the Communist Conspiracy internally" which, he said, was why he joined.

Rousselot lost his reelection campaign in 1962, but he later regained a place in the House and served a total of seven full terms. For several years while not a member of Congress, he served the Society as its Public Relations Director. He emphatically agreed with numerous top California politicians – left-wing and right-wing – about the need for an official investigation of the organization. Only through such "an honest, thorough investigation," he insisted, "can the patriotic, soundly based principles of the Society be brought to the attention of all good Americans." That investigation, soon to be undertaken, was enthusiastically welcomed by the Society.

The other member of Congress who had affiliated with the Society in its early days was Edgar Hiestand, already an eight-year veteran in the House of Representatives. Known widely as an outspoken foe of Communism, he readily signed on as a member after meeting Welch and discovering the Society's determination to oppose the Red menace and preserve America's independence. When California Attorney General Stanley Mosk produced an incredibly nasty report about the Society, Hiestand placed in the *Congressional Record* key excerpts of a rebuttal showing how fraudulent the Mosk report truly was. Compiled by California attorney Thomas Werdel, himself a JBS member, that rebuttal noted of the Mosk report:

> No witnesses were ever called. No information was requested of or opportunity to reply given to the Society.... Without calling witnesses or making a reasonable effort to determine the truth, the [Attorney] General compared the John Birch Society to the structure of the Communist Party itself. The report puts words in strangers' mouths, as alleged members of the society.... Another of the double-standard smear attacks on the Society is the denunciation that it is operating in secrecy for some never defined or explained evil purposes. The John Birch Society is no more secret than the Knights of Columbus, American Legion, Veterans of Foreign Wars, and hundreds of similar organizations.

The Mosk report was soon joined by another attack issued by California Governor Pat Brown. The governor outdid all others in wildly characterizing the Society as "a conspiratorial group," "promoters of the big lie," "operates through secret cells," and "demands absolute obedience to its founder." It was obvious that California's key political leaders, practically all Democrats, had declared their own kind of war on the Society. They used their power and influence to force Congressman Hiestand into a newly carved district dominated by liberals and leftists, a move that cost him reelection.

Facing intense attacks emanating from California, Welch responded on March 22, 1961 with a telegram to Governor Pat Brown requesting the state to conduct an official investigation of the Society. He sent a copy of that telegram to Senator Hugh Burns, Chairman of the California Senate Factfinding Committee on Un-American Activities.

Nine days later, the Society leader sent a similar request to Senator James Eastland, Chairman of the U.S. Senate Internal Security Subcommittee, asking for an investigation of the Society. Dated March 31, 1961, the telegram to Senator Eastland stated in part:

> Because of the charges now being so widely circulated about us, some of which are extreme distortions of fact and many of which are sheer fabrications, The John Birch Society respectfully requests an official investigation by the Senate Internal Security Subcommittee of which you are chairman. As many of our members as your Committee may wish will gladly testify about the background, methods, purposes, and specific activities of the Society.

And we repeat our assurance made recently to the Chairman of a Committee in California that, unlike our Communist enemies, none of our members will plead the Fifth Amendment.

Senator Eastland's Subcommittee never conducted the requested investigation. But the California panel responded immediately. Its chairman, state Senator Hugh Burns, a Democrat as were Governor Brown and Attorney General Mosk, issued a statement announcing his plan to conduct an official inquiry. It stated in part: "Our sole interest in the John Birch Society must go to the question of whether the Society is un-American. We are not interested in investigating the John Birch Society to find out what its views are on Communism. We are only interested in finding out whether the John Birch Society is un-American."

Senator Burns let it be known that the Subcommittee had already been gathering information about the Society because of its explosive growth and expanding influence within the state. Finally, after two years of thorough investigation, the Committee issued its June 1963 report exonerating the Society of the widespread but false charges repeatedly aired in California and throughout the nation.

The Subcommittee told of the Society's origin and growth, discussed in detail the comments made by Welch in *The Politician*, quoted and named numerous area members, admitted sending its personnel into JBS meetings without announcing why they were there, summarized opinions about the organization rendered by some on the right and some on the left including Communist officials, expressed disagreement with the pronouncements of Attorney General Mosk, and gave its conclusions at the end in two short paragraphs. Those conclusions stated:

> We believe that the reason the John Birch Society has attracted so many members is that it simply appeared to them to be the most effective, indeed the only, organization through which they could join in a national movement to learn the truth about the Communist menace and then take some positive concerted action to prevent its spread.
>
> Our investigation and study was requested by the society, which had been publicly charged with being a secret, fascist, subversive, un-American, anti-Semitic organization. We have not found any of these accusations to be supported by the evidence.

After receiving a copy of the report from Senator Burns, Welch immediately thanked the subcommittee and its members for their "honorableness and responsibility." He requested and promptly received permission to publish the report's entire 62 pages in a booklet issued by the Society entitled *The California Report*. Many thousands of copies were put to use by members all across the nation. That panel's work **remains the only official investigation ever conducted about the Society and its work**. JBS officials always expected that the various false and defamatory charges aimed at the organization would cease as a result of the findings of this government agency. But, while the conclusions reached by the California Senate panel did help toward that end, its honest assessment merely slowed the intensity and number of attacks.

Society officials, buoyed by the conclusions about their efforts published in *The California Report*, redoubled their efforts. Welch wrote that the *Report* "reveals a controlling tradition of honorableness and responsibility in the legislative framework of our governmental system which has withstood all the pressures and attrition of the dishonorable decades." And he congratulated the committee members for doing their job "in a completely objective manner."

Chapter 18
Smears From Many; Plaudits From Some

The John Birch Society was only three weeks old when Fidel Castro took control of Cuba on January 1, 1959. Falsely posing as an opponent of Communism, he became an instant hero to many. When the Cuban dictator publicly announced that he was indeed a Communist in 1961, no one in government or the media apologized for all the praises and funding given him. And, of course, none of those who allowed themselves to be taken in, or who knew the truth and were determined to suppress it, bothered to mention that The John Birch Society's Robert Welch had been correct about Castro months before Cuba became the latest Communist conquest.

A few months after Castro "outed" himself as a Communist, a force of 1,400 anti-Castro Cubans invaded their nation at its Bay of Pigs. The April 17, 1961, operation had been planned, financed and controlled by the U.S. State Department and CIA. The men, all volunteers willing to put their lives on the line to reverse the Communist takeover of their homeland had undergone training in Mexico and were then transported in small vessels to their landing point along the southern coast of the island nation. They had been assured that air support would be supplied by the United States, that a force of friendly Cubans would rise up and rendezvous with them, and that success would be theirs. But none of those assurances materialized.

During several days prior to the landing when rumors about its actual occurrence were surfacing almost daily, Welch happened to be away from his office in the midst of a West Coast speaking tour. Everything he initially knew about the coming invasion had been gained from fleeting glances at newspaper accounts. Asked at a public gathering for his assessment of what everyone was expecting, he explained that he had no inside information about the forthcoming operation but was perfectly willing to predict the outcome. He said the mission would fail; anti-Communists throughout Cuba would be lured into exposing themselves where they would be speedily neutralized and immediately arrested;

the U.S. would suffer severe loss of prestige especially throughout Latin America; and Castro would emerge far stronger than ever as "the Communist David who had defeated the great capitalist Goliath." There may have been some immediate scoffers among those who heard Welch's forecast but his predictions were right on target. The Bay of Pigs operation was a well-planned betrayal.

In July 1961, Welch reported that, over the past three months, he had spoken to "twenty audiences totaling approximately 40,000 people." Buoyed by those appearances and the many new members that resulted, he nevertheless warned that anyone "seeking to stop the Communists will face more smears and ridicule and venomous attacks than ever struck Martin Dies or Joe McCarthy." Texas Congressman Martin Dies had chaired the 1930s House of Representatives panel that later became the House Committee on Un-American Activities. Joe McCarthy, the better-known anti-Communist senator from Wisconsin, found in Welch one of his strongest supporters. We encourage skeptics about the work of Senator McCarthy to read *Blacklisted By History: The Untold Story of Senator Joe McCarthy*, a book authored by veteran journalist M. Stanton Evans and published by Crown Publishing Group, 2007.

One of the most "venomous" attacks predicted by Welch came from Senator Stephen Young (D-Ohio) who charged in a speech that "retired lawyer" Welch was "enriching himself" by charging one dollar per person to attend his speeches, that these events produced "tax exempt" money, that he [Welch] "keeps no financial records," that the Internal Revenue Service is not able to know "how much he takes in," that he is "a slick promoter of a secret society whose methods are unconscionable," and that the Society is a "fascist group." All of those charges were totally false. As quickly pointed out by Welch, the truth was that he never was a lawyer; the money collected from attendees went to the sponsoring organization except for a $300 honorarium and the cost of his plane tickets; JBS had never even applied to the IRS for tax-exempt status; the Society had just been audited by a nationally known accounting firm that found nothing out of the ordinary; and the Society was no more secret or fascist than a host of other American organizations. As for enriching himself, Welch laughingly countered with a "hope that this wonderful rain of riches hurries up and happens before my savings run out." Senator Young never apologized.

Society members and Welch himself continued to receive a steady stream of slurs and vindictive characterizations from an array of sources. On April 22, 1961, the Communist Party's *People's World* labeled Welch a "Fuhrer" and claimed the Society to be "fascist." The Communist publication then branded the Society "an ultra right wing group" in its mid-July 1961 issue. Other non-Communist publications added their attacks. In May, *Life* magazine issued a spread entitled "The Unhelpful Fringes" claiming the Society to be "semi-secret" and labeling its message "lunacy." Relying on similar misinformation given Americans over many years, *Life* told its readers that Welch scorns "democracy" and "members occasionally resort to dirty tricks," such as "anonymous calls" in the wee hours. While denying or correcting these charges, Society leaders pointed out that, if any such calls are indeed anonymous, whoever placed them surely couldn't be known.

Not to be outdone or overlooked, the September 26, 1961, issue of *Look* magazine (a popular competitor of *Life* at the time) filled five pages with another report about the Society. After stating that the Welch-led organization "is a semi-secret society," Senior Editor Chester Morrison displayed his mastery of journalistic treachery with:

> The John Birch Society may not be fascist, but it has some trappings of fascism. It may not be cousin to the Ku Klux Klan, but its secrecy arouses suspicion. It certainly is not communist, but has no compunction about adapting to its own purposes the devious propaganda methods of the Soviet Union.

Morrison knew, as any student of journalism knows, that readers will remember the words "fascist," "Ku Klux Klan," and "communist" mentioned alongside the name of The John Birch Society, and many will recall only a hazy connection of all four. The *Look* editor never actually accused the Society of links to such odious groups and their practices. He simply planted seeds of association expecting them to flower in the minds of his readers. When a reader of such journalistic trickery hears "Birch," he will think of fascist, Klan, and communist. The reprehensible style of journalism employed by Morrison and other Society enemies became a fairly regular occurrence.

But, as Society leaders and members found out, all the publicity wasn't negative, and some of it written to cast the Society in a bad light had the opposite effect. On the plus side, California Congressman James Utt placed a remarkably pro-Birch editorial from the Oceanside, California *Banner* in the *Congressional Record* for May 1, 1961.

Beginning in its Sunday, March 5, 1961, issue and continuing for the next four days, the *Los Angeles Times* published reporter Gene Blake's five-part series about the Society. (The Senator Burns-led Subcommittee had mentioned this series in its aforementioned report.) Blake's comments, written after much research and numerous interviews with local members, didn't favor the Society. Nevertheless, Welch asked the newspaper's officials for permission to reprint all five articles – plus the accompanying uncomplimentary editorial written by publisher Otis Chandler.

Welch's request was granted and the six items, plus a letter Welch addressed to Chandler, were printed on a single large sheet of paper folded several times and distributed to members. One of the criticisms issued by publisher Chandler contained the oft-repeated charge that the Society and its members intend "to fight Communists in Communist fashion." Welch addressed that by repeating his standard requirement of members that they never resort to "any sacrifice of morality in the means used to achieve an end." Welch also knew that a prominent member of the Chandler family was already a JBS member – but he never publicized that fact.

In a speech delivered on April 5, 1961, Boston's Richard Cardinal Cushing pointed to Robert Welch as a man he had known for "many years" who should be supported as "a dedicated foe of Communism." The *Boston Herald* noted the Catholic leader's endorsement under the headline, "Cardinal Hails Welch as Enemy of Reds." One year later, the Boston-based Cardinal issued his own 14-page booklet condemning Communism under the title "The Church and Communism." The Society urged members to obtain and distribute copies.

Earlier in 1961, the Society published a 24-page booklet entitled "Appreciation and Encouragement" containing endorsements from scores of individuals in various parts of the nation. Also included were photographically reproduced letters from prominent persons such as former State Department official Spruille Braden, Richard Cardinal Cushing, and former federal government official T. Coleman Andrews. Every member of the Society received a copy of this booklet. A similar booklet carrying the identical heading appeared in 1962 with additional endorsements. In July 1961, the weekly *Human Events* newsletter offered a defense of the Society under a headline "Why the John Birch Society is Under Fire."

On Sunday, May 21, 1961, Welch appeared as the guest on NBC's "Meet the Press." He hoped to use the on-air time to alert more Americans to the threat of Communism, especially noting that Communists had added Cuba to their many previous conquests and were gaining in North Vietnam, Laos and Indonesia. He also hoped to point out that the Supreme Court had issued numerous decisions highly praised by Communists who had celebrated the Court's rulings with their huge rally. Much of the panel's questioning, however, dealt with statements taken from Welch's by-now famous treatise about President Eisenhower – even though none of the panelists had seen the 300-page manuscript.

One of Welch's favorite publications was the *Dan Smoot Report*, an eight-page weekly published in Dallas. Smoot himself had earned two degrees from Southern Methodist University, taught at Harvard University, and then joined the Federal Bureau of Investigation after color blindness kept him from being accepted by the U.S. military. During the nine years he spent with the Bureau, he rose from investigating Communist activity in several U.S. cities to eventually becoming an Administrative Assistant to Director J. Edgar Hoover. In 1955, he left the Bureau and launched his own publishing venture.

In 1961, Smoot showed his approval of the Society by introducing the organization to his readers in one of his weekly reports. He later devoted two separate reports to reasons why Chief Justice Earl Warren should indeed be impeached. Then he issued what Welch labeled "an unbelievably excellent and informative survey of our country's INVISIBLE GOVERNMENT" (emphasis by Welch). For eight consecutive weeks beginning in mid-June of 1961, Smoot provided an expose' of the many well-connected individuals affiliated with such tax-exempt groups as the Council on Foreign Relations, the Foreign Policy Association, and several other left-leaning foundations "pushing America into a one-world socialist system."

Most of the men named by Smoot weren't Communists although some could have been quiet party members. Instead, the bulk of those listed by Smoot were personally ambitious ladder-climbers who were willing to work with and support Communism in its efforts leading to a Communist-led world government. In 1966, Welch would select the term "INSIDERS" when referring to these non-Communist anti-Americans. Smoot had led the way by pointing to this upper level of conspiratorial activity – something that wasn't unknown to Welch, although it was his intention to introduce the topic to JBS members more slowly.

The JBS leader did eventually provide his own assessment of this upper echelon of subversion in an essay entitled "The Truth In Time." It first saw publication in the November 1966 *American Opinion*. (More coverage about this "upgrading" of the JBS beliefs about internal enemies seeking destruction of the U.S. and eventual world government appears in a later chapter.) Smoot subsequently added to what he had already published about these groups and individuals in his 1962 book *The Invisible Government*. Later republished with Smoot's permission by the Society's Western Islands, the Welch essay and the Smoot book became fundamental staples of Society understanding.

In November, Welch asked members to send congratulatory letters to Montana Governor Nutter who had refused to proclaim "United Nations Day" in his state. The Society would later designate October 24th of each year as a day to champion our nation and its system of government rather than celebrate the existence of the United Nations.

Welch noted in the December 1961 *Bulletin* that "we had only four thousand members nearly two years ago," a number that had obviously grown. The year ended with

Welch reviewing Society accomplishments such as a new Speakers Bureau; the Movement to Impeach Earl Warren had introduced many Americans to the subversion being accomplished by the Warren Court; the circulation of *American Opinion* had risen from four to fourteen thousand; book publishing/distribution had increased substantially; and various letter-writing campaigns had achieved partial or complete success. But, in keeping with his long-standing rule, he provided no up-to-date actual membership total.

The *1961 White Book* (the year's *Bulletins* in one volume) closed with several appendices including a four-page letter targeting the horror of foreign aid written by JBS Council Member A.G. Heinsohn, and a separate four-page pamphlet entitled "Why Join The John Birch Society?"

Chapter 19
American Opinion Helps the Cause

Six months after creating the Society (summer of 1960), Welch gifted his stock in *American Opinion* magazine to The John Birch Society. He remained the magazine's Editor and would continue to fill its pages with his perspective about persons, events and issues he deemed important. The magazine, however, would not be the "official voice" of the Society (the monthly JBS *Bulletin* alone held that status). But its valuable content would parallel the Society's efforts, all of it written by authors Welch knew and trusted, plus occasional contributions of his own.

In the early years, every chapter leader of the Society received a complimentary subscription to the magazine. All JBS members were encouraged to subscribe, or to borrow their chapter leader's copy. As noted previously, the magazine grew from the Welch-produced *One Man's Opinion* (published during 1956-57) and adopted the new name *American Opinion* in February 1958, almost a full year before the December 1958 founding of the Society.

Over the years, *American Opinion's* articles have always supplied printed ammunition for various JBS campaigns. Because the magazine has always been part of the Society's educational arsenal, no history of the organization would be complete without mentioning some of its content. While apologizing for the rather staccato method employed here, the list contains some highlights during the earliest years of the Society-owned publication. In future chapters, the year-by-year summary of *American Opinion's* output will be discarded and the focus will simply be on portions of its content that became significant weapons in the Society's educational arsenal.

1958: Welch offered his "Why People Become Communists," and he saluted Senator Barry Goldwater with a highly complimentary biographical sketch entitled "Fighter From Phoenix." Former IRS Commissioner T. Coleman Andrews authored an article about the ravages of inflation. Then the magazine published the ten-page "Report of the Special

Committee of the American Bar Association On Communist Strategy, Tactics and Objectives." Its frightening look at Communist progress within America became a highly popular item in pamphlet form.

1959: The entire January issue provided a brief review of each of the books Welch listed in what he termed "One Hundred Steps to the Truth." Later, Professor Anthony Kubek supplied details about the distortions of history being offered in the schools and by the media. Permission was gained to publish the text of a broadcast made by popular radio commentator Paul Harvey. Articles questioned the federal government's foreign aid program, our nation's entanglement in NATO, and the suicidal disarmament program already being undertaken by U.S. leaders.

1960: Articles detailing the suicidal U.S. disarmament plans and the steady destruction of precious metal-backed money appeared. Former Notre Dame Law School Dean Clarence Manion condemned the Eisenhower administration's contention that treaty law legitimately superseded the Constitution. An article that created a huge amount of interest pointed to a U.S. Air Force publication's exposure of Communist infiltration into America's churches.

1961: Professor Hans Sennholz showed how each of the ten planks of the 1848 *Communist Manifesto* had already been partially or fully fastened on our country. Noteworthy Marxian goals already in place included the federal income tax, the Federal Reserve, and important steps toward a federal takeover of education. Professors Russell Kirk and E. Merrill Root reported about deficiencies in education.

1962: Welch and others penned exposures of Tito, Castro, Sukarno, Nehru, Betancourt, and other Communists or Communist sympathizers. Professor Sennholz explained what could be expected from creation of Europe's Common Market. Medical Doctor F.B. Exner condemned the fluoridation of water supplies as a dangerous precedent that could lead to mass medication. Former Assistant Secretary of State Spruille Braden reported about disturbing developments in Mexico. A full-page ad told readers how to obtain a copy of the revealing book *Toward Soviet America* authored in 1932 by Communist Party leader William Z. Foster.

In October 1962, while Welch retained the title of Editor, young Scott Stanley, Jr. won appointment as Managing Editor of the magazine, a post he continued to hold without interruption until the magazine was discontinued and replaced by the entirely new *The New American* in 1985. A native Kansan, Stanley had graduated from Indiana's Earlham College and was among the dozen young Americans present at the 1960 launching of Buckley's Young Americans for Freedom. A talented orator in addition to his admirable prowess in putting a magazine together, he won a strong following among all subscribers. Never satisfied with Welch's leadership, however, he did involve himself in plans created by a few anti-Welch dissidents to oust the Founder and steer the Society on a different track. His involvement in that behind-the-scenes venture almost cost him his post with *American Opinion*. But Welch, who needed someone to preside over *American Opinion* and who admired the ability of his young appointee, scolded him rather severely, kept him on the team, and took some steps to have him supervised more closely.

1963: Famed national columnist Westbrook Pegler began supplying articles. Popular novelist Taylor Caldwell provided the first of her many offerings with a disparaging analysis of the liberal mentality. Alan Stang launched his many years of association with the magazine and the Society by examining the career of UN Secretary General U Thant. James Lucier debuted as a writer with his expose' of UN favorite Ralph Bunche. He followed that valuable piece with a review of Martin Luther King's numerous connections to Communism. A.F. Canwell told of the personal background and subversive efforts of Defense Secretary Robert McNamara. Hilaire du Berrier warned that South Vietnam's Ngo dinh Diem couldn't be trusted.

The assassination of President Kennedy on November 23, 1963 shocked the nation. A December 1963 issue had already been printed and was about to be sent to subscribers when news arrived about the atrocity. Because one of its articles reported unfavorably on the parade of leftists who had been White House invitees of the Kennedys, Welch prevented its distribution. He wisely felt that presenting unflattering information aimed at the murdered President should not appear immediately after the horrible crime. Copies of this issue of the magazine were never sent to subscribers who were promised an extension of their subscription to account for the never-sent December 1963 issue.

Chapter 20
"One Dozen Candles" Published

Robert Welch never stopped urging people to read. He knew that retention of what one learns from reading far exceeds whatever is heard or seen. And he knew that getting important books into the hands of Society members would help them not only to be better members, but also have them become more successful in their recruitment efforts. So he raised a considerable amount of money and had 12 older books reprinted in inexpensive but easily readable paperback format. He labeled the package of books *One Dozen Candles*.

Promotional materials explained that the name had come from Father James Keller's movement known as *The Christophers* in which he had given wide recognition to the ancient Chinese proverb: "It is better to light one candle than to curse the darkness." Each book would be a single candle shining light on the conspiracy's war against America and the rest of mankind.

The boxed set of *Candles* carried a price tag of $10.00 postpaid – a sizable amount in those days. If the set were purchased as a gift for someone, an announcement naming the donor would be added. The dozen books were:

1. *While You Slept: Our Tragedy in Asia and Who Made It* by John T. Flynn (1951). Flynn had been a leader in the pre-World War II America First Movement. This book focused on the Communist takeover of China and the role played by America's government and media in the tragedy.
2. *The Web of Subversion: Underground Networks in the U.S. Government* by James Burnham (1954). A former leader of the Trotskyite Communist movement in America, Burnham exposed Communists enemies within the U.S. government.
3. *America's Retreat From Victory: The Story of George Catlett Marshall* by Senator Joseph McCarthy (1951). The text of a lengthy speech, actually ghost-written by journalist Forest Davis, was delivered by the Senator on

the floor of the U.S. Senate on June 14, 1951. It tells of the deeds of the famed Secretary of State who failed in his military career but succeeded in contributing to pro-Communist efforts once given a high post in the U.S. government.

4. *Odyssey of a Fellow Traveler* by J.B. Matthews (1938). An idealist who helped in the creation of numerous Communist front organizations, Matthews became totally disillusioned with Communism and spent the later portions of his life working to expose subversive activity within America.

5. *Shanghai Conspiracy: The Sorge Spy Ring* by U.S. Army Major General Charles A. Willoughby (1952). General Douglas MacArthur's Chief of Intelligence, General Willoughby supplied details about the spy ring led by Richard Sorge whose operatives in Moscow, Shanghai, Tokyo, San Francisco and New York contributed heavily to inserting the U.S. into World War II as an ally of the USSR.

6. *From Major Jordan's Dairies* by George Racey Jordan (1952). Assigned by the military as a Lend-Lease expediter based at an air base in Great Falls, Montana, Jordan's work called for him to speed material to the Soviet Union over the polar route during World War II. Suspicious of an unusual amount of "diplomatic" parcels he wasn't authorized to inspect, he opened some and discovered what he later learned were the materials and the plans that enabled the Soviets to develop and explode an atomic bomb far sooner than anyone had expected.

7. *I Saw Poland Betrayed: An American Ambassador Reports to the American People* by Arthur Bliss Lane (1948). As America's top diplomat in Poland (1944-1947), Ambassador Lane saw how American money, prestige and diplomatic intrigue enabled the Soviet Union to subjugate Poland. He gave up his high-level State Department career that had even earned him membership in the Council on Foreign Relations to tell fellow Americans what really happened in Poland and who was responsible. His book was smothered, sold only a few copies, and he died broken-hearted.

8. *The People's Pottage* By Garet Garrett (1953). Three of Garrett's essays supply details about the conversion of America from a republic of self-reliant people into a democracy laden with recipients of government handouts. Garrett was a popular columnist who for a time served as the chief editorial writer for the *Saturday Evening Post*.

9. *The Kohler Strike: Union Violence and Administrative Law* By Sylvester Petro (1961). A Professor of Labor Law at New York University, Petro never ceased believing that all of the administrative law enacted by the federal bureaucracy was completely unconstitutional. His report about Communist activity during the lengthy union strike against Wisconsin's Kohler Company provides a frightening example of subversion within the labor movement.
10. *The Pentagon Case* By Victor J. Fox (1958). Written by a retired military officer using a pen name, this book is the only novel in the package. It shows how planned demoralization can lead to collapse of a nation's military arm.
11. *The Tragedy of Bolivia* By Alberto Ostria Gutierrez (1958). A case history of Communist subversion told by a Professor of International Law at Bolivia's University of La Paz.
12. *Nine Men Against America: The Supreme Court and Its Attack on American Liberties* By Rosalie M. Gordon (1958). A 25-year veteran research assistant for John T. Flynn, Miss Gordon continued the work of her mentor after his untimely death.

Four years later, there would be a newer set of *Candles*, this time published in the increasingly popular – and smaller – pocket size. Three of the original books were replaced by other titles thought to be of more importance. Later, other books in the new format would follow as single-issue titles in Welch's newly created "Americanist Library" series.

Newer Society members found themselves somewhat overwhelmed with items to read. Those who set aside time to do so stayed with the Society. Many who either couldn't or wouldn't find the time to do the reading faded away. The three new *Candles* were:

1. *Seeds of Treason: The True Story of the Chambers-Hiss Tragedy* by Ralph de Toledano (1950). Our nation had become riveted to reports about the 1949 trial of Communist Alger Hiss. Journalist de Toledano spent much of his life writing about the internal subversion ravaging his adopted country.
2. *France, The Tragic Years (1939-1947): An Eyewitness Account of War, Occupation and Liberation* by Sisley Huddleston (1955). An Englishman who spent much of his adult career in Paris reporting for British, Canadian and American publications, Huddleston supplied a first-hand account of the

pro-Communist treachery of Charles DeGaulle.

3. *The Invisible Government* By Dan Smoot (1962). Already described previously, this book provided an introduction to the grip on America already gained by non-communist groups and individuals working to have the U.S. become merely a province of a one-world totalitarian government run by them. It supplied a hard look at the subversion carried out by the Council on Foreign Relations.

On the opening page in each of these new pocket books, Welch explained that an "americanist" didn't have to be an American citizen, only someone who shared the timeless principles that shaped our country from its outset. His page-long introduction to this new set of *Candles* ended with a brief summation of what he meant by the term. He followed that with two lines borrowed from poet William Cullen Bryant:

> *Not yet, O Freedom, close thy lids in*
> *slumber, for thine enemy never sleeps.*

Chapter 21
Stepped Up Attacks Spur More Growth

Welch's Foreword to the Society's 1962 *White Book* noted that new attacks on the Society and on him had come not only from the left but also from "conservatives and rightists." He claimed, "misguided individuals and groups had been beguiled into helping the Communists carry out the Moscow directive [of December 1960] that anti-Communist groups must be destroyed."

Having sent an interim message to chapter leaders in mid-December about the United Nations attack on the peaceful province in Katanga in the Belgian Congo, he repeated his urging that letters protesting this outrage should be sent to the President, members of Congress, and media representatives. Katanga's embattled leader Moise Tshombe had led his province away from the Congo's central government and its Communist leader Patrice Lumumba. The UN's response included a brutal military attack against Katanga to reverse that secession. The UN military effort received strategic help from the United States.

In April 1962, 46 doctors at Katanga's Elizabethville hospital issued a hastily written report about the destructive action carried out by the United Nations. Quickly translated into English from its original French, *46 Angry Men* showed with dramatic photos and accompanying commentary the horror perpetrated by the UN's mercenaries. From the air came jet planes attacking the hospital and churches. On the ground, innocent non-combatants were gunned down. The operation, carried out by the forces of the UN, all clearly sporting UN insignia, demonstrated that the world body had little interest in peace but was, instead, seeking a Communist takeover of the former Belgian colony as a step toward world domination. The Birch Society immediately made copies of this revealing 96-page book available and many thousands were distributed throughout the United States.

Moise Tshombe and the beleaguered Katangans survived the UN's attack and life in the wounded province returned to normal. Some months later, while traveling to Europe to represent his new country at a conference, he debarked from an airplane during its scheduled stop in Algeria and was never seen again. The entire nation soon fell into the hands of Mobutu Sese Seko who used his post to enrich himself in classic dictatorial fashion.

Welch's next move dealt with a response to a matter that shocked even the most well informed Society veterans. In September 1961, the U.S. State Department issued a formal plan to have our nation turn over its military arm to the United Nations. Society members were urged to obtain a copy of the 24-page booklet entitled "Freedom From War: The United States Program for General and Complete Disarmament in a Peaceful World." In rather matter-of-fact language, the document called for "a disarmed world" except that the UN alone would remain fully armed. JBS members were urged to send protests about this plan to President Kennedy and to members of Congress.

Soon, requests for copies of this government booklet were met with an "Out of Print" response. So Welch had thousands (and then more thousands) printed and distributed. For many years into the future, repeated calls to the U.S. Arms Control and Disarmament Agency (ACDA) asked if the plan were still U.S. policy. An appropriate ACDA official always responded that it indeed was firm policy. Confirmation of the continued existence of this amazingly subversive program was customarily followed by assurances that steps were being taken to carry it out. But the ACDA was eventually abolished as a single entity and our own government's incredible disarmament plan continued as U.S. policy that has never been repudiated.

In February 1962, Welch reported that a campaign had arisen over recent months to replace him as the Society's leader. News about such a possibility had reached the Executive Committee of the Council as well as the entire Council. The impetus for such a proposal had come, said Welch, from "the speeches of a prominent publisher of a conservative magazine." He didn't publicly name Bill Buckley as the behind-the-scenes promoter of the plan, but there was no doubt that Buckley was its originator.

The main charge *National Review's* editor laid against Welch was the Birch Society leader's maintenance of "monolithic control," a matter Welch frequently discussed as being necessary in the kind of organization he had created. As long as he encouraged all members to ignore whatever they might disagree with while still working to carry out other recommended courses of action, he contended that no one need worry about the tight rein he held. He also noted that the alternative to one-man leadership would surely lead to fracturing the ability of the organization to function as it should. And he mentioned that it would likely be difficult to find anyone else who would devote as much time, energy and knowledge to the position. The campaign to replace him never gathered any steam among Society leaders and quickly petered out.

Buckley then used the February 13, 1962 issue of his *National Review* magazine to issue a full-scale attack on Welch, accusing him of distorting reality, lacking common sense, maintaining one-man rule, and believing that Communists in and out of government were responsible for any number of national setbacks. The magazine published criticisms of Welch written by author Russell Kirk, Senator Barry Goldwater, Congressman Walter Judd, radio personality Fulton Lewis Jr., and others. Buckley's six-page essay pointed to conclusions Welch had reached in *The Politician*. The Society leader was also held up for scorn for believing that the fiasco at Cuba's Bay of Pigs was planned by Castro in league with disloyal U.S. officials; that Yugoslavia's Tito had never broken with Moscow (as was reported by questionable individuals); that the failed revolts in Poland and Hungary had been arranged by Communist officials in Moscow to destroy anti-Communist fervor; and that NATO wasn't an anti-Communist alliance as much it was a branch of the United Nations.

The case Buckley presented surely swayed some, even me. At the time, I was a subscriber to and a fan of NR and not yet a JBS member. But Buckley's blast angered a considerable number of NR readers, many of whom had been introduced to the Buckley-led magazine by Welch. Attacking Welch led to a sizable flood of cancellations for *National Review*.

I later learned that, within the Buckley criticisms, there appeared several significant distortions of Welch's positions. *National Review's* editor wrote that *American Opinion* "has for several years listed the United States as 40-60% Communist- controlled." And he added: "And this past summer Mr. Welch raised the figure to 50-70+%."

But that wasn't what the Welch-led magazine had stated. Rather, *American Opinion* had given its assessment "of the degree of control over political and economic life exercised, secretly or openly, by the International Communist Conspiracy." There was no claim that the United States as a whole was 50 or 70 percent controlled by Communists. None of the international analysts participating in the *American Opinion* survey – including Welch – believed that the United States was so heavily gripped by Communists. To believe what Buckley had published, a person would have to believe that federal, state and local governments, schools, churches, business institutions, media outlets, and more had been taken over by Communists in more than half of the country. Controlling the political and economic life of a nation is one thing; controlling entire portions of the nation is quite another. But a casual reader or a believer in Buckley either couldn't or wouldn't make that important distinction.

Something else glaringly omitted by Buckley but explicitly stated in Welch's magazine was that the political and economic control being exercised wasn't traceable to a Communist Party here in the United States, or even to the Communist Party in Moscow. It was, as *American Opinion* stated in its accompanying commentary, the work of "the International Communist <u>Conspiracy</u>" whose members were highly placed Americans, Council on Foreign Relations members, ambitious politicians, et al. Buckley refrained from mentioning the word "conspiracy," as he always would diligently avoid that explanation as the genesis of America's problems. Welch and JBS, on the other hand, didn't accept the Buckley-favored idea that many U.S. leaders, their media allies, and others were bumblers trying to do their very best for America, but failing. Or that these highly placed individuals were victims of a long string of bad luck. Or even that some local Communist leaders were dictating U.S. policy. According to the Welch-led magazine, deliberate treachery was the cause of America's numerous travails and, in his view, it all led to the conclusion that a conspiracy existed.

Buckley had effectively declared war on The John Birch Society, especially on the notion of conspiracy. He would boastfully let it be known in several ways that he was determined to "destroy" The John Birch Society, often using that very word when discussing the Society with some of his associates. Years later, I wrote a 250-page book about this favorite of the Establishment and his long career. After reading what I compiled, a sizable number of readers have commented that they knew Buckley's reputation as the great conservative leader wasn't deserved, but they "didn't know how badly he had betrayed the conservative and anti-communist cause." The book, *William F. Buckley, Jr.: Pied Piper for the Establishment*, is available and will help a reader to understand why Mr. Buckley was such a determined foe of Robert Welch and The John Birch Society.

As mentioned previously, Welch and JBS members always considered attacks emanating from known Communists to be an unintended plus, even a badge of honor. But being dishonestly scorned by supposed allies was significantly different. In earlier years, Welch had personally answered Buckley's fund-raising appeals for *National Review* by sending $1,000 even though he had no salary from JBS and was dipping into what remained of his savings. He was gravely disappointed to have been treated so dishonestly by a man he thought was both an ally and a friend. Rather than strike back, however, Welch responded in the April 1962 *Bulletin* by publishing a ten-page listing of recommended books that included four written by Buckley himself and several others authored by Messrs. Kirk, Burnham and Goldwater, the very men cited by Buckley as critics of

Welch. And in that same *Bulletin*, he filled two more pages with recommendations regarding publications and his list included Buckley's *National Review* and its companion, the *National Review Bulletin*.

Having previously noted that there were calls for him to step down as the Society's leader, Welch used the April 1962 *Bulletin* to publish a Council member's statement about the supposed rebellion. The statement, overwhelmingly and immediately approved by Council members, stated in part:

> The Council of The John Birch Society has not been deceived by the falsehoods of the smear campaign or misled by the criticism of those who do not share with us the sense of urgency and imminent peril. We have every confidence in Robert Welch and never for a moment have thought of replacing him or rejecting his leadership. We have not been frightened or discouraged by the frantic efforts of the conspiracy to destroy him and the Society and are resolved more than ever to support him and the principles upon which the Society is built until the battle is won and the Communist menace has passed.

Meanwhile, the weekly *Daily Worker* published attacks aimed either at the Society or Welch in every issue save one during the final six months of 1961. Also, the most important Communist newspaper in the entire world, Moscow-based *Pravda*, managed to outdo the *Worker* with its string of invectives and misrepresentations in a lengthy diatribe dated January 11, 1962. Welch was described in it as "a pallid, grizzled gentleman with stabbing eyes and protruding ears." "He is the Fuhrer of a Fascist organization ... or as described by certain American newspapers, 'the little American Hitler.'" There are, claimed *Pravda*, "military detachments of the Birchists."

The *Pravda* attack was full of factual errors and slurs. Welch used five pages in the March 1962 *Bulletin* to provide members with an English translation and his commentary about it. Among an array of completely false assertions, *Pravda's* correspondent B. Strelnikov claimed that JBS headquarters had "guards who will break your skull" if you try to enter an inner room. He claimed that the Foreword presented in the *Blue Book* "was written by Cardinal Cushing," that "the Society has no shortage of money," that John Birch "was killed in a quarrel with Chinese peasants," and that "Birchists ... aim to create an atmosphere of terror and persecution." All completely false!

Bits of laughter and a touch of pride flowed throughout JBS headquarters when the *Pravda* blast was shown around the office. More emerged when *Pravda* followed on February 7, 1962 with claims that Society members in California were throwing bombs into the homes of ministers and threatening to blow up radio stations. It surely seemed that Communist leaders, who never spent much effort smearing other American groups, certainly recognized they had a formidable foe in JBS. But while Birchers could laugh at what Communists in Russia were saying about their organization and its leader, there weren't any smiles about Buckley's attack, or about a few others from individuals and groups that had always been considered allies.

The rest of 1962 saw Welch warning members that a drive was being launched to create socialized medicine through the King-Anderson bill in the House. He frequently urged protests against what he called "slave labor goods" coming from Communist-dominated counties because such goods provided profit and legitimacy for the totalitarian regimes where they originated. When the Supreme Court issued its ban on prayer in the public schools, the decision supplied more fuel for the Movement To Impeach Earl Warren. The specific prayer at issue had been composed by representatives of the major religious groups in New York State. It left to local officials a decision either to use it or ignore it. Its 22 words stated: "Almighty God, we acknowledge our dependence upon Thee, and we beg your blessing upon us, our parents, our teachers and our country." The Court voted 6 to 1 that this prayer violated the establishment clause of the First Amendment and must not be used. Earl Warren sided with the majority. Two justices were unable to participate.

In May, members in greater Los Angeles placed a full-page ad in the *Los Angeles Herald Examiner* welcoming the House Committee on Un-American Activities and saluting its plan to examine and expose Communist designs aimed at the youth of America. The ad carried the names and locations of 150 chapters of the Society – all in greater Los Angeles.

In other 1962 *Bulletins*, Welch pointed to the unfortunate success achieved by some leftist members of Congress who effectively prohibited using patriotic and anti-Communist programs in courses given to personnel within the military. His alert about this "Muzzling the Military" campaign included a recommendation that members obtain copies of a Senate hearing dealing with that topic chaired by Mississippi Senator John Stennis. In August, the *Bulletin* showed a copy of the "Beliefs and Principles of the John Birch Society" as it had been entered into the *Congressional Record* by Representative John Rousselot. A single sheet printed on both sides, it became a very popular item for members to share with the public, especially at county fairs, speeches, and other gatherings. Members were urged to send congratulatory letters to the governors of six states (Ala., S.C., Va., Miss., Idaho, and Mont.) who refused to proclaim UN Day. The *Bulletin* repeatedly showed photos of "Impeach Warren" billboards erected by members in their communities. Welch suggested that members get involved in local PTA units, even "take them over" where such a step was needed. His "take them over" recommendation led to some strong criticism from anti-Birch forces.

A remarkable friendship developed between Welch and former Secretary of Agriculture Ezra Taft Benson. Without doubt, no single individual received more of the Society leader's time and attention than Benson, the only Eisenhower cabinet official who served during the entire eight years of the recently retired president's term. Benson was especially supportive of Welch's book about Eisenhower (published in 1963) even sending a copy directly to FBI Director J. Edgar Hoover with the urging that he find time to read it through.

In 2010, the *Salt Lake Tribune* unearthed some of Benson's letters showing that the future leader of the Mormon Church (formal name: "The Church of Jesus Christ of Latter Day Saints") had urged Hoover in 1965 to resist pressure from some "soft on Communism groups" who wanted the FBI leader to issue a condemnation of the Society. Hoover never issued anything of the sort. Benson was later urged by church officials to cease being so public about his pro-Welch and pro-JBS attitude. He complied with that request and later became the president of the church. But he still remained very friendly with the Society, its leader, and even this writer who happens to be a practicing Catholic.

Welch found it necessary to respond to blistering condemnations of himself and the Society issued by Michigan Governor George Romney. In a two-page letter written in September 1962, the Society leader defended himself, corrected misrepresentations issued by the governor, and supplied reasons why the Society had been created. Copies of that letter were distributed throughout the nation, especially in Michigan.

The final 1962 *Bulletin* noted that the Society had "doubled our size and strength" during the year but had not "doubled twice" as he had hoped. He then asked members "of whatever faith" to send a get-well card to Father Richard Ginder, a JBS Council Member whose hard-hitting anti-communist columns in the weekly *Our Sunday Visitor* (he was its Editor) literally reached millions of Catholics across America.

CHAPTER 22
1963: PLENTY OF ACTIVITY

Based on an idea shared by Boston policemen Fred Perkins and Arthur Daly, and eventually led by JBS Council Member Lawrence Bunker and members of the Dr. Harold McKinney family, the New England Rally for God, Family and Country gathered an enthusiastic throng of Americanists at Boston's Statler Hilton Hotel for a patriotic rally. It immediately became an annual event attracting concerned Americans from all over the United States. Initial speakers included Ezra Taft Benson and Dan Smoot.

Held year after year for a decade, it became known as a project of The John Birch Society because some of its speakers, such as humorist orator Tom Anderson and former (but soon to be re-elected) Congressman John Rousselot, were well-known members. Robert Welch attended and was honored but did not deliver any of his speeches. Leaders of other patriotic groups were delighted to be among friends who shared their views. Myers Lowman of Circuit Riders, Frank McGehee of the National Indignation Council, author E. Merrill Root and psychologist Edward Hunter were some of the many who gave their views. Area press noted that 27 tables or booths were dispensing literature during the event. Picketing by the NAACP, CORE and the Unitarian Fellowship failed to dim the ardor of the Rally attendees.

When the New Englanders running this Rally ran out of steam, the energetic JBS duo of Bill and LaRita Quinn copied the format and sponsored the Rocky Mountain Rally for God, Family and Country in Colorado. Other rallies, though less ambitious, have been held in several parts of the nation for many years.

The Society drew attention to a serious undermining of the McCarran-Walter Act, the nation's law dealing with immigration. Millions of illegal entrants had already entered the country and the number arriving rose year after year. These intruders were being aided in numerous ways, said Welch, by a Communist front organization known as the "Committee For Protection of Foreign Born."

An announcement of the recently formed American Opinion Speakers Bureau appeared in the *Bulletin*. Some of the earliest speakers included world affairs expert Hilaire du Berrier, Cuban refugee Jose Norman, and well-known American anti-Communist leader W. Cleon Skousen. Soon, another refugee from Cuba, Major Pedro Diaz Lanz, joined them. Once the chief of Castro's tiny air force, he had aided the bearded revolutionary's rise to power but quickly became completely disillusioned after discovering that the man he so highly revered was really a dangerous Communist thug. Diaz Lanz fled to America in mid-1959, discovered The John Birch Society, and spent many subsequent years traveling throughout the U.S. telling what had happened to his native country. Once he learned that Welch had sounded an alarm about Castro **before** the takeover, and had formed an organization to bring truth to the American people, he concluded that "if there had been a single chapter of the Society in Havana working to expose Castro," as Welch had already done in America, "Cuba would not have fallen to Communism."

Welch then informed *Bulletin* readers about a recent Supreme Court decision concluding that Texas farmer J. Evetts Haley had been found guilty of breaking a federal law because he raised wheat on his own farm to feed his own livestock. That ruling by the Warren Court was deemed one more reason why Earl Warren should be impeached.

The March *Bulletin* urged greater use of the recently inaugurated MMM (Members Monthly Message) system. With its small envelope sent along with each monthly *Bulletin*, the program invited members to submit their thoughts, questions, complaints, and contributions to JBS headquarters. Many members complied by turning in their sealed MMMs at each chapter meeting. One of the Society's Council Members later termed the system "the greatest fund raising tool" he had ever seen.

During June 1963, members were reminded about – or introduced to – Manning Johnson, an American Negro who had spent ten years as a member of the Communist Party USA. While serving the Communist cause, he became a candidate for Congress from a New York district. He eventually broke from Communism and supplied valuable testimony that led to the conviction of top Communist Harry Bridges. The Society republished Johnson's 1958 book, *Color, Communism and Common Sense*, an exposure of Communist plans to organize Negroes in a plot to transform a portion of the United States into a branch of worldwide Communism. Johnson, who surely would have been a valuable Society asset, died in a California automobile accident in 1959.

Welch emphasized that the Society wasn't interested in "sunshine patriots and casual Conservatives," but "warriors for God and country [who] mean business in this battle.... men and women of good character, good conscience, and religious ideals of all races and religious creeds who believe in the dignity and freedom and responsibility of the individual." He certainly believed there were plenty of Americans who measured up to those standards and he urged the Society's members to reach out, find them, and bring them into the organization.

Welch then responded to an attack on himself and the Society issued by New York Governor Nelson Rockefeller by filling all 32 pages of the August 1963 *Bulletin* with a response. He began by accusing the governor of being "committed to making the United States a part of a one-world international socialist government." After providing details about Rockefeller's pro-Communist deeds and yet-unfulfilled plans, Welch summarized that, in The John Birch Society, Mr. Rockefeller now had a formidable foe. Copies of this letter were purchased and distributed.

With its 142 pages, the September *Bulletin* shattered a record for length that has never been broken. Because there were so many new members, Welch felt a need to bring all up to date on the Society's positions and projects. After providing information about the organization's very reason for existence, Welch listed the 18 agenda items each member should first understand and then take action where possible toward informing fellow Americans about the matter. The listed agenda items included:

I. RECRUITING: Welch pointed out that his *The Politician* "has now proved to be by far the most effective single help to our recruiting efforts."

II. THE MOVEMENT TO IMPEACH WARREN: Its main weapon was the Impeachment Packet (priced at $1.00) containing seven items targeting Warren and the Warren Court.

III. UNITED NATIONS – GET US OUT!: Welch termed the world body "the most important single instrumentality of the Communists in taking over the remainder of the free world, especially the United States."

IV. UNESCO AND UNICEF: Those two UN organizations were described as "pro-Communist frauds."

V. DISARMAMENT: Awareness of the plan to disarm our nation and create an unchallengeable UN military arm was stressed.

VI. CIVIL RIGHTS: Welch stressed the need to expose Communist plans to create racial warfare leading to the establishment of a "Negro Soviet Republic" within America's borders. The Communist booklets containing those plans were identified. For the first time in JBS-related publications, the revealing photo of Martin Luther King appeared. It showed him sitting alongside known Communists while being trained at the Communist-led Highlander Folk School.

VII. SUPPORT YOUR LOCAL POLICE: Originally suggested by some astute

JBS members, this campaign always stressed the word "local" to raise awareness that its opposite, a national police force, was a feature of all totalitarian governments.

VIII. SLAVE LABOR GOODS: Buying goods made in Communist-controlled countries always helped to sustain Communist rule.

IX. SUPPORT THE LIBERTY AMENDMENT: A project promoted by private citizen Willis Stone, it called for repeal of the Marxian income tax, termination of numerous bureaucratic agencies and projects, and protection of our nation's independence. Working with Stone and his followers provided a clear example of the Society's willingness to partner with other constitutionally oriented organizations.

X. CUBA FREE – IN '63: Welch admitted that there was no chance of accomplishing this goal in 1963. But he emphasized the value of continued demands for freedom in Cuba.

XI. EXECUTIVE ORDERS: Protests were urged about the unconstitutional practice whereby Presidents made law and created federal government agencies.

XII. PUBLIC STATEMENTS: Occasional short statements setting forth the official position of the Society on various issues were already being sent to Chapter and Section leaders for use as letters to the editor and for general distribution.

XIII. AMERICAN OPINION LIBRARIES: Noting that approximately 100 of these "reading rooms that sell books" were already operating, the need for more was repeated.

XIV. GENERAL PUBLISHING: Additional attention was given to the *One Dozen Candles* and a growing number of other titles published by Western Islands and American Opinion.

XV. *AMERICAN OPINION* MAGAZINE: Noting that the primary objective of the magazine "is not circulation, but education," members were asked to help in boosting its subscriber base to many already concerned Americans.

XVI. AMERICAN OPINION SPEAKERS BUREAU: More names were added to the list of available speakers. A courageous Negro lady named Julia Brown who reported on Communist activities while operating undercover for the FBI became an addition to the roster of available speakers.

XVII. MEMBERS MONTHLY MESSAGES: The overwhelming success of this program forced a one-month moratorium to catch up with thanking donors.

XVIII. YOUR OWN READING: All were encouraged to read one book each month from the continually expanding recommended reading list.

XIX. GENERAL AND MISCELLANEOUS COMMENTS: Welch announced that the text of his new speech "The Neutralizers" would be available in booklet form in a month. He then included an extremely incisive six-page review of *The Politician* written by Samuel Blumenfeld. And, as his closing comment, he apologized on page 142 for being so "longwinded."

Shock filled the nation on November 22, 1963, when President Kennedy was assassinated. Americans learned that a former Marine who had previously taken up residence in Russia and become a Communist had been apprehended and accused of committing the crime. That didn't stop a few real bricks from coming through the windows at JBS headquarters. And there were more than a few misguided individuals willing to blame Society members in Dallas for causing "a climate of hate" because they had placed a previously written advertisement in a Dallas newspaper filled with pointed questions aimed at the President just prior to his arrival in their city. Nor did it prevent some commentators and anti-Birch experts from suggesting that the crime had actually been committed by "the right wing."

Two days after the President had been murdered, Lee Harvey Oswald was himself gunned down while in police custody by a sleazy local character named Jack Ruby. Then a mere four days after the Kennedy assassination, the November 26 edition of *The Worker*, the official New York-based Communist Party newspaper, urged President Lyndon Johnson and Congress to appoint "an extraordinary commission … to conduct a searching inquiry into all the circumstances around the assassination of the President and the murder of the suspected killer." The Communist newspaper continued: "Such an investigating committee, **headed by the Chief Justice of the Supreme Court** [emphasis added], should be composed of citizens and experts who enjoy the confidence of the nation." Welch deemed this remarkable call by the Communist newspaper especially revealing in its urging that Earl Warren be selected to lead such a panel. President Johnson's subsequent announcement of the creation of such a panel actually used the exact term, "extraordinary commission," and did name Warren to lead it. Welch suggested that someone in the White House was taking cues from the Communist press.

The investigation led by the Chief Justice eventually concluded that Oswald was the lone killer. And it claimed that he fired the fatal shot from the sixth floor of a building in Dallas just as the presidential motorcade passed by. The bullet hit the back of the President's skull, claimed the Warren-led panel, causing immediate death. But who can forget Oswald revealingly claiming "I'm just a patsy" before he himself was killed? Even more, Dr. David Stewart happened to be in the emergency room at Parkland Memorial Hospital where the President's body had been brought. He always maintained that a bullet that entered the front of his head and blew out portions of its back had caused the wound in the President's skull. Dr. Stewart, a member of The John Birch Society and a friend of mine, certainly never believed that Oswald was the only person shooting at the President, as the Warren Commission had concluded.

The final *Bulletins* for 1963 featured reproductions of several newspaper reports about the Society. One showed a photo of former Secretary of Agriculture Ezra Taft Benson alongside Robert Welch and Mrs. George Birch (the mother of the man whose name and exemplary character was chosen as the Society's symbol). The occasion was a September 23, 1963, testimonial dinner for Welch at the Hollywood Palladium. George Todt of the *Los Angeles Herald-Examiner* reported that "some 2,000" people attended the function.

The December *Bulletin* then reproduced a separate article from the October 13 *New York Times* headlined "Welch Replaced as Birch Leader." It claimed that the Society's founder had been "promoted to a position as the society's elder statesman" as a way "to curb the contentious utterances" he was accused of issuing. The management of the Society, said *Times* writer Jack Langguth, would fall to the Council with no single person named to succeed Welch. There wasn't any truth in this report, wrote Welch, who noted that members of the Society's Council would be pleased to assure anyone that the claim that he was being replaced was a "categorical, complete, and shameless falsehood."

Because the Society had been launched in December 1958, Welch offered some reflections on where the Society stood after its first five years. He recalled his assessment given during the inaugural meeting that the odds of defeating the Communist Conspiracy were "about one in one hundred." Long odds to be sure, but the efforts by members expended during those five years had impressed him sufficiently to reduce his estimate of achieving success to "about one in four." He added to his encouraging look ahead with a discussion about how he wanted the Society to be known. Calling the organization "the finest body of men and women in the whole world today," he reminded its members of the standards he wanted them to continue to live by. He wrote:

> We must take on the responsibilities of leadership, not only by precept and by action, but also by example. In a world where there is so much dishonesty, we must show everybody that there are honest people. In a world where there is so much cruelty, we must have hearts filled with compassion. In a world where conformity to a manipulated public opinion is the rule, we must have the courage to stand up for what is right even when we are the only people to do so. In a world where dependence on and subservience to a paternalistic

government is the increasingly accepted pattern of life, we must demonstrate as well as preach the values of self-reliance.

In a world where it is increasingly taken for granted that the end justifies the means, we must argue for and live up to the principle that honorable means are just as important as worthy ends in any society or any era that aspires to be civilized. In a world where blasphemy is considered smart, we must "let more reverence in us dwell," and show all who will see the worth of that reverence. In a world where falsehood has now become the accepted custom, we must constantly show the value and the necessity of truth. And all of this must not add up to merely a passive and negative quality of refraining from doing what is evil, but to a positive and active quality of opposing evil wherever it is found. This does not at all mean trying to impose on others our ideas of what is good. But it does mean working in all practicable and honorable paths to prevent bad men from imposing their evil ways on us, or on others who do not like them.

But we want The John Birch Society to carry this ambition for excellence even into the realm of taste and behavior and manners – which falls short of involving morality. In our letters, in our printed matter, in our speeches, in our daily contacts of every kind, in all those physical productions and routine actions which represent the Society, or by which it is judged, we want only the best of which we are capable. And we want that <u>best</u> to be so clearly excellent that everybody gradually comes to think of The John Birch Society as unquestionably top-notch in every way…. "Not failure but low aim is the crime," and in little things and large, the aim of The John Birch Society, of its membership, its staff, and its management, must at all times be towards the utmost in quality that our dedication can achieve.

Never seeking power, we shall nevertheless become powerful enough through example, influence, and persuasion. Our only weapon is truth; but whenever and wherever we have taken enough pains to bring it to light, truth will prevail.

Robert Welch (1899 – 1965)
Founder, The John Birch Society
"There is a Conspiracy at work as sure as there is a law of gravity. And to try to overcome its effects by ignoring its existence is exactly the kind of opposition the conspiracy has contrived and created for itself."

— Robert Welch, June 1975

CAPTAIN JOHN M. BIRCH, U.S.A.

While living in China as a Christian Missionary, John Birch joined the U.S. Army on July 4, 1942. He had brought Col. Jimmy Doolittle and his crew to safety after their famous raid over Tokyo earlier that year. John rose to the rank of Captain and was slain only days after WW II ended.

John Birch receiving a well-earned decoration from General Claire Chennault, the commander of the U.S. Army's famous "Flying Tigers." Many who knew of Birch's incredibly important intelligence work felt he should have been awarded the Congressional Medal of Honor.

Mr. and Mrs. Robert Welch (Marian) making some decisions about whom to invite to a future Society function. Mrs. Welch was a valuable member of the editorial staff for JBS-related magazines – *American Opinion* and *The Review Of The News*.

Robert Welch recognized the worth of Senator Joseph McCarthy's anti-Communist revelations. He delivered numerous speeches on behalf of the Wisconsin senator occasionally appearing with him in the 1950s. He later speculated that had The John Birch Society been in existence during the McCarthy era, the senator's effort would have succeeded.

A younger Robert Welch during his years as the Vice President for Sales and Advertising for the James O. Welch Candy Company. Located in Cambridge, Massachusetts, the company was founded by James who happily enticed older brother Robert to join with him. The two created a very successful firm in a highly competitive industry.

The main headquarters of The John Birch Society until the 1989 move to Appleton, Wisconsin. Located at 395 Concord Avenue, Belmont, Massachusetts, it was one of three JBS buildings in the town. The other two housed 1) the editorial and research departments, and 2) the shipping and warehouse facility.

As the Society grew in the early 1960s, a west coast office was opened to facilitate contact with 13 western states. Pictured here is the branch office in San Marino, California, a suburb of Los Angeles. Much of the Society's business for the 13 western states was handled from this building.

In 1989, the Society's Board of Directors instructed CEO Allen Bubolz to close down expensive facilities on the east and west coasts and move to a less expensive location "somewhere in the middle of the country." A lifelong native of Wisconsin, Mr. Bubolz chose Appleton, Wisconsin, for the new headquarters location and the move was made in 1989.

At a student military review held at Holy Cross College in May 1957, John McManus received an award as the top NROTC candidate accepting a Marine Corps commission. The presenter of the USMC's Ceremonial Sword was local industrialist Robert Stoddard. Eighteen months later, Mr. Stoddard was among the 11 men who heard Robert Welch deliver his founding speech at the formation of The John Birch Society.

After filling one of numerous requests to speak to a raucous student gathering at one of the many colleges in the Boston area, John McManus returned to tell Robert Welch about the experience. The engagement occurred during the period when many anti-Vietnam War protests were the norm on college campuses. On this particular occasion and with a smile on my face, I told Mr. Welch that the Society "owed me combat pay." He thanked me profusely for putting myself in such a situation. My request for additional pay, never seriously expected, was never discussed.

The Indianapolis home of Miss Marguerite Dice where the founding meeting of The John Birch Society was held December 8-9, 1958. Miss Dice has been asked by Robert Welch to recommend a place in Indianapolis where a meeting such as the one described to her could be held. She recommended her home and it was, indeed, an excellent place to hold such a private meeting.

At the close of Robert Welch's two-day 17-hour presentation at the founding of The John Birch Society, St. Louis businessman W.B. "Ben" McMillan handed Welch a check for $1,000 and said, "Here, Bob, I guess we're in business." He frequently boasted that he was the "First Member" of The John Birch Society, a claim that no one ever challenged.

One of the men at the founding of the Society, Milwaukee industrialist Wm. J. Grede, was Robert Welch's closest friend. The two had met and become good friends through their membership in the National Association of Manufacturers. Grede, who rose to become the Chairman of the Board of the NAM, was once asked by some of its members to quit the Society. He told them, "If my membership in The John Birch Society is a problem for the NAM, I will quit the NAM. I will not quit The John Birch Society."

Also present at the Society's founding in Indianapolis, Fred C. Koch was among the first members. After graduation from Massachusetts Institute of Technology in 1922, he started building petroleum refineries all over the world, even in the Soviet Union. His awareness of communist designs on America led to friendship with Robert Welch. In 1960, he wrote a small book entitled *A Businessman Looks at Communism* to warn fellow Americans about the horrors of Communism. The companies he built are now led by his sons who have avoided association with The John Birch Society.

A Catholic priest from Connecticut, Fr. Francis Fenton became pastor of church in the southern part of the state where he got to know William F. Buckley Jr. To his credit, Father Fenton never felt comfortable with the man who became the liberal Establishment's favorite. Buckley's mother and one of his sisters became JBS members but were soon urged to quit the Society by "Mr. Conservative." Father Fenton, an early member of the Society's National Council, spent many years writing and speaking for the Society's publications and its Speakers Bureau.

Trained as a surgeon, Dr. N.E. Adamson found himself unable to continue in that branch of medicine because of a peculiar illness. During his recovery, he befriended Robert Welch and read numerous books recommended by his nearby neighbor in Belmont, Massachusetts. When chapters were being formed in the Society's first year, "Nat" Adamson became a chapter leader and held that post for more than 50 years. Named to the National Council, he was its youngest member for several decades and held that distinction until supplanted by Dr. Larry McDonald.

When the Society was not yet a year old and Tom Hill was finishing up his studies at Southern Methodist University, he attended one of Robert Welch lengthy seminars and joined the organization. Hired immediately as a field Coordinator in Texas, he so impressed Robert Welch that he was asked to accept assignment as a top assistant to the Founder at the Society's Massachusetts headquarters. Tom helped the Founder immensely, directed the growing field staff, and was named to the National Council.

In the early 1960s, Arizona resident and aeronautical engineer David Eisenberg became convinced by the mass media that The John Birch Society was anti-Semitic. A Jewish-American, he began studying the Society in order to be better able to oppose it. But he learned by examining the Society itself that he had been victimized by lies. He joined and won a place on the Society's National Council. Always willing to combat the false charge about anti-Semitism, he helped many to overcome that lie.

Born in New Jersey, Robert Stoddard earned degrees from Yale University and Harvard Business School after which he joined the Wyman-Gordon Company in Worcester, Massachusetts. He rose to become its President and Chairman of the Board. A veteran member of the Associated Industries of Massachusetts and the National Association of Manufacturers, he became a close friend and admirer of Robert Welch and was one of the 11 men who met to form the Society in 1958.

Clarence Manion became known for many of his years as "Dean" after leading the Law School at Notre Dame University for 11 years. In 1953, he accepted appointment by President Eisenhower as Chairman of the Commission on Inter-Government Relations only to find that he would not be able to shrink the growing federal bureaucracy. He left that post, returned to practicing law, and launched the weekly television/radio program known as *The Manion Forum*. He authored *The Key To Peace* to explain the U.S. Constitution and happily joined the Society's National Council.

One of the most well known Alaskans, Clyde Lewis founded a mechanical contracting firm in Anchorage and twice won election to the Alaska Senate. He teamed up with Dr. Larry McDonald as two members of the Society's National Council to conduct high-level seminars that resulted in many new members for the Society. Known for his sacrificial generosity to the freedom fight, he energetically and boldly strove to build the Society in his state and elsewhere.

Massachusetts native Laurence E. Bunker earned a law degree and did legal work for the U.S. Army during World War II. Promoted to Colonel while serving for six years as a personal aide to General Douglas MacArthur, he was at the general's side during the occupation of Japan, the Korean War, and the early months after President Truman suddenly dismissed the general. One of the 11 who heard Robert Welch's founding speech in 1958, he served the Society as a member and Council member for many years.

Members who couldn't afford to open and stock an American Opinion Bookstore were frequently able to convert a van into a bookmobile. Some of these libraries on wheels traveled throughout the nation to introduce fellow Americans to the Society.

Countless numbers of "*Get US Out!* of the United Nations" billboards provided awareness that our nation should never have joined the world body. Occasionally a billboard bearing this message became the target of arson and defacement.

Billboards calling attention to the need to Impeach Earl Warren introduced many Americans to the subversion regularly emanating from the Supreme Court. Though Warren wasn't impeached and removed, many Americans were introduced to the pro-communist rulings coming from the nation's highest court.

Though not yet able to vote, the young American in this photo seems quite happy calling attention to the need to "*Get US out!* of the United Nations."

NATIONAL REVIEW

A Journal of Fact and Opinion

THE POPE AT THE UN

OCTOBER 19, 1965 — 50 CENTS

THE JOHN BIRCH SOCIETY AND THE CONSERVATIVE MOVEMENT

The Question of Robert Welch

In the past few weeks a number of conservative spokesmen whose credentials and sincerity are unassailable have made public statements about Mr. Robert Welch, founder of the John Birch Society, calling into question his qualifications to lead a national anti-Communist and anti-statist movement. Russell Kirk, replying to a letter addressed to him by an executive of the John Birch Society, writes that he knows Mr. Welch to be a "likeable, honest, courageous, energetic man" who nevertheless "by silliness and injustice of utterance" has become "the kiss of death" for any conservative enterprise. Congressman Walter Judd said in Minneapolis that he considers Mr. Welch's judgment so flawed as to disqualify him from leadership of an effective anti-Communist movement. Senator Barry Goldwater said he feels Mr. Welch should resign; and, should he refuse to do so, the Society should disband and reorganize under different leadership. Fulton Lewis Jr., at the *Human Events* Conference in Washington, criticized Mr. Welch's direction of the Society. And, it is widely known, some members of the National Council of the John Birch Society are at their wits' end, and one or two have quietly resigned. Their dilemma is, reduced to the simplest terms: How can the John Birch Society be an effective political instrument while it is led by a man whose views on current affairs are, at so many critical points, so critically different from their own, and, for that matter, so far removed from common sense?

That dilemma weighs on conservatives throughout America. It is not a dilemma imposed by the pressure of Liberal or Communist objections to Mr. Welch. If not a single criticism had been made of

FEBRUARY 13, 1962   83

Buckley turned to dishonesty in his newer attack on Robert Welch and The John Birch Society. He converted *American Opinion's* estimate of communist influence into communist control. Reading what he falsely attributed to Robert Welch would have a person thinking that the Society believed a huge portion of the nation was already under total communist control. What *American Opinion* did say was that a sizable portion of the decisions being made in Washington aided the communist cause. Big difference.

In this 1965 attack on the Society, Buckley and his staff converted the JBS slogan *Get US out!* of the United Nations to *Get US out!* of Vietnam. More deliberate dishonesty. The Society never called for pulling out of Vietnam.

Other shadings of Society positions surely made some readers think ill of The John Birch Society. And that was the goal sought by William F. Buckley Jr.

THE LEBANON DEMOCRAT
and Wilson County News

THURSDAY, MARCH 30, 1967 LEBANON, TENNESSEE 37087

Cites Coverups And Deception
JFK Shot From Front
Speaker Tells Rotary

Dr. David Stewart, a member of The John Birch Society, was on duty at the Parkland Memorial Hospital in Dallas when President Kennedy's lifeless body was brought there. Dr. Stewart has always claimed that the fatal bullet entered the President's head from the front and pushed out bodily material on to the back of the vehicle. Dr. Stewart regularly spoke to business clubs and other audiences in order to correct the claim that Lee Harvey Oswald was the killer. He would always add that he did not know who fired the fatal shot.

The 12-page Sunday Supplement pictured here first appeared in a Los Angeles newspaper and drew a most heartening response. Follow up aimed at those who responded led to gaining new members.

The Supplement was then placed in dozens more Sunday newspapers where more prospects for the Society were gained.

The cost of placing this type of advertising, enormous as it was, was borne locally in most instances. This testimony to the loyalty and determination of local members was remarkable. And the response of the people whose Sunday newspaper brought them the Supplement was gratifying.

Mike Culbert...
Whatever Else, Call Him 'Correct'

Editorial Page
Berkeley Daily Gazette

Berkeley DAILY GAZETTE Thurs., Aug. 26, 1971—11

WICHITA — This succinct prediction for the United States was delivered, verbatim, in 1958:

"(1) Greatly expanded government spending, for missiles, for so-called defense generally, for foreign aid, for every conceivable means of getting rid of ever larger sums of American money — as wastefully as possible.

"(2) Higher and then much higher taxes.

"(3) An increasingly unbalanced budget, despite the higher taxes...

"(4) Wild inflation of our currency, leading rapidly towards its ultimate repudiation.

"(5) Government controls of prices, wages, and materials, supposedly to combat inflation."

This panorama was not set forth in any of Samuelson's college textbooks on economics.

It was not rendered in a quarterly report of the Federal Reserve System, was not drawn from a Ford Foundation monograph or a university seminar on economics. The Council of Economic Advisers in no way had anything to do with writing the above predictions.

Points one, two and three were already obvious in 1958, when the prediction was made. Points four and five are now currently in the process of being brought about.

The author? Why, that much-maligned former candymaker, that paranoid monolithicist, that "far rightist," Robert Welch, founder-president of the equally much-maligned John Birch Society.

Welch wrote his gloomy forecast in 1958 in "The Blue Book," not to be found on the shelves of most public schools and libraries.

Now let's give the man his due. Call him rightist, paranoid, monolithic. Call him all those things — but also call him "correct."

Whether he is correct by mistake, correct by coincidence, correct because his monster conspiracy theory is on target, or correct because all that has happened is simply the result of the natural flow of events, this is all of secondary importance to the reality that he is correct.

At least so far.

Welch's precise definition of economic realities that have come to pass, through points 1 to 5 (the dollar IS the process of being repudiated at this very time), should lead us out of sheer interest to ponder the remaining 5 steps.

They are:

"(6) Greatly increased socialistic controls over every operation of our economy and every activity of our daily lives. This is to be accompanied, naturally and automatically, by a correspondingly huge increase in the size of our bureaucracy, and in both the cost and reach of our domestic government.

"(7) Far more centralization of power in Washington, and the practical elimination of our state lines...

"(8) The steady stream of federal aid to and control over our educational system, leading to complete federalization of our public education.

"(9) A constant hammering into the American consciousness of the horror of 'modern warfare', the beauties and the absolute necessity of 'peace' — peace always on Communist terms, of course.

"(10) The consequent willingness of the American people to allow the steps of appeasement by our government which amount to a piecemeal surrender of the rest of the free world and of the United States itself into a Kremlin-ruled tyranny."

Welch's more up-to-date semantics make the seat of his great conspiracy theory other than the Kremlin, and his use of the word "Communist" has very little to do, at least domestically, with the Communist Party.

But, then, who would believe those silly Birchers, paranoiacs that they are? Now, on to the bank...

Reprints of this article, "Call Him Correct" Mike Culbert, are available at twenty copies for one dollar in any quantity. Postage and handling charges: Under $10 — $1; $10 to $24.99 — $1.50; $25 to $49.99 — $2; $50 to $99.99 — $2.50. Order from:
THE JOHN BIRCH SOCIETY
Belmont, MA 02178   San Marino, CA 91108

Having such a column as this appear in a daily newspaper was a wonderful morale booster. That it appeared in the newspaper in Berkeley, California, was stunning. Its author, Mike Culbert, received copious thanks from members. He then wrote other complimentary articles about the Society. The one pictured here was reprinted and distributed by the thousands all across the nation

CHAPTER 23
1964: "NONE CARE CALL IT TREASON"

With the Kennedy assassination still on everyone's mind, the Society placed its "THE TIME HAS COME" advertisement in newspapers in several key cities: New York (2), Chicago, Washington, St. Louis, Los Angeles, Oakland, Salt Lake City (2), and the comparatively small Catholic weekly, *The Wanderer*, based in St. Paul, Minnesota. The major point of the ad stressed that it was "time" for many more Americans to join The John Birch Society.

From the eastern portion of the nation alone, this ad generated 3,415 responses. More than a thousand more arrived at the Western office. Approximately 43 percent had included payment for one of the suggested packets; a mere six percent expressed various forms of hostility; and the remaining 51 percent asked for free information. Also, because all members had received a copy of the ad with their December *Bulletin*, quite a few chapters raised funds to place it at their own expense in their local newspapers.

Welch also noted that Chief Justice Warren had already used "all the power and prestige of his position to prevent any investigation of the [Kennedy] assassination by any agency other than his own commission." There were actually three murders for Texas authorities to investigate. The victims included the slain President, a Dallas police officer killed by Lee Harvey Oswald as he tried to escape, and Oswald himself. But Warren's high-handed action barred the Texas Attorney General, in whose jurisdiction the crimes had been committed, from performing the important task assigned to his office. Such prevention of the state's role was unusual indeed.

The tactic involving paid advertisements dealing with JBS campaigns had by now caught on with many Society leaders. The February 1964 *Bulletin* contained copy for another ad calling for opposition to the "Civil Rights Act of 1963." Labeling the legislation "A Nail For The Coffin Of The American Republic," the ad contained a statement targeting the Act issued by a recent president of the American Bar Association. Over many years, enemies of the Society had continuously – but falsely – claimed that JBS opposition to "civil rights" legislation was rooted in racial bias. But the former ABA leader's opposition squared with the Society's attitude. In the ad, Welch quoted this prominent legal official as follows:

> The proposed extension of federal executive and administrative control over business, industry, individual citizens and the states by the package of legislation called "The Civil Rights Act of 1963" exceeds the total of all such extensions by all decisions of the Supreme Court and all Acts of Congress from 1787 to June 19, 1963. When future generations look back through the eyes of history at this legislation they will recognize ten percent of "civil rights" and ninety percent extension of raw federal power.

While urging increased activity in the Impeach Warren effort, Welch pointed to an example of "cunning rottenness" delivered by journalist Drew Pearson. The self-identified enemy of the Society, who had earned the moniker "muckraker," wrote in one of his syndicated columns:

> Law enforcement officials in the nation's capital are alarmed over reports that right-wing extremists have formed a secret terrorist society which has marked Chief Justice Earl Warren for physical harm.
>
> Members of the society also boasted that they intend to assassinate Dr. Martin Luther King....

Welch pointed to Pearson's clever but nasty wording wherein a never-identified and surely non-existent "secret terrorist society" was accused of concocting a plan to attack Warren and assassinate King. Though he never named The John Birch Society, Pearson avoided using such terms as "group" or "organization" for his target, relying instead on "a secret terrorist **society**" [emphasis supplied], from the "right-wing." He certainly knew that no other national organization on the right had chosen to call itself a society. Readers were left with the inference that The John Birch Society was the unnamed "terrorist" group plotting attacks on Warren and King, even assassination.

The column generated anxiety among some members who, as a result of its publication in their locales, found themselves being accused of belonging to the group referenced by Pearson. Welch assured those members and all members that such a course of action was completely alien to the Society's methods and that such unethical journalism was to be expected of Pearson. He then added: "We would be terribly disappointed to see anything happen to Earl Warren before we can build up enough public understanding of his judicial misdeeds to get him impeached."

Another example of anti-Society media attention occurred when uninvited CBS personnel stormed into the Society's headquarters in Massachusetts and began filming while receiving deserved resistance to their invasion. Subsequent airing of the incident by a smirking Walter Cronkite on his evening news program prompted numerous members to send letters of protest to Cronkite and his employer. The CBS anchorman defended what his colleagues had done when they barged into the JBS building, filmed everyone and everything in sight, and refused to leave until police arrived to put an end to their raucous intrusion. In one of his letters responding to member complaints, Cronkite portrayed the Society as the equivalent of Communists, Black Muslims and the Klan. Other letters from the network's officials admitted that their personnel had indeed gone too far but no such comment was ever broadcast.

The Society began distribution of John Stormer's paperback book *None Dare Call It Treason*. The 254-page compilation of facts showing advances achieved by Communists and the help supplied to them by the U.S. government wasn't the work of a JBS member but the effort of a young Republican activist from Missouri. It quickly became a nationwide bestseller and a most-welcome alarm bell for many Americans. So great was its effectiveness that a counter movement with claims that Stormer's research was faulty and misleading arose. It was neither. The book's survey of Communism's progress and America's decline was indisputable. In little more than a single year, *None Dare Call It Treason* sold seven million copies. The title, boldly emphasizing the word "Treason," borrowed two lines penned by Sir John Harrington (1561-1612) who wrote:

> Treason doth never prosper, what's the reason?
> For if it prosper, none dare call it treason.

Other paperback favorites distributed by JBS members during the busy election year of 1964 were *Conscience of a Conservative* by Barry Goldwater, *A Choice Not an Echo* by Phyllis Schlafly, and *A Texan Looks at Lyndon* by J. Evetts Haley. The Goldwater book, actually ghost-written for him by L. Brent Bozell (a Buckley associate who would later denounce his long-time friend for advocating abortion and associating with "the Establishment") proved very helpful for those who wished to know more about the thinking of the Arizona senator.

The Schlafly book described a meeting of the Bilderberg Movement but it never provided the name of this annual gathering of high-level notables from the U.S. and Western

Europe. Originated in 1956 by Holland's Prince Bernhard and America's David Rockefeller, this extremely hush-hush and invitation-only affair attracted numerous leaders from the worlds of politics, economics, and journalism. Its format, prominent attendees, and deep secrecy gave every reason to believe it to be a conspiratorial confab promoting world government. After its first meeting at Holland's Bilderberg Hotel, the name "Bilderberg Movement" remained even though future meetings were held elsewhere – always at some plush resort in Europe or North America.

The Haley book about Lyndon Johnson supplied unflattering details about the life and deeds of the then-sitting President. While he was seeking election for a full four-year term, Johnson was accurately presented as a grasping politician who would stop at nothing to gain power and then use it to carry out an agenda that did great harm to his country. Each of these books enjoyed widespread distribution during the 1964 political year.

In May, Welch reported about a hoax (the word is an understatement!) perpetrated on Boston's Richard Cardinal Cushing. It grew from a New York City radio appearance by Society Public Relations staffer Tom Davis. The morning after the broadcast, a telegram arrived at the prelate's Boston residence claiming that Davis had, over the airwaves, labeled the recently murdered President Kennedy "a Communist." Reverend Cushing immediately called in the press to publicly denounce the Society.

But Davis emphatically denied that he had made any such accusation. He secured a recording of the radio program, raced to Boston, and presented it to the Cardinal's staff. The result? Cardinal Cushing wrote a letter to Davis admitting that he had been "misinformed" and granted permission for the Society to copy his letter in the JBS *Bulletin*. The next *Bulletin* reproduced the latter.

Displaying ever more determination to create ways "to inform the electorate," Welch announced in June that the "Correction Please" section of *American Opinion* would now be published in its own stand-alone format under that title. This venture morphed several years later into a more professional-looking weekly magazine known as *The Review Of The News*.

Also, in June 1964, the first mention of U.S. military activity in Vietnam appeared in the JBS *Bulletin*. It focused on the plight of seven U.S. Special Forces soldiers being paraded around by the Viet Cong like animals with ropes tied around their necks. Because no known government action had been taken on their behalf, Welch asked members to send letters requesting an explanation to U.S. Ambassador to Vietnam Henry Cabot Lodge, Secretary of State Dean Rusk, and Secretary of Defense Robert McNamara. Lodge eventually acknowledged "the tremendous volume of mail" he received while claiming that he had taken important steps to rescue the men. But nothing of substance was being done. The administration's plans to enlarge the conflict had obviously already been formulated by the Johnson administration. U.S. efforts in Vietnam would soon grow enormously, cost tens of thousands of American lives plus many billions of dollars, and end years later in defeat and ignominious withdrawal.

CHAPTER 24
1964 CONT'D: THE GOLDWATER YEAR

For conservatives and anti-Communists, 1964 was rightly labeled the Goldwater year. The Arizona senator, long openly admired by Welch, steadily moved toward gaining the GOP's nomination for president. Members across the nation involved themselves in activity supporting Goldwater. But the Society itself, in keeping with its fixed policy, never backed, financed, or supported any candidate at any level. All members were always urged to be involved with the political party or candidate of their choice, but never to do so in the Society's name. Welch would later report, and journalists would confirm, that 100 JBS members were among the delegates who did select Goldwater as the GOP's nominee at the July convention in San Francisco.

At this GOP gathering, Nelson Rockefeller used his time at the podium to speak of the need to purge "extremism" from the Party. Before the delegates and a huge national television audience, he targeted "the Nazis, the Klan, the Communists, and the John Birch Society" as detestable groups that the country should shun. Associating the name of the Society with the others that deserved condemnation was, of course, a thoroughly dishonest move. It drew a lusty chorus of boos from many of the delegates.

Welch insisted that Rockefeller wasn't merely wrong, but that he knew exactly what he was doing, and that he even expected to be booed. With the help of his left-leaning allies in the media, the New York governor planted in the minds of millions that the Society was at least as bad – and maybe even worse – than Nazis, Klansmen and Communists. Many uninformed Americans who saw his televised speech remembered only that The John Birch Society was an organization to avoid or combat, and few could remember how they had come to such a conclusion. Nevertheless, after the dust created by Rockefeller had settled, Welch would conclude that the "frantic charges" about the JBS made by Rockefeller had boosted interest in the organization.

Associating the Society with the Klan has always been a nasty tactic. Had anyone cared to ask, Society officials would state that it had always been Society policy never to allow membership to any Klansman. There was, however, one dramatic exception to that rule involving a courageous young American named Delmar Dennis. Serving as an undercover infiltrator into the Klan for the FBI, he received Society permission to ignore the hard and fast policy regarding the ban. Besides the proper authorities, the only people who knew what he was doing within the Klan were members of his JBS chapter, and each was telling no one. At the FBI's direction, Dennis finally surfaced from his years of undercover effort and testified at the 1967 trial of the Klan leaders accused of participating in the murder of three civil rights workers in 1964. It was Dennis who had quietly directed the authorities to the earthen dam where the three bodies had been buried, and it was he who provided the testimony, given at the urging of those authorities three years later, that led to convictions of the killers.

For his courage, Dennis was shot at inside his own home by Klan sympathizers; his wife walked out on him (her father was a Klansman); and he eventually had to flee Mississippi. The Society's Speakers Bureau immediately sent him on a nationwide speaking tour to tell his story. Before numerous audiences throughout the nation, he related his experiences and his first-hand knowledge of Klan leader Sam Bowers' frequent boasts of his admiration for Communism.

In later years, Dennis was occasionally required by U.S. government officials to again provide what he knew about the Klan. While traveling on a speaking tour for JBS several years later, he received an official summons requiring him to appear as an expert witness in a government trial. He immediately called the JBS Speakers Bureau to explain that he was expected to speak that very evening before a gathering in a Chicago suburb and that he had to cancel his appearance. And he asked help in explaining to the local JBS leader why he couldn't appear.

All of this occurred after I had joined JBS, become the organization's employee, and started helping manage the JBS Speakers Bureau. It was I who had initially arranged the Dennis speaking tour and I who received his call. I hurriedly told him to honor the summons, proceed to wherever he was needed, and let me handle what had to be done about the evening speech. With help from a colleague, I called the speech sponsor, told him of the Dennis predicament, suggested that I would immediately leave for Chicago and fill in for Dennis, and gathered what I needed to take with me. I also told the Chicago member not to announce to anyone that Dennis would not appear (it was too late to even try to do that – plus they didn't know who was planning to attend), and to have someone pick me up at the airport. Further, I asked him to bring a decent tape recorder to the hall so we could play a portion of a recorded speech Dennis had made elsewhere.

Off I sped to the Boston airport (Boston to Chicago flights were scheduled almost hourly) and everything proceeded as we hoped. At the event, the emcee explained why Dennis wouldn't be there and introduced me as his substitute. I thanked the audience for its understanding, told them a good deal about the Dennis history, played about 20 minutes of the previously taped speech, and took questions and comments from attendees. The program had been saved but there was no doubt that the audience would have preferred hearing the expected genuine hero.

After being chased out of Mississippi by Klan sympathizers in 1967, Dennis served as one of the Society's full-time staff coordinators in California. A few years later, he had been posted back to Mississippi where members gladly welcomed him as the Mississippi state coordinator. He later told me that he derived the courage to proceed with his dangerous work for the FBI from the Society's courageous members. The last time I saw him occurred when he surprised me with a warm greeting during the Society's 25th anniversary celebration in 1983. He had left the JBS staff and relocated to Tennessee and was no longer actively involved in JBS work. But he said he had come to say farewell to the ailing Robert Welch, a man he so intensely admired. He passed away himself soon afterward.

By 1975, JBS member William H. McIlhany's 1975 book about Delmar Dennis and his extremely dangerous work had become available. Entitled *Klandestine*, it later provided background information for the movie "Mississippi Burning?" In his book, McIlhany had made sure that Dennis's membership in The John Birch Society was known, but the film never mentioned that important aspect of the man's life.

The full truth about JBS efforts regarding the Klan should include the fact that the Society's various efforts had diminished Klan influence more than all other anti-Klan organizations combined. By offering an alternative of solid information and understanding, and counseling against any form of violence and hatred, the Society kept many otherwise confused and worried Americans throughout the South from having anything to do with the Klan – except condemning it. Nelson Rockefeller may or may not have known this when he linked the Society to the Klan in 1964. But even if he had known, it was unlikely that he would have refrained from attacking the Society.

Back To 1964 and the Goldwater Candidacy

The year 1964 saw the arrival of another book that immediately became a member weapon. Society staff member G. Edward Griffin had spent much of the previous year compiling information and then writing *The Fearful Master: A Second Look at the United*

Nations. With a laudatory Introduction written by Congressman James Utt (R-Calif.), the book filled a need for a comprehensive exposé of the world body. Heretofore, bits and pieces of damning information about the UN – its founders, goals, activities, deeds, and supporters – had been made available but never in a single publication. Society officials were delighted when New York City's *Daily News*, then the nation's largest circulation newspaper, published a highly complimentary editorial about *The Fearful Master* on July 24, 1964. Alongside appeared similar laudatory mention of *None Dare Call It Treason*.

In a June 22, 1964, letter sent to NBC newscasters Chet Huntley and David Brinkley, Welch complained strenuously about the content of one of their recent programs. The Society leader noted that, in the particular broadcast he cited, "two men had been captured with a large cache of illegal weapons." Then, another man "with his back to the camera was shown and represented as a U.S. Treasury Agent." This man, Welch's letter continued, "said that the two possessors of the illegal cache had confessed that they were negotiating with The John Birch Society to sell the guns." The whole televised segment, said Welch, was a "staged, bald-faced lie." NBC never aired anything like that again.

In keeping with the newly energized campaign to Get US out! of the United Nations, the June *Bulletin* alerted members about the Xerox Corporation's plan to spend $4 million to promote the UN with televised programming. Names, titles and addresses of a dozen Xerox officials were provided so that letters could be sent to each insisting that lauding the UN was a bad mistake. One of the Xerox executives, Board Chairman Sol Linowitz, would later abandon his post at the company and become the Carter administration's official assigned to deliver the U.S. owned and operated Canal in Panama to the Communist-led Panamanian government.

In July, Welch announced that his newest speech entitled "More Stately Mansions" would stress that "Communists do not fear arms or armies [because] they control too many of the men who might give the order to march." Nor, he added, "do the Communists fear the bombs and missiles of push-button warfare [because] in most cases they now own the men who would push the buttons." This speech, regarded by many veteran Society members as the best ever delivered by the Society's founder, traced the rise of the Conspiracy from the late 18th Century creation of the Bavarian Illuminati to its 20th Century manifestation. He would greatly expand on this topic in the months and years ahead.

July also saw mention of the availability of an article entitled "The Catholic Church and The John Birch Society" written by Council Member S.J. Conner of Wisconsin. It followed by two months an announcement of "A Catholic Priest Looks At The John Birch Society" written by one of the newest Council members, Connecticut-based Rev. Francis E. Fenton. These two items, especially popular among Catholic members but useful for others to share with Catholic friends, helped to dispel the notion promoted in some parts of the nation that the Society was anti-Catholic or had been condemned by Catholic leaders. Simultaneously in other places, strange as it may seem, the Society was being condemned for being overly pro-Catholic!

While addressing the topic of religion, Welch estimated that the preferences of the members was approximately 60 percent Christian (from various Protestant branches), 40 percent Catholic, and one percent Jewish. He stressed that those figures were merely guesswork because no such tabulation had ever been made, nor would ever be made. That guess on his part seems to have remained accurate throughout the life of the organization.

Always willing to provide information about the Society's progress and prospects for the future, Welch noted in July that the Society now had 50 paid Coordinators nationwide. But he wanted 300. And the Society was taking in and spending $2 million per year by the end of 1963. But he hoped to raise and spend $4 million during 1964. Though he didn't reach his 1964 monetary goal, the entire year of 1964 saw explosive growth in membership. Fueled in part by the Goldwater candidacy that exposed many Americans to conservative and anti-Communist thinking, membership swelled. Many who did join, however, were looking for the country to undergo an immediate political turnabout. When they became more aware of the Society's long-range educational strategy and the need for them to become much more deeply informed, some faded away. Gains in membership during this period were still very positive and many of the new Birchers fully adopted the Society's program. Some quickly moved into leadership posts at the local level.

The *Bulletin* for August reported that a letter had been received from a high-ranking Department of the Army official stating: "There are no official restrictions concerning military personnel belonging to The John Birch Society." Anyone needing a copy could simply ask for one. Similar letters from all branches of the military were obtained during succeeding years. But Society members were continuously beset by claims that the name of the Society had appeared on a listing of organizations that members of the armed forces were forbidden to join. That claim was completely erroneous.

In September, news came that a new organization had been created to "tell the truth about the John Birch Society." The National Council for Civic Responsibility (NCCR), led by Arthur Larson of the World Rule by Law Center at Duke University, had already attracted more than 100 pro-world government partisans as members. The group proceeded to spread a seriously distorted view of The John Birch Society. Former Congressman John Rousselot, the Society's recently appointed Public Relations Director, issued a press release expressing his willingness to appear with Larson or any other NCCR member at any time in order to let the public decide which organization is telling the truth. Rousselot asked: "Was it those affiliated with Arthur Larson and the NCCR, or those working with Robert Welch?" No one from the NCCR accepted Rousselot's willingness to debate the matter.

Welch concluded that the Society and its members should feel honored "to have caused some high-level liberals to start seeing Birchers under every bed." In the March 1965 *Bulletin*, he reported that Larson's NCCR "has folded" after only five months of existence.

Welch then accepted an invitation to appear again as a guest on Meet the Press. Expecting to be questioned about *The Politician*, he prepared a 500-word statement and asked for six-to-eight minutes to read it at the beginning of the half-hour program. The moderator didn't allow that and the panel, made up of avid foes of Welch and the Society, peppered him with a variety of questions, none of which he hadn't heard previously. The experience nevertheless proved beneficial because some of the panelists found out that Welch was no fool and could capably counter all of the darts thrown his way.

In October, Welch summarized the importance of efforts to counter the growing threat of the so-called "civil rights" movement. He closed with an oft-repeated statement encouraging greater member activity to deal with this particular topic: "Fully expose the **civil rights** fraud and you will break the back of the Communist Conspiracy!"
It became the standard by which to measure the importance of creating awareness about this significant threat.

The 1964 presidential election saw Goldwater suffer a resounding defeat. One day after the rout, the Society's November *Bulletin* went to press. Departing from the custom of placing an inspirational quote on its cover page, large bold letters spelled out the question: **NOW WILL YOU JOIN THE JOHN BIRCH SOCIETY?** Members were urged to pose that question to "friends, neighbors, and all good Americans who will listen."

Prior to November's Election Day, and probably because he expected the disappointing result it would bring, Welch had asked some well-to-do friends to finance insertion of a 12-page Sunday supplement in selected newspapers. By mid-November, this ambitious and expensive campaign saw the supplement placed in 15 large circulation newspapers whose combined circulation totaled almost six million. Members were then encouraged to purchase a supply of the supplement for their own distribution, and many did so.

In the December 1964 *American Opinion*, Welch placed his 12-page "Reflections on the Election" and immediately offered it as a reprint. Those "Reflections" noted that 42 million had voted for Lyndon Johnson while only 27 million had cast their ballots for Barry Goldwater. The Electoral College vote was even more lopsided in favor of Johnson. Of the 42 million who chose Johnson, Welch stated his belief that "most of them are just as patriotic as the rest of the population." Nevertheless, he believed that they had unwittingly voted to surrender our nation's sovereignty, give billions to Communist tyrants, disarm our military, increase the national debt, swell the already huge federal government, and pave the way for more riots in the name of civil rights. To Welch, the election indicated that the majority of America's voters had chosen "to protect themselves from murder by committing suicide." But he vowed to have the Society keep that from happening.

Early in 1964 during an address to leaders of senior citizen organizations gathered in the White House, President Johnson had boldly stated: "We are going to take all the money that we think is unnecessarily being spent and take it from the haves and give it to the have-nots that need it so much." The mass media never told the American people of Johnson's revolutionary plan, choosing as one alternative the broadcasting of a television ad late in the campaign depicting a small child being victimized by an exploding atomic bomb. The message it conveyed was clear: trigger-happy Goldwater would lead our nation into an all-out nuclear war in which no one would be safe. Arthur Krock of the *New York Times* claimed the ad to be an example of foul play but no official from the Johnson campaign ever apologized for it.

Welch urged his readers not to blame Goldwater for the defeat but to realize that GOP handlers had taken control of his campaign as they worked to make sure their party's nominee lost. He then produced a small handout headlined "If you are one of the 27,000,000 [who voted for Goldwater] then read this…." Designed for members to use in reaching out to others, Welch explained that the people were given "an old-fashioned political campaign which was as unrealistic in our present circumstances as using horse-drawn watercarts to put out a forest fire."

A welcome surge in membership applications followed the Goldwater defeat.

CHAPTER 25
1965: CIVIL RIGHTS REVOLUTION

In a January 1965 report about the previous year's accomplishments, Welch pointed to new Council members, gains in book publishing and distribution, additions to field and headquarters staffs (now totaling exactly 100 employees), a boost in revenue (up to $3.2 million in 1964), and a near doubling of membership between January 1964 and January 1965. He noted the growing popularity of the Society's Support Your Local Police program, especially public realization of the need to retain <u>local</u> control and to resist any moves toward federal involvement and eventual federal takeover.

Opposition to creation of civilian police review boards became a project for members. In cities where these boards had been established, police brutality charges (most often completely unsubstantiated) resulted in bringing the accused officer(s) before a politically appointed board to face possible fines, suspension, demotion, or other disciplinary action. The predictable result saw police officers adopting a look-the-other-way attitude and not performing their customary duties. Welch wasn't surprised that this scheme aimed at destroying police morale and effectiveness was a favorite topic promoted by the Communist *People's World* and the leftist American Civil Liberties Union.

Welch delighted in reporting that 225 American Opinion Bookstores had already been established. Each of these benefited handsomely from sales during the previous political year. But, as soon as the votes had been counted, quite a few became financially burdensome and members could no longer afford them. Many closed their doors and some continued to operate from a member's garage. Years later, when reliance upon the easy course of ordering over the Internet mushroomed, more of these AO Bookstores folded.

In March, the Society's attention turned to Vietnam and the unconscionable policy of sending monetary aid and subsidized trade to European Communist nations while they supplied the Communist regime in Vietnam. Czechoslovakia, Romania, and Poland, for example, were openly sending strategic material that aided enemy forces in Vietnam.

Opposition to sex education in the schools then became a cause for members, as did the "insanity" of various church organizations hosting parties for known homosexuals. The *Bulletin* accused U.S. leaders of additional lunacy for spending taxpayer money to combat poverty in the plush environs of California's Beverly Hills, and for repeatedly turning loose unrepentant criminals who promptly resumed criminal activity. It was these and numerous other seemingly daft policies that Welch insisted weren't happening by chance, bad luck or stupidity, but were the fruits of a behind-the-scenes Conspiracy determined to "subvert the American nation and enslave the American people."

When rioting, burning, looting and anarchy engulfed numerous American cities, Welch stepped up his urging that more attention be given to exposing the so-called "civil rights" struggle. He praised the effective educational campaigns that had already been undertaken by member-created Truth About Civil Turmoil (TACT) committees, and he urged starting more of them. Those who participated weren't asked to join the Society; they were enlisted to help spread sound information that dealt with this single problem. TACT committees sprang up in numerous locales and so did TRAIN (To Restore American Independence Now) and SYLP (Support Your Local Police) committees – all using the guidelines supplied by headquarters.

As part of the campaign to spread truth about civil turmoil, the Society reprinted two small booklets openly published by Communists. These were the 1928 "American Negro Problems" written by Hungarian Communist Joseph Pogany using the alias John Pepper, and the 1935 "The Negroes in a Soviet America" authored by American Communists James W. Ford and James S. Allen. These small publications called for two revolutions – one aimed at establishing Communist control over the nation's southeastern states (creating a Soviet Negro Republic) and the other aiming for Communist control of the entire nation (establishing a Soviet United States). The Ford and Allen booklet spelled out the twin goals: "The revolution for land and freedom in the South and the proletarian revolution in the country as a whole will develop hand in hand."

After Society members distributed these two very revealing publications, Welch produced his own analysis of the Communist designs in a booklet entitled "Two Revolutions at Once." In it, he targeted Martin Luther King as a favorite of the Communists who trained and financed him, and who looked to him to lead the campaign to implement their plans.

Then and now, political leaders and the mass media consistently portrayed King as a champion of non-violence and an apostle of peace. But in a widely distributed article first appearing in the October 1965 issue of *American Opinion*, JBS writer Alan Stang corrected these and several other false notions about King. Regarding the oft-stated claim that King and his cohorts relied on non-violence, Stang presented the King strategy as it had been spelled out by King himself in the April 3, 1965, issue of *Saturday Review*. The "non-violent" Martin Luther King freely admitted that his strategy relied on creating violence and that it couldn't succeed unless some was created. As recounted in *Saturday Review*, the four-step King program called for:

1. Nonviolent demonstrators go into the streets to exercise their constitutional rights.
2. Racists resist by unleashing violence against them.
4. Americans of conscience in the name of decency demand federal intervention and legislation.
5. The administration, under mass pressure, initiates measures of immediate intervention and remedial legislation.

As can easily be seen, the King strategy needed violence whose purpose was to gain "federal intervention and legislation." These goals had been clearly stated in the two booklets published years earlier by the aforementioned Communist strategists. The Society then published Alan Stang's paperback book, *It's Very Simple: The True Story of Civil Rights*. Its 218 pages provided a thorough explanation of the Communist strategy behind the "civil rights" struggle, named the leading players and their backers, and reported on the various organizations working to tear America apart. It then contained recommended steps to counter the planned conversion of a free United States into a mere portion of a Communist-dominated world. Welch wasted no time in promoting the book, even sending a carton containing 100 copies free of charge to each JBS chapter leader. Before 1965 ended, the book had gone through four separate printings of tens of thousands each.

Over and over, Welch repeated the slogan he had created: "Fully expose the civil rights fraud and you will break the back of the Communist Conspiracy." Across the nation, members responded with distribution of literature, parade floats, letter writing, speaker events, and more. In communities throughout the nation, but especially in Southeastern states, members succeeded in hiring halls, gathering audiences, and hosting such knowledgeable experts as ex-communists Leonard Patterson and Lola Belle Holmes, former FBI undercover operatives Julia Brown and Gerald Kirk, widely respected journalist George Schuyler, Rev. Freeman Yearling, Charles Smith, and others – all Black Americans who were totally convinced of the need to expose the Communist threat posing as a crusade for "civil rights." Other speakers, not black but equally determined to expose the King strategy and those employing it, included Alan Stang, G. Edward Griffin, Reed

Benson, David Gumaer, Rex Westerfield, and more.

The efforts of Julia Brown became especially noteworthy. Her appearances in communities across the southeastern United States had regularly attracted large audiences made up of both blacks and whites. A physically small woman with a disarmingly strong voice, she repeatedly calmed both revolution-minded blacks and angry whites in a single hour, frequently bringing partisans of both sides to an understanding that outsiders intended to use them for an evil and destructive purpose. Wherever revolutionary planners intended to increase racial strife and set the stage for Martin Luther King or one of his lieutenants to conduct a parade or mount some other type of demonstration designed to incite a violent response, a call would go out for Mrs. Brown. Over several years, she gladly answered each call, traveled to a targeted community, met with local leaders of both races, delivered her speech, and totally disarmed a potentially explosive situation. In some locales, merely letting it be known that Julia Brown had been contacted and would soon arrive was enough to convince King's front men to pack up and leave town. Her efforts had become so well known and so effective that the revolutionaries knew their schemes couldn't succeed whenever she arrived to defuse the planned violence.

Prior to the successes gained by Julia Brown and others, communities saw revolutionary activity actually achieve the kind of destructiveness sought by its planners. But soon, JBS members succeeded in defusing several potentially dangerous situations through distribution of printed materials. One such example of this kind of courage occurred when Martin Luther King sent top aide Hosea Williams and more than a dozen members of his Southern Christian Leadership Conference (SCLC) to Americus, Georgia, to create a confrontation. Over a two-day period, tensions escalated between blacks and whites and it neared full-scale riot status after a black hothead killed an innocent white man in a drive-by shooting. Led by a local medical doctor who was well-known as a JBS leader, a group of members and allies stepped in and defused the looming explosion. The planned full-scale riot never occurred. Later investigation of this particular incident by officials of the federal Community Relations Service resulted in their conclusion that "members of the John Birch Society" had prevented the planned violence in Americus.

Over in Greenville, Alabama, the same four-step process employed by King and others began when outsider agitators arrived and began implementing the strategy King had clearly laid out. But Greenville was spared the desired violence when JBS members led by a well-known and highly respected local lawyer, who was a veteran JBS member, intervened and defused the situation. Other Birch Society members successfully prevented a looming riot in St. Augustine, Florida.

Over in Sandersville, Georgia, the King strategy had already generated parades and a boycott of local white-owned businesses when a local Baptist pastor contacted Birch Society headquarters and asked for help.

The Society sent Alan Stang, Julia Brown, and me to this small Georgia city in hopes of upsetting the revolutionaries and their plan. In a matter of days, Julia Brown and Alan Stang delivered speeches on consecutive evenings, drawing over 500 the first night and even more the second. In each instance, blacks numbered more than 20 percent of the audience. The determined promoters of violence quietly packed up and left town. Sandersville was spared. The grateful Baptist pastor then took me aside to express his amazement at what had been accomplished. (I was in the community to write an article about what happened and what didn't happen in Sandersville for *The Review Of The News*.) He asked that I include his deeply felt gratitude about what had been achieved. Holding back tears of joy, he said:

> In one single night, I had gathered around my [kitchen] table a Catholic, a Negro, a Jew and some members of my church. Each of us was there to work on a common problem of great importance to all, and no one compromised a single personal principle. We were just being good Americans. Please include in your article my earnest thanks to the staff of TACT, and to The John Birch Society which founded it. They have made me a better man.

Early in 1966, the Society released its 75-minute film "Anarchy USA" to aid member efforts in combating civil rights agitation. The work of Society official G. Edward Griffin, the film presented the Communist strategy given in film clips featuring their own destructive strategy. It then presented Julia Brown recounting her experiences in the Communist Party and her first-hand testimony about being instructed to follow King and implement his strategy.

Experiences recounted by Leonard Patterson during the film were somewhat different from those of Mrs. Brown but he concluded as she had about the fundamental goal of the Communists. In part, he stated:

> When I was a young man only 23 years old, I joined the Communist Party. I knew [Communist Party Leader] Gus Hall and other top-ranking American Communists very well because I trained with them [during the 1930s] at the Lenin University in Moscow. I broke away from the Party when it became clear to me that what the Communists were really up to was to use the Negro people in this country as cannon-fodder in a violent and bloody revolution

aimed at the establishment of an American Soviet dictatorship.... I'm not speaking of things I read about! These are things I personally participated in.

The successful use of "Anarchy USA" along with publicity about this Birch Society-produced film prompted a Boston University Theology School official to request that someone from nearby Birch Society headquarters (Belmont, Massachusetts) show it during one of his classes. The intention was clear: Let the film be shown so that it could easily be debunked as racist propaganda while discrediting the Birch Society for its distortions. I undertook the assignment knowing full well that exposing Martin Luther King, who was featured in the presentation, constituted an attack on their hero who had received his doctoral degree at this very school. It proved to be a very worthwhile expenditure of my time.

After I showed the entire 75-minute film, my expectation of having to answer questions and defend what had been shown never materialized. Instead, the school official promptly dismissed the class and asked that I speedily pack up and leave. There was no doubt in my mind that this man had recognized the full impact of the film and wanted no discussion about it to add to its message. The Society never heard from him again. And no one at Boston University ever asked for a re-showing of "Anarchy USA."

Chapter 26
1965 Cont'd: Buckley's Dishonesty

The October 19, 1965, issue of William Buckley's *National Review* magazine featured a 15-page attack on Robert Welch and the Society. Buckley, who had by now confided to several colleagues and friends that he intended to "destroy the John Birch Society," again used his magazine for that very purpose. Having previously – and grudgingly – noted that Robert Welch had indeed "stirred the patriotism of many Americans," the *National Review* founder and editor, along with several of his staff and other known conservatives, marshaled their arguments and tore into Welch and the Society. There is no doubt that previous sniping by Buckley had already led some Americans to dismiss the Society's efforts. This latest blast would increase those numbers. But it is also beyond doubt that key portions of this newly crafted and comprehensive attack were loaded with deliberate falsehoods.

At the beginning of his lengthy broadside, Buckley himself repeated his previously published distortion of *American Opinion* magazine's claim about communist influence shaping America's economic and political affairs. But as has already been noted in Chapter 21, the magazine never stated what Buckley claimed. Neither Welch nor any of the magazine's editors, international experts, and scribes who claimed to see communist control over a high percentage of U.S. "economic and political affairs" would, even for a moment, offer the distorted view provided by *National Review*'s Founder/Editor.

Frank Meyer and James Burnham, two of the magazine's editors, then offered their claims that Welch had, in the August 1965 JBS *Bulletin*, changed the meaning of the organization's Get US out! slogan from Get US out! <u>of the United Nations</u> to Get US out! <u>of Vietnam</u>. At the time, public support for combating Vietnam's Communist forces was extremely high and any call for abandoning the effort was considered un-patriotic, even pro-Communist. But the claims issued by Meyer and Burnham, intending to show how foolish or radical Welch and his Society were, constituted another exercise in patent dishonesty. Editor Burnham even added a bald-faced lie contending that Welch "advances no other proposal with respect to the Vietnam affair...."

Truth told a very different story. In the August 1965 *Bulletin* referenced by the two *National Review* distorters, Welch had expressed concern because Society members were reporting to him that the short-form Get US out! slogan "was being taken by some individuals to mean Get US Out! of Vietnam," which happened to be an increasingly popular slogan promoted by leftists and pro-Communists. The distortion of the JBS slogan became especially galling to military veterans, current servicemen, and relatives of anyone serving in Vietnam. So Welch quickly suggested to concerned JBS members that they add "of the UN" to make the original intent of the slogan blazingly clear. And he immediately arranged to have newer bumper stickers and signs containing the revised version made available.

Then, in that same August 1965 Bulletin, Welch added the following statement which both Meyer and Burnham chose to ignore. Far from any recommendation to abandon the Vietnam struggle, he wrote:

> The most desirable way of carrying out the exhortation about Vietnam, of course, would be by winning the war quickly and completely, putting the very few remaining anti-Communists of any stature firmly in power, to the great relief and happiness of the long-suffering Vietnamese people, and coming home after issuing an ultimatum which would keep the red murderers of Hanoi and Peiping from even looking in the direction of Saigon.

Responding further to this *National Review* attack, Welch later singled out Burnham's duplicity in a 40-page booklet entitled "Wild Statements" containing his supposedly rash and insupportable utterances over many years. Reviewing comments he had issued about deGaulle, Castro, Achmed Sukarno, the Bay of Pigs disaster, Vietnam, and more, Welch showed that history had proved how "unwild" each of his statements truly was. Addressing Burnham's charge that he had offered "no other proposal with respect to the Vietnam affair" than quitting the struggle, Welch wrote in "Wild Statements":

> The omission makes crystal clear, of course, that the critic was not concerned with spreading truth, but only with seeing how much damage he could do to The John Birch Society. He was obviously hoping that only a few of his readers would ever catch up with his intellectual crime. Which seems a bit naïve for so brilliant a man when you consider that fully one-third and perhaps one-half of the present circulation of that periodical [*National Review*] was created

for it through the endorsement and efforts of The John Birch Society.

Frank Meyer had additionally complained about the Society leader's insistence that a well-entrenched conspiracy not only existed but also was increasingly determining much of what was happening in America. Meyer followed *National Review's* set-in-stone policy that insisted America's decline should be attributed to "liberalism." He urged that the U.S. should combat its internal foes with "conservatism," an undefined and shifting school of thought under whose umbrella a wide variety of serious mischief had already been conducted. Ex-Communist Meyer and ex-Trotskyite Communist Burnham actually displayed early neoconservative [pro-war] tendencies prior to the term becoming more widely employed. Neoconservatives, of course, have always scoffed at any hint of conspiracy.

Buckley, already designated by an array of influential liberals and leftists as their favorite right-wing spokesman, had indeed declared war on The John Birch Society. His denunciations of Welch and the Society carried far more weight than anything emanating from the identifiable left. Many liberals and leftists, including some who might even have been considered conspirators by Welch and others, were delighted. Rockefeller Republicans were thrilled. But Buckley didn't stop there. For many years afterward, *National Review's* Founder continued to use his syndicated column, television program, speeches, and considerable influence to steer people away from JBS. Without doubt, Buckley succeeded in keeping millions of legitimately concerned Americans from examining the Society, and with familiarizing themselves with Welch's considerable – and reliable – output.

Whenever a liberal Republican, leftist Democrat, labor union leader, clergyman, or columnist chose to attack JBS, some damage to the Society resulted. But no one hurt the organization more than Bill Buckley, the man Robert Welch had befriended, recommended, and sent modest personal contributions to help him get started.

Welch always expected and frequently welcomed attacks aimed at the Society by professed Communists. But with considerable justification, he claimed that mainstream U.S. media were taking their lead from what the Communists had issued. Other attacks coming from the Anti-Defamation League (ADL) did their best to disparage JBS with false hints that it promoted anti-Semitism. It remains noteworthy, however, that ADL officials never directly charged the Society with anti-Semitism (stating only that the Society "contributes to anti-Semitism") because they knew such an accusation could not be substantiated. The effect of the ADL's intense campaign undoubtedly kept numerous Jewish Americans away. But when some determined Americans who happened to be Jews formed their "Jewish Society of Americanists" and proudly admitted their JBS membership, the ADL ignored them.

Two years after the California State Senate had released its very welcome 1963 report dealing with the Society, the panel addressed the Society once again. Plainly stating, "… we do not disavow any of the findings we made in our 1963 report," its newer comments stated that "growing incidence of anti-Semitism" had been found in the Society. But it also noted that "the Society as a whole is far from anti-Semitic."

Former Congressman John Rousselot, at the time the Society's Public Relations Director, quickly commented by thanking the subcommittee as he explained: "Widespread repetition of the lie that the Society harbors anti-Semitism has led some anti-Semites to seek us out and join our organization." He noted that it took a considerable amount of effort to dissuade most of those persons from such a notion. "Others," he said, "remained adamant and were removed from our membership rolls." The incidence of anti-Semitism noted by the subcommittee had resulted from falsehoods being aired about the Society, not any change in the organization's fundamental position.

When the surge of new members resulting from the Goldwater campaign waned, Welch contended that the slowdown had been caused by an "organized and synchronized attack on the Society." He insisted that the recent campaign against JBS made all earlier attacks "look like mere rehearsals or pilot operations." Putting a positive slant on it, he contended that the intensified onslaught was actually a response to the Society's numerous successes, especially the effort "exposing the civil rights fraud." But the Society definitely entered a new era where ignoring it and its efforts became the newer method for dealing with the organization's many wake-up calls. Growth descended from a flood of new members to a trickle.

In 1973, while attending a JBS event in Colorado, Welch met with a few local newspaper reporters. With no rancor whatsoever in his question, one of newsmen asked, "When was the low point in the Society's 15-year history?" After a moment of reflection, Welch responded, "It would probably have been the summer of 1966 when the attacks were no longer a daily occurrence and the flood of new memberships had largely dried up." He continued: "That was the period when we urged members to start ad hoc committees like TACT, TRAIN and Support Your Local Police. This got our members going again, and it resulted in good educational work while also bringing some new people into our organization."

Later that very day, I told Welch that the low point he had mentioned just happened to coincide with my joining his staff (August 1, 1966). Without hesitation but with a huge grin on his face, he said, "It surely was our low point."

In late 1965, while he continued to urge members to read good books, Welch altered his habitual recommendation about the need to immerse themselves in factual works and documentaries. Instead, he heaped praise on novelist Taylor Caldwell and her latest work, *Pillar of Iron*. This tour-de-force about Cicero's battle to keep the Roman republic from degenerating into a democracy on the way to tyranny presented numerous valuable lessons for current Americans. Miss Caldwell, a member of the Society, would later be the featured speaker at several JBS events. She also authored several articles for *American Opinion* magazine. Welch, a strong admirer of Cicero, suggested to members that they avoid sinking into pessimism when discovering through the Caldwell book that the Roman statesman's effort had failed. Instead, he urged that Cicero's loss presented a lesson which he summarized as: "In Cicero's lifetime, there was no John Birch Society." In the current struggle for freedom, he continued, "it is exactly what is done by the Society that can make the difference."

The November 1965 *Bulletin*, like the September 1963 issue, filled more than 100 pages. Containing an updated review of Society programs and progress, it announced the availability of long-play recordings of a seminar Welch had recently delivered to a select group in the Midwest. Condensed into 12 albums, the finished product labeled "One Dozen Trumpets" filled 18 hours of listening time and sold for $50.00. He hoped that many no-shows to his two-day presentations, persons who wanted to attend but couldn't for a variety of reasons, might be able to listen to his recorded review of the 200-year-old Conspiracy. Later, the "Trumpets" became available in taped format. These recordings became useful for members who had followed Welch's urgings to form "Study Clubs" where newer members and prospects could be introduced to Welch's history lessons along with his explanation of the Society's program to combat treachery and misinformation.

Among the many pages in this summary *Bulletin*, there appeared a warning about Communist-created division among Canadians who spoke French and fellow Canadians who employed the English language. Welch then warned members not to be deceived into accepting the odious form of anti-Semitism propagated by the *Protocols of the Learned Elders of Zion*. He opined that the book had been "written by Lenin himself, or to his order." He added his belief that "when a Catholic or a Protestant or a Jew, or a Frenchman or an Egyptian, or an American becomes a full-fledged Communist, he is no longer any of these things. His former loyalties are completely erased…. He is now simply a Communist, nothing else." And he ended this section of the lengthy *Bulletin* with a stern warning that no one should allow himself or herself to become a victim of "futility, frustration and despair." He even chided a highly regarded former U.S. Army general who, as far back as eight years ago, had been telling Congressional committees that America was already lost. That military official, believed by Welch to be a patriotic but misinformed ally, would cause others to "let up in the fight." He urged instead that members be aware that the extensive attacks on JBS were evidence of the increasing amount of success already achieved by the Society and its members.

Meanwhile, the monthly *American Opinion* magazine grew in quality and importance as its stable of writers supplied facts and perspective enabling readers to understand and combat forces working to subvert freedom. In the paragraphs below, highlights of the magazine's output during all of 1965 appear. A similar listing of the magazine's articles year after year will not be provided in this book.

In 1965, nationally known author and educator Charles Callan Tansill supplied a detailed account of high-level treachery in Washington that, in 1941, guaranteed our nation's military commanders in Hawaii would be surprised by the December 7, 1941, Japanese attack. Alan Stang warned that Canada's Separatist Movement had the potential of fueling a Communist-style revolution. Editor Scott Stanley analyzed the damaging effects of the "March From Selma." John Stormer supplied a damning look at the nation's press. Economist Hans Sennholz bared inflation's roots under the title "Government's Quiet Thief."

A future regular contributor of important articles, Gary Allen made his debut by tracing the Communist and leftist fueling of malcontents throughout the nation. Former Congressman Martin Dies questioned the findings of the Warren Commission. Former IRS Commissioner T. Coleman Andrews told of IRS selectivity in scrutinizing conservative groups. George Schuyler, the nation's most widely read Black journalist, provided an uplifting essay entitled "For America." In a joyful salute, Alan Stang told of the courageous Negroes of Lincolnton, Georgia, who chased black and white agitators from their community before any of the planned rioting and destructiveness could occur.

September 1965 marked the debut of *The Review Of The News* (TROTN), a pocket-sized weekly magazine. The new weekly would continue publication side-by-side with the monthly *American Opinion* until *The New American*, a biweekly, replaced both in 1985.

Chapter 27
1966: Chief Victory – Staying Alive

Responding to suggestions from members, Welch altered the Society's slogan by adding an acknowledgment of dependence on God. With four newly added words, the slogan would henceforth read: "Less government, more responsibility, and ... with God's help ... a better world."

At this point in the Society's history, many new members had joined after seeing the film of Welch delivering his "Look at the Score" speech. Others had read its text in Chapter One of the *Blue Book*. A chronological survey of the Communist conspiracy's progress during the 20th Century, the message was surely frightening and most who received it felt something had to be done. The Society presented a much-needed course of action, and sign-ups were common.

Members had also begun using a staff-created public relations film, something many had asked for. Entitled simply "What Is The John Birch Society?" its purpose was not so much a recruiting tool as it was a positive depiction of the very nature of the organization. It began with a brief history of Captain John Birch, followed by testimonials from his parents and others, and concluding with a summation of the nature and activities of the organization. It was quite a departure from a Welch-only film that presented no graphics whatsoever in his history-laden monologues. Viewers had always been asking, "What about today?" or "What is happening now?" This film helped to answer some of those questions.

The January 1966 *Bulletin* announced the availability of a newly filmed Welch speech entitled "A Touch of Sanity." Again no graphics, only Welch and his message. But it was different, he explained, in that "Look at the Score" had provided a historical summation of Communist successes beginning with the Bolshevik Revolution. The new "A Touch of Sanity" presented "a horizontal view of Communist activities and poisons all around us." Both films gave viewers a solid dose of the Society's admittedly unnerving convictions. Staff personnel who showed either of these hour-long "Welch only" films were instructed to follow with the 30-minute "What Is The John Birch Society?" This process did bring in new members, but the numbers signing up in 1966 were nowhere near what had been achieved in previous years.

Welch then announced the availability of a filmed speech delivered by former Secretary of Agriculture Ezra Taft Benson. Entitled "Stand Up For Freedom," his message given before a large crowd of enthusiastic friends included a rousing endorsement of the Society. Benson and Welch had become remarkably close through appearances together, voluminous correspondence, and solid agreement to combat the tightening grip of Communist control over the U.S. They likewise agreed on the way to deal with it: creation of understanding among the people.

In addition to the growing number of 16mm films, the Society and a couple of enterprising members started producing filmstrips with accompanying soundtracks on long-play vinyl records and reel-to-reel tapes. Welch pointed to the availability of a new 29-minute filmstrip program providing hard truths about the United Nations. Members who couldn't afford the cost of an expensive 16mm film projector could purchase a filmstrip projector at a much lower cost, and most already had either a record player or a tape machine to provide the accompanying narration. The popularity of this new way to bring a JBS message to others soared and various programs covering an array of subjects became available. Members could now schedule "Monday Night at the Movies" using printed materials supplied by Society headquarters. The Society had actually grown to such a size that several enterprising individuals started producing filmstrip programs to supplement the organization's educational campaigns.

Welch reported that the newly formed Jewish Society of Americanists (JSA) had held a press conference in New York City attended by over 50 media representatives. He also noted that several of the Jewish members (of both JBS and JSA) had participated in a 30-minute taped interview for a CBS news program hosted by Walter Cronkite. As expected, those members capably explained the Society and its programs while refuting the well-publicized charges from the ADL. But no part of this taped program was ever broadcast. Nor did any portions of the well-attended press conference show up in the media. Welch said it was easy to understand that the mass media propagandists who despised the JBS didn't want anything favorable about the Society to reach the public.

The campaign to Support Your Local Police took its place as an increasingly important agenda item. A new book entitled *The Communist Attack on U.S. Police* authored by former Salt Lake City Police Chief Cleon Skousen aided the effort. Skousen had earlier written the very helpful and widely used 12-page article, "The Communist Attack on the

John Birch Society." One of the more significant victories achieved by the Society occurred when possible creation of a Civilian Police Review Board in New York City was overwhelmingly defeated in a city-wide November 1966 referendum. New York City members got plenty of help from others in nearby states, and from non-member citizens who distributed flyers, pamphlets and articles by the thousands. Off-duty policemen, some of whom were avid Society members, contributed in many ways toward defeating the proposal.

A Civilian Police Review Board had long been a goal of Communists and their allies. (Creating such a panel is still a goal of those seeking to disparage police and place them under federal control.) Losing this highly publicized referendum constituted a severe blow to the ambitions of New York Mayor John Lindsay, an easily categorized leftist. Welch attributed the stunning victory to the hard work of members and the policemen themselves while pointing out that it had been achieved because "enough people understood" what was at stake as a result of the distribution of Birch Society material. He claimed the effort to be a victory that could be duplicated by creating enough understanding about other topics and about the entire Communist Conspiracy.

Turning more intensely to the conflict in Vietnam, Welch labeled the purpose of the war "simply to be at war" because war always led to "more government and moral decline." He asked members to send letters to the President, members of Congress, and others asking simply, "When are we going to win this war in Vietnam – and why not?" The Society's campaign dealing with this conflict grew into a permanent agenda item aided significantly by publication of the 292-page book *Background To Betrayal: The Tragedy of Vietnam* written by Hilaire du Berrier. An authority on Asia and its politics, his name led many to believe wrongly that he was not an American. But du Berrier, born and raised in North Dakota, had spent many of his adult years as a soldier of fortune/journalist in Europe, Africa and Southeast Asia. He earned great respect and friendship from French forces in what was once known as Indo-China because he never provided names and whereabouts of the French foes of Japan during World War II. Though jailed, tortured and frequently threatened with death, he survived and lived to continue his reporting of events in the land soon to become known as Vietnam.

Everyone who ever persevered through *Background To Betrayal* considered it a difficult but important read. Keeping track of the many Asian-named personalities and groups was a significant problem. But du Berrier's reporting about the political figures and developments in that country were never challenged. What he provided was completely ignored by all elements of the Establishment-dominated media. Why? Because the author concluded that the American-backed Diem family and American diplomats in both Vietnam and Washington had aided the cause of Communism and harmed the efforts of any significant anti-Communists.

Du Berrier never mentioned the restrictive "Rules of Engagement" imposed on the U.S. military in Vietnam because those hard-to-believe restrictions on our nation's forces hadn't been published. Not until 1985 were these official mandates pried out of the State and Defense Departments and then published in the *Congressional Record* as requested by Arizona Senator Barry Goldwater. They told of restrictions imposed on U.S. forces that guaranteed their inability to achieve victory. Portions of these Rules made public by Goldwater can be viewed in three entries appearing in the *Congressional Record* for March 6, 1985, pages S2632-S2641; March 14, 1985, pages S2982-2990; March 18, 1985, pages S3011-S3018.

Senator Goldwater's revealing commentary about these Rules included his sharp disagreement with incredible limitations placed on our forces. He wrote: "For example, one rule told American pilots they were not permitted to attack a North Vietnam MIG [a Russian-made fighter plane] sitting on the runway. The only time it could be attacked was after it was in flight, was identified and showed hostile intentions. Even then, its base could not be bombed.... In some regions, enemy trucks could evade attack by simply driving off the road.... Another rule provided that SAM missile sites could not be struck while they were under construction, but only after they had become operational."

In April 1966, Welch happily announced that Congressman James Utt (R-Calif.) had introduced a measure calling for complete withdrawal of the U.S. from the United Nations. Members were urged to contact their own congressman to gain support for it. The UN, insisted Welch with plenty of evidence, had been conceived and created by Communists, was still controlled by Communists, and was continuing to propel mankind toward creation of a tyrannical, UN-led, world government.

About our nation's escalating involvement in Vietnam, Welch pointed out: "... this Vietnam action is being conducted on the basis of our treaty commitments to SEATO, with everything we do actually and ultimately under the control and management of the United Nations." That claim could be backed by reading the Articles 52-54 of the UN Charter where authorization for creation of SEATO, and the earlier formation of NATO, appears. These Charter articles specify that "activities undertaken or in contemplation" by such regional arrangements must keep the Security Council informed "at all times." Claiming that his conclusion about the war was "as incontrovertible as sunrise," he urged members to obtain and distribute the $2.00 "United Nations Packet" containing three books: *The Fearful Master, The Bang-Jensen Tragedy,* and *46 Angry Men* along with an assortment of anti-UN reprints and pamphlets.

Under a headline asking "What Hit The John Birch Society?" Welch summarized several of the more recent attacks aimed at the organization and himself. He noted that Arthur Larson's anti-JBS National Council for Civic Responsibility had accepted $50,000 from the Democratic National Committee to aid in its campaign to "destroy" the Society. More brickbats aimed at the JBS came in the Anti-Defamation League's (ADL) distortion-filled 1966 book, *Danger on the Right* authored by the ADL's Forster and Epstein. National Educational Television (NET) sent a crew to JBS headquarters where its personnel were accorded complete cooperation from all staff employees over a period lasting several weeks. Just prior to the airing of their program, its producer boasted in an interview given to a Boston newspaper that her purpose all along had been to damage the Society. Her work failed to accomplish the intended goal.

In 1967, the ADL's Forster and Epstein were at it again with a new 240-page paperback entitled *The Radical Right*. Its first half slammed other anti-Communist and conservative groups and individuals. The other half repeated much of what they had written in 1966. Both of these distortion-filled screeds featured jaundiced commentary about the Society's "War Against Civil Rights." The Society's campaign, as any levelheaded person understood, was never against "civil rights"; it targeted the agitators (many of whom were Communists) who sought to split America by stimulating riots designed to tear the country apart. In its repeated attack, the ADL leaders never accused the Society of anti-Semitism because they knew such a charge couldn't be proved. And, of course, citations from Bill Buckley's consistent anti-Birch campaign buttressed the ADL's attack. Buckley, Americans were told, was the nation's "responsible" conservative.

Welch continued his survey of what had "hit" JBS with details about a Washington gathering of top-level members of the Johnson administration, along with some "moderate" Republican governors and the nation's Attorney General. Given information about this meeting by one attendee, Welch reported that its purpose was to compile information that would enable the Attorney General of the U.S. to issue a formal condemnation of the Society. But the plan fizzled and no such condemnation emerged.

Finally in his listing of attacks occurring from mid-1965 to early 1966, Welch pointed to labor leader Walter Reuther's Committee on Political Action (COPE) and its distribution of millions of copies of a 12-page brochure devoted to warnings about the Society's "proven effectiveness."

Soon, another anti-JBS organization known as the Institute for American Democracy

(IAD) announced its determination to counter "the rising volume of extremist activity, particularly by organizations in the John Birch Society's orbit." This new group had for its leader Dr. Franklin Littell who had received theological training from Reverend Harry Ward, an open and avowed Communist. Littell had earlier written an article entitled "A Cell in Every Church" calling for Communist presence amongst that significant segment of the American people as they planned to worship the Almighty. He later denied his authorship of the piece but Welch claimed to have a copy and supporting commentary about it in his files. This drive to create Communist cells in the churches failed when the House Committee on Un-American Activities exposed Littell and his comrades.

All of these efforts and numerous smaller attacks never mentioned by Welch had significant impact. As noted earlier, the Society's growth in mid-1966 had slowed considerably. Creation of the Littell-led IAD was likely undertaken to insure that the images of JBS as "secret," "un-American," "anti-Semitic," "fascist," "subversive," etc. remained ingrained in the public's consciousness. It took great effort and perseverance for Welch and Society members to continue their efforts. Asked later that year if he could name the Society's chief accomplishment to date, Welch promptly responded, "Staying alive!" And he wasn't trying to be funny.

Beset by attacks large and small, and struggling to keep member morale and activity both healthy and productive, Welch then faced the mid-1966 resignations of Council members Revilo P. Oliver and Slobodan Draskovich. Both made their resignations known to the press which immediately led some eager reporters to predict that the Society was falling apart. Four years earlier, Draskovich had sent an 11-page resignation letter that Welch calmly and successfully countered in the belief that the man's complaints were simply misguided. But when Oliver's resignation earned media attention, Draskovich saw an opportunity to offer himself as a replacement for Welch and Welch decided to let him go. A proud atheist, Oliver's long-standing rejection of anything that smacked of religion finally led him to quit the Society.

Welch announced the departure of these two Council members in a special four-page message to members. It noted that there had been several deaths and several other resignations for "purely personal reasons" or for honest disagreement with JBS policies. But, wrote Welch, such developments should be expected in any national organization and they were "neither new nor fatal in the life of the Society."

Seeing an opportunity to do some significant damage to the Society, Bill Buckley quickly boarded an airplane and traveled to South Bend, Indiana, seeking to persuade JBS Council Member Dean Clarence Manion to resign. The former leader of the Notre

Dame Law School and a one-time Eisenhower appointee as chairman of a commission tasked to streamline government, Manion had become well known nationally through his weekly radio and television *Manion Forum* broadcasts. A long-time friend and admirer of Robert Welch, Manion listened to Buckley's plea, totally rejected it, and sent the would-be Society destroyer back to New York.

Always wanting to keep members informed about the various threats to freedom, Welch announced late in 1966 the publication of two new books. *Ill Fares the Land* written by Dan P. Van Gorder, a veteran agricultural columnist and former speechwriter for members of Congress. His book warned of the growing involvement of the federal government in all aspects of our nation's food production. The other much-needed book, Rose L. Martin's *Fabian Freeway* provided a 550-page survey of the socialist movement – from its origins and destructiveness in Great Britain to how it had crossed the ocean and was now seriously infecting the United States. Unfortunately, many Americans have been led to believe that they could manage to live under socialism while never realizing that its logical next step would be the imposition of its partner, totalitarian Communism.

As 1966 wound down, Welch noted that Drew Pearson had stated in one of his columns, "The John Birch Society, which professes to seek a return to Christianity, is now distributing bumper stickers declaring: 'Kill a Commie for Christ!'" Welch responded:

> Of course we had never even heard of such a bumper sticker, and nothing could be more foreign to the tenets and methods of The John Birch Society. We suspect that, since J. Edgar Hoover has designated Martin Luther King as the biggest liar in America, Pearson is merely striving to regain his lost pre-eminence in that field.

At the close of the year, Welch published the text of his latest speech. Under the title "The Truth In Time," it provided a view of the Conspiracy's history, not from 1917 when Lenin and Trotsky established their base of operations in Moscow, but from the final three decades of the 18th Century and the formation of the Bavarian Illuminati. The goal of that sinister force sought to replace religion, morals, and national governments with diabolically driven world dominance. We lead off our next chapter with our summary of Welch's compelling history lesson.

Chapter 28
1967: Conspiracy Above Communism

As mentioned earlier, Welch had introduced members to the existence of an upper level of conspiratorial activity, something beyond Moscow and the Communist Party in Russia or in the U.S. He began doing so in 1962 when he heaped high praises on the *Dan Smoot Report's* six-part series about the New York-based Council on Foreign Relations (CFR). Readers of Smoot's newsletter, many of whom had become subscribers as a result of Welch's enthusiastic endorsement, were likely wondering what to make of the many high-level government officials, media heavyweights, foundation heads, and other "Establishment" figures who were CFR members but were never Communists. All of these individuals had obviously given their allegiance to something other than the U.S. Constitution. They even made a habit of scoffing at fellow Americans who were concerned about Communist penetration of our nation's government.

Smoot's followers, a high percentage of them JBS members, didn't cease fearing and detesting Communism but many surely wondered about the Kennedy/Johnson appointees who were CFR members. After supplying some background information about the CFR, Smoot listed as CFR members Secretary of State Dean Rusk, Secretary of Defense Robert McNamara, Secretary of the Treasury C. Douglas Dillon, CIA Director Allen Dulles, and numerous other highly placed government officials. President Kennedy had indicated his own CFR membership in a written response to a Smoot inquiry. These individuals by virtue of their CFR membership were favoring U.S. foreign aid programs that were financing Communism's spread, supporting the United Nations, and backing enormous expansion of our own federal government beyond constitutional limitations. Were they themselves Communists? Or were they part of another level of conspiratorial activity parallel to or above Communism? Many wondered.

Welch was well aware of these questions. But he hadn't answered them directly, at least immediately. Instead, he introduced the topic in his 1964 speech "More Stately

Mansions." In that important address, he told of the creation in 1776 of the Bavarian Illuminati, a highly organized conspiracy whose ultimate goals included the overturning of civilization leading to world government. Those who heard or read that speech knew that Welch was suggesting, but not yet stating as fact, the existence of a level of conspiratorial activity higher than Moscow-based Communism. The Society's leader wasn't playing games with his followers. Instead, he was slowly and deliberately bringing them to a better awareness of the immense evil already existing in many parts of the world, especially the toehold it had achieved within the United States.

As 1966 came to a close, Welch answered these questions with what many members considered his best speech. It bore the title "The Truth In Time." No longer just hinting about a sinister force above Communism, he stated with emphasis, "But the Communist movement is only a tool of the total conspiracy." That thunderous assertion and the supporting information surrounding it answered the burning question for many members. Welch explained that numerous conspirators likely weren't actual Communists, though some may indeed have accepted membership in the Party. He would henceforth use the term "INSIDERS" when discussing these individuals and their conspiratorial activity. Within the speech, he would point to their one overall goal:

> The INSIDERS, however, wanted gradually and eventually to bring a concentration of all government power into the hands of the executive department of one central government.

Other questions answered by Welch included: Should Communism be considered an extension, or a front, for an even more insidious conspiratorial group? He wrote:

> ... the INSIDERS were using the Communists, the anarchists, the socialists of various hues and kinds, and dozens of other groups, to promote their purposes.... The enemy which we need to oppose, expose, and destroy, in order to save our country and our civilization, can properly be identified as the Communist conspiracy. But to understand this enemy it is important to remember and understand its roots.

How have the INSIDERS helped to advance the Communist drive for world control? Welch summarized one of the conspiracy's greatest accomplishments:

> Since early in 1945, the most powerful single force in promoting Communism everywhere, and in turning one nation after another over to Communist tyr-

anny – as in Czechoslovakia, and China, and Cuba, and the Congo – has been the help of the United States government to that end.

He then warned members to be forewarned about what they could expect when spreading information about this conspiracy:

Anybody who even starts to point out the truth is mercilessly ridiculed as a believer in the "conspiratorial theory of history"; and anybody who approaches too close to an authoritative exposure of the higher levels of the conspiracy meets the fate of a William Morgan, a Doctor William Wirt, or a Joe McCarthy – a fate which is visibly intended for ourselves.

The text of "The Truth In Time" and the filmed version of this speech were immediately made available. The booklet contained dozens of footnotes directing readers to source materials including such works about the Illuminati as English Professor John Robison's *Proofs of a Conspiracy* and *Memoirs Illustrating the History of Jacobinism* by the French monk Abbe Augustin Barruel. These two remarkable books, both published in Europe in 1798, and both containing indisputable facts about the history and goals of the Illuminati, weren't immediately available. The Society then published the Robison book in 1967. Abbe Barruel's much larger and more comprehensive work became available in 1995 through the efforts of the JBS-friendly American Council on Economics and Society based in Fraser, Michigan. Both authors, who never had any contact with each other, arrived at similar conclusions about the existence and goals of the conspiracy.

Along with the 12-page February 1967 *Bulletin*, Welch enclosed a 24-page booklet entitled "The Truth About Vietnam." As hard-hitting as anything he had ever issued, his summary of the Vietnam struggle included a compilation of disconcerting facts and penetrating questions. He noted that in a recent single week in Vietnam, "144 Americans were killed, 1,004 were wounded and six were reported missing." He then asked 20 questions, provided answers for many, and added comments about each. We summarize some of the points he raised:

    1. The United States is the most powerful nation on earth. Why is it that our forces "cannot lick a puny bunch of half-starved guerrillas in a country the size of Missouri?"

    2. Why fight Communism in Vietnam and help them everywhere else? Welch explained: "Our boys in Vietnam are being killed by Russian bullets

fired from Russian guns, while the Johnson administration sends the Soviets wheat to feed those who are making the guns and the bullets." And he noted that the Communist regime in Poland just sent $13 million to North Vietnam "taken directly out of the much larger sum which Washington had given to Warsaw."

3. The war in Vietnam is being run by SEATO, "a regional subsidiary of the United Nations" just as the war in Korea was justified via the tenets of the NATO pact. Why do our leaders allow this? A war under SEATO is a war controlled by the United Nations.

4. "But if this is war, then what happened to Article I: Section 8, Paragraph 11 of the United States Constitution which decrees that only Congress can put this nation into war?"

5. Why are there "so many incredible handicaps on our men?" The rules under which they fight are preventing the bombing missions from inflicting significant damage and keeping the ground forces from doing the job of which they are capable.

One month after distributing "The Truth About Vietnam," the Society launched a four-page petition addressed to Congress. Its goal? "To have this administration stop, promptly and completely, giving aid in any form, directly or indirectly, to our Communist enemies." Its first three pages pointed to the various forms of aid going from our nation to Soviet Russia and Moscow's European satellites that were supplying North Vietnam. The petition had blank spaces on its fourth page for 17 signatures. One of the many infuriating points raised in it was the claim of North Vietnam's Premier Pham Van Dong: "We shall defeat the Americans with Soviet weapons." Van Dong certainly knew as well as anyone that his forces were obtaining their weaponry from Soviet Russia and its captive nations in Europe. Members immediately went to work gathering signatures and their efforts located many new recruits for introduction to the Society and eventual JBS membership.

The following month (April 1967), Welch added to the Society's anti-Vietnam campaign with a second major booklet. His 20-page "More Truth about Vietnam" focused almost entirely on the numerous ways our own government was feeding, financing and sustaining Communist nations who, in turn, were supplying the Communist enemy in Vietnam. This booklet also devoted four of its pages to the already launched petition to Congress. Filled petitions were to be sent to *The Review Of The News* at the Society's Massachusetts headquarters. Bundles of completed petitions, many filled out at tables set up by Society members at shopping malls or by door-to-door efforts in neighborhoods, were then delivered to selected members of Congress by Reed A. Benson and Robert W. Lee, the Society's staff personnel stationed in Washington.

While many congressional responses to the petition were very encouraging, congressmen who backed the administration's policy kept quiet and allowed the treachery to continue. Welch labeled their inaction "treason" based on the Constitution's Article III, Section 3 where treason is defined as "adhering to [U.S.] enemies, giving them aid and comfort."

Birch Society chapters had been organized and were now functioning in every state – except in Hawaii. In May, a senior JBS Coordinator arrived in Honolulu, contacted the few members already on the rolls, invited several more who had sought information from the Society, and conducted a recruiting meeting at a prestigious hotel in Honolulu. The result: New members and the few already enlisted in the Home Chapter launched the 50th state's first Society chapter.

Four months later, Hawaii's major newspaper discovered the Society's presence and one would think from its front-page coverage that something as explosive as the 1941 Japanese attack at Pearl Harbor had just reoccurred. The newspaper articles relied on the oft-repeated objections aimed at the Society – that Welch had unjustly smeared Dwight Eisenhower; that William Buckley had labeled the Society as the producer of "paranoid and unpatriotic drivel"; and that the Society was racist, anti-Semitic, and secretive. The local chapter leader told the newspaper reporter that the Society had no secrets but would operate as did the Elks, Moose, ACLU and many other organizations that never published the names of their members. He and the newly recruited Hawaiians started work gathering thousands of signatures on the Society's petition seeking to end the flow of aid going to Communist nations.

Hawaiians of all ethnic backgrounds, who were vibrantly aware of the power and influence of the communist-led International Longshore and Warehouse Union (ILWU) and its grip on their state, gladly signed the Society's petition. Some who were introduced to JBS when they were asked to sign the petition became excellent prospects for Society membership. Soon, the very successful JBS chapter leader found himself cut loose by his employer which forced him to return to Mainland USA where he built his own thriving business, and later became a leading member of the Executive Committee of the Society's National Council.

In June, John Rousselot resigned as the Society's Director of Public Relations. Welch accepted his decision with gratitude for his years of service and predicted that John would soon offer himself to voters for some new post. The prediction became reality when John again won election to the U.S. Congress. Reed Benson took over as the new national P.R. Director and Rex Westerfield accepted appointment as western P.R. Director.

Franklin Littell's IAD issued a nine-page blast seeking to blunt the Society's petition and booklets. Welch accused the IAD of having been formed for no other reason than diminishing the overall effectiveness of the Society. Welch told Society members to be encouraged about their growing clout.

The July *Bulletin* contained an insert labeled, "An Early Progress Report On The Greatest Petition Drive in U.S. History." It showed photos of Reed Benson presenting bundles of signed petitions to several members of Congress. Each House member received completed petitions containing roughly 20,000 signatures and each senator received 50,000 signatures. The recipients included House members: Utt (R-Calif.), Williams (D-Miss.), Hansen (R-Idaho), Watson (R-S.C.) and Rarick (R-La.). Senators receiving the larger bundles were Thurmond (R-S.C.) and Byrd (D-Va.). That both Democrats and Republicans happily received these completed petitions spurred the effort nationwide while also canceling a potential argument that its only collaborators were GOP members.

Certainly not ignoring the civil turmoil occurring throughout the nation, Welch composed an eight-page tract entitled "To the Negroes of America." It began with, "Wake up, my misguided friends! They really do think you are stupid." He asked members to distribute it to Black Americans. His message pointed out that the Negro population in America, if measured separately and as a group, was already "among the top five nations of the world" in several economic and cultural categories. And he was delighted to learn that a Negro-led organization in Atlanta was distributing a singe-page flier aimed at fellow blacks that noted: "Our homes get burned; our kids get hurt, our friends get locked up; and we are the ones who get killed." All of that was certainly true while the outsiders who started the trouble all over the nation left town.

The July *Bulletin* also noted the addition of two new Council Members: industrialist and inventor Floyd Paxton of Yakima, Washington, and Dr. Lawrence P. McDonald of Atlanta, Georgia. Dr. McDonald would later perform successful surgery on Robert Welch, build a significant JBS presence in his home area, and win election to the U.S. Congress where he became the acknowledged leader of a hardcore group of anti-communist and determined conservative House members. Dr. McDonald would later be named Chairman of the Society replacing the aging Robert Welch. Only a few months at the helm of the Society on September 1, 1983, he was a passenger aboard Korean Airlines Flight 007 when a Soviet fighter plane attacked it as it headed toward Seoul, South Korea. Neither the plane nor any of its 283 passengers and crew members were ever seen again.

In September 1967, Welch included a 32-page update of the Society's needs and activities entitled "This Is It!" He identified the "Two Main Planks of Current Communist Strategy" as the Vietnam War and the Civil Rights struggle that had just led to the torching of a major portion of Detroit. After summarizing the harm done to the Society by numerous attacks, he wrote that the Society had two main needs: "Reinforcements" by way of more new members, and "money. But we need money first."

He then corrected Los Angeles radio antagonist George Putnam who claimed the Society's leader had made "vast sums of money" while spreading fear about a non-existent conspiracy. The truth, Welch stated, included his never having drawn a salary, putting "half of what little I owned" into the Society's work, and never taking "any pay for any of the articles I have written for *American Opinion*." Years later, Putnam did a surprising but welcome turnabout. After he had become a virtual "has been" on radio, his daily broadcasts were now being aired on a much smaller station where he completely reversed his previous allegiances and became an ardent fan of the Society. Members who recalled his frequent diatribes against the Society and Robert Welch found the man's reversal completely astounding – but most welcome.

After having written numerous valuable articles for *American Opinion* magazine, Dr. James P. Lucier accepted an assignment from Welch to compose in one volume as much as he could learn about the cabal that had come to be known as the Communist Conspiracy. Jim Lucier threw himself into the immense task but never completed it. He eventually turned over what he had written and Welch published its 100 pages under the title *Seventeen Eighty Nine* (the beginning year of the French Revolution).

In part, Lucier's manuscript traced the early careers and ultimate goals of France's Voltaire and Rousseau and the period known as "The Enlightenment." The manuscript then told of Adam Weishaupt's ambitious plans, his successful takeover in 1782 of continental European Freemasonry, the 1784 discovery of and immediate criminalizing of the Illuminati's organization and its members by the Bavarian government, and the subsequent escape of the conspiracy's creator to northern Germany. Toward the end of his fascinating compilation of events in the late 18th Century's largely hidden European and American history, Lucier summarized what he had discovered to be the ultimate goal of the conspirators: "All nations, all sovereignties must perish, all religion must be subdued, all authority subverted, so that the aforesaid elite can create the new and highly visible mechanism for the ruthless government of the world." Today, the unchanged goal of elite conspirators is known as the "New World Order." Robert Welch frequently labeled the ambitious and devious scheme as a "satanic and diabolical" plot. And he would regularly insist that current leaders of the plot haven't deviated even slightly from the plan created in Europe almost 250 years ago.

Ultimate secrecy, of course, has always undergirded the work of any conspiracy. Jim Lucier deftly summarized one of the early goals of the plotters: "The first job of a conspiracy is to convince the world that a conspiracy does not exist." Welch chose that incisive epigram as the lead to his Foreword in the October 1967 *Bulletin*. He quickly followed the use of Lucier's poignant assertion by warning that ridicule of "the conspiratorial theory of history" would surely follow, and would often precede any attempt to consider conspiratorial design as the root cause of what was happening to our country.

In another "Progress Report" about the Vietnam petition, Welch delightedly noted that Reed Benson had delivered bundles of signed petitions against aid to Communist nations to ten more members of Congress. Five House members each received 20,000 signatures and five senators each received 50,000 signatures. The House recipients, again both Democrats and Republicans were Pool (D-Texas), Steiger (R-Ariz.), Buchanan (R-Ala.), Dowdy (D-Texas), and Edwards (R-Ala.). Senators who happily received the larger bundles were Curtis (R-Neb.), Holland (D-Fla.) Talmadge (D-Ga.), Eastland (D-Miss.), and Cotton (R-N.H.).

These new deliveries, all made prior to November 1, 1967, built the cumulative total of petitions already delivered to 33,017 petitions containing 551,908 signatures. Welch continued to insist that the effort should rightly be known as "The Greatest Petition Drive In American History."

Before 1967 ended, Welch reported that recruiting had surely become more difficult, but the creation of ad hoc committees had "doubled our reach, influence and effectiveness." He insisted that the federal Office of Economic Opportunity (War on Poverty) had been created to finance the rioting and destruction needed for a full-scale revolution in America. His mention in 1967 of Saul Alinsky's role in creating such turbulent conditions became of interest to many Americans several decades later because future President Barack Obama and future Senator/Secretary of State/Presidential candidate Hillary Clinton were both Alinsky devotees in their formative years. The Chicago-based revolutionary also trained many others.

Welch closed out the year happily relating that wide distribution of a recent *American Opinion* article by Alan Stang had scuttled the plans of Reies Tijerina, the revolutionary whose goal was to convert the state of New Mexico into the first Communist-led portion of the United States. Welch noted that this attempt by Communists to gain a foothold in New Mexico had failed even while "most of the American people" had no inkling whatsoever that such a plan even existed. Reprints of Stang's article in Spanish had helped the effort to scuttle Tijerina's bold plan.

While growth was still positive numerically, adding new members had slowed. But Birch effectiveness had increased as the new members who joined with JBS veterans eagerly helped to carry out the Society's program. Where the constant targeting of the organization and its Founder had come from enemies on the Left, he would soon face a difficult problem from within the Society itself that we cover in the next chapter.

CHAPTER 29
1968: VIETNAM WAR; COUNCIL DEFECTION

It didn't take long for members to realize that gathering signatures on the Vietnam petition was far easier than getting people to agree that Earl Warren merited impeachment. Members regularly found positive responses when they explained the need to stop sending aid to the Communists who were supplying the Vietnamese enemy with the ability to kill our soldiers. Though all members agreed about the need to put a stop to the Supreme Court's pro-Communism, explaining why the Chief Justice should be removed via the constitutional process for impeachment frequently met with a woeful lack of understanding, both of the damaging role the Court had played and the Constitution's clauses about impeachment. Also, coverage about the rising numbers of American casualties in Vietnam began to dominate the press and the airwaves.

Welch was certainly aware in 1968 that he was asking members to gain signatures on two entirely different petitions. But he kept urging a need for both, even republishing the Impeach Warren petition in the February 1968 *Bulletin*. In July, however, he rearranged the *Bulletin* agenda, moving the Vietnam topic from a "temporary" designation to the "permanent" section where it replaced the Movement To Impeach Earl Warren. The change constituted an acknowledgment that the drive targeting Warren had lost its steam. It ended completely in late 1968 when the Chief Justice announced a date for his resignation.

Earlier, the *Bulletin* cited *The Indianapolis Star's* very welcome comments about the petition being circulated by "an organization called TRAIN (To Restore American Independence Now)." The newspaper correctly pointed out that the U.S. House of Representatives had rejected by 200 to 196 a measure seeking to withhold "foreign aid from any nation supplying North Vietnam." The *Star* noted that there were already "more than 15,000 dead" in the Vietnam conflict, and there was "an American ship seized on the high seas and interned in a North Korean harbor." North Korean Communist forces had indeed captured the USS Pueblo. Its imprisoned crew were held in captivity for almost an entire year. Once released, Navy Petty Officer Lee Hayes, the ship's radioman, met with U.S. reporters who asked what he intended to do when he again set foot in the United States. Hayes immediately responded: "I'm going to join The John Birch Society." Join he did, and he soon embarked on a nationwide speaking tour delivering a strong anti-Communist message for groups gathered by the Society's TRAIN Committees and the American Opinion Speakers Bureau.

Gary Allen's steady stream of articles had by now become a monthly feature of *American Opinion* magazine. His contribution for October 1968 contained his confession that he was once a liberal but had "escaped" to become a conservative. In that article entitled "The Press: How The Left Turned Me Right," the Stanford University graduate who had a degree in history told of having taught misinformation to his high school students. A conservative acquaintance challenged Allen to read several books – most of which came from the Society's set of *One Dozen Candles*. Gary accepted the challenge and intended to show this friend "how little conservatives really know." After plowing through several of the books, becoming very impressed with their content, and then discovering that those books had been completely ignored by national book reviewers, he began to think his conservative friend wasn't so daft at all. Welch delightedly told of Gary's conversion and urged members to never give up trying to gain other converts.

A major portion of the March 1968 *Bulletin* contained the text of yet another of Welch's speeches. "If I Were President" had just been delivered to a huge Birch Society gathering at the prestigious Century Plaza hotel in Los Angeles. In the speech, the Society leader mentioned that he had no intention of actually seeking the office but, if ever he found himself in that role, he would use its authority for the following purposes: tell the truth to the American people; put none but patriots in government posts; restore confidence in the dollar; discontinue all foreign aid; sever diplomatic relations with all Communist regimes; allow our forces to win the war in Vietnam; and withdraw the U.S. from the United Nations. The speech in reprinted form became one of the more popular of the many messages delivered by Welch.

In the midst of gaining numerous small successes, Welch then faced a serious bump in the road consisting of trouble from within. Early in 1968, JBS Council Member Robert Love of Wichita, Kansas, placed a full-page ad in the Wichita newspaper calling for the U.S. to withdraw completely and immediately from Vietnam. Headlined "Let's Get Out of Vietnam Now," the ad's text provided Love's reasons for the recommendation. His urging, therefore, constituted a distinct departure from the JBS call to win the war and then bring the troops home. In addition, Love had mailed a copy of his ad to fellow Council members urging them to place it in their own local newspaper.

The JBS policy at that time authorized Council members to speak officially for the Society. So here was a spokesman for the Society taking a distinctly opposite position about what had become the organization's most important issue. Also, Communist and leftist groups throughout the nation were likewise calling for the U.S. to exit Vietnam. A somewhat angry Welch reminded Love that the Society's position was clear: Win the war first and then leave.

Welch had earlier turned to the U.S. Constitution's definition of treason to define the current administration's policy. (The Constitution states, "Treason against the United States shall consist only in levying war against them, or in adhering to their enemies, giving them aid and comfort.") He believed that supplying aid to an enemy during war was indeed treasonous. He reasoned that congressional tolerance and the fostering of such a policy by most members of Congress (and others in government) would cause many Americans to realize the need for wholesale changes in the U.S. government, even lead many to an awareness about a conspiracy guiding America's policies about the Vietnam War and about numerous other matters. He asked: What other conclusion could one make when U.S. policy included supplying both sides engaged in that escalating and bloody conflict?

The Society's petition had already gained close to one million signatures and had led many Americans who read it and added their names to it to have legitimate second thoughts about their political leaders. If the policy of supplying the European Communists who fueled the North Vietnamese military effort could be sufficiently exposed, Welch reasoned, the American people might bring about a great housecleaning in Washington. And that longed-for development would lead to many more changes, all of which were sorely needed. The opposing stand taken by Robert Love was clearly contrary to the very emphatic position taken by the Society.

After discussing the matter with the maverick Council Member, Welch found no other course but to accept his resignation from both the Council and the Society. Another casualty caught up in this affair turned out to be Wichita's Charles Koch, the son of Fred Koch, one of the attendees at the initial JBS meeting in Indianapolis. The younger Koch had publicly supported Love's move and he too resigned his JBS membership. After receiving a lengthy letter from Welch asking young Koch to reconsider and even accept his invitation to become a member of the Society's Council (where he would succeed his recently deceased father). Charles Koch declined both requests.

In May 1968, the *Bulletin* contained a 16-page pamphlet entitled "Why Join The John Birch Society?" After summarizing the country's present situation, it reviewed past Society efforts and looked ahead to the future. The assassination of Martin Luther King on April 4 prompted Welch to speculate that the nation's most well-known civil rights leader might have been targeted because he would be "worth more as a dead martyr" especially after so many of his Communist connections and calls for violence had been widely exposed.

Welch rightly cited the work of Julia Brown for exposing King's radical efforts. The courageous Negro lady had played a major role in combating King. Welch reported some results of her early 1968 efforts:

> King had been scheduled to speak in Wilmington, North Carolina, for instance, on February 29. When it was announced that Julia Brown would give a talk in Wilmington on February 27, King canceled his forthcoming appearance.... King had been scheduled to proceed to Richmond, stopping on his way for speeches in Danville, Virginia and other cities. But in the meantime, Julia Brown spoke in Danville with between four and five hundred people in attendance. She then went on for speeches in Petersburg and Richmond. On learning of this tour by Julia Brown, King again canceled his own previously publicized appearances. It was worse than futile for him to show up in any city where Julia Brown had just finished telling a small part of the truth about him, about his pro-Communist record, and about his Communist program.

Birch Society members nationwide rightly considered Julia Brown a genuine heroine. She continued to deliver speeches to JBS-gathered audiences for several more years. On June 21, 1979, she testified before the Senate Judiciary Committee as it considered a measure calling for a national holiday to be named after Martin Luther King. Part of her remarks to the senators included:

> While I was in the Communist Party, as a loyal American Negro, I knew Martin Luther King to be closely connected with the Communist Party. If this measure is passed honoring Martin Luther King, we may as well take down the Stars and Stripes that fly over this building and replace it with a Red flag.

In June 1980, Mrs. Brown addressed the JBS Council and several hundred guests at a Society-sponsored event in the nation's capital. Her "Americans, Stop Thinking Like

Communists" speech so impressed Congressman Larry McDonald that he had it inserted into the *Congressional Record* for June 18, 1980. Three years later, she appeared at the Society's gala 25th Anniversary celebration where she received a tumultuous welcome from an extremely appreciative throng. Occasional invitations saw her take the podium in other locations where she recalled her past activity. She died peacefully at 89 years of age in 1989.

Another report about the progress of the Society's petition targeting aid to Communist nations accompanied the July *Bulletin*. The totals delivered to members of Congress had now reached 59,133 petitions containing 982,275 signatures. House members (more Democrats than Republicans on this occasion), each of whom received signed petitions containing 20,000 signatures, were: Dorn (D-S.C.), Abbitt (D-Va.), Brock (R-Tenn.), Snyder (R-Ky.), Whitten (D-Miss.) Nichols (D-Ala.), O'Neal (D-Ga.), Collier (R-Ill.), Adair (R-Ind.), Abernathy (D-Miss.), Broyhill (R-Va.), Long (D-La.), Fisher (D-Texas), and Clawson (R-Calif.). Senators who accepted approximately 50,000 signatures each were: Dominick (R-Colo.), McClellan (D-Ark.), and Bennett (R-Utah). As before, Welch claimed the effort to be "the Greatest Petition Drive In American History."

The March *Bulletin* showed a photo of JBS members marching in a Phoenix Veteran's Day Parade. Each of more than 200 area members carried a small wreath with the name of an Arizona serviceman who had been killed in Vietnam. Parade viewers, many in tears, watched solemnly as the tribute to the fallen men made its way along the parade route. Later, possibly stimulated by the demonstration in Phoenix, a much larger contingent of 1,200 California members carried the names of that many fallen Californians in a Fourth of July parade held in Huntington Beach. Stretching more than two blocks along the parade route, the dramatic demonstration of loyalty to those fallen men, and of anger about the administration's policies, brought both cheers and tears from parade viewers.

After having downgraded the Impeach Warren project to a minor item in the Society's agenda, Welch acknowledged in September that a flood of letters from members persuaded him to prominently reinstate the call for Warren's impeachment. He took that step just as Warren expressed hope that Justice Abe Fortas would be named as his replacement. President Johnson had appointed Fortas to a place on the Court, a move considered payback for the legal help Fortas had supplied years earlier when Johnson escaped charges of fraud in his 1948 primary victory.

At Welch's suggestion, therefore, Birchers cranked up their letter-writing prowess to urge senators to reject the nomination of Fortas for the high post. Many used the slogan, "If you liked Earl Warren, you'll love Abe Fortas." Senators eventually scuttled the plan to have this man, another left-winger, succeed Warren. The efforts of Birch Society members and others had won a significant battle and the hugely disappointed Fortas resigned from the Court in 1969. Acknowledging the Society's role in keeping one of its favorites from becoming Chief Justice, the AFL-CIO's far-left Committee on Political Education (COPE) stated: "Its campaign against Earl Warren helped create the atmosphere in which an Abe Fortas could be denied appointment as Chief Justice."

Georgia Governor Lester Maddox officially designated August 23, 1968, as "John Birch Day" in his state. His formal proclamation told of Birch's early years living and studying in Georgia, the heroic efforts of Captain Birch during World War II, and the eventual naming of "a national patriotic organization" in his honor. A photo of the Governor signing this proclamation showed him surrounded by George and Ethel Birch, Dr. Larry McDonald, and JBS staff personnel William Highsmith, Rex Westerfield and Nelson Sevier.

The October *Bulletin* announced the publication by the Society of David Woodbury's novel entitled *You're Next on the List*. The book focused on the author's belief that fluoridation of water supplies constituted a precedent for possibly adding other substances to drinking water. Frequent media scoffing had often pointed to the supposedly "ridiculous" JBS claim that fluoridating drinking water to prevent dental decay was "part of a Communist plot."

To combat that slur, Welch noted the statements of Tufts University's Dr. Melvin Ketchel appearing *Medical World News*, October 18, 1968. The medical doctor had written: "If the birth rate can't be controlled by voluntary means, then it is, I believe, a necessary and proper function of government to take steps to reduce it." The *Boston Globe* cited Ketchel's further comments: "He suggests that drugs be developed to control fertility in whole populations; drugs that could, for example, be administered to urban centers through the water supply." Welch labeled such an idea "tyranny", and always considered such a possibility a clear example of Communist-style totalitarianism. Some, but not all, of the scoffing about adding substances to the water supply designed to treat people, not the water they drink, ceased.

Years later, in my role as the Society's Public Relations Director, I took a call from a *Newsweek* magazine reporter seeking corroboration of the Society's negativity about fluoridating the water supply. The young lady who called was especially interested in the JBS assertion that such a program was "a typical Communist-style tactic," something she felt was absurd. In a few minutes of conversation, I told her that fluoridating water supplies was a precedent for adding other substances to the people's drinking water. And I offered to "fax" her a news article mentioning approval of relying on the fluoridation precedent to add birth control substances to the water supply. She provided a fax number and the information was promptly sent. *Newsweek* never mentioned the supposed benefit of adding fluoride to the water supply and the obvious plan to show how absurdly extreme the Society was never materialized.

The use by members of less expensive filmstrips had largely replaced their reliance on expensive 16mm films and costly projectors owned by relatively few. Society-produced strips already in wide use included: 1. *The UN: Peace Dove Unmasked* exposing plans to replace U.S. sovereignty with rule by world government; 2. *Show Biz In The Streets* pointing to financing of rioting and destruction accomplished via the federal "War on Poverty"; 3. *The Opinion Makers: Fifty Years Of Managed News* supplying details about the nation's managed press; and 4. *Subsidized Revolution: The War On Poverty* explaining in great detail how government funds were being used to stimulate revolutionary activity in America. Members eagerly equipped themselves with these inexpensive tools and showed them to audiences across the nation.

Confounding numerous enemies, the Society reached its ten-year anniversary in December, a milestone joyfully celebrated at its Indianapolis birthplace. Close to four thousand members and prospective members joined in a full day of festivities. Acknowledging a variety of his many and varied efforts, Colorado sheep farmer Jim Loeffler was named "Bircher of the Decade," an honor all Rocky Mountain area members knew was well deserved. California State Senator John Schmitz – soon to win a seat in the U.S. House and later to become the American Party's candidate for President – delivered one of the many speeches. Wm. J. Grede, the chairman of the Council's Executive Committee and one of Welch's oldest and closest friends, greeted all.

The events at this notable celebration culminated in Welch's speech which followed an amusing exchange between him and Emcee Grede. His good friend asked Welch, "Have you ever actually filled out an application and joined The John Birch Society?" That drew a hearty laugh from the gathering. Quick as a flash, however, Welch jumped from his seat, made his way to the microphone, and confessed, "No, I always thought I could be more effective on the outside." The throng before him burst into even louder laughter and sustained applause. Many had obviously heard that very response from people they had asked to join the Society. Before the entire event had ended, four different individuals wrote out checks to purchase a Life Membership for the man who had created The John Birch Society.

In his "Looking Ahead" remarks on this happy occasion, Welch discussed some plans for the Society he had outlined at the founding – most of which had already been implemented. Among the many victories already achieved, he added one that found many members nodding in agreement. He said, "Our greatest accomplishment has consisted of simply staying alive, through all of the infinitely varied and unbelievably extensive efforts to destroy us." He ended his hour-long presentation with a look ahead and drew a huge burst of approval when he announced a desire to create a Society-run College of Liberal Arts. (A step toward such a goal has actually been taken years later via the Society-affiliated Freedom Project Academy, the Society's on-line home schooling endeavor for grades K-12.)

CHAPTER 30
1989: MOTOREDE AND CULTURE WAR

In January 1969, Welch confessed to being overwhelmed by pleas from distraught members/parents that he create some mechanism for combating the introduction of sex education courses in the nation's schools. When fully informed about what was actually being presented to youngsters, even in kindergarten years, he was shocked. He decided that the Society should indeed get involved to try to stop it.

He admitted further that he had surely intended in the future to start some form of resistance to "the breaking down of modesty, cleanliness, good manners, good taste, moderation in appetites, restraint in behavior, morality and tradition." He then announced that the Society was launching a new ad hoc committee program labeled MOTOREDE, an acronym for the Movement To Restore Decency. And he asked, where possible, that members form a local MOTOREDE group and have it operate just as TACT, TRAIN and SYLP were already functioning.

Welch warned that having MOTOREDE combat the already widespread degradation would not be easy because the sex-ed programs already spreading throughout the nation were being promoted by the National Education Association, the National Council of Churches, the National PTA, the U.S. Office of Education, and "the usual run of leftist organizations, publications and individuals." He also pointed to a new organization that had assumed leadership in the promotion of sex-education for the young, the Sex Information and Education Council of the United States (SIECUS). Its Founder and Executive Director, Dr. Mary Calderone, had already been busily advocating sexual instruction for students at all levels. Well-known in this burgeoning field, she had distinguished herself by asserting: "I don't believe … the old 'Thou shalt nots' apply anymore.'"

Summarizing the goals of the sex-ed promoters and their entry into the schools, Welch pointed to 1) an assault on the family as the fundamental block in the structure of our civilization, 2) the corruption of youth, and 3) the destruction of morality. In addition to providing details about this assault on the young, the Society began to publicize the revealing fact that one of the SIECUS Founders happened to be a member of the Communist Party USA. From the launching of SIECUS in 1964, Communist Party member Isadore Rubin had been serving as the organization's treasurer. Welch saw no contradiction in someone with that background being involved in inundating youngsters with sex information because Communists have always sought to erode morality and destroy the family. Groups and individuals promoting school sex-ed programs then began to ridicule mention of Rubin's tie to Communism as their way of deflecting attention away from the damage being done to youngsters, many of whom became obsessed with the topic of sex at an early age. But the Society's main opposition to sex-ed in the schools was always that it was both hugely inappropriate and decidedly harmful.

Attempting to counter the wave of sex-ed programs being introduced in schools, the Society created a "MOTOREDE Packet" containing a dozen reprinted articles including "A Priest on Sex Education" by JBS Council Member Rev. Francis Fenton and "What To Tell Your Children" by Professor E. Merrill Root. A popular item in the packet was an eight-page "Letter To Landers" in which the popular syndicated columnist received a telling reproach from JBS staff official Chip Wood for her endorsement of school sex-ed programs. Also gratefully received was an easily copied four-page MOTOREDE handout I had written containing statements given by eminent physicians, psychologists and psychiatrists. These opponents of sex education for youngsters objected to disturbing a child's "latency period" and forcing "unnatural sexual preoccupation" on them during their elementary school years. This immediately popular handout contained the following brief summation of the objections to school sex-ed programs:

> We believe that there can be no such thing as a good school course on sex education. It is the parents' right and their responsibility to instruct their children in this delicate area. Although some parents have neglected this duty, usurpation of the rights of every parent is not the solution.

A few months later, Reverend James McHugh, the Director of the Family Life Division of the U.S. Catholic Conference, wrote a magazine article attacking The John Birch Society for its objections to the school sex education programs already in use. Claiming support from the federal Education Commissioner and the head of the National Education Association, Father McHugh generated a response from Robert Welch who pointed to strong denunciations of sex education for youth given by Pope Pius XI in 1931 and Pope Pius XII 1951. But the Society's efforts merely slowed down the forcing of sex education on youngsters. After the Society had drawn attention to SIECUS, the organization made a slight change in its name to <u>Sexuality</u> Information and Education Council of the United States. Its subversive efforts continued.

In February, *American Opinion* featured Gary Allen's "That Music: There's More To It Than Meets The Eye," a startling expose' of the drug-inducing and sex-laden lyrics in music aimed at young people. His survey of the steady output arising from "The Beatles" and numerous other purveyors of such subversion startled anyone who read the article, especially parents whose youngsters had already been harmfully influenced by such stimuli. Following publication of Allen's "That Music," professional musician Joe Crow issued a pamphlet containing the lyrics of 20 current songs, each of which promoted illicit sex, drugs or revolution, and all of which could repeatedly be heard over radio stations beamed at youth.

Society officials then received notification from the authors and distributors of these subversive songs that the *American Opinion* articles had violated copyright laws by publishing the texts of their musical compositions. Legal action would follow, said the complainants, unless distribution of the Society's printed materials containing the lyrics ceased immediately and all remaining stocks of such items were pulled from the shelves and destroyed. Society lawyers reluctantly advised that such action had to be taken. And this form of extremely important proof that America's young people were being targeted by sexual, political, and drug-promoting revolutionaries had to be curtailed.

Chip Wood continued reporting about the Vietnam War and its ever-growing list of casualties. Having already authored the *American Opinion* article "While Brave Men Die," he provided an updated survey of what was occurring on the other side of the globe entitled "The Betrayed: Our Men in Uniform." These reprints and the two Welch booklets showed that the war was actually being directed by the UN's SEATO subsidiary. Also, the hard to believe but truthful fact that a constant flow of U.S. aid was going to the Communist enemy stimulated members to gather even more signatures on the aid and trade petition.

Public Relations Director Reed Benson delivered another huge batch of signed petitions to members of Congress. Welch termed the continuing effort "A Letter With 1,402,622 signatures" that called on Congress to force the administration to cease "giving aid in any form, directly or indirectly, to our Communist enemies." House members happily accepting 20,000 signatures each included: Pettis (R-Calif.), Betts (R-Ohio), McClure (R-Idaho), Thompson (R-Wis.), Scott (R-Va.), Montgomery (D-Miss.), Pollock (R-Alaska), Waggoner (D-La.), Duncan (R-Tenn.), Colmer (D-Miss.), Quillen (R-Tenn.), Foreman (R-N.M.), Saylor (R-Pa.), Fountain (D-N.C.), Andrews (D-Ala.), and Lujan

(R-N.M.). Senators who accepted 50,000 signatures were Gurney (R-Fla.) and Allen (D-Ala.).

In Virginia, the *Richmond Times Dispatch* quoted the encouraging statement issued by JBS Council Member T. Coleman Andrews: "People are beginning to see its [The John Birch Society's] original theories were right…. There is an international Conspiracy." Welch delightedly cited the statement of the former federal official and added: "Our method of opposing that Conspiracy – by education and exposure – is also right."

The Society then began a successful campaign targeting the boycott designed to ruin California grape producers. The overall goal of the leftists led by Cesar Chavez aimed at creating a farm worker movement that would control a major portion of America's agriculture. Grape growers were only the first target. The heavily promoted campaign (assisted by the mass media, left-leaning clergy, and powerful labor unions) eventually failed when JBS members distributed thousands of reprinted articles about the plan throughout the nation. Leftist college students wrongly and somewhat humorously were led to believe that the JBS involvement in blunting the boycotting of grape production stemmed from the Society's campaign to protect the interests of the Welch Company's Grape Jelly. But there was no connection whatsoever between the company and Robert Welch. The misled students soon canceled their ill-advised campaign.

American Opinion's "Sour Grapes" article authored by Rex Westerfield actually followed by two years an earlier article about the grape boycott penned by Gary Allen. Westerfield summarized the overall plan of the revolutionaries: "The object of the boycott is to unite American agricultural workers in a single union under the control of revolutionary leaders – known Marxists and identified Communists." Groups supporting the effort included the Students for a Democratic Society, the Student Non-Violent Coordinating Committee, W.E.B. DuBois Clubs, Black Panthers, Brown Berets, Progressive Labor Party Vietnam Day Committee, and Congress of Racial Equality. Several years of effort to accomplish the takeover of America's agricultural industry didn't succeed, a noteworthy victory for The John Birch Society that had led the way in that important campaign.

In April 1969, *American Opinion* published Alan Stang's article about a highly regarded Chicago police officer who had been convicted of murder for killing a criminal while acting in self-defense. The article received widespread distribution as an example of the on-going campaign to hamper policemen and their work. The fallout from this incident, having little to do with the convicted policeman, came when one of the lawyers targeting the officer, a prominent Chicagoan named Elmer Gertz, sued the Society claiming he had been injured because Stang had labeled him "a member of the Communist

National Lawyers Guild." What Stang had stated was never contested because it was true.

After numerous appeals and a ruling favoring the plaintiff by a six-member jury, the case went all the way to the Supreme Court. There, the high court ruled 14 years after the article appeared that Elmer Gertz was a "private" not a "public" person who was not required to prove actual malice in what was stated about him. The veracity of what Stang had written didn't matter and the Society (the owner of *American Opinion* magazine) was forced to pay Gertz $400,000. Gertz had claimed that linking him to Communism had hurt his ability to practice his profession and earn a living. The truth? He wasn't hurt financially at all. What the ruling actually confirmed is that speaking the truth about someone on the Left can invite trouble, not for the leftist but for anyone who dares to publish facts. Amazingly, the Gertz case, including the Supreme Court's tortured opinion, then became part of law school curricula throughout the nation.

Welch continued providing evidence of conspiracies occurring during previous centuries. He wanted JBS members to understand that their efforts to expose and rout the current manifestation of conspiracy at work could succeed. Pointing to *Anarchy and Anarchists*, an explosive 1889 book written by Chicago Police Captain Michael Shaack after the horrible Haymarket Riot of 1888, he agreed with the author about considering the Haymarket carnage an early work of the same conspiracy targeted by the Birch Society. In that 1888 uprising, eight policemen were killed and 67 were wounded when revolutionaries carried out a planned attack on police stationed at the scene of a leftist demonstration. Captain Shaack had spent a full year studying and then writing about what had happened and why. Welch pointed to the senior police officer's conclusion:

> Let none mistake either the purpose or the devotion of these fanatics, nor their growing strength. This is methodic – not a haphazard conspiracy. The ferment in Russia is controlled by the same heads and the same hands as the activity in Chicago. There is a coldblooded, calculating purpose behind this revolt, manipulating every part of it, the world over, to a common and ruinous end....

Welch wrote that the Shaack book should have been considered a wake-up call for the American people in the late 1800s, just as John Robison's 1798 book *Proofs Of a Conspiracy* had served for the people of England in his day. "It is the same warning which we, in The John Birch Society, have been proclaiming to our fellow citizens for years," stated Welch. He summarized: "The greatest asset of these Insiders, in keeping the existence and growing power of their Conspiracy unrecognized, has been that the whole design was too ambitious, too evil, too fantastic for belief." Exposing and routing the

Conspiracy before rebuilding what had already been torn down continued to be the Society's primary goal.

In September, Dave Gumaer's lengthy article about the American Civil Liberties Union (ACLU) appeared in *American Opinion*. Immediately reprinted in pamphlet format, "The ACLU: Lawyers Playing the Red Game" reported that Roger Baldwin and a group of Communists (William Z. Foster, Harry F. Ward, Elizabeth Gurley Flynn, and others) had launched the organization to defend leftist individuals and campaigns from charges of subversion. Baldwin, who led the organization for decades, revealingly stated years later in his Harvard University reunion book, "I am for Socialism, disarmament, and ultimately for abolishing the State itself... Communism is the goal." Members distributed many copies of this important article.

Former college professor Francis X. Gannon, Ph.D. completed the first of his four-volume *Biographical Dictionary of the Left*. The 614-page Volume I contained background history about dozens of left-wing organizations plus profiles of scores of prominent leftists. Targeted for exposure were such leftists as Saul Alinsky, Roger Baldwin, Abe Fortas, Martin Luther King, Walter Lippmann, Zbigniew Brzezinski, Thurgood Marshall, Walter Reuther, Ralph Bunche, and the Kennedy brothers. The Society would later publish three more volumes in a series that became a much-needed storehouse of information to use in combating leftist individuals and groups. Volume I of a subsequent four-volume set was offered as a bonus for a year's subscription to *American Opinion*.

Welch saw a need to state publicly that the Society wanted nothing to do with a man named Willis Carto and the "half-baked concoction of sophomoric drivel" he was promoting. During 1959, with the Society in its infancy, Carto had been accepted as a JBS employee at the organization's Massachusetts headquarters. After a mere few months, Welch dismissed him without stating any reason for his action. Carto would later found the Liberty Lobby organization whose *Spotlight* publication regularly mixed good information and perspective with unreliable drivel while hinting at anti-Semitism. Birch officials labeled it as a dangerous tangent that should be avoided. Years later, the name *Spotlight* was replaced by *American Free Press*. Neither publication ever received the Society's endorsement.

As the American people started thinking about Christmas 1969, Welch quoted from a letter sent to all U.S. postmasters by postal officials based at their Washington headquarters. It stated that representatives of UNICEF should be permitted to set up tables in local post offices to sell greeting cards during the Christmas season. The Society's response to that directive included a clear urging not to blame the policy on any local postmaster, but on the federal government. To aid in drawing attention to and protesting this misuse of the postal service, Welch urged the distribution of a Society-produced four-page pamphlet entitled "The Truth About UNICEF." It had initially been published to alert homeowners about the practice of using small children to raise money for the United Nations agency while innocently trick-or-treating on Halloween.

This campaign soon proved to be a complete success when the directive granting post office space for sale of UNICEF material was officially rescinded. The form letter sent by postal authorities to those who had protested the policy noted that the reversal had been prompted by the receipt of a huge amount of messages asking for the change of policy. The UN had regularly advertised its UNICEF branch as the beneficial protector of children the world over. However, evidence surfaced showing that UNICEF was supplying North Vietnam with heavy construction equipment worth millions. The UN agency was also guilty of sending material worth millions to such countries as Red China, Communist Vietnam, Zimbabwe and Ethiopia. After he had been elected to Congress, JBS Council Member Dr. Larry McDonald pointed out that the so-called UNICEF medical packs sent to the tyrannical leaders in Zimbabwe were actually combat packs containing weaponry to be used in maintaining brutal dominance in that war-torn country.

The Society's campaign to Support Your Local Police received a boost via an official statement issued by FBI Director J. Edgar Hoover. Although supporting local police gained agreement from most fellow citizens, members frequently found a need to explain the importance of the word "local" in their slogan. Hoover's comment addressed that very point:

> America has no place for, nor does it need, a national police force. It should be abundantly clear by now that … effective law enforcement is basically a local responsibility. In the great area of self-government reserved to the states, counties, and cities, the enforcement of the laws is not only their duty but also their right. Law-abiding citizens and local officials should vigorously oppose concerted attacks against law enforcement and the devious moves to negate local authority and replace it with federal police power.

Added to what Hoover stated, the Society noted that Nazi Germany and all Communist-controlled nations were able to maintain control over the people with centralized national police power. Whenever that point was made, public nods of understanding could be seen.

Chapter 31
1970: JBS Members Win Elections

The January 1970 *Bulletin* led off with Welch's announcement that the last quarter of 1969 was "the most encouraging, in every respect, which we have had in over three years." From the doldrums experienced during the mid-1960s, the organization was again taking in sizable numbers of new members, receiving adequate financial backing, gaining new subscribers to the two magazines (*American Opinion* and *The Review Of The News*), and achieving numerous relatively small victories. Though not widely enough publicized to be known by many Americans, both the Society and its main enemies were vividly aware that the Society's "potential" was being realized.

As was his custom, Welch again provided a brief review of the history and activity of the Conspiracy begun by the Bavarian Illuminati in 1776. He apologized to veteran members for repeating some of what he had written in the past, explaining that he wanted to inform the many new members of the Conspiracy's existence, goals and progress while showing them that many current events in America had historical parallels. For example, he wrote:

> The falsehoods and frame-ups by which Louis XVI and Marie Antoinette were gradually brought to the guillotine were basically the same as those by which [Attorney General] Harry Daugherty and the Harding Administration were disgraced 130 years later; by which Franco and Chiang Kai-shek have been smeared for a lifetime; by which Senator Robert A. Taft was eliminated as America's leader of the opposition to Communism; and by which Senator Joseph McCarthy was hounded to his death. This is also the same technique by which The John Birch Society and its members have been smeared and harassed and persecuted in the effort to destroy so dangerous a threat. The one big difference is that there are a lot of us, and the target is in many places.

He then listed a dozen goals of the Conspiracy among which were wiping out the value of money; transforming the educational system into a subversive propaganda machine; stultifying our spiritual, moral, esthetic and intellectual sense of values; destroying the will to resist; and more. To combat all of it, he wrote, "… there is a continuing, organized body of brave and honorable people who are determined to expose and rout this whole immense, long sustained, and incredibly evil Conspiracy. It is The John Birch Society, something never faced before by the Conspiracy, something that possesses the capability of destroying its already existing grip on the United States and the rest of mankind."

Announcing a plan to boost the number of *Bulletin* subscribers to a million or more, Welch confirmed that the recipients didn't have to be JBS members – though he surely hoped many would eventually enlist. To encourage current members to purchase subscriptions for friends, neighbors, co-workers, et al., he announced that a copy of *The Politician* would be sent to all new *Bulletin* recipients at no extra charge. Why this book? He pointed to Herman Dinsmore, the 1951-1960 editor of the International Edition of *The New York Times* who was currently traveling throughout the United States delivering speeches arranged by the JBS Speaker's Bureau. Dinsmore had sent Welch a letter about the famous book. In it, he gave Welch permission to use his letter as desired. The former *New York Times* Editor had written:

> Reading *The Politician*, which I have just done during December, was for me quite a revealing experience. It is hard for a professional newspaperman to confess that so many things, which he thought were just happening, were actually being made to happen by sinister and conspiratorial forces. But in all honesty, the confession must be made. *The Politician* was a real eye-opener, which caused all kinds of mysterious pieces of a puzzle that still bewildered me to fall rapidly into place. I recommend the book emphatically to every patriotic American who wants to understand not only what is now taking place all around him, but also why. The book is the product of historical research of the first order.

In April, the *Bulletin* carried Welch's essay entitled "What Is Money?" Immediately offered in booklet form it provided a brief history of the creation and use of money from Roman times to the backing of the dollar by gold and silver in the U.S. during the early years of the 20th Century. It also pointed to the steps leading to Federal Reserve currency that has always been backed by nothing. (The final break away from precious metal backing of the dollar, the work of President Richard Nixon, would occur in 1971.)

In May, Welch admitted that he had erred in a previous *Bulletin* with a claim that Illuminati founder Adam Weishaupt was a "renegade Jesuit priest." Some astute Society members had informed him that Weishaupt had been a professor at a Jesuit College but had never become a priest. This error was one of only six he confessed having made in the "one-half million words" he had written during the first decade of the Society's existence.

To keep any future mistakes to a minimum and to take advantage of his prodigious knowledge and solid commitment, Welch "lured" a prominent member of the Society's field staff to be his research assistant and operations director. C.O. "Buck" Mann relocated from Texas to Massachusetts and began to serve as the second of Welch's right-hand men, a top assistant to Welch and a key member of the Society's headquarters staff for the next two decades. One of Mann's first tasks saw him first checking the facts and then publishing the latest Welch speech entitled "What Is Communism?" Asked how he was faring in Massachusetts, Buck responded, "I find it hard to believe that I needed to head **southward** to get to a Society event in New York City."

Buck Mann would work with the staff of *American Opinion* to speed numerous other articles into reprint format, one of the first being an article entitled "Peace Symbols" authored by David Gumaer. Showing numerous photos of the so-called "peace symbol" as it was used not only by Communists but by Germany's Nazis during their rise to totalitarian power, the article answered the questions of many who wondered about its history.

In the *Blue Book*, Welch had discussed his long-standing goal of "a thousand members" in any congressional district. That number of JBS stalwarts spreading sound information and perspective would, he contended, sway a sufficient number of voters to assure the nomination and election to Congress of a constitutionally sound anti-Communist. A new tool that would help members in their efforts to recruit became available with Ed Griffin's two-hour film "This Is The John Birch Society." It had been shown at a recent Council meeting where it received a ringing endorsement from members and guests. Along with the film, Griffin published its complete transcript in booklet form. Both the film and the booklet did help members achieve more success in recruiting fellow Americans.

The petition campaign calling on Congress to terminate the infuriating (and treasonous) aid going to the Viet Cong via European Communist nations ended July 1. The final recipients included Senator Sam Ervin (D-N.C.) who received 50,000 signatures. House members receiving 20,000 signatures each included Landgrebe (R-Ind.), Myers (R-Ind.), Bray (R-Ind.), Roudebush (R-Ind.), Jones (D-N.C.), Henderson (D-N.C.), Jonas (R-N.C.), O'Konski (R-Wis.), Lennon (D-N.C.), Blackburn (R- Ga.), Hebert (D-La.), Schadeberg

(R-Wis.), and Crane (R-Ill.). Approximately 1,800,000 Americans had signed the petition and 67 members of Congress had gladly accepted bundles of signatures in what was likely the largest petition campaign ever conducted in our nation.

Petition gatherers pointed to several examples of restrictions placed on our military as had been reported in several *Bulletins*. One infuriating restriction came in a portion of a letter sent by a U.S. pilot who perished during his 77th mission over Vietnam. Appearing in the January 26, 1967, *Congressional Record*, it stated:

> I am a regular officer and therefore expected to risk my life as part of my job. But why should I do it several times a week on long missions, in a multi-million dollar airplane, so as to knock out an "empty barracks," or an "empty bus'" or a buffalo pulling an irrigation wheel in a rice paddy?"

Why was this highly trained and combat-ready American pilot risking death while being restricted to attacking such inconsequential targets? Welch contended that the reason boiled down to rules issued to all U.S. pilots forbidding them to inflict real damage on the enemy forces that were killing our nation's ground troops.

One of the continuing smears regularly aimed at the Society claimed that the JBS harbored hatred of Jews. After having received several messages about a recent issue of the racist tabloid known as *The Thunderbolt*, Welch reported that both he and the Society had been attacked in it for refusing to maintain that Jews constituted the force behind a variety of ills plaguing America and mankind. Part of this particular diatribe insisted that the Society was guilty of actually helping the Conspiracy by avoiding any mention of its supposed Jewish origin and leadership. An aggravated Welch responded to the charge while noting that "among our ablest, bravest, and most patriotic writers, investigators and speakers" is Alan Stang, an American Jew. He was also pleased to note that there were numerous other Jewish members of the Society including a member of the Council. He insisted that blaming all Jews would violate a "cardinal principle of The John Birch Society, which is that every individual should be judged by his own actions."

The August *Bulletin* reproduced a Scripps Howard report entitled "Birchers are on the rise." Without any of the customary negativity appearing in most reports about the Society, this nationally distributed column told of the Society's increasingly successful ad hoc committee efforts. It even pointed to the elections to Congress of John Rousselot and John Schmitz, both well-known Society members.

Revolutionary activity, most especially including anti-Vietnam War demonstrations, continued to plague the nation. With numerous examples to back up his charge, Welch pointed to the Office of Economic Opportunity (OEO), known as "The War on Poverty," as the hidden financial promoter – along with several tax-exempt foundations – of these disruptive efforts. Citing the government's role in what he termed "the Homemade Revolution," he claimed:

> And by far the most important official medium through which our federal government finances, encourages, foments, and sustains these domestic subversive activities is the Office of Economic Opportunity. In fact, whatever humanitarian pretenses and coloring may be given the OEO, the promotion of the semblance of revolution within the United States is the real reason for its existence.

Articles, books, films, filmstrips, and speeches by Society stalwarts helped greatly to expose this federally funded subversion. Among the speakers targeting the "Homemade Revolution" and related leftist projects were Alan Stang, Julia Brown, David Gumaer, Charlie Smith, Herman Dinsmore, Lee Hayes, General Robert E. Lee Scott, and Joe Crow.

The above lecturers were then joined by American Negro Gerald Kirk who had spent four years reporting to the FBI about Communist-led subversive activities in and around Chicago. He eagerly told his story to fellow Americans. Charlie Smith, another Negro American, became one of the Society's most popular speakers because of his ability to mix humor with his knowledge of domestic revolutionary activity. He explained that he became a conservative while in college when a professor told the class there was no need to worry about the growing national debt "because we owe it to ourselves." When Smith asked the professor how he could obtain his portion of what was owed, the class burst into laughter and the red-faced professor gave no answer. Charlie Smith soon contacted the Society.

MOTOREDE activity swelled throughout the nation. In November 1970, more than two years before the Supreme Court's *Roe v. Wade* decision, the JBS *Bulletin* published my no-nonsense condemnation of abortion as "murder." After focusing on this remarkable departure from basic morality, the MOTOREDE statement predicted that drug abuse, sexual promiscuity, rampant crime, and more could now be expected. At the end of the year, Welch published "The John Birch Resolutions," a 20-page listing of what he termed "the essential elements in the recognized moral code for our Western Civilization." Members everywhere enthusiastically applauded the "Resolutions" while renewing their efforts to bring about less government and more responsibility.

In part, the year 1970 could be remembered as the period when reprinted articles from *American Opinion* became the chief weapons distributed by members to alert the public and gain prospects for membership. Examples of some of the most popular reprinted articles included:

"Prisoners in Vietnam: Why Does America Abandon Her Own?" by Alan Stang

"Black Panthers: Communist Guerrillas in the Streets" by David Gumaer

"Ecology: Government Control of the Environment" by Gary Allen

"Federal Reserve: The Anti-Economics of Boom and Bust" by Gary Allen

"Communism and the Catholic Church in America" by Father Francis Fenton

"The Media: A Look at Establishment Newspapers" by Gary Allen

"Women's Lib: They're Spoiling Eve's Contribution" by Taylor Caldwell

"Pornography: Blue Art and Red Revolution" by Medford Evans

These 1970 articles showed how far ahead of the mass media and general public the Society and its publishing efforts had become.

The very busy and highly successful American Opinion Speakers Bureau (AOSB) operated out of two offices – the major one located at the Society's Massachusetts headquarters and the other at the busy West Coast JBS office in San Marino, California. During the single year of 1970, the AOSB's eastern branch arranged 716 speeches while the California-based division (dealing with members in only the 13 western states) did likewise for sponsors of 475 events. All across the nation, members presented programs under the name of a local TACT, TRAIN, SYLP or MOTOREDE Committee.

Speakers who carried their messages to America's large cities and small communities did so on non-stop tours lasting anywhere from one to three weeks. Their routine called for one-night stands in each location followed by early morning travel to the next stop, mostly by auto. Alan Stang humorously referred to "the body drop" in which his was the body being driven to a halfway point between two speech locations. He would exit the first auto after having discussed the success of the previous night's program with his driver and climb into the second. The first question from the next JBS driver would be, "How did it go last night?" So Alan would repeat much of what he had discussed with his first driver. "It was all in a day's work," claimed the ever-cheerful Alan. Other speakers went through the very same experience with nary a complaint.

Each engagement led to new members, more determination, literature sales, publicity in local media, etc. Whenever possible, speakers would deliver a portion of their message to a noontime service club luncheon, a class at the local high school, an interview on a local radio show, or a visit with community officials.

New members of the Speaker Bureau included retired Detroit Police Lieutenant Leland Brown who discussed the need to retain **local** control of police, and Fordham University Professor William Marra who delivered strong objections to sex education classes in the schools. Navy veteran Lee Hayes continued to recount his experiences as a prisoner of the North Koreans after the *USS Pueblo* had been seized; Charlie Smith insisted that the major civil rights efforts were a "cover for revolution"; young Dave Avery warned of drug infestation in the nation's high schools; professional musician Joe Crow dwelled on the subversive lyrics in much of the music aimed at teens; Julia Brown countered the so-called civil rights movement; Alan Davidson related his experiences as a Green Beret veteran of the Vietnam struggle; retired Brig. Gen. Robert E. Lee Scott, the author of the famous "God is My Co-Pilot" book, discussed the restrictions on U.S. forces in Vietnam; Father Francis Fenton countered myths while telling the truth about The John Birch Society; Herman Dinsmore exposed distortions appearing in the nation's mass media; David Gumaer explained how to combat revolutionary activity threatening the U.S. from within; Alan Stang urged audiences to protest sending aid and trade to the Communist-held European nations that were supplying the North Vietnam enemy; and Gerald Kirk related his experiences as an FBI undercover operative in Chicago-area Communist youth groups. These were only some of the many speakers who delivered important messages throughout the nation.

While sponsoring speaking engagements formed part of member activity, JBS stalwarts regularly took their concerns to friends and neighbors, discussed with co-workers what they had learned, wrote letters to the editor of local newspapers, called radio talk shows, erected floats for parades, shared literature explaining conspiratorial hands behind a variety of problems, and offered their own personal reputation as an advertisement for the Society. The organization that was supposed to have faded away after years of intense attacks was not only still alive; it was flourishing. Enemies who had done their best to kill it decided on a new tactic. The new plan called for ignoring the Society and hoping the American people would conclude it had ceased to exist. But, as we show in the next chapter, that didn't work either.

CHAPTER 32
1971: *OVERVIEW OF OUR WORLD* FILMSTRIP

The year 1971 began with Welch's claim that the previous year had been the best "in every respect" since 1965. The January *Bulletin* contained a photo taken in December during the Society's 12th Anniversary celebration at New York's Waldorf-Astoria Hotel. Pictured shaking hands at the head table were Alabama Governor George Wallace, the event's main speaker, and Charlie Smith, the popular Negro American and Birch Society stalwart. Host Robert Welch appeared in the photo seated between the two speakers.

While carefully maintaining the Society's policy of never recommending or financing political candidates, Welch nevertheless let it be known in several ways that he agreed with Wallace's claim about there being "not a dime's worth of difference" between high-level Democrats and their supposed adversaries, the high-level Republicans. In 1968, Wallace had been the candidate of the American Party with retired Air Force General Curtis LeMay as his running mate. Determined to pose a more realistic threat in 1972 as a Democrat, Wallace's effort all but ended on May 15, 1972, when a would-be assassin seriously wounded him during a campaign appearance in Maryland.

Welch publicly agreed with Gary Allen who had stated in one of his *American Opinion* articles: "Just think. For a mere two or three thousand dollars per year, you can send your children off to college to learn to hate their God, their country, and you. Now there is a real bargain!" The cost of sending a child off to college had grown enormously and the result for many parents was an enormous heartache. As many had already learned, the effect of four years in college on many of their youngsters indeed led to what Gary Allen predicted.

The JBS leader then laughingly told of a man in Texas who attended one of the many TRAIN Committee events believing that he would learn more about old locomotives. Once there, he stayed for the JBS program, agreed with what he heard about the need to protect our nation's independence, became a member of the Committee, and eventually a member of the Society.

The petition campaign seeking termination of aid to Communist nations adopted a new slogan: "SHAME: Stop Helping America's Marxist Enemies." Members were delighted with the acronym and the message it conveyed.

The ever-valiant Dan Smoot contacted Welch to admit reluctantly that age had caught up with him to the point where he could no longer continue writing and publishing his weekly report. Welch immediately suggested that he send his subscription list to JBS and notify all pre-paid subscribers that they would henceforth receive *The Review Of The News* instead. In return, Smoot was asked only to supply the Birch Society's weekly magazine with occasional articles – which he did faithfully. The arrangement benefited both the Society and the highly respected Dan Smoot.

Welch reported that *Life* magazine had shown its utter untrustworthiness by publishing a photo depicting policemen brutalizing some youthful demonstrators during a 1968 demonstration in Chicago. Ten months later, *Life* showed the **exact same photo** with the claim that police had attacked demonstrators at New Jersey's Princeton University in 1967. When dishonest publications such as *Life* have a photo that aids in promoting the views of their leaders, they even lie about what it depicts. *Life*, of course, had earlier joined many other media outlets seeking to harm The John Birch Society with innuendos, misrepresentations and outright lies. Society leaders and members shed no tears when the magazine ceased publication on December 29, 1972.

The Society's book publishing arm, Western Islands, released *Teddy Bare: The Real Story of Chappaquiddick* written by Zad Rust (a pseudonym for former Romanian foreign minister Michel Sturdza). Immediately, the book soared to a high place on *The New York Times* best-seller list, the only Society-published book ever to achieve such recognition. Several hundred thousand copies were sold.

In June, Welch told of the success already achieved by the Project WIN campaign. Developed by field Coordinator Bob Bogensberger, the acronym stood for With Increased Numbers and it sought to gain more members, money and motivation. Presented to members at their monthly chapter meetings by area Coordinators, its fund-raising feature claimed confidently that many would dig more deeply and help the Society financially if they knew all others were making the same sacrifice. The WIN program proved to be an outstanding success raising several million dollars and enabling the Society to move ahead with numerous projects and hire additional staff.

In September, the *Bulletin* announced availability of the new filmstrip "Overview Of Our World." Written and narrated by me, the program sought to help someone who had realistic concerns about America's problems to an awareness about the Conspiracy and the Society – all in a single evening. It provided viewers with information about 1) our nation's basic economic and political foundations, 2) an exposure of America's domestic and foreign enemies, 3) an introduction to the oft-ridiculed "conspiracy theory of history," and 4) an invitation to membership. Welch enthusiastically recommended its use, describing it as "far more valuable and effective than any of us had anticipated." He predicted that there would be 2,000 copies of the filmstrip in use before the end of the year. His prediction was realized.

In October, *The Review Of The News* published its first "Conservative Index," a rating of the votes in Congress made by all 435 House members and 100 senators. This type report about the votes cast by members of Congress had formerly been presented by Dan Smoot. The very first vote it reported dealt with President Nixon's imposition of wage and price controls on the American people. Only 18 of the 435 members of the House had registered opposition. Society members began to order large quantities of reprints of this "Index" in order to distribute locally. Especially useful were distributions of the Index at town meetings where the elected official appeared. Once armed with evidence supplied in the Index, voters registered either their praise or their scorn, and had proof to back up their opinion.

Even though "Overview Of Our World" continued to bring in new members, expectations that most fellow Americans would be persuaded to join the Society after hearing one speech, reading one article, or seeing one film were proving largely unrealistic. So Welch urged members to conduct a series of weekly showings of films, each followed by discussion of issues and literature sales. Members who followed this "Film Series" formula found it very productive both in gaining new members and in energizing the faithful.

Chapter 33
1972: *None Dare Call It Conspiracy*

The year began with more emphasis on the need to Get US Out! of the United Nations. Welch recommended erecting billboards wherever members could afford their cost. And he again urged showing JBS films and filmstrips, and distributing more of the anti-UN material (books, pamphlets, postcards bumper strips, etc.).

Rapid distribution of Gary Allen's privately published *None Dare Call It Conspiracy* generated enormous excitement, notably from Welch himself. The 140-page paperback capably explained the Conspiracy to a huge number of Americans who had only a few inklings about a deliberate plot but had no hard information. Before too long, over 5 million copies had been distributed. In addition, Welch announced a new package of books he labeled "Half A Dozen Searchlights," all published by the Society's Western Islands subsidiary. They were *The Politician* (Welch), *The Fearful Master* (Griffin), *Again, May God Forgive Us* (Welch), *Richard Nixon: The Man Behind the Mask* (Allen), *Teddy Bare* (Rust), and *Nixon's Palace Guard* (Allen). All six could be had for $8.00. Also, the books would be sent at no additional charge to anyone who paid for a $10.00 subscription (or extension) to *The Review Of The News*.

The success of the initial weeklong summer camp program for teens in Washington state prompted Welch to authorize additional camps in 1972, one in California and one in Minnesota. This program would soon expand to ten locations across the nation before becoming too expensive and too time-consuming for staff. It was reluctantly discontinued after 35 years of bringing information about our nation's founding principles – and about its enemies – to many thousands of young Americans.

The May *Bulletin* pointed out that the Society had become "the only" conservative group regularly bringing new recruits into the fight against Communism and big government. Other organizations continued attempts to lure Birchers to work on their pet projects. Meanwhile, Welch excoriated President Nixon for forcing a rise in the price of gold (a $3 increase), a move that devalued the dollar.

While encouraging members to continue their campaigns against rioting and demonstrations generated by the "civil rights" movement, Welch cited the public comment made by FBI Director J. Edgar Hoover that Martin Luther King was "the most notorious liar in America." Then while addressing a recurring problem he dubbed "religious neutralism," Welch announced the availability of a recorded speech given by JBS staffer Delmar Dennis, the courageous JBS member who had infiltrated the KKK for the FBI in Mississippi. A preacher, Dennis relied on his scriptural knowledge to show listeners that work to expose and defeat evil must accompany prayers sent aloft for that very purpose.

In October, all members were urged to participate in the "Day of Shame" exposure of the United Nations. The date chosen was October 24 in memory of the first gathering of world leaders at the UN on October 24, 1945. The Society continued its campaign against any attempts by government to outlaw citizen gun ownership.

Opposition to state ratification of the Equal Rights Amendment next occupied the attention of Society members in many states. Clearly a measure that would lead to a huge increase in federal power, this proposal continued to be a JBS project for several years. Reprints of articles combating passage of the amendment, plus speakers such as Retired U.S. Army General Andrew Gatsis and Oklahoma state senator Mary Helm, and the parallel efforts waged by Phyllis Schlafly's "Stop ERA" organization, kept this revolutionary treachery from being added to the Constitution.

The November *Bulletin* announced a need to combat the new Occupational Safety and Health Administration (OSHA). Describing the work of this government agency as "absolute bureaucratic tyranny," Welch set in motion the new campaign for members. Soon, courageous Idaho Society member Bill Barlow refused to admit OSHA inspectors into his place of business without a duly approved search warrant. The matter ended up in the courts where, a few years later, Barlow's protest won a significant victory at the Supreme Court level in *Marshall v. Barlow's Inc*. The decision removed some of OSHA's teeth but the agency whose supposed purpose had always been capably carried out by business owners in conjunction with the non-governmental National Safety Council continued issuing fines, and intimidating small business owners. The Society formed Nix On OSHA Committees whose efforts were buttressed by reprinted articles from the JBS magazines, speakers from the American Opinion Speakers Bureau, and the Society-produced filmstrip entitled "Threads Of Tyranny."

Western Islands released a new edition of *The Rise of the House of Rothschild*, a 1928 book written by Count Egon C. Corti. Originally published in Germany, the book has always helped readers to understand the role played within the Conspiracy by the famous banking institution.

Welch wasted no time in issuing his comments about the results of the 1972 elections. He concluded wryly that the overwhelming selection by voters of Richard Nixon over far left Democrat George McGovern would "enable Nixon to carry out the McGovern platform."

At approximately 9:00 PM on December 4, three men firebombed the American Opinion Bookstore in Memphis, Tennessee. The fire damaged $15,000 worth of books, pamphlets, films, and projectors. Two witnesses helped police arrest the three young perpetrators within days. Calling the crime "the usual type of Marxist-Leninist attack," JBS Section Leader Mal Mauney told the local press that insurance would cover only part of the losses. He quickly added: "We will not be intimidated. We'll be back in operation before the first of year." That promise was kept.

American Opinion's most widely distributed reprinted articles during 1972 included Susan Huck's "The Orders" dealing with the growing practice whereby presidents bypass Congress and create laws by issuing Executive Orders. Other reprinted articles included "Immigration" of Communist Chinese written by Congressman John Schmitz; "Arthur Bremer" about the man who attempted to assassinate George Wallace by Alan Stang; and "Oshacrats" about the federal government's attack on America's businessmen also by Alan Stang.

Chapter 34
1973: Birch Log and Alan Stang Report

Members began showing a new three-part filmstrip entitled "The John Birch Society: Yesterday, Today, Beliefs and Principles" produced by Public Relations Director Rex Westerfield. Release of the program coincided with his decision to leave the Society's staff. Immediately launching a public relations firm, Rex intended to assist political candidates in their efforts to win election. Welch wished him well while restating the Society's policy of non-involvement in any purely political activity – which meant non-involvement with the Westerfield venture.

A new filmstrip entitled "Peace Dove Unmasked" added to the many tools targeting the UN. Welch specifically commended Oklahoma Coordinator Bill Cherry who had organized members to set up information tables at shopping malls, distribute literature, and invite passersby to attend a showing of a film exposing the threat to national sovereignty posed by the UN. Elsewhere, plenty of encouragement to combat OSHA, especially from business owners, resulted in growing condemnation of this latest bureaucratic attack on freedom.

Headlines across the nation soon blared that "Peace with Honor" had finally arrived in Vietnam. A JBS statement about the conflict bluntly claimed America had "lost" the struggle. Further comments pointed to undeniable proof that our nation had supplied both sides. The Society's statement assessed the costly struggle as a campaign that was "as phony as a nine-dollar bill." In summary, JBS insisted that the effort should become known as "a war on the American people by the American government." Members were urged to continue distribution of the two Welch-authored booklets, *The Truth About Vietnam* and *More Truth About Vietnam*.

After an attack on U.S. Senator John Stennis (D-Miss.), leftists demanded a new campaign against citizen ownership of guns. Bob Lee provided an excellent argument against any form of gun control when he wrote, "Blaming guns for crimes is as senseless as blaming pencils for misspelled words."

Welch confidently assured members that no admitted Communist could ever be elected U.S. President. But in sadness, he noted that recently reelected President Nixon could casually admit that he was "now a Keynesian in economics" and get away with it. Why? Because hardly any American knew anything about British economist John Maynard Keynes. So he set about to overcome that deficiency by declaring that "a Keynesian is automatically the enemy of every economic principle which made the United States the most productive, most powerful, and most prosperous country in the world." More attention was given to exposing Keynes and his socialism by several writers whose work filled JBS publications.

After receiving requests from numerous members for some statement from the Society that could be given to their local newspaper for publication, I mentioned the possibility of creating a weekly newspaper column. I told Welch that I would create a couple of examples of what would fill the need and his immediate response was "Good idea, do it." He didn't need samples; he wanted the project started immediately. Colleague John Fall suggested the column be labeled "The Birch Log." So began publication of a weekly message from the Society that was published in scores, and then hundreds of weekly newspapers. This success led to the creation of a distribution entity known as John Birch Society Features.

Members had already been involved in combating the efforts of a group labeling itself the American Indian Movement (AIM) when Welch told of AIM's revolutionary efforts at Cass Lake, Minnesota, and Wounded Knee, South Dakota. AIM members, using funds supplied by the U.S. government through the Office of Economic Opportunity, set out to seize a portion of territory within the U.S., proclaim creation of their own independent nation, receive diplomatic recognition from Communist-led countries, and proceed to wage war on the United States from within. Combating this totally subversive development became a special project for members in the Dakotas and other midwestern states. Members throughout the nation distributed information about this latest outrage. Reprints of an *American Opinion* article entitled "Red Indians" became very popular and these were helpful in exposing the underlying intent of the AIM members.

Efforts of some courageous native Americans – such as Eugene Rooks, Johnson Holy Rock and Vangie Echohawk – alerted fellow native Americans and many others. Later, Douglas Durham joined AIM, even though he had no Indian lineage. He became a leader within the group and, later, capably helped to expose the threat posed by the AIM revolutionaries with his inside knowledge and eventual speeches. The AIM campaign soon faded into nothingness.

In a speech entitled "Our Only Weapon," Welch recounted 16 separate attacks created by the Conspiracy to weaken and destroy our nation. The various targets he identified included religion, the family, drug and pornography distribution, inflation, bureaucratic rule, and more. Pointing to "truth" as the weapon to defeat the Conspiracy, he urged stronger efforts to use materials supplied by the Society and its two magazines. He then listed numerous JBS accomplishments such as saving the celebration of Christmas, standing firm for <u>local</u> control of police, putting down planned race riots, preventing the revolutionary Reies Tijerina from gaining power in New Mexico, blocking the Cesar Chavez plan to control America's agriculture, and taking the steam out of possible ratification of the Equal Rights Amendment. These victories, Welch stated, were small compared to what had to be done. But each demonstrated that the program he had launched could indeed lead to successes.

Welch then pointed to the action taken by Bernard Goldstein, a man he didn't know but surely admired. A courageous owner of a DC-based meat supply business, Goldstein refused to send 15 pounds of filet mignon to the White House. Asked why, he first pointed to the wage and price controls that had brought on shortages of basic products and then stated, "They started the shortages and don't deserve any better treatment than anyone else."

After its first few months of existence, there were now 28 newspapers receiving the weekly Birch Log. When the U.S. base at Khesanh in Vietnam fell to the Communist forces, a Birch Log column entitled "Remembering Khesanh" gave members an opportunity to show weekly newspaper officials the type of news and analysis they weren't receiving from other sources. In addition to his many articles and speeches, Alan Stang began producing "The Alan Stang Report," a daily five-minute radio commentary about current events written and narrated by Stang himself.

In the midst of the ruckus about the Watergate scandal, Welch suggested that its overblown prominence likely provided a way to replace Richard Nixon as President, not for such solid reasons as his elevation of Red Chinese leaders to respectability, the loss in Vietnam, and other extremely harmful developments, but to get rid of him and not have any of the harm he had done reversed.

Attorney General John Mitchell's outspoken wife Martha created a stir when she announced her understanding of America's real enemies after reading *None Dare Call It Conspiracy*. Her comments earned scorn and then silence from the media. Welch wrote that she was more believable than "anyone in that mass of people connected with Watergate."

Welch's way always included frankness. He reported that actual membership in the Society had peaked "in the fall of 1965." Then came the cumulative effect of a variety of attacks engineered by William Buckley, Nelson Rockefeller, the Republican National Committee, the Anti-Defamation League, Richard Nixon and others. Numerical growth even began to dwindle and the downslide eventually led to "a total decline of some fifteen thousand members." He attributed much of the loss to a problem he termed "religious neutralism." Some members had honestly arrived at the decision to leave the struggle solely in the hands of God. That was their choice although it was one that surprised Welch. But, based on comments he received from members who remained with the JBS program, he thought that relying on religion alone had become a mere excuse on the part of some to abandon the struggle for a variety of other reasons. While the effect on the Society was significant, he added that JBS had already gained back "eight or nine thousand members" and prospects for reaching or exceeding the 1965 membership peak were "very good."

Welch asked members to continue their exposure of OSHA by forming more Nix On OSHA committees and distributing copies of Dan Smoot's timely book entitled *The Business End of Government*. He further announced the availability of *Understanding the Dollar Crisis*, a book written by economist Percy Greaves and published by the Society.

As a telling example of the horrors emanating from the federal government's growing bureaucratic control over various segments of American life, Welch pointed to 185 farmers in a single county of North Dakota who received a grand total of $1,648,261 **for not planting crops** on portions of their land. And he ended the year with the good news that New Hampshire Governor Meldrim Thomson refused to proclaim "United Nations Day." The Governor had instead declared October 21-27, 1973, "Truth About United Nations Week." Governor Thomson soon joined the Society and accepted appointment to its National Council.

CHAPTER 35
1974: McDonald Wins Election

It had become almost laughable to recall the horror expressed in the February 1974 *Bulletin* about the "enormous" national debt that had reached $490 billion. (The admitted national debt when this book first saw publication was $21 trillion!) Once again, Welch repeated his statement published in the *Blue Book* that "the increasing quantity of government, in all nations, has constituted the greatest tragedy of the Twentieth Century."

During consideration of the Equal Rights Amendment in Mississippi, veteran Hattiesburg member Grace Hamilton and two other JBS members convinced their state's legislative committee to reject the proposal. In a letter to the Society, she told of having given her statement to the panel and then wrote:

> Betty Wells, our state chairman [of the Stop ERA Committee], really broke up the audience. She tried to adjust the mike because she is short and it fell out of the holder. After attempts to put it back didn't work, she turned to the TV cameramen and, in her sweet southern drawl, said: "I need a man!" Our side won right then and there!

Professor Antony Sutton of Stanford University's Hoover Institution became a favorite of many Society members. His three volume *Western Technology and Soviet Economic Development* (1968-1973) showed that the Soviet Union had largely been built and sustained by Western aid, most of it from the United States. These three books led to his being forced out of the prestigious Hoover Institution. He went on to write three exposures of damaging financial activity carried on by Establishment banking giants. These were *Wall Street and the Bolshevik Revolution* (1974), *Wall Street and FDR* (1975), and *Wall Street and the Rise of Hitler* (1976).

During the height of the Society's petition drive to have Congress put an end to all aid and trade going from the U.S. to European Communist nations, Sutton's *National Suicide: Military Aid to the Soviet Union* became available. Immediately offered as a bonus for a paid subscription (or extension) to *The Review Of The News*, the book helped build readership for the Society's weekly magazine as well as boost interest in gathering signatures on the aid and trade petition.

The Society then published *Conspiracy Against God and Man* by Reverend Clarence Kelly, a young scholar who became a Catholic priest. He had suspended his seminary studies for a year in order to gather research and write his book. In it, Father Kelly discussed the launching and early history of the Great Conspiracy and the conspiratorial takeover of European Freemasonry by the plotters.

In April, Welch announced that the Foreword to each monthly *Bulletin* would now be written by senior staff personnel, the first such contribution being the work of the Society's librarian, William P. Fall. The *Bulletin* also carried a reproduction of a lengthy *Los Angeles Times* article about Welch's speech to "2,000 John Birch Society faithful." Headlined "Welch Assails Nixon," the article capably summarized the Welch message including his intention to launch a bumper sticker campaign stating "Don't Give Panama Our Canal! – Give Them Kissinger Instead!" The report in the *LA Times* noted Welch's claim that a man like Richard Nixon lives with "a gnawing fear that although he is a peacock today, he may be a feather duster tomorrow."

Welch then published a copy of his protest letter to the editor of a magazine that claimed he had been interviewed by *Playboy* magazine and also that he had previously served as the Imperial Wizard of the Ku Klux Klan. Emphatically denying both of those claims, he added that he had turned down several lucrative offers from *Playboy* for an interview. His refusal to have anything to do with that semi-pornographic magazine, he said, left space in its pages "for the use of such exhibitionists as William F. Buckley, Jr., George Lincoln Rockwell, and Jane Fonda" whose interviews had already appeared. He further stated that he had knowledge of those individuals being interviewed, not because he was a *Playboy* subscriber but because one of its officials had sent him several copies of the magazine hoping that he might reverse his refusal to cooperate and be interviewed. He never did cooperate with *Playboy*.

Continuing the Society's efforts to protect every citizen's right to keep and bear arms, Welch cited a passage from one of Dan Smoot's early columns where his good friend had noted, "Finland with a population of only four million (but with an unusually large number of trained riflemen) was able to resist and humiliate the mammoth armies of the USSR, whose population totaled 170 million." That little-known bit of history about the value of an armed populace occurred during 1939-1940 when the Soviets were beginning their conquests and Hitler was their ally.

Welch then told of a $1,000 contribution given by Society employee Mike Ondre. Mike's daily routine included packaging and shipping books and other materials, collecting items from the Society's three building to be mailed or delivered to the organization's employees, performing a variety of small maintenance jobs, and taking inventory of the many books, pamphlets, films, etc. in the JBS warehouse. When personally delivering his gift to "the boss," Mike mentioned Welch's hope expressed in the *Bulletin* that $25 million was needed. He explained: "I figured out that 25,000 members giving $1,000 each would provide the needed amount – and I want to do my part." For once, Welch was caught speechless, but he recovered sufficiently to thank Mike profusely and then relate the incident in the *Bulletin*.

William Fall's July 1974 Foreword filled the *Bulletin's* early pages with examples of reckless federal spending such as a $15,000 annual expenditure for the District of Columbia's "plant ambulance service" providing assistance to residents whose begonias weren't doing well. Total federal expenditures during 1975 added up to $1,652 billion, a considerable amount at the time but a sum that could easily be labeled "peanuts" when compared to yearly expenditures of many hundreds of billions during later years. After condemning various foreign aid programs, Fall dug out a prediction attributed to Russia's Vladimir Lenin who said, "America will spend itself into national ruin."

Welch pointed to an attack on the Society appearing in the *Wall Street Journal* where readers were solemnly assured that "Red-chasing is no longer exciting." Essentially a claim that there was no Conspiracy propelling our nation toward totalitarian slavery, the article sought to defuse growing acceptance of the Society's insistence that deliberate treachery was responsible for our nation's problems. Welch pointed out that it took more than 600 years for Rome's republic to be completely undermined and replaced by a parade of dictators, and that America should still be prospering after only little more than 200 years of existence. He repeated his contention that oppressive government was deliberately steering America away from its praiseworthy roots and into a tyranny administered by our own government.

The Society received a prepaid order for four copies of Gary Allen's article "Rockefeller: Campaigning for The New World Order" reprinted from the February 1974 *American Opinion*. The order emanated from the Nelson A. Rockefeller Purchasing Department at Rockefeller Plaza in New York City. In his December 1974 *Bulletin* column, Society executive Tom Hill delightedly noted that this order from Nelson Rockefeller's office gave solid evidence of obvious concerns generated by the Society among "the highest circles of the Conspiracy."

In August, the *Bulletin* contained an insert I had written entitled "The Issues." It discussed 17 vexing problems that should concern any American. With an election looming, members purchased and distributed tens of thousands of this timely and useful article. Welch received a late-night telephone call from an Associated Press reporter seeking a comment about the death of Earl Warren. Surprised because he had not heard anything about Warren's passing, Welch nevertheless responded with the Latin maxim "de mortuis nil nisi bonum" which meant nothing to the reporter. So Welch translated it for him: "About the dead say nothing except what is good." The reporter accepted that, thanked Welch, and terminated the call.

Welch used the pages of the September *Bulletin* to share his thoughts about the resignation of Richard Nixon, the elevation to the presidency of Gerald Ford (who had been appointed to the vice presidency upon the earlier resignation of Spiro Agnew), and the choice by Ford of Nelson Rockefeller as the nation's new vice president. Rockefeller's nomination happened to be the second use of Section 2 of the 25th Amendment (added to the Constitution in 1967) where the procedure to fill a vice presidential vacancy is spelled out. Ford's ascension to vice president had been the first use of the new amendment.

Immediately following Richard Nixon's resignation as president, Gerald Ford who had yet to be sworn in met representatives of the media on the front lawn of his Virginia home. In an article I wrote for the *Bulletin*, I noted that Nixon's successor devoted more than one quarter of his remarks to heaping praise on Secretary of State Henry Kissinger without even being asked about that man by the reporters sent to interview him. Note was also made in the *Bulletin* that Ford had previously attended three secret Bilderberg conferences co-chaired by David Rockefeller, Nelson's more sophisticated brother.

In his August 9 inaugural address, the newly sworn-in President Ford summarized: "Our great republic is a government of laws and not of men," but he immediately added, "Here the people rule." That prompted me to add the following comment for the Society's *Bulletin*:

> In other words, according to President Ford, the United States possesses a government of laws, not of men – but the men rule! Or, in terms familiar to members of the Birch Society: This is a Republic, not a Democracy – but it's really a Democracy!

About the obvious leftist-leanings of Nelson Rockefeller, Welch recalled the incident in which the Birch-bashing member of the Rockefeller family had murals featuring complimentary depictions of known Communists erected on the walls of the new Rockefeller

Center. Too much even for the Rockefeller family, Nelson received a scolding and the family had the murals torn out and replaced by something less indicative of the Rockefeller family's true political leanings.

The year 1974 saw Democrat Larry McDonald win a seat in the U.S. House of Representatives. A veteran member of the Society and its National Council, McDonald immediately became a force within Congress as he strengthened the resolve of numerous colleagues. His road to election started with a narrow primary defeat in 1972, victory in a similar primary in 1974, and then triumph over an establishment-supported Republican in the 1974 general election. Society members from Georgia and elsewhere, all acting on their own, helped to pave his road to victory.

CHAPTER 36
1975: FORD FOUNDATION'S SUBVERSION

The year began with Welch recalling the startling 1953 admission gratuitously offered by Ford Foundation President Rowan Gaither to congressional investigator Norman Dodd.

Aware of Dodd having been assigned by the congressional Reece Committee to investigate the questionable work of several tax-exempt foundations, Gaither invited Dodd to his New York City office. During their encounter, the Ford Foundation leader calmly announced that he was operating under "directives issued by the White House" to provide foundation grants that would "so alter life in the United States as to make possible a comfortable merger with the Soviet Union." The startled Norman Dodd asked Gaither if he would state that goal under oath and the Ford Foundation mogul responded that he would not even think of doing so. Nor did he ever name the individuals in the White House whose directives he was following.

The *Bulletin* heaped praise on the small 1850 book *The Law* (80 pages) written by French legislator Frederic Bastiat. Defining the proper role of government and targeting "legal plunder" which was the author's term for various forms of taxation, the book had already become a mainstay for many in the Society. Almost simultaneously, the Society published Karl Marx's 1948 classic *The Communist Manifesto* so that more Americans would understand that Communism's goals were being fastened on America.

Somewhat amazed but pleased, Welch referred to a recent column written by his early nemesis, Chicago newspaperman Jack Mabley. The reporter, who had first aired revelations about Welch's unpublished criticisms of Dwight Eisenhower, claimed to have continued his study of the Society. Expressing surprise at the Society's "staying power," Mabley found himself in agreement with its stands about the Vietnam War, the appointment of Nelson Rockefeller as vice president, and more. Because he was now holding attitudes similar to those held by the Society, the journalist concluded that "things are getting quite confusing." His turnabout regarding the JBS had been shared by many other Americans who had taken some time to learn what the Society says, not merely what others have said about it.

Never a fan of Winston Churchill, Welch expressed great appreciation for the publication of a book entitled *The Lusitania*. Authored by British journalist Colin Simpson, it named the famed Prime Minister of Great Britain as one of the key players in sending the ship into waters controlled by German submarines. Among others, Simpson blamed Churchill for the sinking of the ship by a German U-boat and the loss of 1,200 of its passengers. The incident provided an excuse for the U.S. to enter World War I.

An attempt to have the Consumer Product Safety Commission ban the sale of handgun ammunition generated a wave of protests from Society members. The anti-gun partisans then zeroed in on what they termed "Saturday night specials," a clever term for the small handguns relied upon by many for personal protection.

For $10.00, anyone could purchase a year-long subscription (or extension) to *The Review Of The News* and receive a copy of Taylor Caldwell's *Captains and the Kings*. In this latest of her very popular historical novels, Miss Caldwell supplied details about how a political conspiracy based in America went about implementing its treacherous plans.

Welch's top assistant Tom Hill devoted space in the *Bulletin* to a listing of the Society's various tools to expose the Conspiracy and its willing followers. These were:

The JBS *Bulletin*
The monthly *American Opinion*
The weekly *Review Of The News*
The Birch Log
The Alan Stang Report
Western Islands (book publisher)
American Opinion Bookstores
American Opinion Speakers Bureau
Nationwide network of JBS chapters
National Field Staff
Summer Camps for Youth
Ad Hoc Committees such as SYLP, TRIM, TRAIN, TACT and MOTOREDE

In addition, Hill noted that members throughout the nation were writing letters, gaining signatures on petitions, showing films and filmstrips, and regularly reaching out to fellow Americans. He rightly termed the entire effort "a panorama of productivity."

Welch announced the availability of the long-awaited book entitled *The Life and Words of Robert Welch* authored by veteran staff member G. Edward Griffin. Both members and enemies eagerly sought the biography of the Society's founder. The *Bulletin* happily published a letter sent by Arizona Senator Paul Fannin to a constituent calling for the U.S. to "withdraw its membership and support" from the United Nations. Commenting about this welcome development, Warren Mass wrote that the public stand taken by the Senator amounted to solid evidence that the Society's Get US Out! petition campaign was having a good effect.

The importance of the effort to "Support Your Local Police – and Keep Them Independent" became more obvious after creation of a Ford Foundation subsidiary known as the Police Foundation. It named as the new organization's leader former New York City Police Commissioner Patrick Murphy. Aligning with the goals of others who were seeking national control of police, Murphy pointedly mentioned the forthcoming United Nations Congress on Crime Prevention and then bluntly stated: "I have no fear of a national force ... our 40,000 police forces are not sacred." Without explicit advocacy of a national police force, Murphy let it be known that local control of police was his target.

Displaying his contempt both for socialism and most professors, Welch quoted the deceased but well-remembered polemicist H.L. Mencken who once stated, "The primary purpose of socialism was to get higher salaries for professors." Mencken knew there were far more serious reasons to combat the socialism being preached on campuses but he frequently spiced his writing with bits of humor. *The Review Of The News* published its seventh "Conservative Index," its latest listing of the voting records of all 535 members of Congress.

The Society launched its winning campaign to halt a plan working its way through Congress seeking formal approval of a new "Declaration of <u>Inter</u>dependence." Presidents Eisenhower and Kennedy had previously backed the idea and President Ford had become a supporter. More than 100 members of Congress had already attached their names to the new declaration. An article in *The Review Of The News* by Bill Dunham plus a column in the Birch Log series deftly exposed this fundamental treachery. Letters from JBS members and others soon impelled many in Congress who had already signed the subversive declaration to remove their names from it. This particular attack on our nation's founding document died a well-deserved death.

The Society began a full-scale campaign targeting the Environmental Protection Agency. Created not by Congress but by an Executive Order issued by President Nixon, the agency had quickly demonstrated illicit power to weaken, even destroy, property rights and segments of the free enterprise system. The Society claimed that the EPA could by itself steer the nation into totalitarian rule.

At the JBS Rocky Mountain Rally, Welch found himself temporarily speechless when a parade of members presented him with a small mountain of canvas bags containing 267,000 Get Us Out! petitions filled with the signatures of concerned Americans. Supplemented by members from outside the Rocky Mountain states, this huge number of signed petitions added greatly to the number already collected. I later led a team of members as the Society's Public Relations Director in distributing individual boxes filled with completed petitions to the offices of all members of the U.S. Congress, even to Vice President Nelson Rockefeller at his office in the Senate Office Building.

Nationally syndicated columnist Jack Anderson used one of his columns to attack Congressman McDonald by labeling him the "Freshman Class Clown." Welch concluded that "Dr. McDonald must be doing everything right to get this smear." The Society announced the availability of its newest filmstrip entitled "Dollars and Sense." Written and narrated by me, it featured sound definitions of money and inflation along with sharp criticism of the Federal Reserve. Boldly advertised as a better education in economics than a college student would receive while majoring in economics, it soon became one of the most popular programs ever produced by the Society.

Society officials and New Hampshire members were heartened when the "Live Free or Die" state's Governor Meldrim Thomson issued an official proclamation urging "Withdrawal of the United States from the United Nations." Welch was pleased to reproduce in the *Bulletin* an editorial appearing in the *Arizona Republic* newspaper (the state's largest circulation daily). It noted that the Society's unwavering anti-UN campaign had gained support from many in Arizona.

The *Bulletin* again saluted the work of Professor Antony Sutton, the author of several new books shedding light on well-hidden history of the secretive fraternity at Yale University known as Skull and Bones. His *America's Secret Establishment: An Introduction to the Order of Skull and Bones* (1983) provided important understanding of the rituals and subversive goals of this unusual and eerie campus organization. One of Yale's Skull and Bones members happened to be William F. Buckley, Jr., the prominent American who boldly claimed that he would singlehandedly "destroy" The John Birch Society. He did not succeed.

Dangerous Equal Rights Amendment ratification proposals met defeat in New Jersey and New York. New York Lieutenant Governor Mary Anne Krupsak, an ardent supporter of ERA ratification, reluctantly admitted, "The education process was done better by our opponents." She didn't name the opponents but it was widely known that members of the Society had won the battle. Every JBS member was encouraged to realize how effective the Society's program is, and how many times efforts backed by leftists have been slowed down or canceled because of JBS resistance.

Chapter 37
1976: TRIM Shakes Up Congress

The *Bulletin* reported that the Society's "greatest achievement of 1975" consisted in delivering 804,000 Get US out! petitions containing 4,020,000 signatures to members of Congress. Throughout the nation, JBS stalwarts responded enthusiastically to the launching of the TRIM Bulletin program. California member Bob Reeder, a talented graphics display expert, moved his family to Massachusetts and succeeded in designing the TRIM Bulletin format that enabled members anywhere to publicize their congressman's voting record on tax and spending measures. TRIM had an immediately positive response from many in Congress who applauded the effort. And, of course, numerous others were terribly unhappily about TRIM's ability to show constituents their refusal to uphold the Constitution by voting in Congress for unconstitutional and costly spending programs.

Gary Allen's newly released book, *The Rockefeller File*, reported the history and current deeds of what he termed "America's royal family of finance." Tracing the leftist economic and political preferences played by several generations of Rockefellers, the book showed that they weren't free enterprise capitalists but were, in reality, enemies of free enterprise and advocates of monopolist power protected by government.

The number of summer camps for young Americans reached ten and the Birch Log was now being sent to 125 newspapers. Single Birch Log columns became favorites of many members who reprinted them for use as one-sheet flyers. Subscriptions to the Alan Stang Report soared past the 100 mark. As a result, The John Birch Society's name was reaching many more Americans.

Over the years, members would occasionally ask me to compose a column dealing with a particular issue of major concern in their area. If, for instance, an attempt to create a Police Civilian Review Board was being considered by a city government, I would write a column showing its danger and mention the particular city and the need for good citizens to oppose the dangerous proposal. The column could be mass produced at low cost in that city, but it was also sent to all Birch Log subscribers who published it as national news.

Each week, a copy of the latest Birch Log column was given to all home office employees, and also sent to all members of the JBS field staff. One copy even went to Robert Welch's desk. Imagine my delight when, without any prompting from me, he went out of his way one day to tell me how much he liked my weekly output. He even commented, "You certainly get a lot said on a single piece of paper." From a man who intensely disliked the one-sheet flyer approach, I considered his attitude high praise. I even smiled inwardly about having accomplished creating a way to have a one-sheet flyer targeting a single topic, something that would likely never have been approved had it not been created as a column for newspapers.

U.S. News and World Report published its list of America's "Top thirty leaders" and, to the surprise of no veteran JBS member, most were well-known liberals and internationalists doing harm to the United States. Four pages of the *Bulletin* were devoted to exposing the harmful record of one man on the list, Secretary of State Henry Kissinger. Welch called for him to be fired. The ever-productive Gary Allen aided this particular campaign with yet another book, *Kissinger: The Secret Side of the Secretary of State*.

July 1976 afforded Welch the opportunity to issue his "Bicentennial Message," a 64-page warning about the Conspiracy's already successful efforts to destroy all aspects of freedom and establish a tyrannical New World Order. On the positive side, he announced that the "combined circulation" of *American Opinion* and *The Review Of The News* had reached 100,000. He then noted that, in addition to the number of paid subscribers, reprints of 65 articles from the two magazines over recent years had substantially aided in building the influence of the two JBS-affiliated publications. Member distribution of those reprints throughout the nation dramatically boosted the effectiveness of the two magazines.

Ed Griffin released his newest filmed lecture entitled "The Grand Design," a carefully researched expose' showing that America's internal enemies sought to use fear of nuclear war to bring about world government and the end of freedom. Immediately, a transcript of the film's text became available in booklet form. With Welch and a few other staff personnel, I viewed the premier showing of this film at JBS headquarters. "The boss" registered immediate approval of the program.

Congressman Larry McDonald introduced a measure in Congress to halt federally mandated forced busing of youngsters to schools other than the one nearest their home. When his H.R. 12365 measure became bottled up in a House committee, he started a drive to have House colleagues pry it out the committee via a "discharge petition." Members were encouraged to contact their U.S. representative to urge support for this unique method of moving legislation forward.

The first JBS exposure of the left-leaning, truth-avoiding, and money-making scheme known as the Southern Poverty Law Center appeared in the October *Bulletin*. Gary Allen released his third book in the single calendar year of 1976, a slim pocket book entitled *Jimmy Carter, Jimmy Carter*. With evidence to back up his claim, Allen insisted that the former peanut farmer's race for the presidency was "run on Rockefeller oil, not peanut oil." Allen showed that Carter was surrounded by Council on Foreign Relations members and the former Georgia governor had become an early member of the Trilateral Commission. Formed by David Rockefeller and Zbigniew Brzezinski, this newest Insider organization was clearly created to aid in steering the United States into world government.

Paid circulation of the *JBS Bulletin* (sent to all members and as gifts to several lists of influential individuals) reached 106,000. Welch delightedly announced publication of Congressman McDonald's new book, *We Hold These Truths*, a much-needed survey of the importance of the U.S. Constitution and the techniques many members of Congress were employing to ignore it. Actually ghost-written for him by Dan Smoot, the book stunned some Washington watchers who found it remarkable that at least one member of Congress understood and revered the limitations on government contained in the venerable document.

After highly praising the various works of Professor Antony Sutton, Welch gently chided the former Hoover Institution scholar for attributing the gains of Communism and socialism only to bankers and industrial giants seeking personal financial gain. No, said Welch, the good professor was ignoring – or hadn't yet figured out – the role of an evil Conspiracy seeking to enslave all of mankind. He agreed that some prominent leftists had become wealthy through cooperating with conspiratorial projects but he insisted that the ultimate goal of the Conspiracy had always been acquisition of power, not just amassing wealth.

CHAPTER 38
1977: PROF. QUIGLEY'S REVELATIONS

Revelations given by Georgetown University Professor Carroll Quigley in his monumental 1966 book *Tragedy and Hope* began to figure prominently in the Society's work. Quigley bared information about the existence of a "secret society" working to achieve world rule. Although he never used the word "conspiracy," his boastful knowledge of the aims and methods of the world planners, especially the significant part played by America's Council on Foreign Relations, became very useful information for members. They could now point to corroboration of the Society's view given by a man who had obviously earned the trust of the plotters. Quigley's 1,350-page tome supplied corroboration for much of what the Society had long maintained. Soon, when Cleon Skousen issued his 130-page *The Naked Capitalist*, a competent review of the Quigley opus, Society members had two remarkably useful tools to explain the Conspiracy to fellow Americans.

American Opinion published several articles written by Gary Allen based on the information supplied by Quigley. When members began purchasing copies of the massive book, there were soon none to be had. Understandably, Quigley sought to have his publisher, the Macmillan Company, produce a second printing but he ran into a stall, then an impenetrable roadblock. A Macmillan executive informed the angry author that the printing plates had been destroyed. Quigley became enraged. Even more, a new printing of a pirated edition of his book showed up from Taiwan where copyright practices weren't observed. So the book was again available but its author received no royalties from this pirated edition.

Quigley later met and learned a great deal from Edward Hunter, a friend of The John Birch Society who had experienced similar unwillingness of a major publisher to print more copies of one of his books. Informed about Hunter's experience with Establishment publishers, Quigley began to suspect that the "secret society" he had written about so voluminously in his *Tragedy and Hope* wasn't worthy of the adulation he had given it.

He died soon after his thinking had begun to change. But the information he supplied in his ponderous work has always proven useful to those seeking to explain the self-defeating policies of governments in the U.S. and elsewhere. I summarized what later became known of the Quigley/Hunter friendship in an article appearing in the October 1992 JBS *Bulletin*.

Society executive Tom Hill began suggesting that Society chapters meet twice each month. He asked chapter leaders to continue holding their monthly meeting but to add a second gathering in mid-month for an "Information and Action" meeting. At these newer monthly sessions, letters could be written, films shown, and prospects could be introduced to the work of the Society. Much was accomplished wherever these "I & A" meetings were held. Members were then asked to arrange showings of the filmstrip "Panamania" to mobilize opposition to the Carter administration's drive to transfer ownership of the U.S. Canal to the Communist-led Panama government.

Welch commented about the dangers posed by the various measures proposing gun controls and the corresponding loss of a citizen's right to be armed. He also targeted the planned "giveaway" of the Panama Canal and the strategy behind the "contrived" energy crisis. And he expressed justifiable anger at the refusal of President Carter to welcome New Hampshire Governor Meldrim Thomson to the White House. The Granite State's senior elected official sought to deliver more than one hundred thousand petition signatures seeking to overturn the bureaucratic edicts preventing construction of a nuclear power plant in his state.

Relying on the Constitution's Article III, Section 2 where power is given to Congress to limit the jurisdiction of the Supreme Court and lower federal courts, Congressman McDonald introduced H.R. 4479, a bill to bar federal courts from interfering with the assignment of pupils to a particular local school. His effort sought to cancel the busing of students away from nearby schools in the name of civil rights and racial integration.

McDonald told of a visit to his office of several Boston-area opponents of forced busing. The city had already suffered through numerous demonstrations against the practice, and violence had broken out at many. The Bostonians thought that their presence in Washington would help to reverse the hated use of their children in a detestable government program. Unable to find any of their own representatives available – they were deliberately absent from their offices – the anti-busing stalwarts decided to visit the office of Rep. McDonald. They knew he was on their side.

The Georgia congressman welcomed about a dozen of these frustrated citizens and then gave them a veritable tongue lashing. He said, "You have accomplished nothing except substantial cost to yourselves because of lost time at work, traveling to and from Washington, overnight accommodations, etc. What you should have done is use the money you have just squandered to start a campaign to educate fellow citizens about the need for proper representation in Congress. I hope you won't waste your time and mine in the future." McDonald would tell of that incident, and his advice to the Bostonians to audiences throughout the nation.

When news that a faction within the National Rifle Association had devised plans to water down the organization's stance regarding private gun ownership, numerous members – armed with information from *American Opinion* and *The Review Of The News* – attended the annual NRA convention in Cincinnati. The result saw several top NRA officials sacked and the organization select Retired Vice Admiral Lloyd Mustin as President. Mustin tersely expressed his attitude about gun registration and gun control with two words: "unalterably opposed."

The Society had launched its TRIM (Tax Reform IMmediately) ad hoc program in February 1975. With its "Lower Taxes Through Less Government" slogan and its reporting on the voting records of individual congressmen, the program grew rapidly to 275 committees. TRIM headquarters supplied camera-ready copy enabling members to publish inexpensive TRIM Bulletins showing their congressman's voting record on spending bills. Those TRIM Bulletins quickly became known as the congressman's "report card."

In February 1978, prompted by worries about the TRIM Bulletins showing their record, several members of Congress asked the Federal Election Commission to determine if any laws were being broken by TRIM. House members Jerome Ambro (D-N.Y.) and Helen Meyner (D-N.J.) wanted FEC officials to issue fines and effectively block TRIM leaders from exposing their records. The TRIM chairmen were accused of violating a federal law requiring registration and payment of a fee by any group advocating defeat or victory of a candidate. But no TRIM committee had ever suggested defeat or reelection of any member of Congress.

Nevertheless, after studying the pleas from Ambro and Meyner, FEC officials informed the leaders of the TRIM committees operating in those two districts that they must pay a $100 penalty. Both TRIM leaders responded with denials that they had violated any law. They further contended that paying the $100 would amount to admitting that they actually had done something wrong by not reporting their activity to the federal agency. Jim Hogan, who made his living as a taxi driver, was serving as the chairman of a New Jersey TRIM Committee reporting on Helen Meyner's voting record. He sent a letter to the FEC telling its lawyers to cease their harassment. In New York, TRIM Chairman Ed Cozzette, an aeronautical engineer, also refused to bow to the FEC's demand. His committee was reporting on Jerome Ambro's record.

In August 1978, the FEC sued Cozzette and his Committee. The notification supplied to Cozzette claimed that his committee's "critique of Congressman Ambro's voting record constituted a communication expressly advocating his defeat." That charge was totally false inasmuch as no mention of defeating Ambro appeared on the TRIM brochure. TRIM headquarters had explicitly informed all committee chairmen to avoid any urging by recipients to vote for or against a particular office holder. The FEC's charge additionally stated that Cozzette's group had broken the law by not placing within the TRIM Bulletin a "statement as to whether the TRIM Bulletin had or had not been authorized by a candidate, his authorized political committee, or their agents."

Making the very same charges, the FEC also sued Jim Hogan, the leader of the Northwest Jersey TRIM Committee. Through lawyers, both Cozzette and Hogan let the FEC bureaucrats know that they would not pay any fine, had not broken any law, and wished to be left alone. Similar charges were issued to TRIM Chairman Randy Van Hecke whose committee in Oregon had informed local citizens about the voting record of Congressman Les AuCoin. Several other TRIM Committees and their chairmen were similarly threatened by the FEC.

After the FEC's initial attempt failed to have the targeted individuals pay the fine thereby admitting law breaking, Ed Cozzette received a nasty letter from Congressman Ambro who accused him of receiving money from The John Birch Society. Cozzette, like all other TRIM Committee Chairmen, had actually paid the Society a fee enabling him to receive the TRIM materials. In Oregon, TRIM Chairman Jim Potterf, received a similar letter from Congressman Jim Weaver (D-Oregon). In the nation's capital, the Democratic Congressional Campaign Committee asked all Democratic Party members throughout the nation to forward information about TRIM activity in their district to the seriously worried national Democratic Party office. TRIM had obviously generated enormous concern among big-spending congressmen, most of whom were liberal Democrats.

Pointing to what Welch termed a "truly sizable expense in both time and money," the Society hired lawyers to defend the targeted TRIM chairmen. The entire TRIM operation was on trial and the obvious intent of the plaintiff (FEC) was to put the defendant (TRIM) out of business – and possibly The John Birch Society along with it. After appeals at lower court levels, the case eventually reached the ten-judge panel of the United States Court of Appeals for the Second Circuit in New York. In February 1980, that panel ruled **unanimously** in favor of TRIM and against the FEC. The court concluded that TRIM was simply exercising free speech protected by the First Amendment, and that TRIM's activity should not be regulated by FEC oversight because it did not "expressly advocate the election or defeat of a clearly identified candidate."

In a separate but concurring opinion, Judge Irving Kaufman, the court's Chief Justice, felt so strongly about the FEC's campaign against TRIM's First Amendment rights that he labeled the FEC action "somewhat perverse." He claimed to be disturbed because "citizens of this nation should not be required to account to this court for engaging in debate of political issues."

The Society's victory in that critical test benefited not only TRIM and the Society but it safeguarded the rights of other groups or individuals publishing and distributing reports about how members of Congress were performing. Yet, most of these beneficiaries of the victory not only didn't congratulate and thank The John Birch Society, most continued to bow to the stream of slurs and misinformation about the Society emanating from the media.

While there were some members of Congress who condemned and even ridiculed the TRIM operation, there were plenty of congressional conservative who cheered the effort. James Collins (R-Texas) said TRIM "performed a great community service." Ken Kramer (R-Colo.) was "delighted to receive such a score." Barry Goldwater, Jr. (R-Calif.) enthused: "You TRIM people are the talk of Capitol Hill." Bill Goodling (R-Penna.) told a TRIM leader that the program could be the making or breaking of any member of Congress." And Wally Herger (R-Calif.) thanked a constituent while adding that he was "in complete agreement" with the TRIM effort.

Enthusiasm for TRIM showed when, within ten days after the announcement of its availability, members purchased 40,000 copies of the pamphlet "What is TRIM?" for local distribution. Immediately, a new printing of 100,000 was ordered and these sold in two more weeks. JBS headquarters then placed a third order for another 150,000.

Chapter 39
1978: Exposing SIECUS and Sex-Ed

Members were always encouraged to write friendly, even positive letters to elected officials. Whether requesting support for some measure, sending congratulations for taking a correct stand on another, or gently letting them know their less-than admirable performance was being scrutinized, letters were an effective way to confirm to a congressman that his constituents were watching. Tom Hill noted in the *Bulletin* that a U.S. congressman blamed the Birch Society for surprisingly deciding to retire after serving five two-year terms. In his statement, the veteran legislator included his revealing allegiance to something other than the U.S. Constitution. To those who had been sending letters to him and distributing TRIM Bulletins showing his record, he stated: "They don't understand what this means, to be citizens in the world community. Nobody appreciates what the new requirements are."

"Citizens of the world community?" "New requirements?" Hill congratulated this legislator's constituents who had been publicizing their congressman's record. He added that Birchers are regularly "chided by do-nothing patriots who claim letter-writing to be a waste of time." He insisted, "Nothing could be further from the truth." This incident proved how effective TRIM could be when properly employed.

Although the federal court's decision had safeguarded TRIM from FEC harassment, different problems became obvious. TRIM Committee members continued to distribute issue their TRIM bulletins and JBS officials continued to insist that no committee give any indication of political activity. Sadly, some committees would publish a small number of bulletins (or even none) during periods when elections were not being held and then, prior to an election, distribute large numbers of bulletins. They thereby made themselves potentially liable to charges that TRIM was indeed a political weapon. Society officials requested that such heavily weighted distribution during election seasons never be undertaken. But overly eager members in some local TRIM committees continued to print and distribute their bulletins with this same publishing pattern. They were endangering the very existence of the TRIM program – as well as The John Birch Society itself.

Also by 1980, it had also become almost impossible to find the needed number of spending measures – a requirement TRIM had placed on itself. Many spending bills were now labeled "omnibus" meaning that "pork barrel" expenditures and various unconstitutional spending programs were hidden among legitimate expenditures. Reluctantly, Society officials would soon shut the TRIM operation down. Instead, members were encouraged to rely on *The New American's* "Freedom Index" containing reports on all 535 congressmen and senators, not just on spending bills but on a variety of topics. This Index, published semi-annually by the Society's affiliated magazine, *The New American*, has proven to be a useful substitute for anyone wishing to show an elected official's performance.

Based on reports received at JBS headquarters, the October 1977 anti-UN "Day of Shame" activity had generated coverage in 220 newspapers with a combined circulation of 5,000,000. Additionally, members nationwide had distributed a total of 150,000 reprinted articles, books and other items during the date chosen to expose the world organization's designs on national sovereignty. The publication by the Society's Western Islands of *The Siecus Circle* immediately drew high praise from nationally known educator Max Rafferty and Notre Dame Law School Professor Charles Rice. The book had quickly become touted as a comprehensive exposé of a) the Humanist Movement, b) the invasion of schools by the Sex Information and Education Council of the United States (SIECUS), and c) the continuing assault on the family. It was the first book of its kind offered to the American people.

The Society proudly announced that two of Gary Allen's recent articles showing the control exercised over the Carter administration by the Council on Foreign Relations and the Trilateral Commission would now be available as a single 36-page booklet. The booklet joyfully noted that many fellow citizens had become aware of the completely un-American goals sought by these two Insider organizations. Hence the popular booklet carried the title, "They're Catching On."

Ten pages of the February *Bulletin* contained a review of the subversive plan to transfer the U.S. Canal in Panama to the Communist-led Panamanian government. An article entitled "Carter Against America: The Incredible Panama Story" showed that there were 31 senators opposed to the giveaway, 21 undecided, and 46 in favor. The Senate eventually passed the measure calling for the giveaway by a 69-31 vote, a slim margin when approval by two-thirds (67 senators) was needed.

Because congressional ratification of the Equal Rights Amendment had become unattainable during the seven years allotted for consideration of the measure, some congressional proponents sought passage of a measure granting seven more years for the amendment campaign. Indiana University Law Professor William Stanmeyer spoke against that proposal saying in part:

> If ERA is ratified, it will be left to a few attorneys to decide virtually every question of importance dealing with children's education, husband-wife relationships, the place in society for deviant subcultures, the makeup and readiness of the military, the very existence of all-girl or all-boy schools, and even perhaps the sexual makeup of seminaries and ministerial schools associated with colleges receiving federal aid.

Members sponsoring a speaker from the American Opinion Speakers Bureau were encouraged to sell ads in either a printed program for their event, or place the ads in a newspaper advertisement. Guidelines for gaining such support were supplied to all speaker groups. The November 1978 elections resulted in the defeat of seven senators who had voted for the Panama Canal giveaway. After President Carter had traveled to several states to boost campaigns for the reelection of Democratic party liberals, six of them were defeated. Several others who approved the Canal giveaway would later be voted out of office. The *Bulletin* suggested "the President should have done his own cause a favor by staying home."

CHAPTER 40
1979: *THE INSIDERS* FILMSTRIP

The year started with Welch excoriating President Carter for announcing in mid-December his decision to extend formal diplomatic recognition to Communist China. Members were urged to originate a massive letter-writing campaign to protest the President's move – letters not only to the President but also to elected officials across the nation. The Society leader likened the Carter move to the similar timing in 1913 of passage of the Federal Reserve Act by a numerically small number in Congress. The Federal Reserve gained approval when many members of Congress had already left the nation's capital to be at home to celebrate Christmas.

Gary Allen's newest book, *Tax Target: Washington* received enthusiastic acceptance and wide distribution. The book endorsed the TRIM effort as a way to hold down federal spending. Bob Lee's profiles of the performance of several senators published by *The Review Of The News* (TROTN) were met with joy by subscribers in the home states of those senators. Distribution of large numbers of reprints of those profiles became a major project. In 1976, Senators McGee (D-Wyo.) and Moss (D-Utah) suffered defeat because many voters in their states were given copies of their profiles. In 1978, the same process led to more awareness among the constituencies of Senators Clark (D-Iowa), McIntyre (D-N.H.) and Haskell (D-Colo.), each of whom was defeated. Nationally syndicated columnist Marquis Childs was not alone in pointing to the TROTN reprints as the main cause of these defeats.

Tom Hill cited another encouraging letter received by the Society. It stated:

> Dear Sirs,
> I didn't think I'd ever come to this point, since I was a confirmed "liberal of the Sixties." But I have just finished reading Gary Allen's *None Dare Call It Conspiracy* and this, coupled with other things that seem to be "getting out of hand" in this country lately are driving me to the "Right" very rapidly. Please send info on The John Birch Society.

Receiving such correspondence was not at all unusual. Tom then congratulated the members who had undertaken a widespread distribution of Gary Allen's small but potent book. And he encouraged all other members to do likewise.

On top of everything else the Society was asking of members, Welch announced a new ad hoc program to be known as The American POWER (Promote Our Wonderful Energy Resources) Committee. Former three-term New Hampshire Governor Meldrim Thomson had accepted appointment as Chairman and Welch asked me to be its National Director. POWER began distributing information about untapped domestic and off-shore energy sources while also touting nuclear power as the safest, cleanest and least expensive method of generating electricity.

Bill Dunham happily reported that the legislatures in South Dakota, Idaho, Kentucky, Nebraska and Tennessee had rescinded previous ratification of the Equal Rights Amendment. Gary Handy showed that all ten planks of *The Communist Manifesto* had already been partially or completely fastened on America by our nation's leaders.

Welch then reminded staff and members of his firm commitment to Michelangelo's famous dictum: "Trifles make perfection and perfection is no trifle." To that he added, "What's good enough for some is not good enough for The John Birch Society." In a rather dramatic move certainly felt deeply by the Managing Editor of *American Opinion*, Welch looked through an advance copy of the next issue, found in it "some material that we had no business publishing," and ordered the whole issue destroyed and re-done.

The newest filmstrip entitled "The Insiders" became an instant favorite among members. An initial order of 500 prints had sold immediately and were already in use, and another 500 had been ordered. Naming the members of the Council on Foreign Relations and Trilateral Commission holding posts in the Carter administration, it explained that these were the very government officials who had betrayed Taiwan, spurred the giveaway of the Panama Canal, aided the Communist revolution in Iran, and supported other Communist revolutions in Africa and Latin America.

In the first six pages of the October *Bulletin*, Welch provided a glimpse of his own expertise in the field of science by targeting the fraud perpetrated on the human race – and especially on Americans – by Albert Einstein and his "theory of relativity." He began by noting that Einstein was a Communist who had already assisted the Communist cause by becoming a primary leader in Belgium of the "League Against Imperialism," an organization labeled by Welch as "probably the first worldwide Communist front." Welch's conclusion about Einstein continued:

The plain truth is that his whole international reputation was built up for him by the Insiders of the Conspiracy because of his immense usefulness to them. If scientific absolutes can be downgraded into relativity, then every other absolute – especially moral absolutes – can equally be made relative.

In the field of education, Welch pointed to educator John Dewey whose subversive efforts deserved condemnation, similar to that given to Einstein, for his work in steering so many into dependence upon the state instead of reliance on the family for schooling. According to Welch, some other traitorous individuals who were made into heroes because they had served the Conspiracy's interests were politician Dwight Eisenhower, situation ethics promoter Reverend Harry Ward, diplomat John Foster Dulles, journalist Walter Lippmann, and jurist Felix Frankfurter.

The July *Bulletin* related details about the forcible entry of Michigan-based OSHA inspectors into a local business where they had previously been denied entry by its owner. The inspectors barged into the privately owned facility and eventually found only six minor violations, among which were such "grievous" OSHA requirements about the "proper" placement of safety and exit signs. But signs about safety and exiting had been carefully posted in this particular building and were easily seen by anyone. OSHA personnel said they were not high enough or large enough to satisfy the arbitrary OSHA requirements. In the local newspaper's report about the incident, the outraged business owner commented about the damage done to his building by the forced entry. He stated, "The Gestapo has struck."

Ten pages of the August *Bulletin* listed some of Secretary of State Henry Kissinger's harmful accomplishments. Described in infuriating detail, his leadership had accomplished: the sellout of China; agreeing to the Strategic Arms Limitation Treaty; the demise of our nation's internal security capability; the loss of freedom in Vietnam and Cambodia; and the delivery of prosperous and friendly Rhodesia to Communist-style terrorists who renamed the country Zimbabwe and converted it from a land of plenty into a land of severe shortages.

Requests followed for members to oppose H.R. 2444, the measure calling for creation of a new Department of Education. A Birch Log column issued in June 1980 pointed to the 1932 book *Toward Soviet America* written by National Chairman of the U.S. Communist Party William Z. Foster. This top Communist in America had called for creation of a "National Department of Education," the very goal sought by President Carter and later created by the U.S. Congress.

So successful was the usage of "The Insiders" filmstrip that the text of its soundtrack was issued in booklet form. All members were asked to obtain a minimum of four copies, one to keep and three to distribute. Its heavily footnoted 24-pages also contained the 1978 Trilateral Commission membership list. A letter from Japan addressed to me asked permission to translate the booklet's text into that country's language for local distribution. Permission was immediately given and several copies of the Japanese version of "The Insiders" soon arrived at the Society's Massachusetts headquarters.

Carter administration personnel named as Trilateralists working to build world government included President Carter himself, Vice President Mondale, several cabinet secretaries, six U.S. senators, four U.S. congressmen, two governors, and numerous highly placed officials of the mass media.

Members were alerted via the newly formed American POWER Committee about the availability of the extremely valuable book *The Health Hazards of NOT Going Nuclear*, written by Dr. Petr Beckman, a Czech immigrant to America who was a very popular teacher at a Colorado university. The weekly *U.S. News & World Report* published an interview of Congressman Larry McDonald who ably explained why the United States should withdraw from the United Nations.

The Society's exposure of the CFR/Trilateralist membership of dozens of congressional office holders led many to resign from either or both of these One World organizations. One notable defector was George H.W. Bush who was later excused for exiting both world organizations by David Rockefeller, the Chairman of both. Prominent Insider Leslie Gelb lamented in the *New York Times* that the CFR "is just about being destroyed by the right wing." William F. Buckley defended his CFR membership with insistence that there was nothing subversive about the organization. Congressman McDonald explained that numerous members of Congress had questioned him about the Society's focus on the Conspiracy's Insiders. Some accepted invitations by constituents to view "The Insiders" filmstrip. One rather startled congressman viewed the program and admitted afterwards, "I can see I've got a lot to learn."

Always ready to inject some humor into the Society's efforts, Council Member Tom Anderson responded immediately when told that the January 1980 issue of *American Opinion* would contain an article about the character of Senator Ted Kennedy. "At last," quipped Anderson, "a short article in the magazine!" Welch closed out the year by announcing that Tom Hill had accepted appointment as Executive Vice President of the Society, a move greatly supported by all who knew Tom and had always been grateful for his years of effort.

Robert Welch and former Secretary of Agriculture Ezra Taft Benson addressed 2,000 at the Hollywood Palladium. Mrs. George Birch, the mother of John Birch, provided an enthusiastic endorsement of the organization named after her son. *The Los Angeles Herald Examiner* provided an accurate report about the event.

Three weeks after the banquet at the Hollywood Palladium, (noted at left) the *New York Times* told readers that Robert Welch had been replaced as the Society's leader. There was absolutely no truth to the claim. Welch and Society members enjoyed a good laugh about the Establishment's favorite newspaper. Some suggested that its front page boast, "All the News that Fit to Print," should altered to read "Any way to harm The John Birch Society will be awarded prominent space."

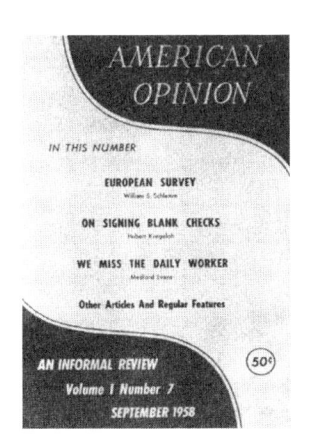

In the September 1958 issue of his *American Opinion* magazine, Robert Welch wrote that Fidel Castro was a lifelong Communist. His revelations about the bearded revolutionary appeared four months prior to Castro seizing Cuba. If private citizen Welch knew of Castro's communist loyalties, top U.S. government officials in the State Department, CIA and elsewhere surely had the same information. But Fidel received critical assistance from the U.S. government and mass media in seizing control of the island nation only 90 miles from Florida.

The 1960 Committee Against Summit Entanglements (CASE), chaired by Robert Welch, sought to prevent President Eisenhower from meeting with and dignifying Soviet Dictator Nikita Khrushchev. Originally left out of the impressive listing of CASE supporters, William F. Buckley, Jr. contacted Welch and, pretending to be a friend of The John Birch Society, begged to have his name included. Welch who was always willing to welcome what he considered credible support for his ventures did indeed add the name of the man who later demonstrated that he was a dishonest foe, not a friend.

At great risk to himself, John Birch Society member Delmar Dennis infiltrated and reported on Ku Klux Klan crimes as an undercover operative for the FBI. Society leaders permitted his early-1960s Klan membership as an exception to their hard and fast rule that no member of the Klan could ever be welcomed as a member of the Society. After several years gathering evidence about the Klan's criminal activity, Dennis became the federal government's chief witness at the trial and conviction of Mississippi Klan leaders. He then completed a nationwide speaking tour for JBS in order to expose the Klan. After delivering speeches from coast to coast, he became the field Coordinator for the John Birch Society in Mississippi.

Enemies of the Society have frequently claimed that Robert Welch's organization was "like the Klan." That falsehood is still occasionally heard. The truth is that the Society did more to diminish the prominence of the Klan than all other organizations combined. As one Mississippi Chapter Leader commented, "The appointment of Delmar Dennis as the Society's Coordinator in Mississippi is a brilliant move that creates a struggle between the Klan and the Society from which one will emerge triumphant and the other will fade into virtual nothingness."

Years later, Hollywood produced a feature film about the work of Delmar Dennis entitled "Mississippi Burning?" Shown in theaters across the nation, the film never mentioned the Dennis name. Nor did it state his oft-stated conviction that he derived courage to proceed with his extremely dangerous work inside the Klan from his membership in and association with members of The John Birch Society.

A genuine American hero, Delmar Dennis passed away soon after attending the Society's 25th anniversary celebration in 1983 where he told this book's author that he came "to say farewell to the boss." Like all who knew Robert Welch's health was in severe decline, Delmar Dennis wanted to thank the Founder for "helping to make me a better man."

Independent, **Huntington Beach, California, July 5, 1968**

Each marcher in this parade carried the name of a Californian who had been killed in the Vietnam War. The 1,200 John Birch Society members and supporters created their remarkable demonstration in the 1968 Fourth of July parade at Huntington Beach, California. Their effort filled two long blocks of the parade route. Crowds of onlookers burst into applause and then into somber silence or tears when they realized that each marcher was carrying the name of a fallen American.

Two Blocks Long, Twelve Hundred Strong

Members of The John Birch Society march in the annual Fourth of July parade at Huntington Beach, California. See Page 19 inside for further details.

Page One of the AFL-CIO's "exposure" of The John Birch Society gave evidence that the left-leaning labor giant was remarkably concerned about the work of Robert Welch's creation. Society members obtained many copies of this six-page handout and distributed them to prospects for membership. The AFL-CIO actually paid Robert Welch's organization a huge compliment with its attack. It showed the Society to be an effective antidote to the liberalism and pro-communism of Big Labor.

Even though an interview published in the December 13, 1983 issue of *USA Today* never gave the Society's address, more than 300 Americans wrote to the Society. Their requests for additional information were answered promptly.

Many articles appearing in *American Opinion* were reprinted by the thousands (at times, hundreds of thousands) and then distributed throughout the nation. Whenever an issue needed attention, Editor Scott Stanley and one of his writers would produce an effective expose' and members would purchase copies for distribution in their communities.

Equally popular were reprints of articles from *The Review Of The News*. JBS members and magazine subscribers distributed large numbers of reprinted profiles of elected congressional figures that had originally appeared in the Society's weekly news magazine. Many in Congress had a hard time defending their record once these profiles were distributed.

The Birch Log started as newspaper column provided to community and county weeklies. Columns discussing a particular current issue were also printed as handouts for widespread distribution. One rather famous use of *The Birch Log* saw Society members pass out copies of an exposure of communist agent Alger Hiss to audiences at several eastern colleges where the convicted former government official had been invited to speak. Neither Hiss nor the leftist professors who gave him a platform to defend himself and his treason appreciated distribution of the truth about the famous traitor. Many students who were coerced into attending the Hiss speech found the handout they received most interesting.

After a 1985 financial analysis showed that having both a monthly and a weekly magazine was a huge financial drain, CEO Clifford Barker decided to close down both *American Opinion* and *The Review Of The News* and combine the work of both magazines into a completely new publication. *The New American* debuted in September 1985. Under the very able leadership of Gary Benoit, the new biweekly magazine became a leading journal for accurate news and hard-hitting perspective. Conservative Caucus leader Howard Phillips frequently told John McManus, "*The New American* is the very best among all the publications claiming to stand for conservative or constitutionalist values."

Prominent John Birch Society member Dr. Larry McDonald won election to the U.S. House of Representatives in 1974. He quickly became a leader of no-nonsense fellow House members. Reelected four times and increasing popular in his home state of Georgia, he was one of the victims of the attack on Korean Airlines 007 by a Soviet fighter plane on September 1, 1983. He had been named the successor to Robert Welch as top leader the Society in March 1983.

After several members of the Society's Executive Committee formed a "Search Committee" to select a successor to Dr. McDonald, they chose one of their own committee members, A. Clifford Barker. A highly regarded veteran Society member and a member of the National Council, he accepted appointment as the organization's Chief Executive Officer in 1984. He served until 1986.

Society officials then turned to long-time staff official Charles "Chuck" Armour to lead the organization. Armour had left a promising career in the insurance field in the early 1960s to accept a Society leadership post in California. The only man ever to hold the title "District Governor" (the post created by Robert Welch to be the overseer of field activity in a multi-state region), he became well known throughout the Western states as a speaker, trainer of junior staff officials, and spokesman with all elements of the media. He served as CEO until 1989.

In selecting Allen Bubolz as the Society's leader in 1989, the organization had turned to someone who had earned undergraduate and graduate business degrees. It was expected that he could help the Society focus more than previously on its business concerns while continuing the organization's primary work protecting sovereignty and exposing conspiratorial projects. When the death of Allen's father left a void in the Bubolz family's Secura Insurance Company doing business in several midwestern states, Allen stepped aside from Society's leadership post in 1991 while remaining a member.

Veteran JBS staff official Don Fotheringham accepts a plaque acknowledging his 50 years of continuous service on the staff of the Society. Presenting the award are the Society's three leaders who served in their posts from 1991 until 2005. Left to right: CEO G. Vance Smith, President John McManus, and Vice President Thomas Gow. Each of these men possessed decades-long experience in all aspects of the Society's work.

The Society wanted President Bill Clinton impeached and removed from office, not merely for his disgraceful personal conduct but more importantly, for accepting bribes from American and Communist Chinese sources seeking favors. The House of Representatives did impeach the President for his disgraceful conduct but the Senate did not vote to remove him from office. Hard evidence about Mr. Clinton accepting bribes from Communist Chinese and American industrialists was ignored.

A massive Society effort succeeded in preventing the United States Congress from canceling our nation's independence by joining a proposed North American Union (NAU). Proponents of the scheme made clear their intention to have membership in the NAU become a major step in uniting Canada, Mexico and the U.S. The actual proposal sought to expand the already harmful NAFTA pact into a ceding of sovereignty on the way toward the creation of a Free Trade Area of the Americas.

Birch Society Week-long Summer Camps for teenagers were conducted in ten locations scattered throughout the nation. Classes focused on history, political systems, economics, and morality along with sporting events, campfires, and other customary summertime activities. The photo above was taken at a camp located in Pennsylvania. The youngster in the front row was the son of one of the camp's staff personnel whose family had come to the site to see what their son and daughter were enjoying.

During afternoon recreation time at a Society camp in Wyoming, all youngsters were afforded an opportunity to enjoy white water rafting down a portion of the Snake River. The gal in the rear of the raft steered the vessel safely through some pretty turbulent rapids.

Washington/World

Experience: From left: Harold Brown (Secretary of Defense for President Carter), Lawrence Eagleburger (State, George H.W. Bush), James Baker (State, George H.W. Bush), Colin Powell (State, Preside[nt]... (Defense, Nixon and Ford), Defense Secretary Donald Rumsfeld, Vice President Cheney, President Bush, Secretary of State Condoleezza Rice, George Shultz (State, Reagan), Melvin Laird (Defense... Defense, Kennedy and Johnson), Madeleine Albright (State, Clinton), Alexander Haig (State, Reagan), Frank Carlucci (Defense, Reagan), William Perry (Defense, Clinton) and William Cohen (Defens[e]...

Cabinet members give Bush their 2 cen[ts]

[Secret]aries of State, Defense offer ideas for victory in Iraq

[N]— President Bush held [a meetin]g about Iraq on Thursday, [that] featured something un-

[...]on administration diplomat [...]right and other Democrats [W]hite House in a group of 13 [secreta]ries of State and Defense, as [he urg]ed new outreach on the [war in] Iraq.

[Everyb]ody around this table agreed [that if w]e go into Iraq, I fully un[derstood,"] Bush said in the Roosevelt [Room. "The]se are good solid Americans [who fear th]at we've got to succeed [over] there."

[He and] others said they offered a variety of suggestions for improvements in Iraq. Albright said she told the president that Iraq was "a war of choice, not of necessity," but now "getting it right is a necessity, not a choice."

Even some of the Republicans there had questions for the president: "Some of the things he heard he probably didn't like too well," said Melvin Laird, Defense secretary for President Nixon and author of a recent piece in the magazine *Foreign Affairs* in which he said Bush had done "an uneven job of selling his (Iraq) message."

White House spokesman Scott McClellan called the meeting "part of the effort to broaden the outreach."

Faced with falling public approval ratings for his presidency and for the war, Bush launched a series of speeches and events that began with the Nov. 30 release of a new "Strategy For Victory" in Iraq. He has provided statistics that he says show that Iraq's security, infrastructure and political development are improving. But he has also admitted mistakes and setbacks since the March 2003 invasion.

Polls show about half of Americans think the war was a mistake, and fewer than half — 42% in a Dec. 16-18 USA TODAY/CNN/Gallup Poll — say Bush has a plan to achieve victory in Iraq.

Critics have accused Bush of having a secretive and narrow management style, restricting himself to a tight circle of advisers. Lawrence Wilkerson, chief of staff to former secretary of State Colin Powell, attributed the decision to invade Iraq and other actions to a small "cabal" led by Vice President Cheney and Defense Secretary Donald Rumsfeld.

Wilkerson, who did not attend Thursday's meeting and has emerged as a critic of the administration since leaving the State Department, said Bush's outreach effort is in part an attempt "to send a signal the administration is not so insular." But, he added, "whether that really means he's opening up, I doubt seriously."

Powell attended the meeting of former secretaries, saying later through a spokeswoman that it provided "a good exchange of views."

The meeting came on a day when at least 100 people died in new attacks in Iraq, including five U.S. troops. The ex-secretaries heard briefings from officials in Iraq via teleconference, and later had a group discussion with the president.

"It all went very quickly, frankly," said Albright, who served as United Nations ambassador and secretary of State in the Clinton administration. "It's very hard to be really able to have a sustained discussion."

Some members of past [ad]ministrations praised Bush['s effort] to reach out.

Lawrence Eagleburger, se[cretary] for Bush's father, said, "I thin[k a] good deal more openness" [by] the president "has got to tal[k] with the American people [as he] has in the past."

Former Nixon Defense [...] praised Bush's recent aggr[essive position?]... "In the last four weeks, [...] well." Laird said he told B[ush] about the Army having eno[ugh...] bright said she expressed [concern over] America's standing in the w[orld].

Harold Brown, Defense [Secretary for] President Carter, said the n[ext steps] are "crucial" in Iraq and c[alled it a] tough situation." Asked if [there] were sources of advice o[n ad]dressing, Brown said: "W[e will wait] and see, won't we?"

On January 6, 2006, President George W. Bush gathered 16 former Secretaries of Defense and State to ask what he should do about Iraq. Other than the President himself, everyone in the photo was a member of the world-government promoting Council on Foreign Relations (CFR). The CFR is one of the key organizations in what has been termed "The Deep State." This photo counters claims by CFR defenders that the powerful pro-world government organization is merely a forum for a variety of ideas, is not subversive, and does not set our nation's policies.

STAR-GAZETTE

Elmira, N.Y., September 1, 1983 — 25 Cents

Missing jet lands safely

SEOUL, South Korea (AP) — A South Korean jumbo jet that was missing for hours while en route from New York to Seoul with 269 people aboard, including a U.S. congressman, landed safely today on a Soviet island, Korean Air Lines said.

The airline did not say why the plane had landed on the island of Sakhalin, although a KAL spokeswoman in New York, Bonnie Villarico, said she had been told it was a forced landing. She said arrangements were being made to send another plane to the isalnd to pick up the passengers.

The Boeing 747 had been unaccounted for since it last gave its position southeast of Hokkaido, Japan's northernmost main island, more than six hours before the first report that it had landed on Sakhalin. The Soviet island is north of Hokkaido.

Among the passengers was U.S. Rep. Lawrence P. McDonald, D-Ga. His staff said he was going to South Korea to attend a ceremony marking the 30th anniversary of the U.S.-South Korea defense pact.

In Atlanta, Harold P. McDonald Jr., the congressman's brother, said, "we've just heard from the State Department ... that the plane is down and apparently the passengers are safe."

There apparently was at least one other American on the flight.

Yoo Sung-Wha, the wife of a professor from the University of Pittsburgh, said her husband, Yoo Chung-Sum, was on board.

South Korea and the Soviet Union have no diplomatic relations.

In April 1978, a Korean Air Lines jet, with 110 people aboard, was fired upon by Soviet aircraft and forced to land Murmansk, a Soviet city. The Soviets alleged the Korean jet had violated their air space while en route from Paris to Seoul. Two passengers, a Korean and a Japanese, were killed and 13 others injured in the incident.

KAL Flight No. 7, which had stopped in Anchorage, Alaska, was scheduled to arrive at Seoul's Kimpo airport at 5:53 a.m. today (4:53 p.m. EDT Wednesday).

On September 1, 1983, a Soviet fighter plane attacked Korean Airlines Flight 007 after it had refueled in Alaska on its way to South Korea. One of the 269 passengers and crew members was John Birch Society Chairman Larry McDonald, a congressman from Georgia. Early press reports, such as the one shown here, claimed that the plane landed safely on Sakhalin Island. And the U.S. State Department immediately notified Harold McDonald, the congressman's brother, that all aboard were safe. Only a few hours after these reports, however, the official story changed and our nation was told that the plane crashed into the sea. None of KAL 007 passengers, dead or alive, was ever seen again.

"Some even believe we are part of a secret cabal working against the best interests of the United States, characterizing my family and me as internationalists and of conspiring with others around the world to build a more integrated global political and economic structure one world, if you will. If that's the charge, I stand guilty, and I am proud of it."

- David Rockefeller, *Memoirs,* 2002

In his own 2002 autobiography entitled *Memoirs*, David Rockefeller wrote of his and his family's efforts to build "one world." He boldly described his efforts as "conspiring with others around the world…." And he ended his revealing admission by insisting, "I stand guilty, and I am proud of it." His boastful frankness confirmed what John Birch Society publications have long stated of him and the Rockefeller family.

Rocky Mountain News, December 2, 1966

Rocky Mou

A Scripps-Howard Newspaper

108TH YEAR, NO. 224

Superiors Blocked Early Space Test, General Declares

BOSTON, Dec. 1 — (UPI) — Retired Army Gen. James M. Gavin said Thursday night that prior to the launch of Russia's Sputnik 1, he was given a "written order, forbidding him from developing an Earth satellite.

Gavin said that in 1956, more than a year before Sputnik was sent aloft in its history-making flight, Wernher von Braun "had launched a Jupiter nose cone more than 700 miles into space.

"We believed then that we had the capability of orbiting a satellite," Gavin said in a speech at the annual meeting of the American Institute of Aeronautics and Astronautics.

"On the basis of this, I made several entreaties to the Department of Defense seeking authority to launch a satellite, and shortly thereafter I was given a written order forbidding me to do so. This admonition was passed on to Von Braun," he said.

Gavin said it was clear by late summer of 1957 that the Soviets were about ready to launch a spacecraft, but "assertions of this were received with skepticism if not ridicule."

Gen. James M. Gavin

In 1957, the Soviet Union successfully orbited a small satellite that circled the earth. Immediately, fears were spread throughout the United States claiming that the Communist-led nation was technologically and scientifically superior. Accordingly, proposals sailed through Congress that expanded bureaucracy, dramatically increased the federal government's meddling in education, and added countless billions to the federal budget. But in 1966, the U.S. Army general who led our nation's space program when the Soviet satellite shocked the world told of being ordered by the Defense Department prior to the Soviet "triumph" not to launch a U.S. satellite. Some scoffers about claims of a conspiracy might find the above article interesting.

Art Thompson wrote a small book entitled *Exposing Terrorism Inside the Terror Triangle* in 2009. In it, he pointed to the training of international terrorists, including islamic killers, conducted by Russian experts.

Arthur R. Thompson started life in Seattle, Washington in 1938. Educated at Washington Military Academy and the University of Washington, he worked for the Boeing Corporation and spent many years reporting on subversive activities in the Seattle area.

An early member of The John Birch Society, he served at a field Coordinator in the Northwest for several years. He then left the Society's staff and started his own manufacturing businesses. Traveling throughout the United States enabled him to gather material for his 2016 book *To the Victor Go the Myths and Monuments*.

He returned to the staff of The John Birch Society in 2000 and won the Board of Director's appointment as CEO in 2005.

In 2014, his *International Merger by Foreign Entanglements* book exposed the planning of conspirators to scuttle national independence via so-called free trade agreements.

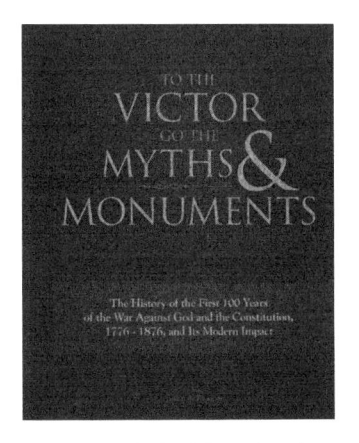

After several decades of gathering information about conspiratorial activity during the first 100 years of the United States as a nation, he produced the monumental 2016 book, *To the Victor Go the Myths and Monuments*.

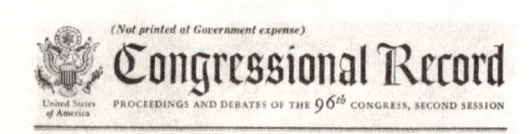

AMERICANS, STOP THINKING LIKE COMMUNISTS

PLEADS A FORMER COMMUNIST AND PATRIOTIC AMERICAN NEGRO

(Not printed at Government expense)

Congressional Record
PROCEEDINGS AND DEBATES OF THE 96th CONGRESS, SECOND SESSION

REMARKS
OF
HON. LARRY McDONALD
OF GEORGIA
IN THE HOUSE OF REPRESENTATIVES
Wednesday, June 18, 1980

• Mr. McDONALD. Mr. Speaker, Julia Brown, who was for many years an undercover member of the Communist Party of the United States for the FBI, addressed the Council of The John Birch Society here in Washington on June 9, 1980. She felt it appropriate at that time to restate her testimony before the Senate Judiciary Committee of one year ago pertaining to the possible enactment of a Federal paid holiday in honor of the late Martin Luther King. Her testimony, then, as now, is deserving of wider attention. This lady has given a lot to her country and her views are not popular in some circles but they are valid in my view. I commend it to the attention of my colleagues.

Her testimony follows:

For much of the 1950s, Cleveland resident Julia Brown spent many hours working as an undercover operative for the FBI in the Communist Party. She eventually testified at the trial of several Communist Party members who were duly convicted of crimes against our nation.

Mrs. Brown then joined The John Birch Society and traveled throughout the nation warning Americans about the subversive plans of Martin Luther King and numerous agitators working with him. Her ability to deliver speeches to Americans of mixed racial backgrounds about plans for riots and ethnic struggles frequently led King and his forces to cancel their planned forays in numerous communities. She later tried to convince Congress not to honor King's memory by naming a holiday after him. Her testimony and accompanying speech to a Birch Society gathering in 1980 so impressed Congressman Larry McDonald that he had it transcribed and entered into the *Congressional Record*.

CHAPTER 41
1980: LEFT-WING SENATORS EXPOSED

Prior to the TRIM operation being reluctantly shut down by Society officials, members continued to demonstrate its remarkable impact. Welch reported the work of North Dakota members who placed the entire four-page TRIM Bulletin in the thirteen largest newspapers in their state (total circulation 212,000). Other distribution efforts included 122,000 in a single California district; 110,000 in Jackson, Mississippi; 87,000 in northeast Massachusetts; and 48,000 in Pensacola, Florida.

An amusing exchange between a Texas congressman and one of his constituents began when an astute lady complained in a letter to Congressman Hightower about his vote for a big spending measure. He wrote back and told her "not to depend on TRIM, a part of the John Birch Society." But the lady knew nothing about the TRIM effort and, after doing her own digging, found some local JBS members who had indeed formed a TRIM Committee. She happily joined with them and wrote a letter to Mr. Hightower thanking him for steering her to the area's TRIM Committee.

In January, Welch noted that the American Opinion Speakers Bureau had placed speakers before 2,000 audiences in the past year, a portion of these engagements conducted in addition to the featured evening program. Some of the speakers delivering messages across the nation included:

> Congressional Medal of Honor recipient **Lewis Millett**
> Lithuanian-American immigrant **Vilius Brazenas**
> Foreign policy expert **Patricia Hurley**
> Economics authority **Robert Adelmann**
> Highly decorated Vietnam veteran **Patrick Mahoney**
> Research specialist and future editor **Gary Benoit**
> Author and researcher **William McIlhany**
> Second Amendment scholar **William Caru**th
> Energy authority **Cliff Nolte**

Free enterprise stalwart **Frank Fortkamp**
Regulatory agency opponent **Charles Smith**
Veteran writer/speaker **Alan Stang**

These fruitful efforts then became supplemented by seminars conducted under the label **BEST** (Birch Educational Service Team). The most prestigious **BEST** seminars featured the tandem of Alaska State Senator Clyde Lewis and Congressman Larry McDonald. These two members of the Society's Council had already delivered six seminars in 1979 and they continued to present their powerful commentaries in the months ahead.

A measure calling for a national holiday in honor of Martin Luther King had been defeated in the previous session of Congress. But it was reintroduced and eventually passed despite the efforts of JBS members who contacted members of Congress and shared Society-produced pamphlets full of damaging information about King's background and career.

The Society issued commentary about a new form of deceiving the public entitled "A Communist Is A Communist." Exposing the on-again, off-again designation by the U.S. government of Communist dictatorships as good or bad, its few words showed how the American people were being buffaloed with assurance that the USSR was good and Communist China was bad. Then, a few years or even a few months later, the Moscow-led Communists were labeled bad and the Beijing-led Communists became good. Back and forth went the designations of good and bad Communists. This incredible style of switching designations of America's enemies occurred regularly. Written by me, reproducible master copies of the flyer were supplied to JBS members for their own distribution. The flyer invited readers to send for a copy of *The Insiders* book. Interest in the book increased.

Sales of *Teddy Bare* received a sizable boost when the book received an endorsement from the Scuba diver who retrieved the body of Mary Jo Kopechne from Senator Ted Kennedy's submerged auto. Like many others, the diver never accepted the explanation given by the Kennedy team. The author of this revealing book, Prince Michel Sturdza of Romania, happened to be a determined foe of Communism and a close friend of Robert Welch. A frequent visitor to the United States, Sturdza's book showed how 200 years of Massachusetts law had been brushed aside so that Kennedy would not be held accountable and prosecuted for his role in the tragedy.

Soon, the Society recommended another book about Senator Kennedy and the entire Kennedy family. *Ted Kennedy: In Over His Head* by Gary Allen told of the tawdry exploits of the family's patriarch Joseph and the last of his sons, Senator Ted.

The conversion of Rhodesia from a prosperous nation to a land of shortages and terror had finally been completed. Robert Mugabe's terrorist faction had succeeded in a complete takeover. A substantial number of Rhodesians had actually formed their own JBS chapter in the city of Bulawayo. These good people were obviously distraught after Mugabe had successfully seized power. The development amounted to a clear victory for Communism engineered by Henry Kissinger – something the Society had tried to prevent. The May *Bulletin* published the text of one of many letters sent by these Rhodesians to Society headquarters. In part, it stated, "We now have a Marxist-terrorist Prime Minister in Rhodesia, soon to be Zimbabwe."

Book sales continued to boost morale at JBS headquarters. One of the largest book wholesalers in the United States ordered more than 2,000 copies of *None Dare Call It Conspiracy*. The husband and wife team of James and Marti Hefley asked for and received help from the Society for researching and then distributing their book, *The Secret File On John Birch*. Welch announced that sales of *The Blue Book of The John Birch Society* had passed the one million mark.

A new JBS filmstrip entitled "Feast or Famine" showed how federal regulations were financially starving many small farmers and steering America's food supply into the hands of several huge corporations. The program contained comments from two congressmen: Georgia's Larry McDonald and Idaho's Steve Symms. Welch condemned the U.S. government's delivery of $4 million to Panama's Communist leader – which meant that our nation had not only transferred ownership of the American-built canal to a Communist-led government but had paid its Communist leaders to take it.

The success achieved by showing "The Insiders" filmstrip and distributing its text in booklet form led Society staffer and *Bulletin* columnist Bill Fall to urge more showings and distributions. Claiming that the use of these two items had "soundly jolted the Conspiracy," he pointed out that David Rockefeller, the leader of both the CFR and the Trilateral Commission, had found a need to defend the Conspiracy's one-world scheme in a speech before the World Affairs Council in Los Angeles. A lengthy portion of his remarks showed up in several key newspapers. What he said showed him being seriously rattled. His concerns were made obvious even in publications friendly to him and his one-world scheme.

JBS educational successes created so much angst within the Establishment that various portions of the liberal media began mentioning the Society again. Much of this attention insisted that the Society was a small fringe group deserving of no attention, an obvious contradiction. House Speaker Tip O'Neill (D-Mass.) weighed in with his claim that "the John Birchers control the Republican Party." That was a strange claim inasmuch as the lone Society member in Congress at the time was Larry McDonald – a Democrat. Tom Hill commented about this new flurry of attention by recalling Welch's response when he was accused 20 years earlier of "stealing the Republican Party." Welch countered immediately that it was "the first time I've ever been accused of petty larceny."

The Society's Western Islands book division published *Nicaragua Betrayed*, a book written by journalist Jack Cox after he had conducted many interviews with Nicaragua's now-deposed former leader, Anastasio Somoza. Having fled for his life to Paraguay, Somoza provided details of the many steps taken against him and his country by the Carter administration. A graduate of our nation's West Point military academy and a great admirer of the United States, Somoza found himself betrayed by numerous U.S. officials he thought were friends. He was later gunned down in Paraguay where he had expected safe haven. Part of his comments appearing in the book included the following warning to Americans:

> When the United States assumes leadership, in conspiratorial fashion, to annihilate anti-Communist nations, I believe it is my duty to speak out. When I have factual evidence that the United States of America had actually aided and abetted the evil forces of Communism, I believe the people of the United States should share in such facts and incontrovertible manifestations.

A version of *Nicaragua Betrayed* was soon issued in the Spanish language and shared with many in Latin America.

The Birch Log exposed a plan developed by UNESCO to gain control of journalists and their work by requiring them to register and receive credentials from the UN agency. The scheme drew outraged opposition from Birchers and their friends – and from several angry journalists – and was soon scrapped. It proved to be another small victory achieved by the Society. Welch then mentioned a small book published by Larry McDonald's Western Goals organization about what had befallen Nicaragua's Somoza. *Ally Betrayed ... Nicaragua* covered the Somoza story in 120 pages, a more easily read version than the 448 pages in the Cox book mentioned above.

The *Bulletin* noted with delight that the American Legion, meeting in its annual convention, had issued a resolution calling on Congress to investigate the Trilateral Commission and the Council on Foreign Relations. The concluding paragraph of the Legion's Resolution 773 stated:

> *RESOLVED, by the American Legion in National Convention that we demand in the best interest of our country that the Congress of the United States launch a comprehensive investigation into the Trilateral Commission and its parent organization, the Council on Foreign Relations, to determine what influence has been and is being exerted over the foreign and domestic policies of the United States.*

Copies of this resolution were immediately made available for Society members to share with the public, and especially with leaders of the Legion in their own communities. They were urged to offer to show "The Insiders" filmstrip at the local Legion post. Some local officials of this prominent veteran's organization did view the program and then scheduled a time for a showing so their members could see why the Legion itself had issued the resolution.

The November *Bulletin* contained a reproduction of Congressman McDonald's four-page "Open Letter to President Carter." Initially published in mid-October as a full-page advertisement in the *New York Times*, its text questioned the Carter administration's role in helping to advance Communism in Nicaragua, El Salvador, Panama, Cuba, Red China, South Korea, Cambodia, Rhodesia, South Africa, Afghanistan, and Iran. Coming as it did only a few weeks before the 1980 presidential election, the "Open Letter" surely impacted the thinking of some voters. President Carter did suffer defeat at the hands of Ronald Reagan in that November 1980 election.

Commenting on the recent congressional elections, the December *Bulletin* noted that 29 senators who supported the Panama Canal giveaway had either suffered defeat for reelection or had decided to retire. The most important Senate vote for or against the giveaway (there was no vote in the House) occurred on March 16, 1978. It passed 68-32, which meant that a shift of two votes away from favoring the giveaway would have defeated the measure because of the need for two-thirds support. In 1978, President Carter had worked hard for the reelection of numerous Democrat senators. He ruefully admitted that his efforts favoring the Canal giveaway had cost him – and numerous senators – their posts.

The 19 defeated senators (not all in the same year and not all Democrats) were Anderson (Minn.), Clark (Iowa), Haskell (Col.), Hathaway (Me.), McIntyre (N.H.), Brooke (Mass.), Case (NJ), Bayh (Ind.), Church (Idaho), Culver (Iowa), Durkin (N.H.), Gravel (Alaska) Magnuson (Wash.), McGovern (S.Dak.), Morgan (N.Car.), Nelson (Wisc.), Stone (Fla.), Talmadge (Ga.), and Javits (NY). Ten other pro-giveaway senators chose not to run for reelection. These were Abourezk (S.Dak.), Hatfield (Mont.), Hodges (Ark.), Humphrey (Minn.), Sparkman (Ala.), Pearson (Kansas), Muskie (Me.), Ribicoff (Conn.), Stevenson (Ill.), and Bellmon (Okla.).

In the final *Bulletin* of 1980, Welch reemphasized that the overall plan of the Society would continue to rely on education first and action that followed. He stressed the necessity of helping fellow Americans understand enduring principles, unvarnished history, current events, and the need for creating awareness among the people. He insisted that political victories would follow only after a sufficient number of Americans were made aware of the wonders of our nation's foundations and the threats posed by enemies from within attempting to destroy them. He then listed numerous accomplishments that the JBS efforts had brought about. These included:

- Wider understanding about the United Nations;
- The need to Support Your <u>Local</u> Police – and keep them Independent;
- Blocking the plans of homegrown terrorists such as New Mexico's Reies Tijerina, the leaders of the American Indian Movement, and various Civil Rights activists;
- Stopping passage of dangerous federal legislation such as the Genocide Treaty, Atlantic Union Pact, postcard voter registration, Common Situs Picketing, and various gun control measures;
- Calling attention to the harm being done by sex education in the schools;
- Blocking passage of the Equal Rights Amendment;
- Publicizing the incredible giveaway of the Panama Canal and providing voters with sufficient information to have supporters of the giveaway defeated or forced into retirement;
- Protecting the First Amendment's free speech clause with the court victory that exonerated TRIM and protected the right of all Americans to publicize the voting record of their elected officials;
- Numerous smaller victories at state and local levels.

CHAPTER 42
1981: REAGAN DOESN'T DELIVER

Ten pages of the initial 1981 *Bulletin* carried the text of a speech given by JBS Council Member Father Francis Fenton at the 1980 Rocky Mountain Rally For God and Country. Entitled "Can We Win? – Will We Win?" the Connecticut priest won high praise from the throng who attended the very successful event. Especially impressed with the speech was JBS Executive Vice President Tom Hill who considered it "one of the finest speeches ever given."

The text of several radio broadcasts of the Alan Stang Report stressed the vital "need for guns." Stang also focused attention on the Trilateral Commission (TC), the Council on Foreign Relations (CFR), and members of either or both who held key posts in the disappointing Reagan administration. Certainly included among those causing concern were Vice President George H.W. Bush, Secretary of State Alexander Haig (soon replaced by George Shultz), Defense Secretary Caspar Weinberger, Secretary of the Treasury Donald Regan, and Secretary of Commerce Malcolm Baldridge. All had CFR or TC credentials – or both. Welch cautioned members to refrain from over-optimism about the forthcoming Reagan administration.

Members were then encouraged to distribute copies of "Social Security Is Broke," Dan Smoot's analysis of the costly program and his recommendations for corrective action. Welch wrote of having received his niece's request for an assessment of the Electoral College. After supplying some facts about its origins and history, he summed up his attitude about the unique method of choosing a President with a terse "Leave it alone!" Members were urged to purchase and read *The Tax-Exempt Foundations*, Bill McIlhany's valuable exposure of Rockefeller, Ford, Carnegie, and other foundations that had not only escaped taxation but were major supporters of a variety of left-wing groups and causes.

Bill Dunham compiled numerous reasons why everyone should read Donald Lambro's book, *Fat City: How Washington Wastes Your Taxes*. Dunham remarked that he had sent a copy to the Washington office of David Stockman, the Director of Management and Budget, and was then pleased to note that the federal government had ordered copies for all cabinet secretaries. Members were then asked to promote passage of bills introduced in Congress to abolish OSHA and the Departments of Education and Energy. President Reagan had promised to dissolve these two cabinet-level departments. But he never even tried.

As federal indebtedness increased, the Society launched a campaign entitled "No Trillion Dollar Debt." Members distributed reprints of pertinent articles about the rising debt from *The Review Of The News* and *American Opinion*. Readers were requested to write letters to their congressman about rising red ink totals. Note was made of Alan Stang's arduous schedule of speaking events. In a five-week period during July and August, he delivered his "No Trillion Dollar Debt" speech 25 times. Other speakers completed similarly grueling tours, though none as demanding as the one Stang had just completed. The Society then produced a single-page proclamation calling for "No Trillion Dollar Debt." It featured spaces for citizens to place their signatures and directions about how to forward copies to appropriate members of Congress whose names were listed on the document.

Welch recommended Phoebe Courtney's booklet discussing the top-heavy infestation of members of the Trilateral Commission and the Council on Foreign Relations into the Reagan Administration. After having strongly indicated that he would not let it happen, President Reagan had reversed course and named numerous INSIDERS to key posts, a development that severely disappointed many supporters.

Welch then cited a portion of a letter received from a New England based professor of economics. After viewing the filmstrip *Overview of Our World*, the professor commented: "I have been fighting this thing all my life and never knew until now what I was really fighting." He happily joined the Society.

The plight of POWs began to receive well-deserved attention. Combined with a cry of "No Reparations" for the Communist governments that had now overrun Vietnam and neighboring nations, an article from *American Opinion* entitled "Bring Them Home" became a campaign weapon. Many Society members had already been distributing reprints of "The Missing," an *American Opinion* article penned by Bill Hoar. All who would subscribe or extend their subscription to *The Review Of The News* would receive a copy of Bob Lee's carefully written and thoroughly documented new book, *The United Nation's Conspiracy*.

Within his new essay "Confusion Worse Confounded," Welch mentioned that the genesis of what he termed his "most infamous book," *The Politician*, was a lengthy 1954 letter he sent to J. Howard Pew, one of his close friends who was at the time President of the Sun Oil Company. He also mentioned his visit in Dallas with N. Bunker Hunt, another close friend known for his involvement in the petroleum industry. Hunt, who later became a member of the Society's Council, showed Welch a huge map hanging on a wall in his office. It pointed out the Hunt-financed pipeline in Libya that was built to carry oil to a Mediterranean port for shipment anywhere in the world. When asked, Hunt said that building that pipeline had cost $74 million. Hunt didn't know at the time that Muammar Gaddafi would soon confiscate the Hunt-owned Libya creation.

CHAPTER 43
1982: ERA SUFFERS DESERVED DEFEAT

In the first *Bulletin* of 1982, Gary Handy cautioned all "who should know better" that Ronald Reagan's election did not mean victory over the Conspiracy. Yes, he noted, several prominent left-wingers in Congress had been defeated. Yes, the 1980 election produced a President who promised what conservatives surely wanted. And yes, there was an apparent tilt toward creating a strong national defense. Also, the expected passage of the Equal Rights Amendment had been blocked and it appeared that some tax cuts would follow. There were "numerous reasons for optimism" wrote Handy. But a close look at what had been accomplished showed a need for much more work before celebrating a rout of well-entrenched forces determined to establish world tyranny.

Under the heading "Opportunities for the New Year," Handy pointed to the need for members to devote time toward a) the still sputtering economy that could be revived if members could create wider use of the still-existing TRIM program; b) educating many more about the Federal Reserve and promoting its eventual replacement by sound money; c) alerting fellow Americans about the attack on the nation's religious and cultural underpinnings with widespread distribution of the anti-Humanism book *The Siecus Circle*; d) urging Congress to put clamps on the judiciary; e) informing fellow Americans about the plight of POWs and MIAs left behind in Southeast Asia; f) maintaining the right to keep and bear arms; and g) building more support for the drive to withdraw from the United Nations.

The *Bulletin* provided a brief accounting of the remarkable economic and political stability achieved in Chile after Chileans rescued their country from Communist control in 1973. Members were asked to send letters to President Reagan encouraging him to increase efforts on behalf of POWs still held captive in Vietnam. The Society's filmstrip program *Marijuana: A High Risk* received praise from Congressman McDonald and numerous chiefs of police, some of whom sent letters to the Society endorsing the program. The filmstrip's text became available in booklet format.

Members were reminded of the American Legion's 1981 resolution asking Congress to investigate the Trilateral Commission and the Council on Foreign Relations. Not to be outdone, the Veterans of Foreign Wars followed with their own resolution seeking a similar investigation of the two world-government-promoting organizations. Bill Guidry expressed concern about the many liberal and internationalist-minded Reagan appointees and the willingness of the administration to soft-pedal or even back-pedal on promises candidate Reagan had made during the 1980 campaign.

Gun control enthusiasts throughout the nation were dismayed by the action taken in Morton Grove, Illinois, where an ordinance banning the possession of handguns within the community had been enacted. Several months later, Mayor Darvin Purdy of Kennesaw, Georgia, steered a measure through his city's governing body that required every head of a household to possess a firearm and a supply of ammunition. His suburban community near Atlanta had been victimized by repeated burglaries and armed attacks committed by Atlantans who had committed their crimes and speedily headed back to Atlanta.

When the ordinance requiring citizens to have a gun in their homes received wide publicity, the burglaries and armed attacks in Kennesaw ceased. Then, when Mayor Purdy learned that San Francisco Mayor Diane Feinstein had copied the program given by Morton Grove and enacted a measure banning gun ownership, he sent her a request that she send to Kennesaw all the guns collected as a result of her city's new campaign. He explained he wanted to give some of those weapons to his city's poorer residents. Mayor Purdy then traveled to San Francisco where he delivered the featured speech at the Society's November 1982 Council Dinner.

Council on Foreign Relations President Winston Lord defended his organization for three hours on a Nashville, Tennessee, radio station. As the Society's Public Relations Director, I accepted the station's invitation for a three-hour rebuttal. The host for both programs confessed that even though he had listened to the CFR President for three hours, he learned far more about the CFR from the Birch Society spokesman. Note was made in the *Bulletin* that, in past years, the Society had to defend itself on radio shows. But now, the CFR was forced to defend its record, a welcome change.

Note was made of President Reagan's changed attitude whereby he would now seek only a "cut in the rate of increase" in taxation, not a cut in the amount of taxation itself that he had promised. Welch warmly congratulated me for Birch Log column showing the duplicity of Mr. Reagan.

Reprints of Bill Guidry's *American Opinion* article "Hanoi Jane" became instantly popular. In booklet format, Bill supplied details about movie star Jane Fonda's disgraceful trip to North Vietnam, her hob-nobbing with the North Vietnamese killers of Americans, and her willingness to be paraded before American POWs in their prison. While in North Vietnam, she even posed for photographs showing her happily seated at an anti-aircraft weapon of the very type regularly employed to down America's fighter planes.

An intensified campaign spreading fear about a possible nuclear war had already shaped the thinking of many Americans. Propaganda calling for a "nuclear freeze" on the production, deployment and testing of nuclear weaponry led many to support American-Soviet agreements, and even have our nation freeze its own arsenal no matter what the Soviets did. To combat this subversive campaign, the Society issued a six-page pamphlet I composed. Entitled "What About Nuclear Madness?" it sought to dispel fears spreading across the nation about nuclear weapons. The pamphlet helped good sense prevail.

Congressman McDonald's Western Goals Foundation announced the availability of a 58-minute film entitled "No Place To Hide: The History and Strategy of Terrorism." The very first program created to explain how terrorism is regularly employed to destroy a nation or propel new leaders to power, this film did much to alert JBS members and their audiences to a threat that would become an even greater concern in the years ahead.

Society members were delighted when a newsletter from the United Nations Association of the United States pointed to the success being achieved by the JBS Summer Camp program. West Coast Society official Joe Mehrten cited the following excerpt from the pro-UN organization's newsletter *The Inter Dependent*. It stated:

> The John Birch Society is employing a new weapon in its crusade against liberal internationalism. According to *Newsweek*, the group runs a chain of 11 summer camps which, in addition to sports, offer seminars with titles like "The United Nations – Get the US Out," and "What Is Communism?" Birch officials seem to be winning the battle for the minds and hearts of the young. Three-quarters of the campers go on to enlist in the Society.

In August, Welch announced the inauguration of a new petition – this one addressed to the President and members of Congress with the title "Stop Building Communist Missiles." It pointed to the U.S. policy of sending the Soviet Union and its satellite nations such strategically vital items as ball-bearing manufacturing equipment, sophisticated computers, advanced optical devices, an entire truck factory, and loans and credits to purchase all these items. The petition sought to have our nation cease supplying the Communists with the equipment and the financing needed to build the weaponry used to threaten the West. Many of the transactions involved in transferring material to the USSR had to gain U.S. government permission, a formality that was rarely denied.

To aid members in gathering the signatures and finding prospects for membership, the *Bulletin* quoted from an April 1982 speech delivered by Senator William Armstrong (R-Colo.). In remarks to his fellow senators, he stated:

> In the last ten years alone, the United States and other Western nations have sold to the Soviet Union and its satellites more than $50 billion worth of sophisticated technical equipment the Communists could not produce themselves. This equipment has been used to produce nuclear missiles, tanks and armored cars, military command and controls systems, spy satellites, and air defense radars. In addition, the Soviets have been able to purchase entire factories, designed and built by Western engineers and financed in large part by American and Western European banks. Much of the production of these factories is devoted to the manufacture of military transport, ammunition, and other logistical items for the Soviet war machine. It is difficult to overstate the extent to which the West has contributed to the military threat that now endangers our very existence.

To assist in this newest petition endeavor, the Society gathered ten previous articles from its publications and issued them in a 24-page tabloid-style newspaper format. Each of the articles contained details about the various ways American equipment, technology and financing had been transferred to the USSR and its satellites. This tabloid became a very popular item among members who purchased copies in bundles of 50, and even larger bundles of 1,000.

Book reviewer Sally Humphries pointed to the availability of *Fire In the Minds of Men*, a 677-page history of secret organizations from their birth at the time of the 1789 French Revolution to their maturity during the Russian Revolution of 1917. Authored by Professor James H. Billington, a CFR member and a scholar with numerous left-wing credentials, Billington's work nevertheless corroborated JBS contentions about the Illuminati and its successor organizations. Educated at Harvard and through the Rhodes Scholar program in England, Billington became the Librarian of Congress and served in that post from 1987 to 2015.

Reprints of the text of my speech "Let 'Em Crumble" became the next offering for member use. It called attention to the various ways U.S. aid and trade continued to sustain the Soviet Empire and the infuriating fact that all of it was encouraged by the Reagan administration. Gary Benoit's "To Wage 'Peace'?" article exposed the government's constant reliance on fear of nuclear war to pave the way for U.S. surrender to a UN-led world government. Both of these items appeared in the October *Bulletin*, and each became a weapon in the October 24 anti-United Nations "Day of Shame" campaign.

Bob Lee's review of the accomplishments of the Society and its two affiliated magazines appeared in both the *Bulletin* and *American Opinion*. Bob noted the Society's constant stream of books and magazines and the contributions of radio broadcasts of The Alan Stang Report and the Birch Log columns. Lee also pointed to the successes achieved via the Society's summer camp program for youngsters. His own carefully researched profiles of the performances of liberal senators appearing in *The Review Of The News* had been blamed for the defeat of 10 liberal senators. The accomplishments cited in Bob's single article greatly encouraged all members.

One of my Birch Log columns excoriated the 130 U.S. Catholic Bishops who had endorsed surrender of our nation rather than remain militarily strong so that no enemy would dare attack it. The bishops were asked, "Why no outcry against supplying computers, sophisticated electronics equipment, loans, credits or anything to the tyrants running the Kremlin?"

Postal regulations requiring annual publication of paid subscription totals showed that the number of persons receiving the *Bulletin* had shrunk from 107,000 in 1981 to 52,000 in 1982. Tom Hill explained that generous donors had paid for 60,000 gift subscriptions (sent mostly to doctors) but were unable to continue financing such a program because of the economic slowdown.

Chapter 44
1983: Frail Welch Steps Aside

The year 1983 marked the 25th anniversary of the founding of the Society. With a celebration scheduled for December, preparations began early and continued throughout the year. Meanwhile JBS efforts on many fronts continued.

An announcement appeared about the availability of audio and video tapes of Congressman McDonald's superb speech "Reversing the Recession: Congress Is the Key." In it, the Georgia Congressman pointed to the deficiencies of the Reagan administration while stressing that Congress, especially the House with its power of the purse (see Article I: Section 7 of the Constitution), could cure many serious problems.

Members throughout the nation were successfully combating attempts to have government leaders at all levels approve nuclear freeze proposals. Heavily promoted initiatives were paving the way for disarmament, even acceptance of unilateral scrapping of all weapons. Several reprinted articles exposed these hard-to-believe plans.

Ten pages of the January *Bulletin* carried Bill Fall's "Get America Up In Arms!" article. Written to demonstrate that citizens not only possessed a right to be armed but were duty-bound to be able to defend themselves and their country, Fall's 10-page essay became a very popular weapon in the fight to keep and bear arms. One journalist from a major newspaper stated that he originally disagreed with the contention that individuals should be armed. But after reading Fall's essay, he reversed his stance.

Bob Lee provided little-known background information about the history of the Social Security system in the January issue of *American Opinion*. While Society members were busily spreading information and enlisting new recruits, some observant Birchers began to wonder about the health of Society Founder Robert Welch. They noted the absence of any Welch contributions in recent *Bulletins*.

After the *New York Times* published a complimentary article touting the "achievements" of the Council on Foreign Relations, the Society pointed to the utter falsity of the CFR's repeated claim that it was merely a place where important people voiced a variety of opinions without reaching any conclusions. Taking credit for "achievements" certainly required reaching conclusions.

The CFR's "achievements" named by the *Times* included our nation's post-World War II planning, acceptance of Communist domination of China, and the "framework" for an end to America's military involvement in Vietnam. The *Bulletin's* response insisted that such planning saw "the United States descend from undisputed world leadership and being admired by virtually all nations to being militarily threatened by the USSR and despised by practically everyone." Hardly achievements! Getting in bed with Red China and the disgraceful capitulation of years of effort in Vietnam by abandoning the mission were some of the nation's monumental setbacks, not achievements.

The announcement that nationally syndicated columnist Dr. Walter Williams would be the featured speaker at the March Council Dinner in Los Angeles spurred ticket sales. The Society's first formal stand against acceptance of homosexuality appeared in the February 1983 *Bulletin* when Father Enrique Rueda's book, "The Homosexual Network," received an unqualified endorsement. His much-needed examination of this topic pointed to federal funding of various homosexual groups.

After a decade of its successful use in filmstrip format, the extremely popular "Overview Of Our World" seminar became available in videotape format. Tom Hill praised its ability to tell "enough of our story so that the message has lasting value to the viewer." This new version of "Overview" presented its valuable perspective about political systems and basic economic principles, but it also included details about Insider influence within the Reagan administration. Tom Hill reported that, after announcing its availability only a few weeks ago, the Society found itself "swamped" with orders for the new production.

Members were urged to distribute copies of a laymen-produced "Open Letter To Each of the Catholic Bishops in the United States." It countered the support by the Catholic leaders of the ongoing drive toward national disarmament. That it was being backed by numerous high-ranking members of the clergy shocked, disappointed and energized many readers, not all of whom were Catholic.

At the March 12th Council Dinner in Los Angeles, Executive Committee Chairman William Grede announced the first leadership changes in the Society's 25-year history. Henceforth Lawrence P. McDonald would be Chairman; Thomas N. Hill President; and Robert Welch would step aside to become Chairman Emeritus.

Veteran members of the Society present at this momentous "changing of the guard" weren't terribly surprised by the changes. But they expressed long and thunderous gratitude to Welch and warm acceptance of the changes. Most already knew that a successor to Welch had to be appointed because of his failing health, and no one questioned the choice of Congressman McDonald and Vice President Hill to fill the organization's leadership positions. In his brief message given after the leadership changes had been announced, Welch noted that he would still be "on hand" to offer advice and support and he wished the new appointees "great success." He added, "Retirement for me from the standpoint of the normal interpretation of that word is out of the question." His remarks generated a few tears but all joined in expressing profound thanks to "the Founder" and heartfelt support for the new officials.

The Society's Speakers Bureau announced that Israeli citizen Avraham Shifrin was now available for speeches in the United States. A Russian Jew, he had spent 10 years in Soviet prison camps plus four more years in what was termed internal exile. Finally free of Soviet brutality and scrutiny, he and his wife fled to Israel where they formed an organization designed to publicize their knowledge of Soviet prisons and concentration camps. Strong opponents of U.S. aid being sent to the USSR and other Communist-led nations, this courageous couple happily affiliated with the Society and supported its efforts. The Shifrins would complete several speaking tours throughout the United States over the next several years. In each speech, Avraham told of his knowledge of Soviet tyranny and the need for the American people to publicize the fact that U.S. aid was keeping it alive.

While traveling through Virginia's Tidewater area to deliver one of his speeches, Shifrin accepted an invitation to be interviewed by Pat Robertson at his Christian Coalition's lavish headquarters. Expecting to discuss the highpoints of his speech over the Christian Broadcasting Network, he was told before the interview not to discuss the aid being supplied the USSR. Shocked and angered by such a demand, he promptly walked out of the building and never did appear on any CBN program. He reported the incident to the Society's Speakers Bureau leaders and summed up his anger about the treatment he received. "Those people are not to be trusted," he insisted. Shifrin would later produce *The First Guidebook To Prisons And Concentration Camps Of The Soviet Union,* a devastating compilation of maps, photographs, facts and testimonies about the criminal activity of the Soviet Union, all of which was being sustained by U.S. aid and trade. The *Bulletin* then informed readers about a huge response to two of my national television appearances – one on PBS and the other on C-SPAN.

The Society published a second 24-page tabloid. Under the heading "Americanist Issues," this new report contained nine major articles from *American Opinion* and *The*

Review Of The News. Most countered propaganda about the nuclear freeze hysteria sweeping the nation. The tabloid's first offering carried the headline, "Soviets Are Behind the Freeze Campaign." In addition, the smaller "Some Sober Facts About Nuclear War" written by Society ally Dr. Petr Beckmann led numerous business owners to join in the campaign against the nuclear freeze proposals.

While publicizing the "Youth Needs Truth" Summer Camp program, Joe Mehrten selected three letters among many the Society had received from parents and camp enthusiasts themselves. Here are a few encouraging examples:

> (1) *We sent our grandson to camp and even though he went with no knowledge and against his wishes, we are amazed at what he learned. He is talking everyone's ear off.... He was a non-reader and now he reads every chance he has.*
>
> (2) *I've been a member for eighteen years and many times I have been going to write and try to heap upon you just some of the praise I believe you deserve. But when my son came home from camp full of enthusiasm and added wisdom, I had to send you a big thank you! It is without a doubt the best money ever spent on my son. He plans on going again and says he has never been in the company of finer young people or had a better time.*
>
> (3) *This is my second year going to camp and I've already learned more than I could in my whole life at school. I want to thank you for making that possible.*

Topics covered at the camps included What Is Americanism, Peace Versus War, What Being a Civilized Person Means, Free Enterprise Economics, The Media and the Environment, Drug Attacks on Youth, Gun Control, Support Your Local Police, and How To Communicate With a Member of Congress. Afternoons at each camp found the campers involved in swimming, volleyball, and other sports. Evenings always featured a campfire, a variety of skits, and the singing of patriotic songs.

The May *Bulletin* summarized the lengthy effort and success in the fight against ratification of the Equal Rights Amendment. Congress had approved the measure and sent it to the states for ratification in March 1972. A time limit of seven years was set. Several states ratified quickly because their legislators had been convinced that the ERA dealt merely with equal pay for women and protection of basic human rights. But when others learned that the ERA would threaten numerous other rights while upsetting existing laws regarding marriage, childcare, inheritance, child custody and property rights, the bandwagon leading to passage hit a brick wall.

After the seven years had elapsed, the required 38 state ratifications had not been gained. Amazingly, in a highly unusual departure from precedent, Congress added another three years and three months for consideration by the states. By now however, legislators in several states had rescinded their previous approval. The campaign to add the ERA to the Constitution seemed to be over. And it did die when, after the additional three years and three months had not led to the number of needed ratifications, even the proponents had to admit defeat.

Announcement that retired Army General George S. Patton Jr. would be the featured speaker at the Denver Council Dinner in June spurred excitement throughout the Rocky Mountain states. The son of the famous World War II general (himself an Army general) discussed "The Dangers of the Peace and Freeze Movements."

With indisputable figures and documents to back his contentions, Gary Benoit showed in an important *Bulletin* article that the Reagan administration had not slowed federal spending, had not blocked another boost in the ceiling on the national debt, had not led Congress to become a right-wing body, and had not ceased providing financial assistance to Communist-led nations. Alongside these claims, the *Bulletin* showed a photo reproduction of a Federal Register document containing President Reagan's signature on an official proclamation stating that it was "in the national interest" of the United States to approve an Export-Import Bank credit to Communist China of $68,425,000. The document indicated that the loan had been extended to the Chinese government so they could purchase "steel making equipment." Gary Allen followed Benoit's analysis with his *American Opinion* article "The Terrible Cost of the Reagan Compromise."

Bill Guidry lauded an article by Bob Lee showing that the Department of Education's National Commission on Excellence in Education had reported additional decline in student performance. Nevertheless, as Guidry pointed out, the commission recommended more federal interference. Instead, the JBS scribe suggested complete removal of the federal government from education along with abolition the federal Department of Education.

Four years earlier, President Jimmy Carter had submitted a bill to Congress seeking to establish a national holiday to celebrate Martin Luther King's birthday. Even though support for the measure had grown, sufficient resistance in the Congress had kept it from passage. Introduced anew however, it sailed through to passage and gained approval from President Reagan in November 1983. The JBS *Bulletin* for September 1983 commented about the proposal as follows:

It is hard for us to believe that any Congressman remains unaware that the FBI, acting under authorization granted by Attorney General Robert Kennedy, instituted wiretaps and other forms of surveillance over King's activities for six full years. Or that this action was undertaken specifically because the FBI had evidence that King was collaborating with and being manipulated by known and secret Communists. Or that, as was done with George Orwell's fictional memory hole, a court ordered the records and tapes of this surveillance to be sealed in the National Archives until the year 2027. Or that the hiding of this material is reason enough not to honor King.

Opponents of the measure even turned to King's assessment of the Vietnam War. Congressman John Ashbrook had inserted several of King's comments about the War in the *Congressional Record* for October 4, 1967. According to King, the U.S. was "the greatest purveyor of violence in the world today," and he falsely insisted that U.S. troops "may have killed a million South Vietnamese civilians – mostly children." Referring to the Vietnamese people, King likened the efforts of U.S. forces to those of Hitler's Nazi Germany when he stated, "We test out our latest weapons on them, just as the Germans tested new medicine and new tortures in the concentration camps of Europe." Whatever one thought about the Vietnam War, these insults directed at the men who put their lives on the line constituted a pack of outrageous lies.

Far more detailed information about King's background and subversive efforts had already appeared in Society publications over the years. But all of it wasn't enough to dissuade Congress and President Reagan from honoring him by establishing the third Monday of January as a national holiday in his name.

Chapter 45
1983 Continued: McDonald Aboard KAL007

The beginning pages of the September 1983 *Bulletin* eerily dwelled on three important points raised by JBS Chairman Larry McDonald. In what turned out to be his last communication to members of the Society, McDonald called for expressions of gratitude for Founder Robert Welch, an urging to members to work even harder, and a reminder about the forthcoming 25th Anniversary celebration scheduled for early December. By the time members throughout the nation received this *Bulletin*, however, news reports informed all Americans that 269 passengers and crew members, including Chairman McDonald, were aboard a Korean Air Lines commercial jet plane when it was attacked by a Soviet fighter on September 1, 1983, on its way to Seoul, South Korea. McDonald intended to participate in ceremonies marking the 30th Anniversary of the end of the Korean War's hostilities.

On September 1, U.S. newspapers carried an Associated Press release stating unequivocally that the missing KAL plane had landed on the Soviet Union's Sakhalin Island just east of the Russian mainland. Under the headline "Missing jet lands safely," the AP quoted Harold McDonald, the missing congressman's brother who immediately relayed that message to others: "We've just heard from the State Department … that the plane is down and the passengers are safe," he stated. Harold McDonald was certainly relieved to have that assurance. The September 1 *New York Times* stated: "Early reports said the plane … had been forced down by Soviet Air Force planes and that all 240 passengers and 29 crew members were believed to be safe." But not a single one of the 269 aboard that plane has ever been seen again.

After the president of Korean Air Lines received word that all aboard the plane were safe, he started out from Seoul to go to Sakhalin Island in order to greet the plane's passengers and crew and arrange for another plane to take them to South Korea's capital city. He got as far as Japan when he was told that Japanese authorities had received word from

Soviet sources that the plane had plunged into the sea. New reports about the incident then began providing this completely different explanation about what had occurred.

After much digging, *American Opinion's* investigative reporter Robert W. Lee found sufficient evidence to conclude that the Soviet fighter had launched a heat-seeking missile hitting one of KAL 007's four engines. Further and most importantly, stated Lee, the plane had been damaged but not destroyed. He also discovered that the International Civil Aviation Organization (ICAO) had tracked the plane's descent for a full 12 minutes after it had been hit. He believed that KAL's pilots had obviously controlled the wounded plane for that length of time and the giant Boeing 747 had not crashed into the sea but was searching for a place to land. Lee concluded that they found such a place on Sakhalin Island just as the early reports of the incident claimed.

Lee's important report about the incident noted that other Boeing 747 planes had survived near catastrophic incidents and managed to land safely rather than crash. His article containing this far more plausible explanation was written after his extensive investigation and consultation with experienced airline pilots. It appeared in the September 10, 1991, issue of *The New American*. A full year later, Soviet officials delivered to South Korean personnel what were reputed to be the "black boxes" from the Korean airliner. Examination showed that they contained no information whatsoever.

For several years after this incident, while carrying out official duties as the Society's Public Relations Director, I was frequently asked to respond to questions about the incident during radio and television appearances. The most common was "Did the Society believe the plane had been attacked because McDonald was aboard?" The answer I gave over and over, was – and still is – "Yes that is our belief because nothing else makes sense. But we cannot prove it."

The front page of the October *Bulletin* carried a statement set in large bold type, "We Will *Not* Forget!" Numerous following pages carried an appropriate "In Memoriam" about Dr. McDonald written by Society President Thomas N. Hill followed by the text of the speech given by *American Opinion* Managing Editor Scott Stanley to 4,000 who gathered in Washington's Constitution Hall to remember Larry McDonald and his many fellow passengers who disappeared. The Society issued a press release urging that the United States should "recognize the Soviet Union for what it is – an outlaw, criminal regime – and withdraw diplomatic recognition." Sadly, that demand received next to no backing in the Congress.

Larry McDonald's last comment to members – appearing in that September *Bulletin* – stated: "The John Birch Society has the formula and is supplying the tools. This is the time for members and staff to fill the role in history that stands as a challenge before us."

Mourning Put Aside; Society's Work Continues

Without either Robert Welch or Larry McDonald as its leader, the Society plunged ahead under direction supplied by President Hill. Immediately, the campaign known as "Stop Building Communist Missiles" and the continuing call for terminating all aid and trade with Communist nations was appropriately renamed "The Larry McDonald Crusade To Stop Financing Communism." JBS staffer Joe Mehrten had proposed the change, received the go-ahead from President Hill, and then served as its chairman while also carrying out his other duties at the Society's office in San Marino, California. The plan for this new Crusade included publishing reports on how the 100 senators were voting on measures dealing with aid and trade sent to Communist nations.

Mehrten then compiled a 140-page collection of "Aid and Trade Documents" containing a veritable mountain of evidence proving that our nation was indeed supplying Communist enemies. Society leaders would later suggest that the organization's efforts publicizing this treachery – the petition mentioned previously, the speeches delivered by numerous Society members and allies, the distribution of numerous articles and reprints, and the work of the Larry McDonald Crusade – led to the implosion of the Soviet Union several years later. Why that occurred has never been satisfactorily unearthed except for the revelations given by Soviet defector Anatoliy Golitsyn in his remarkable 1984 book *New Lies For Old*. A veteran of many years of high level intelligence work for the Kremlin, Golitsyn quit communism and did his best to warn the West about the coming implosion of the Soviet Union. He predicted that the Berlin Wall would be torn down, a younger leader with a liberal image (Mikhail Gorbachev?) would emerge, and a neutral socialist Europe would be created. All of what this high level former Soviet official suggested did indeed occur.

In the November *Bulletin*, Mehrten quoted a portion of the May 25, 1983, commencement speech given by Secretary of the Navy John Lehman to the graduating class at the Naval Academy. Lehman told the latest group of newly commissioned Navy and Marine Corps officers:

> Within weeks, many of you will be looking across just hundreds of feet of water at some of the most modern technology ever invented in America. **Unfortunately, it is on Soviet ships.** (Emphasis added.)

The leader of the Larry McDonald Crusade then cited several other protests about the aid going to Communist countries. He was happy to include a statement given by *New York Times* columnist William Safire who, after listing several examples of help being supplied to our nation's chief enemy, concluded, "Not only do we aid the Russians militarily, we strengthen them economically and strategically."

A second edition of my "The Insiders" paperback book became available. The new book's Part I contained the terse but vivid description of both the Council on Foreign Relations and the Trilateral Commission and their domination over the Carter administration. Its Part II dealt with similar domination by members of these one-world promoting organizations over the Reagan administration. The book's Appendix published the latest membership rosters of both the CFR and TC. The small book's popularity soared.

The final *Bulletin* for the year 1983 led off with one more invitation to all to attend the Society's 25th Anniversary celebration in Indianapolis on December 9-10. Executive Committee Chairman Wm. J. Grede thanked all members for their "unselfish labors and many sacrifices … despite significant obstacles along the way." He congratulated all "for their successes and the positive influence we have had on the American people for a quarter century." In the last short piece he ever wrote for the *Bulletin*, Welch led off with the text of his short poem initially published many years earlier in the old *Boston Record*.

AT TWENTY

If, fifty years from now, when I survey
The scanty roll of things that I have done,
I find a score of visions unfulfilled
And victories I dreamed of still unwon,
I'll doubtless see mistakes that I have made
And places where I lost because I picked
the losing side;
But not a failure shall I find
In the trail I've left behind,
Where I might have won but didn't, just because
I never tried.

The extremely successful 25th Anniversary celebration turned out to be a combination of joy over the Society's many accomplishments, sadness over the loss of Larry McDonald, and the failing health of Robert Welch.

At the anniversary's December 9 morning session emceed by Alan Stang, messages were delivered by me, staff members Bill Cherry and Joe Mehrten, Council Member

General Andrew Gatsis, Major League baseball star Eric Show, and the greatly loved Julia Brown. Her final comment evoking a tremendous response stated, "Martin Luther King had his dream; Jesse Jackson had his scheme; but Julia Brown is part of a great team – The John Birch Society."

Following the event's luncheon, with Western District Governor Charles Armour acting as Emcee, a member of the Indianapolis City Council, a Society member himself, presented the Keys of the City to Welch. Armour then introduced five Council Members who shared their memories and experiences in a session labeled "What the Society Has Meant to Me." They were: Glenn Schmitz from Minnesota, Elisha Poole from Alabama, Nelson Bunker Hunt from Texas, Walter Ruckel from Florida, and Clyde Lewis from Alaska. Nelson Bunker Hunt's comments ended with:

> Rome wasn't built in a day. And a well-entrenched Conspiracy's grip on our country isn't going to be removed in a day. But there is hope that the job can be done. And there is no organization that has the potential for doing it other than this one. For that, we thank Robert Welch.

In a stirring speech winding up the afternoon session, *American Opinion* Managing Editor Scott Stanley urged everyone to never forget Larry McDonald.

The evening banquet saw Robert W. Stoddard and Wm. J. Grede, both founding members of the Society, share Emcee duties. After the invocation by George Birch, the father of John Birch (Mrs. Birch had passed away), Dan Smoot discussed the disarray of the conservative movement 25 years earlier and heaped praise on Welch for founding the Society and giving the movement new life and the American people new hope. Mrs. Larry McDonald told of her late husband's tireless efforts to promote the Society's principles and goals. New Hampshire Governor Meldrim Thomson stressed the horror and idiocy of supplying aid and trade to avowed Communist enemies. President Tom Hill spoke on behalf of the Society's tens of thousands when he turned to the Society's Founder and stated, "Thank you, Robert Welch, for giving us that which you have given, and most importantly thank you for making it possible for us to fight this battle effectively – and to win it!"

In a very emotional and fitting finale, Wm. Grede introduced Founder Welch as "a man who had accomplished the impossible, a man I am very proud to have long called my friend." After thunderous applause, the frail Robert Welch delivered the final message he would ever give to his faithful followers. To those before him and to all members throughout the nation – and in foreign nations – he said:

Thank you for all that you have done and will be doing in this epic undertaking. And, God be with you till we meet again.

The applause was resounding and lengthy as the great throng of Society members stood to show their gratitude and respect. With the celebration over, Welch went back to Belmont, Massachusetts where he continued to share his wisdom and insight with President Tom Hill, me and other staff personnel. Two days after Christmas in 1983, while in his office, he suffered a crippling stroke that took away his ability to speak, even to swallow. He spent a month in a Boston hospital and was then moved to a nearby nursing home for care. He died on January 6, 1985. A fitting memorial program, held at the Belmont, Massachusetts High School shortly afterward, drew family, Society members, and admirers from many parts of the nation.

Chapter 46
1984: Barker Named CEO

Members got a boost when the first monthly *Bulletin* of 1984 reproduced in its entirety a prominently placed *USA Today* interview of this writer. Appearing in the newspaper's December 13, 1983 issue under the headline, "Stop making deals that help Russians," numerous JBS positions appeared without any distortion or misinformation. The interview generated a tidy flood of inquiries from readers, many of whom soon became JBS members.

Included in the many comments about the 25th anniversary celebration, my Birch Log answered a question on the minds of many Americans about the Society's stress on education rather than reliance on political strategy, a course regularly recommended by many others. The column stated:

> Does the Birch program work? Ask former Senators McGovern, Bayh, Church and a dozen more. Ask the American Indian Movement, the Equal Rights Amendment promoters, and scores of ex-Congressmen. Ask the millions who have been helped to understand so many issues and so many politicians because they benefited from a Birch perspective. Ask those who have a better appreciation of the American system that should have been provided in school, and about the performance of the nation's politicians. Then, ask many politicians how they benefited from a Birch perspective. It does indeed work, and it continues to reach more millions day by day.

Growing disapproval of the United Nations throughout the nation led to an announcement by a State Department spokesman that the United States would withdraw at the end of 1984 from the United Nations Educational, Scientific, and Cultural Organization (UNESCO). Society leaders justifiably claimed some credit for that development. A somewhat nervous Secretary of State George Shultz, quickly pointed out that the step soon to be taken "does not presage any wider disengagement from the United Nations or its specialized agencies."

Alongside the many Speakers Bureau regulars delivering their important messages throughout the nation, the Bureau added the team of Roy and Sandy McKesson who unabashedly condemned the nation's public school system. In addition, KGB defector Thomas Schuman told audiences of his inside knowledge about "Communist Use of the Free World's Press," and young Costa Rican Willy Solis who, as a leader of an anti-Communist youth movement in his country, was able to discuss "The Communist Threat in Central America." Sadly, this courageous young man was murdered shortly after returning to his home in Costa Rica.

The *Bulletin* aimed sharp criticism at President Reagan for welcoming Communist China's Premier Zhao Ziyang to America, for granting Most Favored Nation status to the Beijing regime, for refusing to allow the sale of fighter planes to the anti-Communist government in Taiwan, and for signing agreements resulting in transfers of technology and guidance systems to the Communist dictators in Beijing.

Leaders of The Larry McDonald Crusade To Stop Financing Communism included Mrs. Kathryn McDonald (Honorary Chairman), Retired U.S. Army Brigadier General and JBS Council Member Andrew Gatsis (National Chairman), and Joseph Mehrten (National Director). A six-page pamphlet describing the Crusade's work focused attention on the transfer to the Soviet Union of precision ball-bearing machines, computer technology, entire computer systems, and a huge truck manufacturing facility.

After the loss of JBS Chairman Larry McDonald, Executive Committee Chairman Wm. J. Grede filled the now-vacant leadership post on a temporary basis. Aided in every detail by President Hill, Bill Grede then created a "Long-range Planning Committee" made up of veteran members of the Society's Council who were tasked with the responsibility of recommending a new Chairman. After a great deal of discussion, the Committee members chose one of their own, A. Clifford Barker. The selection won speedy approval from the Society's Executive Committee and the full Council. Barker's acceptance of the post was then publicly announced at the Los Angeles Council Dinner on March 3. 1984. The Society again had a full-time Chairman/CEO.

Born in Arizona in 1933, A. Clifford Barker (who always preferred to be known as Clif with a single "f") distinguished himself early in life as a concert-level musician and brilliant scientist. He served as an electronics instructor for the U.S. Marine Corps while still a student at UCLA. He graduated with honors, advanced his education in the field of electronics, won several awards, and actually held posts in several aerospace firms while earning graduate degrees. In 1973 he formed Navidyne Corporation, a leading producer of satellite navigation systems for ships at sea. A member of the Society since 1961 and a diligent student of its program, his admiration for Robert Welch and what that man had accomplished was second to none.

The March *Bulletin* began with my Foreword entitled "Time Is Running Out." Dwelling on rising federal indebtedness and its eventual consequences, it was immediately reprinted and distributed widely at a time when the admitted national debt had not yet reached the $1 trillion plateau. Many Americans who read it became aware of some basic economic facts. The eight-page article also pointed to the failure of the Reagan administration to live up to its claim of being a bedrock opponent of deficit spending.

At their annual meeting in their home state, the South Carolina congressional delegation (two senators and six House members) heard five-minute messages from the six South Carolina TRIM chairmen. And the South Carolina JBS Coordinator then used additional time to explain to all of those elected officials what TRIM Committees were doing nationally and how each local effort was generating opposition to reckless federal spending. The eight congressional members from the Palmetto State became even more respectful of The John Birch Society's educational program.

The Society's newly created Birch Research Incorporated (BRI) division produced a 64-page "Directory of the 98th Congress." The booklet contained helpful instructions about how to contact members of Congress, the voting records of members of the previous Congress, how to conduct meetings, and much more.

Tom Hill chided President Reagan for publicly claiming that the U.S. and Communist China may have "some differences … but there are many things we have in common that can be mutually beneficial." In his statement, Mr. Reagan had explained that America had an unofficial relationship with the anti-Communist Chinese on Taiwan but that it was "with the people of Taiwan, not Taiwan itself." In other words, the betrayal of the Nationalist Chinese ally would continue. On another topic, Charles Armour contended that the nuclear freeze promoters would have "great difficulty attracting a crowd" if they didn't include rock music bands and Hollywood stars at their rallies.

John Fall reminded Society members in his "Bring Them Home" section of the *Bulletin* that "almost 2,500 Americans left behind in Southeast Asia have yet to be accounted for." He urged wider distribution of the *American Opinion* article "The Missing," especially to candidates for political office and their supporters. Very few of the 2,500 left behind were ever seen again.

During his visit to China, President Reagan signed a treaty enabling U.S. firms to sell China nuclear reactors, fuel, and engineering services. The President received a promise from Chinese authorities that none of this material would be used for nuclear weaponry.

Bill Guidry commented, "… if the Communists in China keep their promise as faithfully as they have all others, President Reagan might go down in history as the most imperceptive U.S. negotiator since General Custer."

Reporters Discover Baseball Players in JBS

Eric Show was not only a successful pitcher for the San Diego Padres baseball team, he was also well versed in a variety of academic pursuits. His teammates often referred to him as "the Professor." On a summer day in 1983 when baseball didn't consume most of his time, Eric happened by the San Diego American Opinion Bookstore. Intrigued as he was by books, he chatted with the Society volunteer and soon purchased a copy of Gary Allen's *None Dare Call It Conspiracy*. He read it, told several teammates about it, and purchased copies for them. Soon a regular customer, he devoured several other Birch-recommended books and joined the Society. Before too long, teammates Dave Dravecky and Mark Thurmond, also became JBS members.

The three baseball players soon appeared with local Society members at a JBS booth erected at the annual fair in nearby Del Mar. They greeted passersby, signed autographs, and urged the people to purchase some JBS literature. All of this was deemed remarkable by local newspapermen who wrote about the three in the sports section of the local newspaper. Then a lengthy article about the trio and their connection to JBS appeared in the *Los Angeles Times* where interviews with other players and team officials were featured. Then, the Associated Press issued its own report claiming there were confrontations between the three Birchers and their black teammates. Sports pages across the nation then repeated that nasty falsehood.

Garry Templeton and Alan Wiggins, two black Padres teammates, quickly sought to correct the false claim of racial unrest within the team. Templeton said, "I've known that Eric was a member of the John Birchers for two years, and it was never an issue. We've kidded about it, just like I kid around about a lot of things. I think someone is trying to distract us." Alan Wiggins added, "I saw the eleven o'clock news and it really got me angry. They stated that Wiggins and Templeton charged three Padres with racism. It really blew me away." The two knew that the Society members had been falsely accused but Wiggins indicated that the integrity and character of those teammates stood for something. "They're good guys, good Christians," he said while refusing to corroborate the accusations blared by the press. Show responded to the completely false charges of racism and anti-Semitism with, "We're against any 'ism' that takes away from God, country, and love. My lawyer is Jewish, my financial adviser is Spanish, and I support a Black minister."

After several days of whirlwind coverage attempting to disparage the three Major League players who had joined the Society, each actually pitched a complete game shutout. Players on other teams sought information about the Society from Show and his mates, or from the Society itself. Some from other teams soon joined the Society. There was joking about the possibility that the Society would field its own baseball team. As mentioned previously, Eric Show then gladly accepted the invitation to speak at the Society's 25th anniversary celebration where he was warmly welcomed.

Staff official Joe Mehrten then happily told of the very positive press coverage of the Society's summer camp program. Articles appeared in California's *Santa Ana Register* and Colorado's *Rocky Mountain News*. The Associated Press repeated portions of those reports, and its coverage appeared throughout the nation. The *Bulletin* announced the availability of Bill Hoar's magnificent history book entitled *Architects of Conspiracy*. Anyone purchasing a year's subscription to *American Opinion* received a copy of the $19.95 book.

Chairman Clif Barker told of visiting with Welch at the nursing home. He and several other colleagues detected no improvement in the condition of the Society's Founder. Barker commented:

> Let us never forget what this man has done to make it possible for us to continue enjoying the freedom our nation's founding fathers gained for us. In 1958, Robert Welch was capable of enjoying life to its fullest. His intellectual pursuits ranged from pure mathematics to poetry, from history to languages. He loved to travel and he loved being a host, especially for small groups of friends, where he could entertain them with a recitation of poetry, argue the probability of some obscure mathematical theorem, or pursue the reasons why all tomato products should be outlawed.
>
> Mr. Welch was more thoroughly prepared to enjoy and to be fulfilled in later years of life than anyone I have ever met. But sometime in the mid-1950s, he made a conscious decision to forego all chance of enjoying any of the intellectual, social, and travel pleasures he enjoyed so much. When he founded The John Birch Society, he decided to lay down his life, not in a single dramatic act of heroism, but slowly, bit-by-bit in a twenty-five year effort to build the one body of men and women that could win this battle between the forces of light and the forces of darkness.

CHAPTER 47
1985-86: FINANCIAL WOES; ARMOUR CEO

The remarkable individual who launched the Society and directed it for 25 years passed away at age 85 on January 6, 1985. Appropriate tributes and memories appeared in both *American Opinion* and *The Review Of The News*. In the Society's *Bulletin*, Chairman Barker delivered some of his own thoughts about the death of the man revered by all Birch Society members. Among numerous personal attributes and accomplishments that had set Robert Welch apart, Barker pointed to the extraordinary determination of the Society's Founder. In 1958, as Welch brought his two-day presentation to a close, he told the group before him, "… there is no force and no discouragement which would make me quit or even put less of my life and energy into the struggle." That struggle, of course, could be summed up as the fight to preserve our country – indeed our civilization – from being overcome by a godless conspiracy seeking to enslave all of mankind.

Barker also saw fit to quote a centuries-old passage from Edmund Burke that aptly portrayed the role played by Welch over many decades. Burke wrote:

> How often has public calamity been arrested on the very brink of ruin by the seasonable energy of one man? … One vigorous mind without office, without situation, without public functions of any kind … I say one such man confiding in the aid of God, and full of just reliance on his own fortitude, vigor, enterprise, and perseverance, would first draw to him some few like himself, and then multitudes hardly thought to be in existence would appear and troop around him.

Describing Welch as a "beacon of hope" and "a powerful and courageous force for truth," Barker spoke for all Birchers in saying that "we have been blessed with the privilege of knowing this great man through his millions of words of wise counsel, penetrating insight, and clear purpose." As "recipients of his gifts of wisdom and understanding, we are well-equipped to carry on his work in this great struggle."

No Break in the Society's Work

There was joy among Birch Society staff and members when President Reagan withdrew the U.S. from UNESCO. A closer look at the President's proclamation, however, showed that the U.S. would resume membership "when UNESCO returns to its original purposes and principles." For all the years of its existence, however, UNESCO's purpose had been to promote Marxism. The UN agency had even taken steps toward a freedom-destroying "New International Economic Order." Also, the funds no longer going to UNESCO were being forwarded to other UN agencies. UNICEF put its share to use by supporting such pro-Communist organizations as the terrorist South West Africa People's Organization (SWAPO) and the Communist-led government in Zimbabwe. A clear break from the UN itself remained the only sensible course for America.

Among other projects and organizational decisions marking Barker's two years at the helm of the Society, he should be remembered for deciding that producing two magazines (a monthly and a weekly) was far too costly and completely unnecessary. He was aided in making this assessment by a comprehensive report written by Bill Fall who acted on my suggestion. After seeing the enormity of the financial drain in having two magazines, he agreed to combine the monthly *American Opinion* and the weekly *The Review Of The News* into a single newly named publication. It would be *The New American*, a name he drew from the title of a 1957 Welch speech entitled "The New Americanism." In that timely message given even before the founding of the Society, Welch lamented that the term Americanism had degenerated "into something negative and defeatist." In 1985, when targeting Americanism had become even more obvious throughout the world, Barker felt a need to reverse the trend and one small way of accomplishing his goal was to clothe the new publication with the positive name "American." He also wanted the magazine's name to refer to its readers, the remarkable people who either were already Birch Society members or who would join in the future. The new magazine made its debut on September 17, 1985.

Then in April 1986, Clif Barker officially separated the Society from the many Ronald Reagan cheerleaders with a short but devastating summary of the Reagan record. Labeling his own conclusions a "less happy observation," his assessment appeared in the *Bulletin* where he wrote:

> When Ronald Reagan leaves office [in January 1989], he will be able to boast

that he imposed the largest single tax increase in U.S. history; that he raised the annual federal budget to over $1 trillion; that he more than doubled the national debt by adding well over $1 trillion in deficits; that he finally succeeded in getting the UN's Genocide Treaty ratified.... He also saved the Communist-terrorist P.L.O. from extinction – twice – and has striven to raise Communist China to the level of a superpower with dramatic increases in aid, trade, and even military armament.

The Society's CEO also took aim at the numerous "groups and individuals" who were constantly referring to Mr. Reagan as "the most conservative and anti-Communist U.S. president in the last fifty years." At the close of his heavy indictment of the sitting President where he insisted that Reagan was neither conservative nor anti-Communist, he wrote:

In short, never has the world been in more urgent need of The John Birch Society, which remains as the only genuinely Americanist organization with sufficient know-how, means, and determination to expose and stop the monstrous Conspiracy that is now rapidly consolidating the New World Order over the planet.

Society activity continued with extensive distribution of TRIM bulletins; attempts to put an end to the U.S. campaign against South Africa; publicizing the enormous flow of aid and trade going to Communist-controlled nations; protecting the U.S. Constitution from organizations and individuals planning to rewrite or completely scrap it during its 1987 bi-centennial year; and more. But all was not well in the Society under the leadership of Clif Barker. The problem was red ink, something Barker had inherited but failed to deal with.

An emergency meeting called by leading Executive Committee members led to their request to me to write a letter that would be sent to every Society member summarizing the organization's dire financial condition and asking for help in erasing it. No changes were made in the rather blunt two pages and it was immediately sent to each member. Replacing the monthly *Bulletin* for June 1986, it began: "There will not be a Monthly *Bulletin* for June." Then came the frank discussion of the Society's extremely precarious financial condition that included indebtedness totaling "nearly $1,600,000." The letter noted that Society expenses were "exceeding income by approximately $40,000 per week." Signed by Barker and a senior representative of the Executive Committee, the letter suggested that 1,600 recipients sending $1,000 each would retire the debt but that whatever anyone could afford would be gratefully accepted. It ended with a promise to "never again let such a situation develop."

All across the nation, members dug in and responded promptly and generously. Approximately three weeks later, two men known to no one at the JBS entered Society headquarters and asked the receptionist if the letter had accomplished its goal and drawn the desperately needed funds. The two weren't Society members but they had somehow come to know the contents of the admittedly stark appeal for financial help. They were immediately taken to my office where I told them the needed amount had already arrived via U.S. mail. Somewhat surprised, one said there must have been "several five- or six-figure donors." Assured that this was not the case, they were told that a sizable number of the responses did include a check for $1,000, but most had included checks for smaller amounts.

The two strangers had let it be known that they were writers for one of the left-wing tabloids currently available in the Boston area. It became pretty clear to me they had intended to write about the Society's imminent demise. So, to assure them that this wasn't about to happen, I asked if they would care to see the huge pile of letters still needing the Society's expression of gratitude. Taken immediately upstairs where several employees were working on the thank you letters, they were shown a long table with piles of unanswered letters whose checks had been removed and deposited. One of the two inquisitors blurted out, "There's no other organization in this country that could have accomplished what that one letter brought."

Glad to have such a realistic response from someone who obviously wasn't a friend of the Society, I asked if the two had any further questions, offered them samples of Society literature, and bid them farewell. Neither of the two ever wrote a word about what they were surprised to discover about the loyalty and love the members of The John Birch Society had for their organization.

In late June 1986, the Executive Committee of the Society's Council then announced Clif Barker's resignation and the appointment of veteran West Coast staff official Charles Armour as his replacement. All who knew Clif Barker respected his decision to leave the post and thanked him for his willingness to fill the leadership gap after Robert Welch and Larry McDonald were no longer with us. It had become known, even through Clif's own frankness often stated to me, that he was not psychologically equipped to ask people for the funds needed by the Society, a daunting task facing every Society leader. He returned to the field of electronics and has remained a friend of the Society. Congratulations and thanks then came in a flood for Charles "Chuck" Armour, the newest holder of the Society's CEO post.

William F. Jasper then supplied an array of facts and figures to show that President Reagan had broken his promises and shattered the peoples' expectation that he would bring real change and a return to our nation's admirable roots. Over 14 fact-filled pages, Jasper indicted Reagan in *The New American* for rising indebtedness, cave-ins to the New World Order, appointments of Establishment Insiders, continuation of military disarmament, expansion of aid and trade to Communist-controlled nations, etc. Especially noteworthy, Bill pointed to the President's failure to deliver on his explicit campaign vow to abolish the Departments of Education and Energy. But Mr. Reagan never even tried to rid the nation of these unconstitutional, costly, and harmful departments.

Bill Jasper's assessment aside, the American people were continuously being told that their "conservative and anti-Communist president" was providing outstanding conservative leadership and solving America's problems. Less than a month after he took office, the President indicated clearly that he didn't intend to cut spending. As noted previously in this book, Mr. Reagan had clearly stated, "It is important to note that we are reducing the rate of increase in taxing and spending. [Emphasis added.] We are not attempting to cut either taxing or spending to a level below that which we presently have." Birchers weren't just surprised about that capitulation, they were angry about it.

President Armour thought it worthwhile to remind older members and inform newer ones about the worth of their organization given by an important Communist publication 20 years earlier. In 1967, *People's World* had grudgingly issued the following comment, a hard admission for the Communist publication to make after repeatedly trying to destroy the Society:

> The John Birch Society is the largest and most sophisticated "anti-Communist" organization in the United States. The Right is a seething mass of over 4,000 organizations, bewildering in their titles, aims and diversity. Of all the groups, only 30 distinct organizations appear to be of national importance, and the prime one is The John Birch Society.

One staff official commented wryly: "Finally, the Communists offered some truth about our Society!"

CHAPTER 48
1987-88: PROTECTING THE CONSTITUTION

As the nation headed toward celebrating 200 years of government under the Constitution, Society members were called upon to block numerous plans to alter or possibly discard the venerable document. All were encouraged to refer to the revealing 1984 book authored by James MacGregor Burns entitled *The Power To Lead*. The Williams College Professor held high positions in both the Committee on the Constitutional System and Project '87, two groups loudly calling for a new Constitution. In his book, Burns wrote:

> Let us face reality. The framers have simply been too shrewd for us. They have outwitted us. They designed separate institutions that cannot be unified by mechanical linkages, frail bridges, tinkering. If we are to "turn the founders upside down" – to put together what they put asunder – we must directly confront the constitutional structure they erected.

Such boldness amounted to an unintended compliment given the Constitution. But it also signaled there would be a full-bore attack on the nation's 200-year-old governmental system. Supported by a host of left-leaning politicians and opinion molders, an array of the Constitution's enemies called for centralizing even more power at the federal level, destroying remaining checks on federal highhandedness, and turning "the founders upside down." Their effort had to be confronted if the Constitution were to survive. So members went to work writing letters, sponsoring speakers, distributing articles, etc. Victory was achieved when the bicentennial year passed and the Constitution was still the "supreme law of the land."

The efforts of the Tulsa, Oklahoma, TRIM Committee over a ten-year period finally saw the district's voters replace a 14-year veteran leftist. The *Bulletin* reminded all that there is no quick and easy way to overcome decades of brainwashing – but it can be done!

In an "Open Letter To Lt. Col. Oliver North," the Society congratulated the USMC officer for standing firm during the grilling he received from two congressional committees. The letter discussed the aid Colonel North had been able to secure for the Nicaraguan Contras in their fight to keep the Communist Sandinistas from conquering their nation. But the JBS missive also sought to alert North himself about the formidable left-leaning and conspiratorial enemies within the U.S. government who were targeting him. Members were asked to distribute copies of the letter in their communities and to send a copy to the embattled Colonel. Many did as asked.

The Society's Larry McDonald Crusade To Stop Financing Communism started collecting signatures on the new petition to Members of Congress. Headlined "Stop Helping Communism – Here, There or Anywhere," it not only focused attention on the equipment, technology and credit going to Communist-led governments, it warned that "Communism is being built here without a shot being fired." From the Hoover Institution, Professor Antony Sutton's book, "The Best Enemy Money Can Buy," provided infuriating examples of strategic aid going to Communist enemies from the West, chiefly from the United States. The information compiled by Sutton generated impressive energy for the petition campaign.

Efforts by the Society to blunt the worldwide acceptance of Communists ascending to leadership in South Africa met with little success. The supposedly horrible existence for Blacks living in that country conveniently ignored the fact that Black people from other nations were continually streaming into South Africa while Blacks within South Africa were not fleeing to go elsewhere. Also, though many leaders of the Insider-favored African National Congress (ANC) were Communists, America's political and media leaders continued to promote them as humanitarians who would capably serve as new national officials.

Mention appeared in the *Bulletin* about an end-of-camp quiz given to the young people who had just spent a full week enjoying the JBS camp experience. Soon, numerous members were asking, "Can I see the quiz?" They wanted to know what sort of instruction campers were given and how well they themselves would fare if presented with the test. The 25-question exit exam went promptly to all who sought a copy. Recipients were delighted to know that the campers were expected to have answers to meaningful questions.

New video presentations included staff-produced "A Program for Responsible Citizenship," my "Keeping Faith With America," and Bill Jasper's "Who Shall Teach?" The Jasper analysis of the deficiencies in our nation's education system (text available in booklet format) spurred numerous anxious parents to look to private and home schooling alternatives for their youngsters. "In Cold Blood," another book published by the Society, told of the horrors occurring in Afghanistan at the hands of Soviet invaders. Author Abdul Shams, a former high-ranking official of the Afghan government now living in America, warned that the widespread death and destruction in his home country might soon be duplicated in the United States. Veteran JBS member Sterling Lacy authored "Valley of Decision," a small but excellent paperback book whose major contribution was its defense of the oft-challenged belief that conspiracy was the stimulus behind many of our nation's problems.

Under the headline, "Plenty of Prospects Out There," staff official Charlie Everett reported that as a result of my appearance as a guest on the Dallas-based "Point of View" radio show, the hour-long program generated "hundreds of responses" from listeners. Each sent $3.00 for a package of JBS literature. The *Bulletin* published numerous encouraging comments from many of those listeners – a solid indication that there were indeed many prospects who would seek information after being introduced to the Society.

Giving appropriate credit to the effectiveness of hard-working members, Society CEO Charles Armour recalled Robert Welch's early estimate that 1,000 JBS members in any congressional district would be sufficient to alter the district's voting results. A few years later, however, Welch revised his estimate downward to 500 members per district. Armour explained that even Robert Welch had "no idea of the positive effect that could be brought about by the dedication, determination and commitment of our members." Armour's message sought to spur all to step up their recruiting efforts and enlist more Americans into the Society.

Nicaragua Betrayed, a book written by Jack Cox about former Nicaraguan leader Anastasio Somoza's valiant effort to save his country from a Communist takeover provided another case history showing the U.S. government and media combining to deliver a friendly nation into Communist hands. Then the John Wayne-narrated film "No Substitute for Victory" became instantly popular among members. Its sharp criticism of America's flawed foreign policy, especially the stream of aid and trade going to Communist nations, gave members another tool to use in recruiting. Showings of Ed Griffin's film "The Grand Design" demonstrated to viewers that U.S. foreign policy was leading America toward cancellation of independence in favor of "a Communist-style world government."

While political and media leaders continued to describe President Ronald Reagan as a hardcore economic skinflint, the JBS showed a graph produced by the U.S. Office of Management and Budget dramatically demonstrating otherwise. Deficits during the Reagan years far exceeded shortfalls amassed by any of the seven previous administrations.

A lengthy excerpt from a speech by Senator Jesse Helms (R-N.C.) opposing any merger of our nation with others in a "new world order" filled the beginning pages of the July 1988 *Bulletin.* The Society produced a video program entitled "Premeditated Merger." Narrated by CEO Armour, it helped members fight the campaign leading toward the planned "new world order." Once "Premeditated Merger" became available in August 1988, it was immediately employed by members to alert fellow Americans about plans to cede U.S. sovereignty to a world government. Two months later, "Out of Control: The Immigration Invasion," a filmed documentary authored by Bill Jasper, explained the duplicitous strategy behind the absence of substantive efforts to close our southern border. These films helped members everywhere to gain more recruits for the organization.

Because members and staff were often asked why the Society didn't change its name, a short discourse on that topic appeared in the October *Bulletin*. I began it by stressing that John Birch's life and deeds had always been a fitting symbol for the organization. But, I insisted, the most compelling reason for not changing the name has always been that many Americans would, in the future, flock to the organization once they became even partially aware of the treachery emanating from our nation's highest offices. Also, a change of the name would indicate a degree of cowardice or an admission that the organization had done something wrong and had good reason to hide its name. There was, of course, no cowardice and no wrong had been committed. Therefore there would be no name change. Every JBS member was asked to combat suggestions that a new name for The John Birch Society would be a wise move.

The Shadows of Power: The Council on Foreign Relations and the American Decline by James Perloff quickly became the most popular book published by Western Islands since the 1960s. Still selling well after 25 years, it capably introduces readers to the Council on Foreign Relations and names that pillar of the Establishment as a seat of *Insider* power working to create a world government.

A member of the Society living in Eastern Massachusetts, Jim Perloff had worked part time at the organization's Research Department. He had never previously written anything that had been published anywhere. But he did ask Society executive Buck Mann to consider publishing an article he'd composed about the CFR. Mann read it, and found it "excellent" but too lengthy for inclusion in our magazine. So he asked Jim if he had more information dealing with the topic. When Perloff responded, "Yes, plenty more." Mann suggested that he put it all together because it would make an excellent book. Which is precisely what happened. *The Shadows of Power* soon helped countless tens of thousands to gain an awareness about the harm to our nation emanating from the Council on Foreign Relations.

The Society then recommended Douglas Hyde's small book "Dedication and Leadership." A former news editor for the Communist Party's *London Daily Worker*, Hyde had broken with the Communists and joined the Catholic Church. His book relates the successes Communists had regularly achieved through personal contact, inspirational dedication of members, and more. JBS members were urged to duplicate the successful employment of such moral means as letter writing, speakers bureau, personal contact, etc. in their efforts to gather more Americans into Society membership.

Before the year ended, Bill Jasper and I happened to be in Washington on separate assignments. We eventually got together and went to interview Soviet defector Ken Alibek (who had shortened his name from Kanatjan Alibekov). Several journalists and government personnel had already cited him as an authority on the USSR's chemical and biological warfare experimentation. Dr. Alibek was most cordial and cooperative during the interview at his northern Virginia office. When Bill had finished gathering the information he planned to use in a subsequent *New American* article, I asked Dr. Alibek, "You were a member of the inner circle in the Kremlin, the nomenclatura as it is called. Can you tell us what became of the passengers and crew of the Korean Airliner that was attacked by a Soviet fighter plane while on its way to South Korea in 1983?"

To put it mildly, Dr. Alibek froze at that point. Quickly recovering from being somewhat startled by my question, he terminated the meeting and ushered us out of his office. He never answered the question. Outside, Bill and I discussed what had occurred and we agreed that nothing the man had said during the course of the 20-minute interview could be believed. We figured that his swift reaction indicated his knowledge of something about the fate of the 269 aboard KAL 007. But he wasn't about to divulge anything. We never again met with Dr. Alibek.

Chapter 49
1989: Move To Appleton; Bubolz CEO

The January 1989 *Bulletin* carried a "Special Announcement" informing members that Wisconsin native G. Allen Bubolz had been named as the Society's new Chief Executive Officer. The change resulted from a decision reached by the Society's Board of Directors. A member of the Council himself though not holding a place on the Board of Directors, Bubolz succeeded Charles Armour who received the thanks of the Board for his many years of dedicated service in numerous posts. He remained a member of the Council.

Under the headline "KAL 007 Update," JBS investigative reporter Bob Lee responded in an article to a November 1, 1988, letter about "the loss of KAL 007" sent to him by Assistant Secretary of State J. Edward Fox. Pointing to the questions raised by Bob in his earlier article dealing with the loss of the plane and its passengers, Lee noted that the State Department official had failed to answer how the plane could have remained airborne for 12-plus minutes after being hit by a heat-seeking missile, why there was so little debris in the claimed "crash" area, and more. Lee always insisted – backed by plenty of evidence – that the wounded plane had landed on Sakhalin Island with minimal harm to passengers and crew. Members were asked to demand answers to the many unanswered questions Lee had raised about the September 1, 1983, tragedy. But meaningful answers to those questions have never been supplied.

Continuing to demonstrate the tragic absurdity of helping Communist nations with aid and trade while simultaneously considering them enemies, the *Bulletin* asked, "Why fight them with one hand and feed them with the other?" Plenty of evidence followed to show that the U.S. was indeed feeding its supposed enemy. The Society then issued a video and a 24-page booklet entitled "Keeping Faith With America" written by me. These two items helped in the campaign to keep state legislatures from issuing official calls for a constitutional convention.

Bill Jasper alerted members about the cozy relationship between the Communist periodical *People's Daily World* and Mary Hatwood Futrell, the President of the 1.9 million-member National Education Association. Actually a labor union, the NEA had consistently favored imposition of Communist and socialist goals on our nation. Jasper recommended alerting public school educators about the NEA's subversive activity.

JBS member Bill Caruth's 30-minute video program entitled "More Than a Right" capably defended the right of all law-abiding citizens to keep and bear arms. Members were urged to celebrate John Birch Day on or near the May 27 birthday of the remarkable missionary-turned-soldier. Note was made of the strong relationship between President-elect George H. W. Bush and former Secretary of State Henry Kissinger. Even before Bush took office, he had designated Kissinger, a leading advocate of a sovereignty-destroying New World Order, to travel to Russia to represent the incoming administration in discussions with Soviet leader Mikhail Gorbachev.

Society CEO Allen Bubolz acted on the mandate given him by the Board of Directors and closed down JBS offices in Massachusetts and California. For a new headquarters location "somewhere in the middle of the country," Bubolz chose Appleton, Wisconsin, his hometown. Employees packed up and moved during June and July 1989. Many veteran stalwarts were unable to uproot and had to be replaced. Gary Benoit, a key individual in the JBS hierarchy, did move his family to Wisconsin where he continued to hold the reins as Editor of *The New American*. I continued to serve as Director of Public Relations. From California came senior field staff Coordinator Tom Gow who replaced Buck Mann as Chief Operating Officer. And from Colorado came Coordinator G. Vance Smith who replaced Charlie Everett as Director of Field Operations.

Work to combat the drive to have state legislatures pass a resolution calling for a Con-Con coincided with efforts in other states to persuade their state legislatures to rescind previous Con-Con calls. Almost immediately after the Society opened its new headquarters in Wisconsin, Chinese forces conducted a bloody suppression of freedom in Beijing's Tiananmen Square. The Society responded with a commentary entitled "China: No One Should be Surprised."

A new campaign had members formally requesting the 14 U.S. senators who were CFR members to explain why they had affiliated with an organization seeking to cancel our nation's independence. A single-page flyer headlined, "Why would anyone who professes to be an American hold membership in the Council on Foreign Relations?" was made available to accompany member inquiries. This project soon grew into asking that same question to hundreds more CFR members. Each was sent a copy of *The Shadows of Power*.

Noteworthy responses to this ambitious program came from: *Wall Street Journal* Editor Robert Bartley who said he "would rather rely" on the CFR than on The John Birch Society; *National Review* Editor Buckley who claimed he had "detected no bias in their choice of speakers"; *Washington Times* editor Arnaud DeBorchgrave insisted that he was able to "provide some balance" within the CFR; *Washington Post* Chairman Katharine Graham claimed that the CFR was "a harmless organization;" and Notre Dame University President Emeritus Father Theodore Hesburgh gave assurance that the CFR "is no more subversive than the Girl Scouts."

This program, financed through special contributions from Society members grew to have the Perloff book sent to each member of the House and Senate, as well as to members of some state legislatures and many of the nation's corporate leaders who happened to be CFR members. The campaign certainly caused concern within that organization's ranks and it delighted members of the Society who liked the idea of being on the offensive. One certain effect saw members of the CFR being identified in articles they authored and in news items where they were mentioned.

Chapter 50
1990: Bogus Environmentalism

After welcoming Associated Press reporter John Solomon to the Appleton headquarters, Society leaders were greatly encouraged when his balanced and barbless article appeared in hundreds of newspapers throughout the nation. AP had also sent his report to radio and television stations where it generated another round of welcome publicity. The AP reporter wrote about the skepticism held by Society leaders about the breakup of the Soviet Union's empire and the questionable claims of Communist leaders. Soviet Union leader Gorbachev and many others had in a matter of days sought to portray themselves as mere socialists instead of previously wanting to be known as Communists. Gorbachev himself had written of his lifelong commitment to communism.

The attention given the Society by the AP had resulted from the placement in a Chicago newspaper of a full-page Society ad carrying the headline "Aid to Poland? Hold on a Minute!" Pointing to Poland's new leaders, all Communists or collaborators with Communists, the ad also targeted U.S. national indebtedness and bluntly stated, "The heavily indebted U.S. government should hardly be giving away money."

Answering the question, "What is Communism?", the lead essay in the January 1990 *Bulletin* stated, "Communism is not an ideology in which men believe; it is a Conspiracy in which men participate." As for socialism which many Communists were now claiming to be their life-long choice, the article continued, "Socialism is domination of economic life. Redistribution of wealth (a cardinal goal of socialists) presupposes power to control wealth. When people depend on the state for their jobs, housing, food and health care, they become slaves of state power." That, of course, is the goal of Communism.

The *Bulletin* then pointed to Gorbachev's explanation that his numerous references to "perestroika," joyfully accepted by President George H.W. Bush, Secretary of State James A. Baker, and the U.S. mass media, were nothing more than calls for some restructuring that would lead, stated Gorbachev, to "more socialism and more democracy." The Russian leader would later describe the newly created European Union as "the new European Soviet." JBS leaders weren't surprised to find so few political leaders, journalists, and others citing these revealing admissions of the Russian leader.

Instead of relying on Gorbachev and the mass media, the Society again urged placing confidence in the works of Communist defector Anatoliy Golitsyn whose books *Perestroika Deception* and *New Lies for Old* could be ordered through American Opinion Books.

The excellent nationwide reception accorded Perloff's *The Shadows of Power* led to a program in which the Society mailed single copies of the book to 2,000 college libraries, the Washington and district offices of all members of Congress, and 1,700 political editors of daily newspapers. Included with the book was a copy of the one-page flyer asking, "Why would anyone who professes to be an American hold membership in the Council on Foreign Relations?" The campaign soon began to receive responses from CFR members who were obviously unhappy to have received the book.

Preparing to counter the environmental extremism scheduled for Earth Day, two important articles from *The New American* were made readily available in reprinted format. Gary Benoit's "The Greatest Sham on Earth" debunked many of the claims published in *The Environmental Handbook 1970*. His analysis included a top environmentalist's open recommendation to employ fraud when promoting environmental claims. That recommendation, given by Senator Tim Wirth (D-Colo.), a Director of Earth Day 1990, revealingly stated:

> We've got to ride the global warming issue. Even if the theory is wrong, we will be doing the right thing in terms of economic and environmental policy.

The other reprinted article, "Six Crises" by Bob Lee, provided a scientific debunking of claims made by many environmentalists about acid rain, the greenhouse effect, ozone depletion, deforestation, overpopulation, and auto emissions. Lee cited numerous experts who supplied solid information to counter the excesses of the environmental extremists. He claimed, with justification, that many of the near hysterical claims of the doom-saying environmentalists were based on fabricated or exaggerated evidence.

Another single sheet advertisement entitled "You Be the Judge" presented a variety of stands taken by environmentalists alongside counter stands presented by reliable scientists and economists. The December 1990 *Bulletin* showed a sample of this popular single-sheet flyer/ad. Placed in 18 newspapers with a combined circulation of 1.6 million readers, it invited all to send for a $5.00 packet of "facts and analysis." Several hundred readers did exactly that. The Society also created a press kit containing a variety of items capably debunking the claims of radical environmentalists. Sent to 1,730 daily newspapers, 3,723 college newspaper editors, and 100 radio talk-show hosts, the effort proved to be a success when Society officials were invited guests on 15 different radio shows on Earth Day (April 22nd) alone. Those guest appearances led 1,300 listeners to order a $5.00 packet of information.

With hopes of increasing the American peoples' awareness about the Council on Foreign Relations, the *Bulletin* offered a new eight-page brochure formatted to fit into a business envelope. Entitled "Americans Have a Right To Know – About the Council on Foreign Relations," this new educational weapon quickly became a very popular item among Society members.

Because CFR members customarily described their organization as a mere "forum for discussion" where no particular policy or goal is ever recommended, the Society urged distribution of my 12-page pamphlet quoting CFR members and leaders who certainly did champion various foreign policy initiatives. "How the CFR Sets Policy" countered the dishonest insistence of CFR officials and members that it was nothing more than "a talking shop" or "a place, not a cause."

Don Fotheringham warned that the latest cry for amending the U.S. Constitution to outlaw flag burning would lead ill-informed Americans to suspect that the Constitution itself was deficient, not the Congress and the judges who were regularly ignoring its many restraints. He expressed concern that this newest attempt to alter the Constitution might lead to support for a Con-Con (constitutional convention). Members were again urged to oppose calls for a convention and to work at getting some state legislatures to rescind previously issued calls.

In addition to the newest single-sheet "Mandela A Hero?" flyer/ad, the Society's Speakers Bureau sent Tomsanqa Linda on a speaking tour throughout the U.S. The black mayor of South Africa's Port Elizabeth township (population 400,000), Linda had done his best in his home country to counter the propaganda favoring Nelson Mandela and the Communist-led African National Congress (ANC). For his efforts in his home country, Linda saw his business looted and later burned to the ground. His life and that of his wife and children were also threatened. As he traveled through the United States delivering his speech exposing Mandela and the ANC, he received excellent press coverage including a 45-minute news conference in Washington broadcast nationally by C-SPAN. But his effort, combined with that of JBS members nationwide, couldn't stop some U.S. leaders from ignoring the Communist leadership of ANC, glorifying Mandela, and having this Communist-favored individual become the leader of the South African nation. Mandela came to the U.S. where he toured the United States as if he were a rock star celebrity.

Prior to Mandela's appearances in the United States, Tulsa, Oklahoma, chapter leader Bob Bell arranged to have his area newspaper publish a press release supplying details about Mandela's Communist connections. Retaliation from the local NAACP and others called for a boycott of the Bell-owned amusement park. Bell refused to back away from spreading the truth about Mandela and his Communist-led African National Congress.

The Society dared bare the truth about Iraq's 1990 invasion of neighboring Kuwait. What the American people were told was that President George H. W. Bush formed a coalition of military forces under UN command and used it for his oft-repeated goal of creating a "new world order." The Society responded with a new JBS video program entitled "Mideast Masquerade." It accused President Bush of using the incident to propel the United States into a UN-led world government.

The city of Fort Wayne, Indiana, hosted a citizen's forum entitled "America's Role in the New World Order." Sponsored by the area's newspaper and Indiana University, its presenters included CFR member William Maynes, nationally known columnist David Broder, and Indiana Senator Richard Lugar. Considered by JBS to be an event that would be duplicated across the nation, a JBS "Quick Response Team" operating out of the Society's headquarters took immediate action. The Team placed a newspaper ad explaining the significance of the term "New World Order" and followed it with a JBS press conference, radio interviews, and several other events. As they entered the hall, each of the more than 600 persons who attended received JBS material from more than 60 Indiana JBS members who had answered the call for opposition to this "new world order" forum. No similar events were held anywhere in the United States. Numerous attendees at the Fort Wayne event became prospects for JBS membership.

CHAPTER 51
1991: NEW LEADERSHIP TEAM

Gary Benoit led off 1991 explaining in *The New American* that war, which Welch had frequently identified as "big government's best friend," had also become "the United Nation's best friend." Completely ignoring the Constitution's grant of war-making power to Congress alone, President George H. W. Bush sought and gained authorization from the world body to form a coalition of forces from several nations that would attack Iraq and reverse Saddam Hussein's invasion of neighboring Kuwait. In one of many similar statements made by Mr. Bush, he revealingly insisted:

> Out of these troubled times, our fifth objective – a new world order – can emerge…. We are now in sight of a United Nations that performs as envisioned by its founders.

The president repeated his intention to create a "new world order" again and again. His doing so prompted numerous previously uninvolved Americans to contact the Society and ask for membership. James Drummey's new book, *The Establishment's Man*, provided a thorough look at Bush's career – from his Skull & Bones involvement at Yale, to membership in the Council on Foreign Relations and the Trilateral Commission, to being appointed to some of the highest government posts such as Director of the CIA, being tapped to be Vice President, and finally to becoming the nation's 41st President.

Under the headline "Republican Presidents Are More Harmful," the *Bulletin* pointed to the erroneous attitude held by many Americans that a GOP president would surely reverse America's dangerous drift into socialism and world government. The article quoted Stanford University researcher Thomas Gale Moore's advice for voters given ten years earlier. To those who wondered which candidate they should choose to be the next U.S. president, Moore wrote:

> … a voter who wants a liberal policy should vote Republican; conversely if he

yearns for a conservative policy, he should cast his ballot for a Democrat.

After the Society again urged distribution of the State Department's 1961 *Freedom From War* document, startled Americans began asking questions about its call for the U.S. – and all nations – to turn over their military arms to the UN. Was America's government actually intending to carry out such a plan? Had the 1961 document ever been revised or superseded? Some digging produced answers.

A. Richard Richstein, the General Council of the U.S. Arms Control and Disarmament Agency, confirmed in a May 11, 1982, letter that the U.S. "has never formally withdrawn this plan." In January 1991, William Nary, the official historian of the Arms Control and Disarmament Agency, bluntly stated during my telephoned inquiry that "the proposal has never been withdrawn." Birch Society officials have long believed that the plan never reached completion because of resistance generated by Society members. But that doesn't mean that its suicidal path to disarmament and UN control of the planet won't be resurrected at any time.

A newly produced four-page "Did You Know?" handout became a popular item. Containing ten current news headlines followed by short commentary about each, it aimed to provide reasons why an American should resist the way the country was being run, and how the mass media was unreliably reporting the news through either distortion of facts or completely ignoring important information. The fourth page contained a brief description of the Society and an invitation to send $5.00 for a packet of information. Many newly alarmed Americans did exactly that.

In June, at its regularly scheduled meeting held in Chicago, the Society's Council accepted the resignation of G. Allen Bubolz as Society CEO/President. Mr. Bubolz cited as the reason for his resignation a need to attend to numerous personal affairs as a result of the recent death of his father who had founded and built a well-respected insurance firm doing business in several midwestern states. At a subsequent meeting of the Council's Executive Committee, three new officers were named: National Director of Field Activities G. Smith became CEO; from Public Relations Director, I became President; and former Senior Field Coordinator Tom Gow accepted assignment as Vice President of Operations.

The new leadership change meant that, after the disappearance of Larry McDonald, the Society had enlisted three men to serve in its leadership posts, each for approximately two years. There was no turmoil among members because of this turnover of the reins of leadership. Society members kept reaching out to fellow Americans. The educational work of the Society continued and membership grew though growth never reached the numbers any leader or member wished.

Because President Bush had employed the phrase "New World Order" so frequently, the Society published a 28-page display of newspaper headlines showing the use of that chilling phrase by Fidel Castro, Mikhail Gorbachev, Nelson Rockefeller, Richard Nixon, several CFR luminaries, and others. A quick glance at page after page swiftly demonstrated to anyone that the oft-repeated phrase was a signal to identify its user as a proponent of world government. The front page of this 8.5 x 11 booklet carried the title "NEW WORLD ORDER" followed by two penetrating questions: "Where did the phrase originate? What does it mean?" The 28-page booklet became a useful tool in the Society's efforts to awaken many sleeping Americans.

The New American published an additional report about the 1983 attack on KAL 007. In it, author Bob Lee supplied more evidence claiming that the wounded plane didn't crash into the sea. Members were urged to contact their senators to have them conduct further investigations of the chilling incident. It was hoped that the fate of the missing persons aboard that plane (Society Chairman Larry McDonald and 268 others) would finally be known. But no government investigation resulted.

The *Bulletin* asked members to send letters to senators supporting the nomination of Judge Clarence Thomas to the Supreme Court. Members were also apprised of dangers inherent in the newly proposed North American Free Trade Agreement (NAFTA). All were urged to read and share Jane Ingraham's *New American* article explaining the pitfalls in the NAFTA proposal.

As part of a campaign to counter the flattering portrayal of Mikhail Gorbachev, the *Bulletin* suggested posing the following question to fellow Americans, and especially to representatives of the mass media:

> Why is it that our government officials, cheered on by the media, continue to hound octogenarian ex-Nazi corporals for their alleged participation in the crimes of Nazi Germany 50 years ago while they ignore Gorbachev's rape of Afghanistan in the 1980s and the past crimes of so many other Communist officials?

The *Bulletin* described Gorbachev as an arch criminal who spent his entire adult life ascending to higher and higher posts within Russia's Communist Party. Members were requested to protest the granting of any form of aid to him or to the collapsing Soviet Union.

In 1997, when Gorbachev visited the St. Louis area to deliver speeches and receive awards, he was met by a fusillade of unwanted opposition generated by local JBS members. Operating as the hastily formed "Committee to Expose the Real Mikhail Gorbachev," the group arranged widespread distribution of information about the Russian leader's meteoric rise within the Communist apparatus and his emphatic claim given in a December 1989 speech to the Soviet Congress in Moscow assuring all that "I am a communist, a convinced communist; for some that may be a fantasy, but for me it is my main goal." The committee's information also told of Gorbachev's part in the Soviet attack on Afghanistan that included dropping booby-trapped toys for children to pick up and have their limbs and eyes blown away. The effort didn't keep Gorbachev from coming to Missouri, but it did result in informing many unaware citizens about "the Real Gorbachev."

The Society's first videotaped warning about questionable "global warming" appeared in the October 1991 *Bulletin*. A 30-minute interview of professional meteorologist H. Read McGrath showed him condemning the questionable claims about global warming, the greenhouse effect, and the depletion of the earth's ozone layer.

The *Bulletin* announced the start of a campaign to send a copy of *The Establishment's Man* about President George H. W. Bush to thousands of Americans. When a front-page *Wall Street Journal* article sought to portray the Society as irrelevant, the Society answered by asking: "How insignificant can we be when the *Wall Street Journal* uses space on its front page to tell the world we are insignificant?" JBS ally Phoebe Courtney continued her excellent analysis of the problems facing America with a new 16-page pamphlet entitled "Why a Tax Revolt Is Brewing."

The newest addition to the list of many flyer/ads carried the title, "Why We Still Say Get US Out! of the United Nations." These single-page flyer/ads continued to be very popular with members who could place one as a paid advertisement in a local newspaper or take it to a local copy shop and have dozens or hundreds made for hand-to-hand distribution.

The TRIM Committee distributions of an individual congressman's voting record received credit for the defeat of 21 big-spending members of the House in the 1990 elections. Never a political weapon, it was always a strictly educational offering. TRIM officials explained:

> If a voter wants higher taxes and more government, he will be pleased when TRIM informs him that his representative in Congress is voting that way.

Another may be delighted to learn that his representative is trying to hold back taxes and spending that threaten to drown America in red ink. TRIM neither endorses a candidate for any office nor recommends that any candidate be defeated.

Chapter 52
1992: Saying No To UN Army

The *Bulletin* reminded readers of the damage one should expect from any government intrusion into the private sector. In Welch's discourse during his 1958 two-day dissertation at the Society's founding meeting, he stated:

> A government trying to step in and improve the workings of a free market is exactly like a man who takes a lighted lantern outdoors at noon of a bright June day to show you the sun. A government's answer to any criticism of the inadequacy of the lantern is always to bring more lanterns, and then more lanterns – until eventually the smoke and glare so seriously interfere with and shut off the light of the sun that everybody has to work mainly by lantern light.

Numerous politicians across the country continued to be stung by TRIM. In Tennessee, Representative Marilyn Lloyd sent a JBS member couple a three-page letter attempting to defend the five votes she had cast for higher taxes and more government. In Arizona, Representative Jim Kolbe voted for higher taxes and more government 11 times out of 15 opportunities chronicled by TRIM. He actually contacted the local TRIM Chairman requesting a meeting where he presented a 17-page defense of what he had supported. Mr. Kolbe hoped that TRIM would cease spreading those nasty TRIM Bulletins around the district. Farther out West, the TRIM Chairman in Representative Randy Cunningham's Southern California district passed out TRIM Bulletins at a public meeting and forced the rattled congressman to try to defend his vote for a $25.4 billion foreign aid bill. In Northern California, Congressman Frank Riggs showed up late at a meeting he and his staff had arranged and it cost him dearly because, when he finally did appear, everyone in the large crowd had already read the TRIM Bulletin – twice! Mr. Riggs tried in vain to justify his seven out of eight votes for increased spending and larger government.

In Arkansas, Representative Ray Thornton sought to discredit TRIM's report about his voting for more government by claiming that, although he did vote for the spending bill as reported, he hadn't co-sponsored it. That amazingly weak defense of the indefensible got him nowhere. In New Mexico, Congressman Bill Richardson sought to discount his voting eight out of eight times for more spending and larger government by claiming that, overall, Congress was working to reduce government spending – a complete falsehood. And back in California, Representative William Thomas claimed that he really was a spending opponent even though he had voted 40 times for more spending out of the 53 votes he had cast.

In Maryland, Congressman Steny Hoyer's aide told two young female Birch Society members that they couldn't legally distribute TRIM Bulletins on county property. Persuaded that their distribution plan would indeed have been illegal, they prepared to leave when a witness to the confrontation introduced himself as a reporter for the local newspaper. He found their effort to be worthy of a story in the local newspaper. Instead of having TRIM Bulletins passed out to only a few dozen voters at the congressman's meeting, the reporter's complimentary article about the completely legal activity planned by the two ladies ended up as a feature piece in the very next issue of his newspaper. It showed the claim of Hoyer's aide to be a complete falsehood, and it also included publication of the entire TRIM Bulletin. So, instead of passing out copies of the TRIM Bulletin to several dozen attendees at the meeting, the two gals were delighted to know that the TRIM Bulletin was reproduced in the local newspaper for 10,000 subscribers to read.

The March *Bulletin* published my eight-page article entitled "The Story Behind the Unwarranted Attack on The John Birch Society." It became a favorite for members who used its detailed information to counter attacks aimed at the Society. Most were shown to be outright falsehoods.

Members were alerted that Rotary International's monthly magazine, *The Rotarian,* presented articles glorifying the United Nations. Numerous members requested Rotary International to publish an opposing view. Their pleas were ignored.

An initial concern about the UN's *Agenda 21* plan to revise virtually all aspects of mankind's life and activity appeared even before the document became obtainable by the general public. A product of UN planning, *Agenda 21* surfaced at the "Earth Summit" held in Rio de Janeiro in June 1992. Bill Jasper, who attended the Rio Conference where the document was unveiled, had brought home a copy of the massive plan. Opposition to it became a significant JBS project in subsequent years.

In July 1992, the *Bulletin* listed numerous ways the enemies of freedom were creating and using environmental hysteria to propel mankind into world government. Distribution of tens of thousands of the entire "Resilient Earth" issue of *The New American* began. Soon, many more thousands of the entire issue of the magazine had to be reprinted.

H. Ross Perot drew national attention with his surprising run for the presidency. The chief effect he had in the 1992 and 1996 presidential contests saw him helping Bill Clinton win both elections. Perot's record showed him favoring gun control, abortion, and a rewriting of the Constitution via a Con-Con. He had earlier been endorsed for membership in the Council on Foreign Relations by his GOP opponent, George H. W. Bush. Like numerous other "shooting stars" in the political world, Perot arrived, quickly gained massive media attention, rose to national prominence, and just as quickly faded away.

The Society's headquarters staff honored me with a small celebration on the occasion of my 1,000th Birch Log column. While publication of the column in county weeklies and small-city dailies never reached the numbers we sought, numerous single columns had been widely used as educational advertisements and as handouts at county fairs and parades. At the University of New Hampshire, members eagerly distributed a column about the Communist connections of Alger Hiss at his speech. The same was done at other college-sponsored speaking engagements. The convicted felon even complained publicly about the attention he was receiving, telling a Long Island, New York reporter, "Everywhere I go to speak, The John Birch Society shows up."

The Society produced a four-page handout entitled "Rely on Science!" Members were urged to question, even discount, the claims of environmentalists while heeding the truth given by numerous men and women of science. Opposite positions about numerous topics were shown including global warming, ozone depletion, carbon dioxide and acid rain. A careful reading of the information presented in this brief format helped many to understand that the claims of numerous environmental extremists were far from credible.

The third edition of *The Insiders: Architects of the New World Order* became available. Containing an analysis of the Carter, Reagan and Bush administrations, the 134-page pocket-sized book became an important educational tool. Following the pattern set in previous editions, *The Insiders* listed the latest membership rosters of the CFR and the Trilateral Commission.

The campaign to Get US out! of the United Nations received new energy from members with the publication of Bill Jasper's *Global Tyranny ... Step By Step: The United Nations and the Emerging New World Orde*r. This 350-page book presented a compelling warning to Americans to understand that the world organization was not created to benefit mankind and was not a do-nothing collection of blowhards who posed no real threat to anyone. It was instead an organization designed to establish total power for the world body over the earth and all its inhabitants.

Early salvos aimed against U.S. acceptance of the North America Free Trade Agreement (NAFTA) appeared in the *Bulletin* and *The New American*. Congress eventually approved the NAFTA trade pact in a very close vote supported by various members of the Clinton Administration.

A great deal of JBS-generated attention had already been paid to the revelations given in Professor Carroll Quigley's 1350-page book *Tragedy and Hope*. But who was Quigley? Why did the Macmillan Company cease publishing his book? And did Quigley ever come to a realization that the "secret society" he so glowingly lauded actually amounted to a Conspiracy to rule mankind? These questions were answered in ten pages I wrote for the October 1992 *Bulletin*. This revealing look into the late stages of the Georgetown University professor's life was reprinted in pamphlet format under the title "Bill Clinton and Carroll Quigley."

UN Secretary General Boutros Boutros-Ghali announced a plan to create a UN standing army and President George H. W. Bush wasted no time in seconding the idea. UN leaders have long sought their own military arm. Because of resistance to the plan, the UN continued to use the forces of individual nations in its "peacekeeping" operations. JBS members stepped up their exposure of the UN by putting Bill Jasper's *Global Tyranny* book into many hands. The plan to build a UN standing army was scrapped – at least temporarily.

CHAPTER 53
1993: C-SPAN HELPS JBS CAUSE

The first 1993 *Bulletin* reminded readers via a bold headline that the well-known moniker for our nation should remain "Uncle Sam" not become "Uncle Globocop." The reminder appeared because of outgoing President Bush's plans to send U.S. forces into Somalia. Our nation's ambassador in neighboring Kenya, Smith Hempstone, along with several U.S.-affiliated journalists, urged President Clinton to reverse his decision to have our forces involved in that nation's tribal warfare. But some U.S. troops were sent anyway, and several came home in body bags while strife continued to plague one of the poorest of Africa's nations.

A new single-sheet flyer/ad entitled "It's Still the Same Old Story" showed that the new Clinton administration, like numerous predecessors, was top-heavy with CFR Insiders. Sixteen high-ranking officials, including Mr. Clinton himself, were members of the world government organization, and half of them were also listed on the Trilateral Commission's roster. This newest handout urged recipients to purchase and distribute copies of *The Insiders*.

Although his surprising run for the presidency didn't bring him victory, Ross Perot used his newly acquired notoriety to push hard for a Con-Con. Interviewed on several television programs, he delightedly claimed that only "two more states" were needed to force Congress to create the convention. Members in key states continued to warn state legislators about the likely harm to the entire Constitution should there be a Con-Con. Society members led in the campaign to persuade state legislatures to rescind previous calls for a convention.

A newly activated U.S. Commission on Improving the Effectiveness of the United Nations held an event at UCLA. Formed by several CFR members and funded by CFR led tax-exempt foundations, the Commission had already met in Philadelphia and its second meeting in Los Angeles attracted Mayor Tom Bradley (CFR) and several other CFR schemers. But two UCLA students were on hand to greet attendees and hand each a flyer urging readership of Bill Jasper's *Global Tyranny ... Step by Step* book and a recently published article from *The New American* entitled "UN: A Threat To Liberty."

Given a chance to speak to the 200 attendees at the UCLA event, one of the courageous students delivered a short statement pointing out that the UN's claim to favor peace was deceitful because its own Charter explicitly described its war powers. He added that the UN was already guilty of war atrocities such as its attack on Katanga in 1961. He ended his brief message with: "Please join me in calling for the U.S. to get out of the UN." Unexpected applause from many in the audience caused the Commission's co-chairman, Trilateral Commission member Congressman James Leach (R-Iowa), to attempt saving face with the quip, "It's always nice to hear an opposing viewpoint."

Bill Jasper spent large portions of the next three months on a coast-to-coast tour delivering a speech urging withdrawal from the United Nations and autographing copies of his *Global Tyranny ... Step by Step*. With short breaks during his extended forays into various parts of the nation, he traveled through 33 states and delivered his major speech 49 times. At many stops, he also met with the press, gave a short version of his speech at luncheon meetings, and took advantage of opportunities to speak to high school students. His guest appearances on television shows numbered 14 and he participated in 57 interviews on radio stations. Other Society speakers had completed similar tours but none had been "on the road" as successfully as my good friend Bill Jasper in 1993.

Five pages of the May 1993 *Bulletin* carried major excerpts from a 1969 Welch speech warning about the attitude known as anti-Semitism. Also, the Society's four-page article "Rely On Science!" had become an increasingly popular item even though a few members had complained about its title after some recipients thought it to be supportive of bogus science. After due consideration, the article was re-issued with a new title, "Stop Environmental Hysteria!"

Repetition over radio and TV interviews of the pithy summation "A Communist is nothing but a Socialist in a hurry" continued to attract Americans to the Society. Plans were announced to create widespread distribution of the May 17, 1993 issue of *The New American* headlined "Regulation in America: Is This Still the Land of the Free?" Focusing totally on the harm being accomplished throughout the nation by federal regulatory agencies, the usefulness of this particular issue of the magazine soon paralleled the successful distribution of the previous year's "Resilient Earth" issue.

Publication of two important books debunking environmental claims heartened members. These were *Sound and Fury: The Science and Politics of Global Warming* by University of Virginia Professor Patrick Michaels and *Environmental Overkill: Whatever*

Happened to Common Sense? by Washington Governor Dixy Lee Ray. Both proved helpful in the effort to prevent dangerous proposals from being enacted to deal with questionable environmental claims.

The text of testimony given by Society official Don Fotheringham to a Louisiana government body filled four pages of the July *Bulletin*. Don spoke in opposition to a measure seeking to have the state of Louisiana call for a Con-Con. After listening carefully, many of that state's legislators responded favorably and refused to issue a convention call.

In a recent TRIM "report card" showing his record over the past few months, Congressman James Inhofe (R-Okla.) was shown to have voted seven times for higher taxes and more government. Members in his district let him know of their displeasure. Months later when the next TRIM Bulletin appeared, Mr. Inhofe's record showed eight votes for lower taxes and less government and none for the opposite stances. During the next election cycle, Representative Inhofe won a seat in the U.S. Senate where he has been a conservative stalwart and a challenger of much of the dangerous environmental nonsense for many years.

The *Bulletin* published the Society's expression of deep gratitude to Brigadier General Andrew Gatsis, U.S. Army (Ret.) whose numerous speeches and occasional articles in *The New American* had contributed significantly to Society campaigns. General Gatsis accepted appointment to the Society's National Council.

Continuing its reports about educational decline, *The New American* showed the harm being done in the nation's schools through the United Nations influenced "Outcome-Based Education" program. Members were asked to contact their congressional representative urging support for a measure that would have the Federal Reserve audited, something that had never been done in the Fed's 80 years of existence. Under the title "Memories of Larry McDonald," the *Bulletin* carried a well-deserved tribute to the late Society leader on the 10th Anniversary of his disappearance with 268 others aboard KAL 007.

Members made an instant bestseller of my newly published book, *Financial Terrorism: Hijacking America Under the Threat of Bankruptcy*. The book won praise for having "demystified" the field of economics and made the so-called "dismal science" understandable for anyone. Topics explained in layman's terms included a definition of sound money, the truth about inflation, the horror of national indebtedness, and the conspiratorial planning aimed at seeking the nation's financial destruction.

The *Bulletin* continued to encourage strong opposition to the proposed North American Free Trade Agreement (NAFTA). Members were asked to show David Rockefeller's support for this dangerous proposal. Heaping praise on the NAFTA proposal, Rockefeller who, at the time, held top leadership posts in both the CFR and Trilateral Commission had stated, "Everything is now in place – after 500 years – to build a true 'new world' in the Western Hemisphere. I don't think that the word 'criminal' would be too strong a word to describe rejecting NAFTA." His heavy endorsement spurred many to work harder to block congressional support for the pact. The effort did not succeed however, as NAFTA won approval in Congress and thousands of jobs and even entire factories soon went to Mexico.

Many members and friends journeyed to Indianapolis for the Society's 35th anniversary celebration. In addition to an array of Society speakers, Army veteran William Miller related details of his friendship with and admiration for Captain John Birch when the two worked together in China during World War II. As a young Army lieutenant fresh from graduation at West Point, Miller's facility with the Chinese language led to his being immediately assigned to the Far East war zone. He worked closely with Birch whose exploits he knew well, and whose death at the hands of Chinese Communists he sadly reported to superiors. Miller told of the great respect all Americans serving in China had for the man Robert Welch lauded in his book, *The Life of John Birch*. He also told of gathering area Catholic chaplains to offer a Solemn High Requiem Mass and burial for the man he and others believed should have been awarded the Congressional Medal of Honor. After retiring from the Army, Miller spent the rest of his years in the West Indies. He greatly appreciated the opportunity to meet with and speak to members of the Society.

CHAPTER 54
1994: COUNTERING WILD RUMORS

An early 1994 *Bulletin* reported the success that Society members had achieved with letters of protest about the choice of militant leftist Morton Halperin for appointment to a high Pentagon post. The embattled Halperin withdrew his name for consideration. Critics of the Society had often scoffed at the ineffectiveness of letter-writing campaigns. But Halperin's withdrawal (almost certainly because of the uproar created by JBS members) showed that the tactic frequently works. In later years, acting on the advice of friendly members of Congress, Society leaders urged telephone calls in place of letters as the best way to contact their elected officials. Because of anthrax scares and other blockages, letters sent to Congress were being routed through a time-consuming screening process. Telephone calls, either to an office in Washington or to a local district office, became the more effective way to get a congressman's attention.

As the seemingly endless campaign to prevent a Con-Con heated up once again, Don Fotheringham spelled out the real reason why some wanted a convention "They want to wreck or replace the Constitution itself," he claimed. "It's a gross absurdity," he added, "to insist on a convention to add a Balanced Budget Amendment when Congress already has power to balance the budget via the Constitution's Article I, Section 7." Such a sensible use of what's already in the Constitution would certainly not "endanger the entire Constitution," he added. And he showed the folly of another supposed need for a convention: the clamor for limiting the terms of office holders. His comment? "We already have a term limitation mechanism; it's called voting."

Among the first to warn about the dangers inherent in any strengthening of the General Agreement on Tariffs and Trade (GATT), Society members did their best to block such a move. But the Clinton Administration prevailed. Soon, GATT became the World Trade Organization (WTO), another meddlesome and dangerous United Nations subdivision.

Member enthusiasm for the April 4, 1994, issue of *The New American* headlined "Toward a Police State" resulted in repeated calls to the printer for additional printings of tens of thousands. That issue of the magazine became even more useful when the leftist's phony campaign against "assault weapons" posed an attack on every citizen's right to keep and bear any firearms.

When numerous portions of the nation were inundated with claims that "black helicopters" were about to transport UN troops to take control of domestic enclaves and their inhabitants, the Society capably put that rumor to rest. No such plan ever existed. As had been done in numerous other instances, the Society's efforts showed that this particular rumor of impending calamity was completely without merit.

After C-SPAN aired my speech about the misuse of our nation's military, the staff of a Virginia-based training school for Marine Corps Majors and Lieutenant Colonels arranged to have me speak at the school. Drawing from its budget to bring "expert commentators" to address the officers, the school paid for this JBS official to deliver the Society's thoughts on the proper and improper employment of our nation's military. Here we had a former Marine Corps officer telling active duty USMC officers how they were being required to carry out assignments that were constitutionally questionable – all at U.S. government expense. A first? Yes indeed.

During the Q&A session following my prepared remarks, one of the Marine officers wanted to know the Society's position when people in other lands were being systematically slaughtered "such as Bosnian Muslims." Without hesitation, I answered: "The purpose of the U.S. military is to safeguard the lives and property of the American people. Placing U.S. military forces in the midst of a struggle that has been going on for centuries is not among the vital interests of this nation. The situation you mention is tragic, but it is not an American problem." And I added: "It has always been true that liberals are very generous with other people's money; it has become additionally true that liberals are also generous with other people's sons, daughters, fathers, and brothers." The USMC officer who asked the question nodded his agreement with my response.

An announcement about the passing of Ezra Taft Benson filled an entire page in the *Bulletin*. Robert Welch and the Society itself had benefited greatly from the outspoken support given by the former Eisenhower administration Secretary of Agriculture (1953–1961). Benson would later serve as the top official of the Church of Jesus Christ of Latter Day Saints (the Mormon Church).

Several years after Mr. Benson was no longer a cabinet official, a Salt Lake City newspaper published excerpts of his letters written during the mid-1960s. Of particular interest were those he sent to J. Edgar Hoover urging the FBI leader to resist any pressure to condemn The John Birch Society. The letters from Mr. Benson to Director Hoover also contained his suggestion that President Eisenhower had helped Communism, not impeded its progress.

In a warning about impending pro-UN initiatives, Bill Jasper listed the following proposed UN treaties: Biodiversity, Rights of the Child, Law of the Sea, and five separate "Human Rights" pacts. Articles about the dangers posed by each of these had already appeared in recent issues of *The New American*. Reminding members of the many dangerous designs of the world body was hardly necessary, but doing so generated more anti-UN activity.

The *Bulletin* announced the availability of two new video presentations: 1) "Who Is Bill Clinton?" a 29-minute expose' of the life and career of the man then serving as President the United States; and 2) "Revolution By Treaty," an explanation of the portion of the Constitution dealing with treaties – emphasizing that treaty law does **not** supersede the Constitution. Both presentations were immediately put to work by many members.

Another Special Issue of *The New American* reported the deficiencies of our nation's education system. Entitled "What Went Wrong?" it received huge accolades from readers who ordered extra copes to share with the growing number of parents who were finding the government schools deficient, even dangerous places for their offspring.

1994 proved to be a banner year. Recruiting increased 79 percent; literature sales doubled the total reached two years earlier; subscriptions to *The New American* grew at the same rate; and the significant impact of TRIM on members of Congress continued.

Chapter 55
1995: Gingrich Exposed; New Books

The year 1995 began with Republicans holding majority control of both Houses of Congress. House Speaker Newt Gingrich unveiled his "Contract With America" described by Bill Jasper in *The New American* as a dangerous proposal that was far from something any knowledgeable conservative should support. He explained that passage of its call for a presidential "line-item veto" would shift power to the Executive branch; its "term limits" provision would erode accountability of elected officials; its proposal for a balanced budget amendment would turn out to be more unnecessary face-saving not monetary saving; and its intention to fund police departments would be a step toward creation of federalized police power. Jasper insisted that the real "Contract With America" was the U.S. Constitution and each member of Congress had already sworn a solemn oath to uphold it, not the phony substitute being offered. Members throughout the country immediately began sharing copies of this particular issue of *The New American* explaining in greater detail that Gingrich's "Contract" was fraught with danger.

Speaker Gingrich had already expressed great admiration for *The Third Wave*, a book by Alvin and Heidi Tofler. Their book boldly stated that our nation's governmental system was "increasingly obsolete, oppressive and dangerous." Instead, it called for the U.S. Constitution to be "radically changed and a new system of government invented." His heavy endorsement of such revolutionary thinking combined with spreading awareness that he was a veteran CFR member helped to diminish Gingrich's stature and effectiveness.

Pointing to the horror of mounting federal indebtedness, the *Bulletin* noted the obvious disdain toward their oath of office exhibited by many government officials. Knowing that oath-taking had become a mere formality without substance, the Society summarized: "If our congressmen would follow the Constitution they've sworn to uphold, the federal government would shrink to approximately 20 percent its size and 20 percent its cost." The Society's list of unconstitutional programs and agencies that should be abolished included: Foreign Aid, Food Stamps, the Departments of Energy, Education, and Housing and Urban Development, and the practice of creating law with executive orders issued by the president.

While on a speaking tour through Montana, I stressed the above points before an audience of approximately 100. After the meeting and its Q&A session, a huge rancher, still in his overalls, arrived at the podium and stated rather brusquely: "You said the government would shrink by 20 percent. How about five?" I quickly responded, "You might be correct and I'll keep your comment in mind." Only then did he smile and indicate that he was glad to have attended the program.

The Society produced two new books; my *Changing Commands: The Betrayal of America's Military*, and *Freedom on the Altar: The UN's Crusade Against God and Family* written by William Norman Grigg. Soon after these two books became available, the Fourth Edition of *The Insiders: Architects of the New World Order* also arrived from the Society's printer. This latest in the series of my popular small paperback books provided sharp criticism of the past four administrations and an updated listing of CFR and Trilateral members.

Don Fotheringham continued providing state legislative committees with "in person" testimony about the dangers inherent in a Con-Con even if such a goal was hidden in a call for a Conference of the States. In a short space of time, he spoke before state legislative bodies in Colorado, Nevada, Maryland, Pennsylvania, New Mexico and Montana. Meanwhile, other JBS members were combating the drive to create a Con-Con in their states.

Gary Benoit set the stage for widespread JBS exposure of the United Nations in October 1995, the 50th anniversary of the initial meeting the world body's members. In addition to the books, pamphlets, and videos already available, he recommended obtaining copies of the special issue of *The New American* headlined "Coming Your Way: The United Nations, Global Government … and You!" The May *Bulletin* led off with a six-page "Open Letter to Members of Congress." Prominently labeled a message from the President of The John Birch Society, it reminded federal legislators of their solemn oath to stand by the Constitution's limitations on the powers of government. Members responded by sending copies of this "Open Letter" to senators and congressmen.

Two new pamphlets arrived to aid in the campaign to Get US out! One bore the title "A Dozen Reasons" to withdraw from the UN and the second bore the title "Why Not World Government?" Both were used by members to alert fellow Americans about the danger posed by membership in the world body. But a curious problem arose when members found that sharing the "Why Not World Government?" pamphlet needed a new title. The one already in use seemed to be promoting the United Nations with its title, not calling attention to reasons why the United States should withdraw. It was replaced with a more understandable title.

CEO Smith delightedly announced that the Society had just purchased its headquarters building and an adjacent building that would henceforth house the Society's research files, shipping/warehouse space, and *The New American* editorial office. He wrote glowingly of the gratitude the Society owed to all who had provided the funds to accomplish such a great step forward. Those funds, largely provided by well-to-do members and friends for the special purpose of buying two buildings, did not tap into normal revenue streams.

Soon, construction of a tunnel linking the two buildings began – an addition greatly appreciated by all who regularly needed ready access to both buildings. The underground passageway has always delighted users but especially during the frigid winter months. One of the walls in the lengthy tunnel would later become adorned with dozens of photos of Robert Welch – from his earliest days as a boy in North Carolina and his years at the Naval Academy and the Welch Candy Company to his founding and leadership of The John Birch Society. Visitors to the Society's headquarters have always been greatly impressed by the obvious professionalism present in these buildings. An early announcement appeared in July for the "Open House" planned for October.

A second edition of *The Secret File on John Birch* became available. Authors James and Marti Hefley had initially published their book about John Birch in 1980 after consulting with JBS staff officials who helped them with information and contacts. Drawing on additional details gathered from relatives and friends of John Birch, plus the declassification of some government documents, the Hefleys produced their second book, an excellent study that proved to be well worth any reader's time.

Members were advised to keep in contact with their congressmen, especially because liberal GOP leaders were now pressuring many fellow Republicans whose past showed them to be opponents of dangerous legislation. Speaker Gingrich, in particular, had begun steering House members to support harmful measures. The suggested method of dealing with such a problem was more TRIM Bulletin distribution and more use of the Conservative Index published semi-annually by *The New American*.

The September *Bulletin* repeated a lesson given by Larry McDonald 20 years earlier. It involved a JBS member claiming to have found a conservative candidate for Congress in his area. The excited individual contacted McDonald to ask for advice about getting his newly found candidate elected. Larry's immediate response was, "How many chapters of the Society are there in your district?" When told there were very few, McDonald responded by telling the eager Bircher that he would be wasting his time and money. He continued, "The way to get a really good person elected to Congress is to build the Society beforehand." Which is what he had done before he announced his own candidacy.

Gary Benoit reported on the revelations dug out by Bill Jasper about the bombing of the Murrah Building in Oklahoma City. Bill had convincingly shown in articles published in *The New American* that bombs had been set off within the building and there was a "John Doe #2" who collaborated with Timothy McVeigh. Yet, the authorities probing the disaster were determined to reach other conclusions. Nationally known columnist Sam Francis stood virtually alone in commenting that Bill Jasper's work dealing with the Oklahoma City bombing "deserved a Pulitzer Prize."

After U.S. Army Specialist Michael New refused to add UN insignia to his uniform and serve under a UN commander in Europe, he was disciplined and eventually removed from the Army. Arguing that he joined the United States military, not the UN military, he stood his ground and sent a shock wave throughout all levels of the military.

I sought from numerous military personnel an answer to the simple question, "Is a potential recruit told that, if he joins one of the branches of the U.S. military, he might be placed in a UN unit?" Practically all of the military spokespersons I eventually contacted admitted an inability to answer that simple question and each directed me to contact a more senior officer at some other location. I did as suggested and one after another said they couldn't provide an answer, adding that I should direct my question to a higher authority. At each of these inquiries, I identified myself as a reporter for a national magazine. My quest for an answer had begun with military personnel in Massachusetts, then to senior officers at an Air Force base in New York, who directed me to contact senior officials at another Air Force base – this one in Texas. Finally, I was given the phone number of an officer at the Pentagon, a lieutenant colonel. I asked the above question and he immediately said he didn't want to be quoted by name. Once he had assurance that I would not name him, he stated, "You're absolutely correct in asking about the way our forces are being shifted around. But I'm retiring in three weeks which is why I asked not to be named." Transfers of U.S. forces to UN control continued. The Society would later state with abundant evidence that U.S. forces serving in NATO-authorized operations – in such locations as South Korea – were undoubtedly under UN control.

Many hundreds of members happily attended the Open House held at JBS headquarters. They all appreciated touring the facilities and meeting members of the staff. A sense of significant accomplishment combined with an obvious need to continue the Society's work permeated the thinking of the many visitors. An evening banquet followed where a parade of Society officials provided encouraging reports about the Society's work and the organization's plans for the future.

CHAPTER 56
1996: "CONSPIRACY" TARGETED IN TNA

Bill Jasper led the way in 1996 by showing that the Clinton plan to send U.S. forces into Bosnia was really a continuation of efforts to have our nation inch toward submission to a tyrannical world government. He reached back in history with details about the plans to have World War I spur U.S. acceptance of the League of Nations, a goal never achieved. But the horrors of World War II led to our nation becoming a founding member of the United Nations in 1945. Once our forces were committed to the former Yugoslavia, members started repeating a new slogan, "Bring 'Em Home!"

Members in and around Indiana raised the funds to have a "Get US out! of the United Nations" banner flown over Notre Dame stadium during a Notre Dame-Navy football game. Soon, another banner flew back and forth over many thousands of beachgoers along the Delaware/Maryland coasts. Dozens of large signs appeared throughout Los Angeles calling for the U.S. to withdraw from the world body. Members created floats and banners depicting the same message for display in local parades and similar events.

A front-page story in the *Salt Lake City Tribune* told of Governor Mike Leavitt's utter dismay over his inability to have Utah's legislature call for a Con-Con. He blamed The John Birch Society. Nevertheless, the drive to create a Con-Con continued in other states where it ran into similar opposition from determined JBS members.

Responding to repeated suggestions from members, Society leaders began financing a national plan to place *The New American* on newsstands across the nation. Many sent special donations to fund the project. So a contract was signed with a national news distributing firm. Despite all the effort and expense over several months, newsstand sales never came close to paying for the venture and it was soon canceled. The lesson learned: Robert Welch's emphasis on person-to-person contact had been proven correct once again.

A special issue of *The New American* dealing with the exploding immigration problem won praise from readers who ordered additional copies. As has so often been the case with many matters, the Society and its magazine led the nation on this issue.

A new "Open Letter to Congress" focused attention on the transfer of authority over U.S. military units to UN control. Calling attention to the process required explaining to members of Congress that NATO was – and always had been – a subsidiary of the United Nations. This Open Letter, sent to every member of Congress and distributed by members throughout the nation, cited the subversive thoughts of Professor James J. Schneider, an instructor of senior military officials at the U.S. Army Command and General Staff College, Fort Leavenworth, Kansas. Schneider repeatedly stated the case for UN control as he told his senior officer students that "the future [of the military] will be dominated by a single overwhelming presence – the United Nations." He boldly called for open "transformation of NATO [North Atlantic Treaty Organization] from a regional security arrangement to a future role as the UN's military arm." Society resistance to this truly subversive plan continued.

In May 1996, another special issue of *The New American* contained a series of articles about the Oklahoma City bombing. Written by Bill Jasper, members in Oklahoma distributed several thousand copies to legislators, police officials, and the general public. Wherever the magazine was shared, the response included gratitude along with questions about why the authorities weren't acting on the information it contained.

As the nation slid even further away from its commendable roots, Bill Jasper cited a passage from famed British jurist Sir William Blackstone whose 1765 *Commentaries* are customarily referenced in law schools. Blackstone didn't hesitate when pointing to the foundation given man by God Himself. He wrote: "Man, considered as a creature, must necessarily be subject to the laws of his Creator...." Sadly, the highly regarded legal scholar who insisted that all law must be based on God's law would not fit well in many of our nation's current institutions where future lawyers are taught.

Spreading the importance of maintaining local police and shunning a national police force had already produced such a good effect in many quarters that the Society found it hard to believe that a Ph.D. "expert" had begun accusing the Society for stimulating homegrown terrorism. Dr. John Nutter pointed to a distorted view of several JBS books and films in his talks given to law enforcement groups. The truth, as Bill Jasper quickly pointed out, is completely opposite what Nutter was claiming. The Society had already built a deserved reputation as an opponent of terrorism and civil unrest while continuously reminding anyone that control of police should be local, not national as it had become in Nazi Germany and Soviet Russia. Talks by Dr. Nutter and like-minded "experts" have nevertheless continued to spread a totally false depiction of the Society's efforts.

Immigration expert Michael Rodriquez became the newest star of the Society's American Opinion Speakers Bureau. As far back as 1980 when he was a prominent faculty member at the Indianapolis-based Defense Information School of Journalism, Rodriquez pointed out the Marxist beginnings of the Sanctuary Movement, the subversive program known as Liberation Theology, the mistaken emphasis placed on bilingual education, and more.

Distribution of the "Conspiracy" issue of *The New American* inched toward the 400,000 mark and it continued to be a primary tool for members reaching out to influence others. Along with it, my hour-long videotaped speech exposed the leftist career of House Speaker Newt Gingrich. The program, entitled "Newt Gingrich: Building the New World Order," showed that Gingrich was tightly tied to the CFR and its globalist agenda, and also to the New Age Movement, expanded government power, and internationalism – all of this while the U.S. news media continued to portray the House Speaker as a committed conservative. Copies of the speech, reproduced in DVD format, became useful during several of Gingrich's later efforts to become the GOP nominee for president or a cabinet official in a future administration.

JBS moviegoers who paid to see Mel Gibson's "Conspiracy" film were surprised – and pleased – to see *The New American's* "Conspiracy" issue prominently displayed at one point in the movie. Years afterward, I happened to meet Mel and, after telling him that I was the magazine's Publisher, I asked how he happened to show it in the film. He responded, "One of my assistants had a copy, showed it to me, and suggested that it might fit well in the story we were telling. So we used it." I told him that all the writers, editors, and others associated with *The New America* enjoyed knowing that a cover of their magazine had appeared in a Hollywood production.

Members throughout the nation were surprised and disappointed when one of their heroes, North Carolina Senator Jesse Helms, wrote an essay lauding the United Nations for the CFR's *Foreign Affairs* magazine. The Helms article in the September/October 1996 issue dignified the notion that the UN was useful in helping sovereign states work together. The article contained nothing about the UN's provable and consistent attack on sovereignty. Society members continued to call for the U.S. to withdraw from the world body. Obviously feeling the heat generated by the Society, the CFR then created pro-UN discussion groups in a project financed by Hungarian born and New York based billionaire George Soros, a prominent leftist who had distinguished himself by financing subversive groups and individuals.

CHAPTER 57
1997: CLINTON IMPEACHED BUT SURVIVES

In a compelling defense of the "fact" of conspiracy and its goal to create a tyrannical New World Order, Bob Lee demolished a dozen arguments employed to steer fellow Americans away from concluding that the harm being done to our nation stemmed from deliberate design. Carefully stating each of the arguments employed by conspiracy scoffers, he capably reinforced the original insistence about conspiracy spelled out by JBS Founder Robert Welch. One of the more commonly heard arguments claiming to debunk the existence of a conspiracy follows:

> If this Master Conspiracy actually exists, wouldn't at least a few prominent Americans who have stumbled across it have been willing to risk their careers and reputations, if need be, to come forward and tell what they know?

The reality is that numerous individuals, usually at great cost to themselves, have done exactly that. Lee summarized the efforts of several who did "risk their careers and reputations" to warn fellow Americans about a sinister plot to destroy the independence of our nation and the freedom of the American people. Among others, these patriotic individuals were:

Dr. William Wirt, an educator who, after being invited to Washington in 1935, listened to plotters openly boast of gaining effective Communist control over President Roosevelt and his administration. He also focused attention on the subversion already underway in our nation's schools. His efforts to prevent Communist gains failed when his credible revelations were discounted and the U.S. government's takeover of education proceeded.

Major George Racey Jordan who discovered that shipments of the plans and parts for building an atomic bomb were being sent to Russia during

World War II. He alerted senior authorities in Washington and not only was nothing done to stop the shipments, the transfers of critically important information and equipment continued and grew. He detailed what he discovered in his book, *From Major Jordan's Diaries*.

Arthur Bliss Lane resigned his post as U.S. Ambassador to Poland and wrote *I Saw Poland Betrayed* in 1948. Had his revelations been widely known, they would have shocked the nation. But a boycott of his book proved effective and it created hardly a ripple of revulsion against the pro-Communist control in Washington. Lane who gave up his career to alert the nation soon died broken-hearted.

Senator Joseph McCarthy placed his reputation on the line in the 1950s to warn about Communist infiltration of government, media, and the military. He was so wrongfully portrayed that many Americans still think he was an enemy of true Americanism instead of actually being one of its greatest defenders. The full truth about what this single man tried to do appeared in the excellent 2007 book *Blacklisted By History* authored by journalist M. Stanton Evans.

The efforts of these Americans should have produced headlines but that didn't happen. Senator McCarthy received headline treatment but it was dishonest, distorted and made useful by the enemies of freedom. The few individuals named above were prominent and credible Americans who risked their careers trying to alert the American people about treachery emanating from high places. Had there been a John Birch Society to help spread the important information these and others provided, the conspiracy's activity – and numerous conspirators – would have been set back, possibly even thoroughly exposed, and properly dealt with by appropriate authorities.

Readers of the *Bulletin* were reminded of the brilliant epigram penned by James Lucier in his study of the early history of the Conspiracy entitled *Seventeen Eighty-Nine*. He stated: "The first job of conspiracy is to convince the world that conspiracy does not exist." And, of course, widespread debunking of the notion of conspiracy has become common among people who aren't themselves involved in any element of conspiracy – except that they are being used by a force they believe does not exist.

After President Clinton selected leftist Anthony Lake to be the Director of the Central Intelligence Agency, Bill Jasper traced the man's incredibly subversive history for an article in *The New American*. A Society initiated letter writing campaign based on the Jasper research proved how important such a tactic could be when Lake withdrew his name for consideration. The incident resulted in condemnation of The John Birch Society and Bill Jasper by name in the *New York Times*, the *Wall Street Journal* and several openly leftist publications.

Colorado members raised the funds needed to place Jane Ingraham's *New American* article about the 1941 attack at Pearl Harbor in the *Rocky Mountain News* (406,000 subscribers). She told of the successful breaking of the Japanese code and the refusal of President Roosevelt and other senior government officials to warn U.S. commanders in Hawaii about the impending attack. A simple telegraphed message to either General Short or Admiral Kimmel about what was about to happen would have surely lessened the loss of life and some of the damage inflicted on U.S. ships and planes. Mrs. Ingraham concluded that President Roosevelt wanted to involve the U.S. in war and the horror at Pearl Harbor provided him with sufficient reason to proceed.

The *Bulletin* acknowledged that it and *The New American* were steady conveyors of bad news mixed with occasional victories. JBS Vice President Tom Gow addressed the complaints of many by quoting our nation's second President, John Adams, who stated:

> Liberty cannot be preserved without a general knowledge among the people … they have a right, and indisputable, unalienable, indefeasible, divine right to that most dreaded and envied kind of knowledge, I mean the character and conduct of their leaders.

An announcement reported the release of a new video program entitled *Which Way America?* written and narrated by me. It told of the early history of the Conspiracy in Part I. Then, the use of war, subversion, and the spreading of misinformation was explained in Part II. Particular emphasis was presented in this program about the decline in the quality of education and the corruption of religion.

A Nebraska member sent copies of the entire "Conspiracy" issue of *The New American* to each of his 285 fellow Nebraska chiropractors, and then to 120 law enforcement officials, numerous state government officeholders, and others – a total of 550 magazines in all. In California, JBS Council Member Cliff Goehring and several area members distributed 1,000 copies of the "Conspiracy" issue at the state's Republican Central Committee meeting.

Texas Congressman Ron Paul introduced a measure to have the U.S. withdraw completely from the United Nations. Brought to the floor for a vote, it won the support of 54 House members, the first such vote ever recorded. (218 Yes votes were needed for passage.) Members were urged to congratulate and thank the 54, and to ask other congressmen to support the measure when it again comes up for consideration.

Through all the years of the Society's existence, leaders of other organizations have sought JBS support for their various causes, publications, etc. The response by Society officials led to cooperation with some and, for solid reasons, a refusal for others. Whenever the Society declined a request that would have amounted to an alliance with another group, or merely remained silent about a questionable proposal, some seekers of Society backing for their effort responded by attacking the Society, even to accusing Welch and other leaders of being "on the other side." Their evidence to support such a charge was always ridiculous.

One individual who sought JBS backing for her "cause" learned after being told the Society would not cooperate with her that, half a century ago, Welch had been a member of the socialist League for Industrial Democracy (LID). She either didn't know or refused to acknowledge that Welch had openly stated a good while back that he had once subscribed to the LID's publication, a move that meant he automatically had become one of its "members." But he had wanted to see the publication in order to know what that leftist organization was supporting and planning. Similarly, he had subscribed to several other leftist publications. To accuse him of being a partisan for leftist goals because he read their publication was a gross absurdity. But claims seeking to disparage the Society based on such flimsy "evidence" have regularly bedeviled the organization and its leaders.

In mid-July, UN Secretary General Kofi Annan told the Associated Press of his hope "to reverse the perception, widespread within the United States, that the United Nations is a bloated, ineffectual organization that wastes American taxpayers' money." As the Society's Public Relations Director, I issued the following comment:

> Rather than be upset at finding this attitude among Americans, the Secretary General should be delighted. If the American people think the UN is merely a do-nothing bureaucracy, any desire for U.S. withdrawal will be minimal. After all, many will conclude that an ineffectual UN can't be much of a threat. Astute UN watchers, however, know that the UN is actually hiding behind the image of ineffectiveness. It is both steadily tightening its grip on the sovereignty of nations and working toward becoming the unchallengeable world government its creators envisioned it to be.

The New American had earlier published convincing evidence about some individuals having prior knowledge of the plan to bomb the Oklahoma City federal building.

Bill Jasper had verified that personnel employed by the Bureau of Alcohol, Tobacco and Firearms (ATF) had been instructed not to go to work on that fateful morning. A witness called by the county grand jury two years after the bombing told of having gone to the building immediately following the explosion to look for his wife who filled a position within the building (though she was not employed by ATF). When he arrived at the site, he was told by an ATF agent that he would find no ATF personnel there because they had been alerted not to come to work that morning. This particular witness, a man named Bruce Shaw, testified for 90 minutes before the grand jury. His startling claims impressed the grand jurors but the coverup of what really occurred on that day continued.

Among the constant stream of recommended books, the Society pointed to *Windswept House*, a novel about infiltration of the Catholic Church by individuals – including some clergymen – who sought to bring the Church into the "new world order." The author, Catholic priest Malachi Martin, had become "laicized" (a term used for priests who no longer wished to function in that capacity). Before he received lay status, he had spent years as a member of the Vatican staff, and after finding himself amidst numerous clergymen whom he deemed to be enemies of Catholicism, and without any ability to do something about such penetration, he resigned his post. Soon making his way to America, he spent years writing and speaking about his first-hand knowledge of subversion within the church. My interview of this fascinating individual appeared in the June 9, 1997, issue of *The New American*.

The Society and its magazine regularly published information about issues and persons who would be featured months – or even years – later by the mainstream media as newly discovered newsmakers. One excellent example of JBS being "ahead of the curve" was the cover article in the October 12, 1998, issue of *The New American*. Under a headline asking "Is This The Face of Terror?" the magazine provided a photo and a brief history of Osama bin Laden, the wealthy Saudi exile who had been accused of being responsible for the bombing of U.S. embassies in Kenya and Tanzania and was later believed to have masterminded the 9/11 attacks on our nation. Long before most Americans ever heard of this man, Bill Jasper stated: "… there is no secret that bin Laden has declared war on America." Three years later after pointing to this man and his intentions, the horrific attacks on New York's Twin Towers and the Pentagon were carried out by bin Laden's Al Qaeda. The wealthy terrorist immediately claimed responsibility for the death of 3,000 Americans, the destruction of the buildings in New York, and the attack the Pentagon. No longer were Americans able to insist that terrorism would never occur in the United States.

The November 1997 *Bulletin* announced a new Society project entitled IMPEACH CLINTON NOW! Reasons for such a dramatic demand were given in several issues of *The New American*, the *Bulletin*, and in various pamphlets and flyers created by the Society. The initial move in this campaign saw the Society launch the ad hoc committee ACTION (Activate Congress To Improve Our Nation). Anyone could obtain information by calling 1-888-LEAVE DC. As part of the effort, the Society started a petition campaign seeking to have the House of Representatives impeach the President as a needed step toward having the Senate decide if he should be removed from office.

The Constitution's Article II, Section 4 states that a president, vice president, and other federal officials can be removed from office if impeached [by the House] and convicted by two-thirds of the Senate for "treason, bribery, or other high crimes and misdemeanors." Clinton's conduct with White House intern Monica Lewinsky certainly fit the category of "misdemeanor" inasmuch as it demeaned the office of President of the United States. But the tawdry affair Clinton had with the young female was not the issue on which the Society focused its attention.

Instead, there were numerous instances where bribes were accepted by Clinton, the Democratic National Committee, and the Clinton campaign for reelection. Large amounts of money flowed into Clinton coffers followed by presidential action favoring the designs of the donors. Millions came from such individuals as Charlie Trie, John Huang and Johnny Chung, each of whom had ties to Communist China. Chung, who was considered important enough to have been awarded 51 visits to the White House, even remarked with a smirk, "I see the White House is like a subway – you have to put coins in to open the gates." After providing $640,000 to one of the Clinton organizations, Charlie Trie was scheduled to be subpoenaed by Congress. So he promptly fled to China, his home country.

American citizen Bernard Schwartz, the CEO of Loral Space & Communications Company, gave $1.3 million to Clinton's political campaigns. It just so happened that he needed approval from the federal government to supply China's military arm with highly sensitive equipment and technology for its space and missile programs. Both the U.S. Defense and State departments had properly refused Schwartz's pleas to waive existing U.S. prohibitions on selling such items to a potential enemy. But, after Schwartz gave his large donation to Clinton's reelection effort, the President transferred grant-making authority for this particular proposal from Defense and State to the Commerce Department that immediately provided the needed waivers. Schwartz, therefore, was significantly aided in his desire to sell sensitive military equipment to the Chinese. Later, he was additionally rewarded for his large donation to the Clinton machine with a White House party created to celebrate his birthday.

On December 19, 1998, the House considered four impeachment charges and approved two – perjury and obstruction of justice. Neither of those charges addressed the matter of bribery. The only approved charges against the president stemmed from the Lewinsky affair. At the Senate trial on February 12, 1999, where 67 votes were needed to remove Clinton from office, only 50 senators voted to convict the president on the obstruction of justice charge and only 45 found him worthy of removal from office on the perjury charge. Therefore, President Clinton, only the second President in our nation's history to be impeached, escaped removal from office.

After my visit to the *Washington Post* headquarters and my showing a top reporter samples of the items the Society was using in its Impeach campaign, the newspaper reluctantly admitted that among the "early activists" who succeeded in having Clinton impeached "were the leaders of the John Birch Society." The article noted further that the Society's drive to put Clinton on trial "predated" the headline-grabbing revelations about the Lewinsky affair.

CHAPTER 58
1998: OPEN HOUSE AT HEADQUARTERS

In a dramatic example of the effectiveness of the TRIM operation, ten-term California Congressman Vic Fazio startled his supporters in late 1997 when he announced his decision to forego a run for reelection. Having frequently run unopposed, he had steadily risen to important leadership positions within the Democratic Party and become a favorite of his home area's dominant newspaper. Fazio's claim that he wanted to "give more time to family life" didn't satisfy even his most diehard followers. The Fazio-friendly newspaper said he was a victim of "burnout," a claim ridiculed by the area's Birch Society members. Working under the leadership of Dr. John Burns and Council Member Cliff Goehring, the local TRIM Committee had distributed over 400,000 TRIM Bulletins during recent years, most via door-to-door delivery. Congressman Fazio wasn't a "burnout" victim; he knew he was about to be defeated by voters who had been made aware of his big spending and frequent trashing of the Constitution.

When the Associated Press announced that the federal government was no longer guilty of deficit spending, TRIM director Jim Toft did some digging and found that the Congressional Budget Office had fudged the figures. He pointed to the $5.23 trillion indebtedness figure supplied on October 1, 1996, and the indebtedness figure of $5.42 trillion posted exactly one year later. While announcing that he hadn't earned "an advanced degree in mathematics," Jim said he was nevertheless able to show that the total amount of red ink added during that year came to $190 billion. The phony claim given by the press ignored "borrowing" from Social Security and other federal trust funds. Yet, for decades into the future, government officials and unreliable press coverage continued to tell the American people that President Clinton may have had "some problems," and may have been guilty of naughty behavior, but at least he didn't run up the deficit as did his Republican predecessors. Was this type of government created misinformation the norm? Of course!

C-SPAN's airing of my "Impeach Clinton" speech spurred thousands of viewers to call the Society's toll-free telephone number to request information and purchase packets of "Impeach Clinton" literature. That speech and JBS activity nationwide had quickly generated over 5,000 inquiries.

Satisfied with the convictions of McVeigh and Nichols for the bombing of the Oklahoma City federal building, Clinton era Attorney General Janet Reno announced that the investigation was now closed. But she even admitted that many Americans remained unsatisfied, that they believed the full truth about the crime had not been told. Bill Jasper, whose investigative work and subsequent articles published in *The New American* continued to point to the involvement of others, remained convinced that a monstrous cover-up had been achieved. The *Bulletin* noted that the *Tulsa World* newspaper had published polling results showing that 71 percent believed McVeigh and Nichols were not alone in committing the terrible crime.

Even before the Clinton impeachment trial, Republican leaders in Congress formally criticized the White House for its veil of secrecy surrounding the shipment of missile guidance equipment and technology to China. Congressman Dana Rohrabacher (R-Calif.), the chairman of the House subcommittee dealing with space and aeronautics matters, commented: "I am very sad to say that [the Chinese] now have the capability of landing nuclear weapons in the United States, and we are the ones who perfected their rockets. United States national security has been harmed."

Generated in large part by the Society, resistance to the Kyoto Treaty that blamed human activity for increases in the earth's temperature resulted in a U.S. refusal to sign the document. Vice President Al Gore claimed that 1997 "will be the hottest year since records have been kept." But the Society's *Bulletin* reported the existence of opposite findings published by numerous environmental scientists including those at the Virginia-based Science and Environmental Policy Project. That group reported:

> … temperature readings taken from U.S. weather satellites, the most reliable and only global temperature data available, put 1997 among the coolest years since satellite-based measurements began.

Society efforts continued to resist unnecessary and costly programs proposed by environmental extremists who favored the dictates and restrictions contained in the Kyoto Treaty.

Having slowed down the plunging of our nation into a UN-controlled "new world order," members were now urged to generate resistance to two new proposals clearly advocating steps toward that goal. The new attacks on sovereignty called for 1) expanding NATO into a world government, and 2) creating a UN International Criminal Court to deal with "international" crimes. A new group carrying the name World Federalist Movement (not to be confused with the older and still dangerous World Federalist Association) rose to promote a "world federation." The promoters of world government seemed to have abandoned their previously touted "new world order" terminology. That constituted another small victory for The John Birch Society!

In the November *Bulletin*, members were reminded of the caution expressed by the ever-perceptive Tom Hill given in 1976. Tom wanted members to include in their recruiting efforts some mention of the positive promise of what can be built in an atmosphere of freedom. Well aware that many good members had become "bearers of bad news" (and there certainly was enough of that to share!), he counseled all to promote the long range goals of the Society even while gaining the attention of potential recruits by informing them about the latest threats to freedom. Recalling that Robert Welch had frequently reminded everyone that the Society should never be just an opponent of a Conspiracy, that it should be known for its long-range goal of preserving the American system while helping to create a world where freedom abounded.

More than 600 hundred members and friends traveled to Appleton for a gala "Open House" and celebration of the 40th Anniversary of the Society. All marveled at the extensiveness of the two buildings and the professionalism of the staff. One visitor said what most were thinking: "Because of the favorable reports I had heard about the facilities, I expected to be impressed. Seeing it for myself exceeded my expectations." The evening banquet featured brief talks by me, CEO Smith, VP Gow, and field staff veterans Mike Armstrong, Larry Waters, and Jim Fitzgerald.

While admitting that more work was needed, Society leaders claimed partial success in such campaigns as Support Your Local Police, Get US out! of the United Nations, Awareness of Conspiracy, Book Publishing, Speakers Bureau activity, Video Production, Preserving the Constitution, Protecting the Citizen's Right to be Armed, Voter Education, Putting Down Wild Rumors, and more.

The New American published a listing of Society accomplishments in conjunction with its 40th anniversary. Heaping praise on the organization, Congresswoman Helen Chenoweth (R-Idaho), a JBS member, lauded Society members "who are unashamed to advocate love of country, defense of our nation, and an abiding commitment to our Constitution." Congressman Ron Paul (R-Texas) said it would be "hard to overestimate the beneficial, educational impact of The John Birch Society over the past four decades." Columnist Joseph Sobran asked, "Who else still recognizes tyranny where our ancestors would have recognized it?"

Chapter 59
1999: "Get US Out" Campaign Grows

In addition to the Society's effectiveness in exposing Newt Gingrich as a false conservative, the GOP's poor showing in the November 1998 congressional elections contributed to his decision to abandon his Speaker of the House post. Widespread showing of the JBS produced video "The Real Newt Gingrich" surely encouraged him to bow out. Shortly afterward, he even announced his plan to leave Congress. GOP leaders looked to Robert Livingston (R-La.) to succeed him as Speaker but he suddenly withdrew from consideration. Dennis Hastert (R-Ill.) then rose from relative obscurity to acquire the high post. Years later, I asked Ron Paul how the Republican leaders had reached down so far in their ranks to choose Hastert, a former high school teacher and wrestling coach and a man hardly known to anyone outside of his district. Dr. Paul responded, "Gingrich was heavily responsible for that choice." Hastert filled the Speaker's post for a while and then retired. He eventually went to prison for attempting to hide numerous sexual improprieties and subsequent hush money payoffs that he hoped would keep his criminal activity from being known.

New video programs included "Injustice for All" designed to counter the drive for creation of a UN International Criminal Court, and "The United Nations: A Look Into The Future" to portray what an all-powerful UN would mean to nationhood and the world's people. *The New American* published a "Special Issue" labeled "Chinagate" containing numerous examples of Chinese money flowing illegally into Clinton coffers. Those "donations" were followed by favors given the Beijing regime by Mr. Clinton and his subordinates.

Continued urging spurred many members to purchase and read *Philip Dru: Administrator*, the 1912 novel written by arch-conspirator Edward Mandell House. Published anonymously, House was quickly identified as its author and never shied away from being so named. In the book, he outlined plans to seize the presidency and convert the U.S.

into a dictatorship under his leadership. He effectively accomplished many of his goals through his unusually close association with President Woodrow Wilson. House would later lead the group that founded the Council on Foreign Relations after the U.S. Senate refused to have our nation sign on as a member of the new League of Nations. Larry Greenley's eight-page "Guide" to help readers better understand the somewhat cryptic message given by House was sent to all who requested it.

Congressman Bob Barr (R-Ga.), a leader in the failed campaign to remove President Clinton from office, congratulated the Society and its members for having the president impeached. He noted that the Society "had a lot of impact" in the worthy but only partially successful campaign.

Gary Benoit pointed to the statements of Senator Robert Byrd (D-WV) expressing awareness that President Clinton had committed perjury and was guilty of "high crimes and misdemeanors." But Byrd nevertheless voted to acquit the President. Gary reminded all about this senator's previous membership in the Ku Klux Klan and his history of parading falsely as a constitutional conservative. The *Bulletin* quoted Congressman James Sensenbrenner (R-Wis.): "It's obvious to me that Senate Democrats were opposed to the impeachment. They didn't care about the evidence. They just wanted to vote 'no' and that's what happened."

The "Panama Canal Giveaway" information supplied by *The New American* spurred former Chairman of the Joint Chiefs of Staff Admiral Thomas Moorer to express his complete agreement with the stand taken by the Society. In an interview published by *The New American*, the former Chairman of the Joint Chiefs of Staff pointed out that U.S. leaders had not only given the incredibly strategic canal to a Communist-led government, the transaction also included paying them to take it. Along with the canal, U.S. leaders had also helped Chinese firms gain control of U.S. bases built to guard the strategic waterway. Admiral Moorer would then appear as the featured speaker at the Society's October Council Dinner held in Salt Lake City where he received an enthusiastic welcome.

The Society urged sending letters of thanks to 74 members of the House of Representatives who voted to cut off funding for the United Nations. Four of those congressmen were Democrats: Virgil Goode of Virginia, Matthew Martinez of California, Collin Peterson of Minnesota, and Gene Taylor of Mississippi. That 74 would take such a public stand was encouraging to Society members and cause for heightened alarm among UN officials and their supporters.

Society members and readers of *The New American* were introduced to the subversive strategy urged by Italian Communist Antonio Gramsci. Tom Gow provided an in-depth analysis of this man's sinister plan that called for winning control of a nation for Communism, not through political or military successes, but through capturing its culture. Gramsci urged gaining control of churches, labor unions, media, political parties, universities, foundations, etc. Gramsci died in 1937 but his subversive strategy continues to be systematically and steadily employed in America. Its harm has become more obvious daily.

The Society announced availability of a small but hard-hitting pamphlet entitled "The Right To Keep and Bear Arms." Members were encouraged to add it to the numerous items already dealing with the God-given right to be armed. Immediate response from JBS members indicated that retaining the right to be armed would always be a high priority. The Society closed the year 1999 and ended the 20th Century by offering a new recruiting video entitled "Membership: Making a Difference."

CHAPTER 60
2000: JBS Never Worried About Y2K

Members were surprised – and overwhelmingly pleased – with the new shape of the *Bulletin*. From the customary 32 pages and 6x9 size, the *Bulletin* was now 16 pages and 8.5x11 in size. Also, full color gave the monthly message from headquarters a very beneficial sprightliness.

The first messages of the new century told of the importance of recruiting. CEO Smith and I discussed the vital need to swell the membership rolls. As far back as 1964, Robert Welch urged everyone to consider themselves assigned "to build the organization." He frequently insisted, "Our greatest need is obviously more hands in the fight." In 1971, he expanded on that observation even while chiding himself for asking too much of every member. He wrote:

> But on the whole you good people, and even our staff, have been too busy with all of our projects (and sometimes with other people's projects). There has not been put into recruitment the concentrated effort that was needed.

Nearly 30 years had elapsed since Welch published that observation. Continuing with his thought, I added: "Our challenge is no different today. We must rapidly build this organization with more members, more chapters, and more of everything that is 'Birch,' not busily using our efforts to undertake other group's projects…."

Then, because the need was always present to stop the enemy's advances, the *Bulletin* urged members to ask their own congressman to support a measure declaring the Panama Canal Treaty and its transfer of the Canal to Panama "null and void." Immediately, 26 co-sponsors had agreed and signed on to H.J. Res. 77 introduced by Idaho Republican Helen Chenoweth. At a press conference held in the nation's capital, retired Admiral Moorer and I met with reporters at the National Press Club to issue a warning about the transfer of ownership of the Canal and the possible threat posed by Chinese taking over management and ownership of the strategic waterway. But what turned out to be a valiant try on the part of JBS members and some in Congress failed. Ownership of the Canal did shift to the ultra-leftist government in Panama and to their friends from China who were delighted to receive control of one of the world's most important shipping channels.

Concerns were then raised about the FBI's "Project Megiddo" and the 32-page "Report" the Bureau had just released. In it, the Society found itself added to a list of organizations and individuals constituting a terrorist threat to police departments and to the nation as a whole. Members were urged to contact their own police department to assure them that, rather than a threat to local police and law and order, the Society's long-standing Support Your Local Police program was as good a friend of police as could be found anywhere. Happily, Project Megiddo did little harm to the Society while accomplishing little good in targeting the real enemies of law and order. One consequence of this misguided report was the FBI discrediting itself with JBS members who had regularly supported the work of the bureau.

According to the predictions of many "experts," the dawn of the year 2000 would bring a cataclysmic worldwide shutdown of computers. In mid-1998, an analysis by Dennis Behreandt carrying the title "Millennium Mayhem" (*The New American*, September 14, 1998) had calmly provided reasons why no one should fear what was termed "Y2K." After January 1, 2000, had passed and computers kept functioning, Joseph Nocera of *Money* magazine wrote, "I never thought the day would come when I found myself in agreement with the John Birch Society, but I think those boys got this one (Y2K) exactly right." Did he then begin agreeing with more of what the Society and *The New American* were saying? No evidence showed that he did. In all likelihood, he knew little about the Society other than the nasty portrayals of our organization given by politicians and the mass media for many years.

Members were hardly surprised when reading the report in *The New American* containing CNN founder Ted Turner's categorization of himself as "a socialist at heart." He made his remark while delivering a speech in China at an event marking the 50th anniversary of the Communist takeover of that huge country.

As the UN stepped up its efforts to become the world's undisputed leader, members were reminded of four current proposals put forth by the world body. These were:

1. Creation of a world court that could bring to trial anyone from anywhere.
2. Establishment of UN world taxation in the name of protecting the environment.
3. Further steps leading to abolition of the right to be armed and enforcement of that ban by a UN military force.

4. Terminating national sovereignty in favor of world law and world government.

Members were called upon to increase their exposure of the growing threat posed by the UN. The work already accomplished over 40 years had kept these current UN goals – and numerous others – from being reached. With real but limited success already deserving of accolades, all in JBS were encouraged to arrange for showings of pertinent DVDs, distribution of more literature, sponsorship of more speaking engagements, and helping many more fellow Americans realize the need to Get US out!

The *Bulletin* announced availability of a new recruiting tool, a 20-page large size and full-color booklet entitled "Gateway to Freedom." It became a favorite of many members who used it to introduce the Society through page by page discussion of the Society's history, programs, successes, and plans for the future.

More ammunition for the Get US out! campaign came with a Special Issue of *The New American* entitled "Building the Global Gulag: The UN's Design for Millennial Tyranny." Among the many topics covered were the UN's International Criminal Court, the UN's phony Declaration on the Rights of the Child, UN Population Control, and the use of Italian Communist Antonio Gramsci's plan to subvert the human race by corrupting religion, schools, and other portions of a nation's culture.

Members were urged to voice opposition to H.R. 4453 introduced by Leftist Congressman James McGovern (D-Mass.). His bill called for the formation of a miniature UN army. After letters from JBS members warned of its consequences, the measure received very little support.

Despite candidate George W. Bush's claim to be a pro-life constitutionalist, his claim that "the Supreme Court has settled the abortion issue for all time" showed him to be a pro-abortion fellow traveler. The *Bulletin* likened his stance on this sensitive issue to that of Ronald Reagan who also claimed to be ardently pro-life but then appointed pro-abortion Justice Sandra Day O'Connor to the Court. The *Bulletin* continued to advise readers that the 2000 presidential race between Bush and Gore was asking voters to choose between "TweedleBush and TweedleGore." The recommended way to deal with such a poor choice remained directing attention to the House of Representatives where "the power of the purse" has always resided.

Don Fotheringham asked members to refrain from becoming "amendment happy." He wanted all to be able to explain to others that several amendments being promoted were either unnecessary or harmful. For example, he pointed to the proposed Balanced Budget Amendment (BBA) and a Term Limits Amendment. The BBA had so many loopholes in it that budgets would still easily be unbalanced, The effective way to cease deficit spending was already present in the Constitution (Article I, Section 7) which gave a majority in the House power to reject any spending measure. As for an amendment to limit terms, the experience of limiting a president to two four-year terms had not brought about any welcome change. Nor would limiting congressional terms do any better. Fotheringham also suggested that an amendment to ban abortion and another to punish flag burning are not necessary, that the goal sought by each – and several other proposed amendments – could be reached via legislation instead of cluttering the Constitution with unneeded amendments. CEO Smith used five pages of the August 2000 *Bulletin* to remind members about Welch's timeless "Warning Against Anti-Semitism."

Will Grigg explained the trap contained in the UN's program that awards "Non-Governmental Organization" (NGO) status. With approximately 1,500 NGOs already named, these mostly left-leaning religious, political, humanitarian, and activist organizations have claimed an ability to influence the world body from within. But, Will pointed out, groups seeking such a designation have to pledge their support for the "purposes and principles" of the UN to earn the desired NGO status. They could never call for the U.S. to withdraw from the world body. Nor could they oppose UN projects without jeopardizing their supposed power to put a brake on the UN. The world organization's NGO program effectively neutralizes groups and individuals who might otherwise be effective opponents of the world body and its designs.

An announcement appeared in the *Bulletin* about the selection by Reform Party presidential candidate Pat Buchanan who had selected JBS member and retired Los Angeles schoolteacher Ezola Foster as his running mate. Members were reminded that building the Society should be undertaken before they could expect any political victories. Bill Jasper reported on the gathering of 150 world leaders at what was called the "UN Millennial Summit." Warren Mass told of the concern expressed five years earlier by Establishment favorite Strobe Talbott, a current Deputy Secretary of State. Noting that opposition to the UN was "growing and having an impact in Congress," Talbot warned that, if the U.S. should diminish or end its support for the world body, it "might very well quickly join the League of Nations on the ash heap of history." Birch Society members applauded that assessment. Editor Gary Benoit pointed to the less-than-complimentary comments made in *The New American* about the Harry Potter phenomenon.

Members were reminded of Welch's February 1962 comments about Communist and Insider use of what he called "the principle of reversal." It had been employed against 1952 Presidential candidate Senator Robert Taft ("I like Taft but he can't win") and Senator Joseph McCarthy ("I like what McCarthy is trying to do, but I can't stand his methods"). And it was then employed to harm the Society ("The John Birch Society is a wonderful group of people, if they would only get rid of Welch and his dictatorial control.") Welch explained that the use of this principle involves recognizing some gain achieved by Conspiracy foes and then turning it around so it helps the Conspiracy and harms its enemy.

In sadness, CEO Smith told of the trial and conviction for tax evasion of long-time JBS stalwart Alan Stang. The popular writer and speaker had ignored the Society's advice, even Welch's personal urging that he abandon his one-man tax protest. Stang's many fans were certainly opposed to the income tax and the use of funds taken from Americans for questionable, even treasonous, purposes. But the Society's advice always included a recommendation that the way to deal with such injustices was to gather sufficient strength to have Congress cease the treason, abide by constitutional restraints, and eventually abolish the tax, not take on the federal government in what many others had already found to be a losing endeavor.

An announcement of the availability of a handsome book containing a compilation of *The New American's* "20th Century Heroes" caught the attention of many. Short biographies of such noteworthy persons as Chiang Kai-shek, Joseph McCarthy, Ezra Taft Benson, Taylor Caldwell, Robert Welch, Captain John Birch, Jozsef Cardinal Mindszenty, G.K. Chesterton, and others filled the book's 208 pages. Along with the "Heroes" book, members were urged to obtain David Shippers' blockbuster entitled "Sellout." Having served as the Chief Investigative Counsel for the House Judiciary Committee, Shippers accused democrats and republicans of concealing damning evidence of President Clinton's "impeachable, even criminal offenses."

CHAPTER 61
2001: *TWENTIETH CENTURY HEROES* PUBLISHED

Counting occasional "Interim" *Bulletins*, the January 2001 *Bulletin* happened to be Number 500 in the series begun decades ago. Its front page stressed continued standing for principle, even when many others preferred expediency or self-aggrandizement. Of particular note at the time was a reaffirmation of the important thinking behind the Society's classic slogan, "This is a Republic, Not a Democracy. Let's Keep It That Way." The nation's Founders gave us the rule of law rather than rule by a mob. Even though educators, elected officials, media representatives and others repeatedly referred to the U.S. system as a democracy, many Americans had become aware, not only of the Founders creation of a republic, but of their detestation of democracy.

In the wake of the extremely close presidential election that saw George Bush eventually triumph over Al Gore, the *Bulletin* urged the need to protect the Electoral College. Don Fotheringham explained the thinking of the nation's Founders when they created the unique constitutional system for electing a president. He stressed their intention to insure that small-population states had a voice in the process, something that would disappear should popular national voting and its potential for enshrining majority rule become the method of choosing a president. Keeping the Electoral College was, he wrote, one way of maintaining the republic and shunning democracy.

The 1983 pamphlet "Back to Basics" had long been a helpful tool to explain the American system in just a few words. Gary Benoit's small gem had always received due praise and members were again being urged to use it as an initial introduction to "Birch" thinking. An article in *The New American* signaled an alert about the Gramscian "Culture War" being waged against the nation.

Another warning about the possible creation of the UN's International Criminal Court (ICC) appeared in the *Bulletin*. As one of his last acts as president, Bill Clinton authorized our nation's participation in the sovereignty-compromising court. Contacting members of Congress became a project because of the court's dangerous claim of authority to prosecute officials of any nation, even uniformed members of the military serving in a foreign country.

Like its predecessors, the George W. Bush administration had selected numerous CFR and Trilateral Commission members. Off to a late start because of the delayed decision about the vote count in Florida, its highest posts went to reliable Insiders such as Dick Cheney, Donald Rumsfeld, Condoleezza Rice, Paul Wolfowitz and Colin Powell, all CFR members. Fresh from his formal swearing-in and his solemn pledge to uphold the U.S. Constitution, new Secretary of State Powell hustled himself to New York as one of his first public acts. Before an assemblage of reporters at United Nations headquarters, he displayed his woeful contempt of U.S. independence as he told reporters, "When it comes to our role as a member of the Security Council, we are obviously bound by UN resolutions and we're not trying to modify that." Placing UN power above the U.S. Constitution should have disqualified Powell for any government post. But only The John Birch Society made special note of Powell's terribly misplaced allegiance.

The struggle to preserve the U.S. Constitution received a boost when legislatures in both Utah and North Dakota withdrew previous calls for a Con-Con. Society members in those two states, and all across the nation, breathed a sigh of relief as they celebrated these hard-won achievements.

Society leaders delightedly announced the availability of Bill Jasper's newest book, *The United Nations Exposed.*

JBS Vice President Tom Gow said that the book was loaded with documented evidence of both the subversive history and current activity of the world body. Well-known intelligence specialist Dr. Joseph Douglass joined the Society's Speakers Bureau and released his important book *Red Cocaine* showing the Communist Chinese to be behind the surge in hard-core drugs entering our nation.

Bill Buckley continued to spread misinformation about the Society. Considered by Establishment figures and their docile followers as the most reliable authority about the JBS, Buckley occasionally bared his own preferences. The *Washington Times* published a revealing exchange in which this leading anti-JBS figure was asked, "If you were graduating from college in 2000, what kind of politics would a youthful Buckley embrace?" The so-called leader of the conservative movement replied, "I'd be a socialist ... a Mike Harrington socialist. I'd even say a communist!" (Michael Harrington had been a congressman from Massachusetts before he became the Founder of the Democratic Socialists of America.)

With numerous facts cataloging its history, Warren Mass showed that the European Union constituted a significant step toward world government for the nations it had lured into membership. The EU's bait consisted of such "gifts" as new highways (in Greece and Estonia), bridges (in Scotland), water purification plants (in Ireland), etc. He added that the various trade pacts into which the U.S. had been taken by Congress and recent presidents would do to the United States precisely what the EU had done to Europe – cancel national sovereignty.

Support for Ron Paul's measure calling for U.S. withdrawal from the United Nations became a regular task for members. Being able to show prospects that there indeed were members of Congress who wanted the U.S. to quit the world body helped to have more Americans accept and read pamphlets and books presenting the unvarnished truth about the UN.

For several days at the end of June 2001, Society field staff employees from all over the nation gathered at JBS headquarters for fellowship and instruction about plans for increased Get US out! activity. One of the speakers at the event was JBS member Vilius Brazenas, the Lithuanian native who twice lived under Communism and once under Nazism before fleeing to America. Telling of his personal experiences and his love for The John Birch Society made him a very popular speaker throughout the nation and especially at the many JBS summer camps he attended.

The campaign to Get US out! continued to supply members with books, pamphlets, videotapes and speakers. A new set of six colorful trifolds targeted the UN for its plans to gain control of population, military, land, guns, and children – and then create a UN taxation scheme to fund its activities. Each of those pamphlets encouraged recipients to obtain a copy of Bill Jasper's *The United Nations Exposed*. Another weapon in the anti-UN campaign was Will Grigg's 150-page paperback *Global Gun Grab: The United Nations Campaign to Disarm Americans*.

Renewed attention was drawn to the 1962 State Department document entitled "A World Effectively Controlled by the United Nations." Authored by CFR member Lincoln P. Bloomfield, it laid out plans for step-by-step acquisition of control over nations leading to the goal of world government. As subversive as the entire study was, it was particularly infuriating to know that it was paid for by taxpayers.

Members were asked to obtain and distribute another new trifold pamphlet. With a color photo of the flames shooting out of New York's Twin Towers, the pamphlet carried the appropriate headline, "Fight Terrorism: Get US out! of the United Nations."

Prominent citizens in Switzerland sponsored an appearance in their country for me as a JBS spokesman and a knowledgeable opponent of membership in the United Nations. I delivered several speeches about the wisdom of staying out of the UN. What I stated was what these good people wanted to hear. It did surprise me, however, to be questioned by some wanting to know if the UN "was dangerous from its inception." I assured all that it was. When the Swiss people voted in a subsequent national referendum, 11 cantons rejected the plan but 12 approved and Switzerland did become a member of the world body. Some of the friends I had made in that remarkable country suggested that the vote count had been rigged in at least one of the cantons. But there was nothing they could do about their suspicions.

CHAPTER 62
2002: NEW BOOK EXPOSES BUCKLEY

Bill Jasper carefully explained how leftist groups in America have succeeded in hamstringing law enforcement and intelligence agencies and left our nation wide open to terrorist attacks such as the 9/11 catastrophe. He summarized:

> The campaign has been led by such groups as the American Civil Liberties Union (ACLU), the National Lawyers Guild (NLG), the Communist Party (CPUSA), and the Institute for Policy Studies (IPS), funded by such revolutionary founts as the Ford and Rockefeller Foundations, and promoted by the Council on Foreign Relations, the *New York Times*, the *Washington Post*, CBS, NBC, CNN and other co-conspirators in the national media.

In addition, as Bill affirmed, the porous border had enabled millions to cross into the United States. Among the illegal entrants were terrorists, common criminals, and drug dealers who should never have been allowed into our country.

Jasper lamented the failure of Congress to back H. Res. 48, a measure designed to reestablish the House Internal Security Committee (once known as the House Committee on Un-American Activities). The measure had originally been introduced years earlier by Congressmen Larry McDonald (D-Ga.) and John Ashbrook (R-Ohio).

Traffic to the five JBS web sites continued to grow. In 2001, over four million visitors accessed the sites seeking information, or wanting to order JBS books, pamphlets, DVDs, etc. The surge amounted to a 46 percent increase during 2002 over the number of visitors in 2001.

Will Grigg's pocket-sized 150-page book *Global Gun Grab* continued much in demand, especially among defenders of the Second Amendment. One individual, not a member of the Society, purchased 2,000 copies of the book and conducted his own personal distribution.

Demonstrating that the Society had provided valuable leadership by alerting Americans to the threat of terrorism, the *Bulletin* showed a listing of articles dealing with the topic beginning in 1968. The first of many was Gary Allen's article entitled "Terrorism" published by *American Opinion* in December 1968. Through succeeding years, articles by Welch, Larry McDonald and numerous others spelled out the tactics and individuals involved in or suspected of terrorist activity. More information about this topic appeared in the important video program "No Place To Hide, The Strategy and Tactics of Terrorism" produced by McDonald's Western Goals Foundation and shown by Society members throughout the nation.

Detailed information appeared in the *Bulletin* about creating local committees to publicize the need to "Get US Out of the United Nations." Impetus to do so grew when Mikhail Gorbachev's enthusiasm for the European Union (an important step toward a UN-led world government) received media attention. The former leader of the USSR had stated during a 2000 visit to London that the EU is "the new European Soviet." The Society agreed with that assessment.

The ever-valuable Bill Jasper cut through all of the favorable verbiage about the plan to have the 2001 Quebec Summit recognized as the first step in creating a European Union-style pact called the Free Trade Area of the Americas (FTAA). President George W. Bush declared that his goal was to have Congress approve U.S. entry into FTAA by 2005 and then have all of the Western Hemisphere nations (except Cuba) enlisted by the year 2010. Bill showed that all of the organizations promoting this sovereignty-destroying scheme had ties to David Rockefeller and other members of the Rockefeller family.

Jim Toft alerted members about the national debt breaking through the $6 trillion plateau. Warren Mass pointed out that the UN was again seeking independent taxing authority in addition to its drive to create and empower an International Criminal Court. Members were urged to contact representatives in Congress to oppose such conspiratorial plans.

Television's History Channel broadcast a riveting program about the 1942 U.S. bombing raid over Tokyo and the remarkable American who rescued lead pilot Jimmy Doolittle and his crew from occupied China. The program actually devoted much of its content to the exploits of then-missionary John Birch and his subsequent years as a commissioned officer in the U.S. Army serving in China. It boosted JBS morale everywhere to know that John Birch was finally receiving some praise for his heroic work

A call went out to oppose creation of the Department of Homeland Security because it would amount to federal meddling in police work and possible federal control of local police. All who received the alert were informed (reminded?) that a similar agency had been created in Germany during Hitler's rise to total power.

Jim Toft sought to energize more members either to start or to beef up TRIM activity by pointing out that two farms in upstate New York had been paid close to half a million dollars by the federal government over five recent years to do little or nothing with their land. The owner of the two farms? Billionaire banker David Rockefeller.

Veteran staff official Don Fotheringham relied on his extensive field coordinator experience to compile warnings about attitudes and programs capable of luring JBS members away from important issues and programs. His valuable treatise entitled *Tangents* has always helped many to keep their eye on the JBS ball rather than become ensnared into quick fix, dead-end, and cleverly designed fringe alternatives taking them away from important activity.

The *Bulletin* announced the Society's publication of my long-awaited book *William F. Buckley, Jr.: Pied Piper for the Establishment*. It shows how Buckley regularly carried the ball for more government and more entangling alliances – while being praised by liberals and leftists as "the responsible voice of the conservative movement." Buckley, who never missed an opportunity to smear Welch and the Society, eventually acknowledged the book's existence but said the only condemnation of him was the fact that he had joined the Council on Foreign Relations. It did that on a single page of the 250-page book. But other pages showed his pro-UN, pro-abortion, pro-Big Government, and dishonest anti-JBS stances. Not one fact in the book has ever been challenged.

When a number of world government crusaders began promoting a "New World Religion," the Society responded and soon had members and pastors across the nation sharing articles and booklets about this latest subversive UN activity. Its major promoters – Steven Rockefeller, Mikhail Gorbachev, and Maurice Strong – actually displayed a made-to-order replica of the Old Testament's Ark of the Covenant. They dubbed their blasphemous creation the "Ark of Hope" and showed it in various U.S. communities in hopes of building enthusiasm for the UN's consistent refusal to acknowledge God's very existence. Once the scheme became known to JBS members, they combated it with a special issue of *The New American* entitled "The New World Religion." In Indiana, JBS leader Al Foreman wrote enthusiastically about the willingness of numerous pastors to help in the distribution of the magazine to their congregations. This UN program eventually suffered a welcome death.

CEO Smith eagerly announced a plan to purchase yet another building near the Society's Appleton headquarters to house Robert Welch University. Already functioning, RWU had plans to develop materials for home-school education, manage the summer camp program previously run by the Society, develop a college/adult-level curriculum, and more. RWU never accomplished the goals set for it and was eventually replaced by the more-successful Freedom Project Academy discussed in a later chapter.

National, even global attention zeroed in on Iraq and especially on its leader, Saddam Hussein. Accusations were spread worldwide that he possessed an arsenal of "weapons of mass destruction" (WMD) and was about to use them against others, including the United States. The American people weren't told that he obtained most of his arms from the United States. Nor was any proof ever offered that he indeed had created some fearsome WMDs. It seemed mostly that someone had to pay for what was done to America on 9/11 – even though all but a few of the airplane hijackers were Saudis, not Iraqis.

President Bush eagerly signed H.J Res.114, a measure giving him a congressional green light to invade Iraq. The U.S. Constitution granting power to send the nation into war to Congress alone was again ignored. During a press conference, Mr. Bush was asked about WMDs and his answer included backing away from the podium and slowly turning 360 degrees as if he were searching for something. His incredible mockery of the claims of those insisting there were no such weapons in Iraq infuriated Society members and many other Americans. The president had signaled a willingness to send American forces into an undeclared war. And he obviously knew there were no WMDs in the country he was prepared to invade. As usual, authorization to proceed with the invasion came from the United Nations. The second war against Iraq would soon begin.

The final chapter of my immediately popular book about Buckley carried the heading, "The JBS: Alive, Well, and Growing." Deemed an excellent introduction to prospective members by several headquarters staff personnel, it was reprinted separately and used as an aid in recruiting. Promoters of the UN's godless religion switched some of their emphasis to a campaign calling for earth worship. Members quickly exposed this "New False Religion" as part of their effort to counter the "New World Religion" and its United Nations sponsor. Both of the UN's attempts to denigrate religion failed and no more was heard about either of these proposals.

CHAPTER 63
2003: GAY MARRIAGE OPPOSED

Jim Toft unearthed a remarkable 2002 statement offered by Ben Bernanke, then a member of the Federal Reserve Board of Governors. It was remarkable because it contained an unvarnished assessment of the value of the dollar, the non-existent legality of government creation of money out of nothing, and a credible awareness of inflation. Speaking at the D.C.-based National Economics Club, the man who would be named Federal Reserve Chairman four years later stated:

> Like gold, U.S. dollars have value only to the extent that they are strictly limited in supply. But the U.S. government has a technology called a printing press (or, today, its electronic equivalent) that allows it to produce as many U.S. dollars as it wishes at essentially no cost. By increasing the number of U.S. dollars in circulation, or even by credibly threatening to do so, the U.S. government can also reduce the value of the dollar in terms of goods and services, which is equivalent to raising the prices in dollars of those goods and services. We conclude that, under a paper-money system, a determined government can always generate higher spending and hence positive inflation.

Jim pointed out that Bernanke's remarks were prepared for delivery, not off-the-cuff meanderings. Of course, missing in what the future Fed Chairman said was any condemnation of inflation and any mention of the Fed by name. Bernanke would soon be named Fed Chairman and the sound perspective he provided at the National Economics Club was never uttered again.

The next Society-produced video program carried the title "Behind the Big News." Issued alongside a special "Media Cartel" issue of *The New American*, the two items capably exposed the unreliability of the mass media. Since many Americans had already concluded that the media was generally untrustworthy, distribution of these two items proved helpful in prospecting and recruiting.

On the heels of exposing the media, the Society's video department released a blockbuster program entitled "Indoctrinating Our Youth in Earth Worship." Only 22 minutes long, it was designed for use at many of the nation's noontime service clubs. Its message showing the UN behind this form of subversion also proved especially useful in energizing parents of high schoolers who were being subjected to this newest example of pro-UN propaganda.

The March 2003 *Bulletin* announced publication of *Inside the United Nations* a 136-page book exposing the goals of the world body. Steve Bonta's small but excellent introductory look at the world body helped many readers to understand the need to Get US out! of the United Nations. The *Bulletin* then carried the sad news that Jim Toft had suddenly passed away. A talented writer and speaker, Jim had only recently been feted on the 30th anniversary of his work as a member of the Society's staff.

Veteran members were reminded and newer members introduced to one of the oldest and most glaring examples of INSIDER treachery: the 1961 State Department document entitled "Freedom From War." In just 19 pages, this official U.S. government plan listed steps designed to have the U.S. and all nations not only disarm but also turn over their weaponry to the "U.N. Peace Force." The Society reprinted many copies of this remarkably subversive document for sharing with fellow Americans.

The campaign to block creation of a Con-Con received a boost when former Idaho Assistant Attorney General George Detweiler, a JBS member, explained in a short essay that the goal should be "Amend the Court, Not the Constitution." Warren Mass urged distribution of a reprint of my article in *The New American* entitled "Irreconcilable Differences," a report about how a few determined senators blocked entry into the League of Nations soon after World War I. Its bottom-line message was that protecting national sovereignty by staying out of any world government organization was wisely accomplished on one occasion, and withdrawing from the United Nations would be a current expression of similar wisdom.

The *Bulletin* reminded readers that late 19th Century British Prime Minister Benjamin Disraeli once demonstrated his awareness of conspiracy when he stated: "The world is governed by very different personages from what is imagined by those who are not behind the scenes." Catherine Drinker Bowen's *Miracle at Philadelphia*, a riveting book about what occurred during the Constitutional Convention of 1787, earned high praise.

Far ahead of most in America, the *Bulletin* made note of the loss of 2.5 million manufacturing jobs during the first three years of the George W. Bush administration. Much of the lost industry went to Mexico or China courtesy of NAFTA and other job-killing pacts.

Society members were urged to contact members of Congress to have them block further losses by refusing to approve President Bush's call for creation of the EU-style pact known as the Free Trade Area of the Americas (FTAA).

On July 15, 2003, 74 members of the House of Representatives backed an amendment to the Foreign Relations Authorization Act. It called for terminating any funding going to the United Nations. Although the measure didn't pass, the simple fact that Congress considered it sent a message about rising sentiment throughout the U.S. to quit the world body. Among the 74 who voted to cease funding the UN via this method was future Vice President Mike Pence, then a congressman from Indiana.

In suburban New York City, a weekly newspaper asked readers in over a million homes to respond to a survey asking if the UN posed a danger to the "sovereignty of the U.S." A whopping 88 percent responded that it did. The JBS campaign to Get US Out! continued to produce greater awareness of the dangers connected to membership in the so-called "peace" organization.

The Society delightedly pointed to claims by national journalists that the plan to create the FTAA by 2005 had become unrealistic. The work of JBS members in alerting fellow Americans about the scheme was paying off. Rather than sitting back and becoming complacent, however, members were urged to continue, even redouble, their efforts because the enemies of freedom "never sleep." The *Bulletin* reminded readers of the cost of participation in various foreign entanglements by pointing to the World Trade Organization's ruling against the U.S. in a dispute over steel tariffs. The WTO had arbitrarily imposed sanctions on American shipments of steel to Europe that cost U.S. firms $2 million.

George Detweiler told of Supreme Court Justice Sandra Day O'Connor's willingness to rely on foreign judicial rulings in her work. The Reagan-appointed jurist obviously had little regard for her oath to abide by the U.S. Constitution. Detweiler said of Justice O'Connor's attitude, "America constitutional law must necessarily and properly be based on the words in the Constitution. There is no room for decisions from courts in other countries."

While pointing out the wrongness of relying on authorization supplied by the United Nations to go to war against Iraq, Gary Benoit strongly recommended "Behind the Deception," a reprinted article about the topic recently published in *The New American*.

CHAPTER 64
2004: SAYING LOUD NO TO FTAA

The year 2004 saw the *Bulletin* place greater emphasis on the need to block U.S. entry into the Free Trade Area of the Americas (FTAA). All members were urged to distribute copies of the eight-page pamphlet entitled "Say NO to FTAA!" President George W. Bush had set 2005 as the year for completion of the negotiations that would expand the sovereignty-compromising elements of NAFTA and pave the way for eventual rule by the UN. One revealing item in the new pamphlet contained the May 2002 statement given by Mexico's President Vicente Fox. He confidently stated: "Eventually our long-range objective is to establish with the United States, but also with Canada our other regional partner, an ensemble of connections and institutions similar to those created by the European Union." President Fox was certainly aware of what the EU has meant for European nations, and what NAFTA had already meant for the United States, Canada and his country. The *Bulletin* showed a display of a dozen items available for use in the Stop the FTAA campaign. Members ordered considerable supplies of flyers, pamphlets, DVDs, pass-along cards, etc. for distribution in their areas.

The *Bulletin* contained my "Open Letter to Members" explaining that I was stepping "sideways" (not down) by relinquishing the title of President while continuing to serve the organization as a writer, spokesman, lecturer, and consultant. I announced that I had accepted the very important post of National Chairman of the Society's "Stop the FTAA" campaign.

In the *Bulletin's* popular column entitled "Suggested Talking Points for a Letter to the Editor," the Society recommended opposition to "gay marriage," especially the claim by proponents that advocacy of this revolutionary change was simply a matter of civil rights. The column pointed out that "thousands of years of recorded history have defined marriage as the joining of one man and one woman." It further stated, "Call such newly created unions whatever you want, but don't call them marriages."

Announcement of a new occasional column in the *Bulletin* entitled "Ahead of the

Curve" noted the early prediction by the Society that there would be no catastrophic crashing of computers as predicted by many when Y2K (year 2000) arrived. Others had claimed with certainty that computers and everything associated with them would fail, or break down, and usher in a national, even worldwide, calamity. The *Bulletin* column would remind readers of other positions taken by the Society and *The New American* that were not only correct but were way ahead of anyone else. Examples: Castro was named as a Communist while being feted by the Eisenhower administration and the media; President Bush's plan to create an amnesty program for illegal aliens while calling it something else; the Iraq War known as "Desert Storm" would further empower the United Nations; and more. In these and numerous other instances, the Society and its magazine were not only entirely correct, but were months or years ahead of everyone else.

The fifth edition of the very popular book *The Insiders* became available. It showed how the George W. Bush administration, like its predecessors, was heavily populated with Insiders who were either determined conspirators or useful aides doing the work of the Conspiracy. As in the past, this new edition of *The Insiders* published the current membership rosters of the CFR and Trilateral Commission.

Letters to senators asking for opposition to the UN's Law of the Sea Treaty (LOST) were requested. The LOST pact contained a power grab over the world's oceans and seas. Members were disappointed to learn of National Rifle Association CEO Wayne LaPierre's willingness to support a Con-Con if the Campaign Finance Reform Act were not repealed or defanged.

Will Grigg's *America's Engineered Decline* paperback book appeared. Focusing on economic matters, the book realistically pointed to the attack on business and the related transfer of manufacturing jobs out of the U.S. It further presented facts and figures about the harm resulting from America's open borders and the plan to compromise U.S. sovereignty via the FTAA.

In a *New American* article, Bill Jasper noted that the two candidates for President in the 2004 election (John Kerry and George W. Bush) were both members of Yale's secretive Skull & Bones organization. After describing what had become known about this bizarre conspiratorial group, he noted that each had given no information about it when asked during their Meet the Press appearances. "Why is this not a major election-year issue?" asked Jasper. The answer, of course, is that a conspiracy covers up what it does not want the public to know.

The *Bulletin* boldly claimed, "FTAA is not about free trade. It is about repealing our Declaration of Independence." The anti-FTAA campaign adopted the slogan, "If NAFTA hasn't crushed you, the FTAA will." Billboards with that very message proved helpful wherever members raised funds to erect one. George Detweiler cautioned that the proposed constitutional amendment containing a traditional definition of marriage could do harm. While acknowledging that the harm he saw was certainly not the intention of its promoters, he explained that the amendment would "shift power over marriage from a matter of state law and transfer it to the feds" where it "would further concentrate power in federal hands." The proposed amendment never attracted the support it needed to be added to the Constitution.

The August "Talking Points" portion of the *Bulletin* pointed to the Bush administration's delight in announcing the creation of 248,000 jobs. But, it was noted in this same *Bulletin*, "more than 70 percent of these jobs were low paying domestic service positions that can't be farmed out overseas." Senator Fritz Hollings (D-S.C.) addressed the continuing loss of jobs when he stated, "The world power that loses its manufacturing capacity is no longer a world power." Tom Gow urged members to contact their congressman and senators to inform them that opposition to trade pacts isn't only about losing jobs but about loss of independence. He suggested that many in Congress needed to be awakened to this fact.

To buttress claims that the FTAA was more about national independence than about jobs, the *Bulletin* cited an article appearing three years earlier in Atlanta's *Journal Constitution* newspaper. It stated:

> The ultimate goal of any White House policy ought to be a North American political and economic alliance similar in scope and ambition to the European Union.

This influential newspaper urged support for the proposal offered by several members of the Georgia congressional delegation to have the headquarters of the FTAA (when formed) located in Atlanta where an estimated 27,000 jobs could be filled and $500 million per year would be generated. Expecting that FTAA would need 27,000 new employees to manage something using the word "free" in its very name provided more evidence that FTAA wasn't about "free" trade, but about a gigantic bureaucracy that would manage trade and transfer jobs out of the United States.

Chapter 65
2005: Change in JBS Leadership

While generating opposition to the Free Trade Area of the Americas, members were alerted to a measure soon to be placed before Congress that would have the U.S. withdraw from the World Trade Organization. A suggested letter for members to send to Congress stated that, as a result of membership in WTO, "our nation has been forced to accept rulings dealing with our tax laws, steel tariffs, oil imports, cotton subsidies, even the purchase of bananas." All of this and more, it continued, added up to impacting "our nation's ability to act independently."

Further commentary about U.S. involvement in the WTO included the 1994 statement of then Speaker of the House Newt Gingrich urging congressmen to vote for immersion in the WTO even though it would accomplish "transferring from the United States at a practical level significant authority to a new organization." Gingrich knew what he was supporting as he led the way toward U.S. membership in WTO. Reprints of a timely article entitled "The WTO Trap" became a popular item to share with fellow Americans, almost all of whom had no knowledge whatsoever of even the existence of the WTO.

The pernicious consequences of entangling our nation in so-called trade pacts became obvious after the state of California came up with a plan to chop up discarded automobile tires and mix this "crumb rubber" with asphalt for use in paving roads. The state's legislature passed a measure to initiate the program but Governor Schwarzenegger voted it while proclaiming that it violated international trade pacts such as NAFTA and WTO. Disposing of 32 million scrap auto tires in this sensible and useful way might seem like a small matter but the inability to proceed as desired showed that the real issue underlying trade pacts like NAFTA and WTO was the ability of nations to act independently.

An announcement appeared about the availability of an English-language edition of Abbe Augustin Barruel's 1798 classic *Memoirs Illustrating the History of Jacobinism*, a lengthy study about the rise and spread of the Illuminati conspiracy. Paired with John Robison's *Proofs of a Conspiracy*, also originally published in 1798, the Barruel book added more important history about the roots of the Great Conspiracy.

As illegal immigration from Mexico continued, the Mexican government actually published an illustrated booklet describing for its own people – in the Spanish language – how to enter the U.S. illegally. That Mexico would officially take such a stand without forceful retaliation by the U.S. government starkly indicated an absence of proper leadership of our nation.

Speakers for the Spring 2005 tours included Council Members Bob Bell and Art Crino, veteran *New American* contributor Bill Jasper and me. Each speaker would address the need to "Stop the FTAA." In the midst of the campaign to create the FTAA, Congress started consideration of a measure known as the Central American Free Trade Agreement (CAFTA). Accurately described as a "mere steppingstone to the FTAA," CAFTA eventually won passage in the House by the slimmest of margins (217-215).

The New American for March 21, 2005 forcefully exposed Hollywood's ongoing "Culture War" against America. There would be more attention paid by the Society to the deliberate attempt to destroy morals, manners and all else that constitutes a nation's culture.

Welch's long-ago warning about what he termed "Booby Traps" appeared as the lead article in the *Bulletin*. A "Booby Trap" was a problem in which false information was being supplied for the dual purposes of muddying the waters of an investigation and discrediting anyone who exposes the planned conclusion. Welch stated in his original 1968 warning: "There are several good reasons why we do not go rushing in to take a position, and ask you to take action, on every new source of excitement which the Insiders arrange." He pointed to the frequent spreading of false information, especially the proliferation of unsubstantiated rumors that are directed to JBS members in hopes that they will indeed discredit themselves. In its May 2, 2005 issue, *The New American* presented facts and countered fiction with several articles about "Conspiracy Theories."

Instead of calling for the U.S. to exit the United Nations, Secretary of State Condoleezza Rice confirmed her own pro-UN stance with her choice of John Bolton to be U.S. ambassador to the world body. During a period when Bolton was being portrayed as a conservative opponent of the UN, Ms. Rice stated:

> John Bolton is personally committed to the future success of the United Nations and he will be a strong voice for reform at a time when the United Nations has begun to reform itself to help meet the challenging agenda before the international community.

Here, members of the Society were once again given important information about a highly praised individual who had been nominated for a key government post. The UN, as the Society had always maintained, cannot be reformed. Calling for such a goal is a deliberate attempt to downplay the increasing demand that the U.S. withdraw from the world body.

The May 2005 *Bulletin* urged members to obtain and share copies of Dr. Tom Woods' instant best-seller *The Politically Incorrect Guide to American History*. Described as a book full of "facts you were never taught in school," it listed "Books You're Not Supposed to Read," and glimpses of little-known or disregarded American leaders such as President Calvin Coolidge who once stated, "I look upon one of my chief accomplishments minding my own business." Wouldn't it be wonderful if a current president or candidate for the office would credibly say that today?

The Society had never agreed with the dire claims of Al Gore and others regarding global warming. When climatologist Dr. Patrick Michaels issued his book *Meltdown: The Predictable Distortion of Global Warming by Scientists, Politicians and the Media*, it received a strong endorsement from the JBS.

Members were urged to send letters opposing the McCain-Kennedy-Kolbe measure proposing amnesty for millions of illegal entrants to our country – and for millions more who would take advantage of such legislation encouraging them to come to the U.S.

Society stalwarts were heartened with the news that French and Dutch voters refused to ratify the proposed new Constitution for the European Union. Their refusals should have been enough to kill the plan and lessen the EU's power. But EU leaders immediately produced a virtual duplicate of the proposed Constitution in the form of a treaty and sent it to the leaders – not to the people – of the various EU member nations. There would be no more leaving the matter up to the vote of the people! Without exception, the leaders promptly endorsed the new constitution. By doing so, they bypassed the will of the voters and submerged all EU nations into a pact under the overall leadership of the UN. The *Bulletin* reminded all that what had just occurred in Europe was precisely what was intended for America.

The *Bulletin's* "Talking Points" section reminded all that it is totally wrong to consider a Supreme Court decision as "the law of the land." The very first sentence in the U.S. Constitution plainly states that "all legislative power" is vested in Congress, none in the Judicial Branch. Allowing the law-making function of government to be usurped by the high court – or by a presidential executive order – demonstrated ignorance of or contempt for the Constitution.

When promoting the plan to create a Free Trade Area of the Americas, the George W. Bush administration joined forces with counterparts in Canada and Mexico to form the Security and Prosperity Partnership (SPP) of North America. In the U.S., the name of Robert Pastor, the leading proponent of the Security and Prosperity Partnership, unsurprisingly showed up on the CFR's membership list. In Mexico, the SPP leader was Jorge Casteneda who happened to be a veteran member of Mexico's Communist Party. Members spread information about the real goal of the SPP (eventual creation of the hemisphere-wide FTAA) and support for the SPP waned.

The November *Bulletin* contained an important one-page letter addressed "To Members of The John Birch Society" announcing the resignations of G. Vance Smith as CEO/President and Thomas G. Gow as Vice President. The letter further stated that the Society's Board of Directors had unanimously appointed Arthur R. Thompson as CEO and me as President. At a subsequent meeting one week later, the JBS Board of Directors appointed Larry O. Waters as Vice President. No reasons for these moves were given. Across the nation and at Society headquarters, there had been widespread dissatisfaction with the Society's leadership. The changes noted above, which seemed both necessary and beneficial, were readily accepted by members.

In a subsequent letter, also published in the *Bulletin*, Robert Welch's two sons (Robert H. Welch III and Hillard W. Welch) expressed their concern about the retention of leadership over Robert Welch University by the Smith/Gow duo. Those two former JBS leaders were requested to accept the termination of their relationship with the fledgling educational institution. But the wishes of the Welch brothers – and JBS leaders – were never realized.

The first warning about potential control of the Internet by the UN or one of its agencies appeared in the December 2005 *Bulletin*. All readers of the *Bulletin* were asked to alert fellow Americans about the need to gather support for S. Res. 273 introduced by Senator Norm Coleman (R-Minn.). His measure stated rather bluntly and firmly, "The United Nations and other international organizations shall not be allowed to exercise control over the Internet."

Warren Mass called for additional attention to House measure H.R. 698 that sought to correct the constitutional loophole known as granting citizenship to "anchor babies." These were infants born in the U.S. who were automatically recognized as full U.S. citizens even though their parents weren't citizens and were illegal entrants to the U.S. This practice conferring immediate citizenship on newborns, sometimes referred to as "birthright citizenship," stemmed from a misinterpretation of the intent of the 14th Amendment. Its result produced the welcoming of entire families of foreigners who claimed a relationship to a newborn, almost always the child of an illegal immigrant. A reprint of the *New American* article "A Bold Remedy to a Grave Threat" helped to draw attention to the problem — but the measure never received needed support in the House of Representatives and the "anchor baby" practice continued.

The December *Bulletin* threw a well-earned bouquet to JBS members whose opposition to the creation of the FTAA had triumphed — at least for a time. President Bush's assurance, given to internationalists throughout the Western Hemisphere that he would deliver the FTAA proposal to Congress in 2005 for speedy approval had been deemed by the president himself as unworkable. The realization that it wouldn't be approved by Congress forced his retreat. The *Bulletin* told why: "Had there never been a John Birch Society, the FTAA would likely have already been created and our nation would now be entangled in a duplicate of the sovereignty-destroying European Union." Members were elated to have succeeded in killing a potentially serious undermining of our nation's independence.

Chapter 66
2006: CFR Leader Trashes Sovereignty

Members were encouraged to realize that an *Investor's Business Daily* editorial stated: "The thinking that inspired those bumper stickers that read 'Get the U.S. Out of the U.N. and the U.N. Out of the U.S.' is legitimate." Obviously, the Society's decades-long campaign to have the U.S. withdraw from the world body had gained an important ally.

A Council on Foreign Relations/Pew Research Center poll found that less than half of the American people "express a positive opinion of the UN, down from 77 percent four years ago." The CFR's statement acknowledged, "Public views of the United Nations have become much more negative over the past four years…."

Those who enjoyed reading Dr. Tom Woods' *Politically Incorrect Guide to American History* were pleased to learn that Tom Bethell's *Politically Incorrect Guide to Science* had become available. Its commentaries about global warming, nuclear power, evolution, and numerous other topics were most welcome. A photo of JBS member Greg Butko showed him in his army uniform reading the latest issue of *The New American* while stationed in Baghdad. It was a joy to know that the magazine made its way to a war scene on the other side of the globe.

The *Bulletin* called on members to spread realization of the fact that **"The United Nations isn't taking over our country. Instead, our nation is being delivered to the world body."** All were encouraged to include that summation in any discussion with fellow Americans about the world body. A reminder about the little known but terribly important 1945 United Nations Participation Act followed. Passed by Congress a few months after the birth of the UN, this Act gave illegitimate authority to a U.S. president to send American forces into a UN mission without any consultation with Congress. The measure clearly bypassed Article I, Section 8 of the U.S. Constitution which states that Congress alone shall have power to send the nation's forces into war. A popular issue of

The New American carrying the front-page headline "Bring 'Em Home" urged the return to America of U.S. armed forces stationed in Iraq.

To those who regularly condemned America because of its history of permitting slavery, the Society urged the following response: "Slavery should be condemned but Americans should take pride in noting that ours is a nation where slavery was abolished, a step that made America an even better place."

Instead of taking action to prevent illegal immigration, U.S. leaders were justifiably criticized for 1) allowing Mexican consular documents to be used as a substitute for properly issued U.S. documents; 2) reneging on promises to beef up the Border Patrol; 3) providing welfare, education, and various benefits to illegal entrants; and 4) tolerating the distribution by Mexican authorities of their "Guide for New Immigrants" booklet containing information about how to live in America printed in both English and Spanish languages.

At a Council Dinner held in Southern California, former CEO Charles "Chuck" Armour received a well-deserved welcome from all. In his brief speech, he delighted old and new friends by recalling the years "when the Society was being blamed for everything." He then urged all to work harder so that a day would soon arrive "when The John Birch Society gets blamed for getting the U.S. out of the UN!" The *Bulletin* showed a photo of a UN organizational chart with the World Trade Organization (WTO) appearing as a UN subsidiary. This relationship was always denied by liberals and internationalists who regularly claimed that the WTO was an independent agency.

CFR President Richard N. Haass had recently visited Taiwan where he informed Free Chinese leaders that national sovereignty was a thing of the past and, therefore, "the time has come to rethink this notion." His desire for all nations to give up their independence came as no surprise. But his public acknowledgment of such a subversive attitude, even in faraway Taiwan, wasn't expected.

The Society announced availability of a DVD that soon became the most popular single weapon ever produced by the organization. In 28 minutes, "Overview Of America" told of the wisdom of the Founding Fathers, their successful creation of a republic rather than a democracy, and the basic economic considerations that led to America becoming the envy of the world. As its author and narrator, I would later note that portions of the program had been lifted by some groups and individuals who presented it as their own creation. My summary of that development included: "Imitation has been replaced as the highest form of flattery. Thievery is now higher."

Larry Greenley summarized what Congress should do about the immigration invasion while calling for letters to Congress protesting 1) Illegal immigration; 2) "Birthright" citizenship; 3) Amnesty proposals; and 4) Guest Worker programs. The "Suggested Letters to the Editor" column mentioned approval by Congress of four boosts in the debt ceiling during George W. Bush's administration and, further, the president had not vetoed a single debt ceiling increase during his five years in office. A poll conducted by a Chicago firm found 22 percent of Americans could name all five characters in "The Simpsons" television program but only one person in a thousand could name the five freedoms protected by the First Amendment.

C-SPAN taped and then broadcast my speech about the immigration problem. Delivered in California, the talk emphasized the Constitution's Article IV, Section 4 requirement that the federal government "protect each of them [the states] from invasion." With that portion of the Constitution in mind, I pointed out: "Right now, there are somewhere between 11 million and 20 million illegal aliens within our borders. Practically all have entered by crossing the border separating our nation from Mexico. If this isn't an invasion, what is it?"

In an attempt to adopt popular business practices to promote the aims of the Society, new Marketing and Public Affairs Managers were hired. Neither man had any knowledge of the Society or the unique problems it has always faced. After several months, the experiment was deemed a failure and the two men were let go. CEO Thompson did adopt one suggestion made these managers by changing the format of the *Bulletin*. From a glossy 16 pages, the monthly message to members would now be produced in tabloid newspaper style.

Thompson then provided evidence leading to the conclusion that many government policies were designed to divide and conquer the America people. A column listing basic economic principles pointed out that 1) wealth is productivity, not paper shuffling; 2) sound money, not unbacked paper currency, stimulates a healthy economy; 3) money should be a commodity that does not need to be managed; 4) Congress was granted power to "coin money," not issue it; 5) Inflation is not rising prices but is an increase in the quantity of currency that lowers the value of existing currency; and 6) any heavily indebted nation should hardly create a foreign aid program to give money away.

As a way to cover up its past choices of human rights abusers for places on its Human Rights Commission, the UN General Assembly changed the name of this panel to Human Rights Council. But the General Assembly continued the practice of elevating the abusers of human rights to the newly named branch of the world government. Appointments of China, Cuba, Pakistan, Russia, and Saudi Arabia to the panel amounted to mockery of the very mention of human rights. Having these nations serve on such a watchdog panel is laughable – except that it's not funny. Opponents of the UN now had another reason to want the U.S. to withdraw. Suggestions for letters to the editors of local newspapers included the need to have U.S. forces removed from Iraq where Shiite and Sunni factions continued to war with each other – as they have for 15 centuries.

A court case initiated by former JBS CEO Smith resulted in a decree that Smith and his associate were the rightful owners of Robert Welch University – even though the two had resigned their JBS leadership positions. In the past, a resignation from the Society's top post meant resignation from all related corporations. Messrs. Barker, Armour and Bubolz resigned only from the Society itself and their doing so was considered resignation from several related corporations. Surprisingly however, the presiding judge didn't see the matter that way. Therefore the infant Robert Welch University became the property of individuals who were no longer serving as leaders of the Society.

Smith and Gow claimed to be planning creation of a home-schooling program but progress toward that goal was virtually non-existent. Over subsequent years, Robert Welch University accomplished next to nothing while a newly created program led by JBS CEO Thompson began. Freedom Project Academy has been teaching hundreds of K-12 students via the Internet as well as leading the way in exposing the deficiencies and downright harm in forcing government schooling and its Common Core program on the nation.

In August, an independent video producer based in New York City arranged for a debate about the United Nations between three participants wanting the U.S. to withdraw and three praising the world body. Bill Jasper and I were joined by Ron Paul staffer Kent Snyder as opponents of the UN. UN Under Secretary General Shashi Tharoor, former State Department official William Vanden Heuvel, and President of the United States Association of the U. S. William Luers defended the world body. Vanden Heuvel and Luers were veteran CFR members. The show, known as "Debates, Debates" did air in a very few locations and its producer enthusiastically said he would contact the JBS participants for additional shows. He never did. Nor did the minimal airing of the encounter stimulate anyone to contact the Society for further information.

Efforts to expose the goals of the Security and Prosperity Partnership (SPP) and FTAA remained a primary project for the Society. Showing the SPP plan to build super highway corridors from Mexico to Canada through various portions of the U.S. proved helpful in combating the drive to create a North American Union – which was the ultimate goal of those calling for creation of the FTAA.

Conservative Caucus Chairman Howard Phillips and I decided to form the "Coalition to Block the North American Union." Its five-member Steering Committee included Phillips and me plus Eagle Forum Founder Phyllis Schlafly, American Policy Center Chairman Tom DeWeese, and popular author Jerome Corsi. In the weeks and months ahead, more than 60 conservative leaders from across the United States joined the coalition. The efforts of this group, plus the work of JBS members throughout the nation, successfully blocked the merger of Canada, the U.S., and Mexico. World government planners received a formidable setback.

Among the many projects leading to successful blocking of the NAU, the distribution by JBS members of one million copies of the October 15, 2007, edition of *The New American* stood out. Personal delivery of the magazine to legislators, editors, business owners, clergymen, and others led to awareness among many who previously knew nothing of the plot. In addition, more copies of the magazine alerted Americans via the internet. Explaining what the planned North American Union would mean for our nation, the magazine's writers covered all aspects of the "Merger in the Making." The U.S. House of Representatives eventually approved a measure cutting off funding for the SPP. Also, 18 state legislatures considered resolutions opposing creation of the NAU. Many state officials obviously approved what JBS members had requested of them.

Asked as he was exiting a press conference what Iraq's involvement in the 9/11 terrorist consisted of, President Bush answered "Nothing!" as he sped away. His answer was significant because blaming Iraq for the 9/11 attack had persuaded many Americans to support the second invasion of that country. That enormously costly campaign – in lives and treasure – was no longer being justified as retaliation for the death of thousands at the World Trade Center. Mr. Bush never pointed out that almost all of the hijackers who guided planes into the buildings were from Saudi Arabia, not from Iraq.

The October 2006 *Bulletin* pointed to the refusal of MIT professor Dr. Richard Lindzen to concur with Al Gore and others who insisted on blaming humans for global warming. One of America's most prominent authorities in the field of atmospheric science, Dr. Lindzen would readily concur that the Earth might be a bit warmer but he would emphatically add, "We don't know why!" Several renowned international authorities then condemned the UN's Convention for the Elimination of All Forms of Discrimination Against Women (CEDAW) for its backing of abortion and other morally objectionable practices.

Canadian author Mel Hurtig attended a closed meeting held in Banff, Alberta, Canada whose purpose sought to spur acceptance of the North American Union proposal. He publicly denounced the gathering attended by some Canadian leaders and such American participants as NAU godfather Robert Pastor, State Department official Thomas Shannon, former Secretary of State George Shultz, and former U.S. Trade Representative Carla Hills. These U.S. participants were all members of the CFR. Hurtig stated:

> We're talking about such an important thing. We're talking about the integration of Canada into the United States. For them to hold this meeting in secret and to make every effort to avoid anybody learning anything about it, right away you've got to be hugely concerned.

All JBS members were grateful to Mel Hurtig for his report about the Banff gathering. That it was intended to be kept secret, a cardinal element of conspiracy, was no surprise to JBS members.

CHAPTER 67
2007: NEOCONSERVATISM EXPOSED

George Detweiler asked *Bulletin* readers to spread awareness that there are no federal "mandatory appropriations" except salaries for the president and federal judges. He noted that even the pay received by members of Congress is set by law, and the amount they are given is whatever that body decides. It could even be nothing, a highly unlikely development.

Detweiler wrote in response to a claim by a prominent left-wing congressman that Congress had no choice in funding an array of federal spending programs because these were "mandatory" expenditures. Among them were a variety of entitlement programs, foreign aid, payments to the UN, Medicare, etc. He discussed the "myth" claiming that once a federal spending program is established, "there is a continuing obligation on the part of Congress to fund it."

Incoming UN Secretary General Ban Ki-moon demonstrated "worthiness" for his position when he lauded predecessors U Thant and Kofi Annan, both of whom had expressed antipathy toward the independence of nations. The appointment of the South Korean diplomat simply added more fuel to the Get US Out! campaign.

CEO Thompson corrected an attitude being heard from Society opponents that there was a split amongst the organization's leaders. He pointed to a similar claim appearing in the *Wall Street Journal* 40 years earlier. When smears and misrepresentations didn't kill the Society, he stated, another tactic had to be employed. It, too, failed to accomplish destroying the Society.

There were now 3,000 fatalities among our forces in Iraq. Playing the dangerous role of referee between the Shiite and Sunni Muslims had become the task of U.S. forces – hardly a proper use of our nation's military. Meanwhile, U.S. Border Patrol Agents Jose Compean and Ignacio Ramos were given totally unjust prison sentences for the non-fatal shooting of a drug smuggler at the Mexican-U.S. border. Promises to plug holes in the border and begin meaningful treatment of illegal border crossers continued to be utterly empty.

One answer to the oft-repeated question about the failure of religious leaders to join in combating the conspiracy's influence within our nation came when the CFR's *Annual Report* listed Richard D. Land as one of its newest members. Land was serving as the president of the Southern Baptist Convention's Ethics and Religious Liberty Convention. CEO Thompson pointed out that Land's membership was "by no means the only example of CFR influence in the Christian Right."

Jim Fitzgerald reported in his *Bulletin* column that U.S. Department of Labor had acknowledged the eligibility of 1,800,000 working Americans for NAFTA's Transitional Adjustment Assistance Program. These Americans had lost jobs because of NAFTA. Jim repeated the call for repeal of NAFTA. Yet, there were still some supposedly competent commentators who claimed NAFTA to be beneficial to the U.S.

Two dozen members of the new Coalition to Block the North American Union met in the Cannon Office Building to plan strategy and tactics. The new eight-page JBS pamphlet headlined "Preserve Our American Heritage of Freedom" was adopted for wide distribution. Calls for exiting NAFTA, not merely tinkering around its edges while leaving it to fulfill its purpose, were deemed unacceptable. The reason the Coalition had been formed was to provide evidence showing that the U.S. should completely avoid being dragged into a sovereignty-destroying North American Union. Society members were reminded that exiting NAFTA would constitute a crippling blow in the drive to create the NAU.

Prompted by JBS members, the Idaho and Montana legislatures passed measures opposing any partnership among Canada, the U.S. and Mexico (the fundamental goal of the NAU) as well as the related plan to build new NAFTA highways through America's heartland.

Members were advised to obtain a copy of Dr. Ted Baehr's annual *Movie Guide* for help in selecting appropriate viewing material for moviegoers. Dr. Baehr continued to gain influence in our nation's movie industry but he acknowledged that much more needed to be done.

CEO Thompson identified Russia's presence in the training of terrorists. Referring to the work of the late Congressman Larry McDonald and relying on the evidence supplied by numerous authors and reporters, he told of close cooperation between Moscow and various known Islamic terrorists.

Bill Jasper provided details about his successful three-week visit to Australia hosted by veteran Australian JBS member Douglas Giddings. The well-known JBS author, speaker and commentator filled guest appearances on numerous media programs, spoke to several groups of concerned Australians, and boosted the morale of the many Aussies he encountered who were concerned about the same topics bedeviling them that concerned many Americans.

Another book in the "Politically Incorrect Guide" series appealed to JBS members. Written by Attorney Christopher Horner, a Fellow at the Competitive Enterprise Institute, *The Politically Incorrect Guide to Global Warming* included the author's summation that his book was an antidote to "more Chicken-Little hysteria."

With production costs already covered through the sale of DVDs, the Society dramatically dropped the price of a single JBS-produced disk to $1.00, and even lower for quantity purchases. JBS official Sam Antonio won the admiration of TV host Glenn Beck on his CNN program. Beck stated over the air, "Sam, I have to tell you. When I was growing up, I thought the John Birch Society was a bunch of nuts. However, you guys are starting to make more and more sense to me." Beck then hosted me as JBS President on his radio show. He mentioned that in its 27-year history, no one from JBS had ever been interviewed by CNN. Shortly after these JBS appearances, Beck was cut loose by this network begun by Ted Turner. It had become one of our nation's most intense promoters of socialistic big government and internationalism.

When the National Council of State Legislators held its annual meeting in Boston, delegates were met by JBS members and a large table stocked with JBS material and manned by Society Coordinator Hal Shurtleff, Council Member Ed Clements and his wife Diane, and other area members. The JBS team received thanks from many delegates who had traveled to Boston from all 50 states. They eagerly accepted copies of *The New American*, gladly took suggested resolutions for consideration by their legislative bodies, and loaded up on various pamphlets and DVDs providing background information about immigration, the proposed NAU, and other issues. Many of these legislators asked to be contacted by JBS members in their states. Ed Clements remarked: "It was great having legislators come to us for information instead of struggling to get an appointment to visit with them."

My exposure of neoconservatism appearing in *The New American* helped members understand why so many Republicans thought to be conservatives were really closet socialists and internationalists. The article explained that these individuals, while pretending to be principled conservatives, preferred socialistic big government and support for using our nation's military for undeclared wars and policing the planet.

CEO Art Thompson explained the value in having everyone in JBS working on "the same agenda, with the same direction, under the same leadership." He also reminded members that not all issues should receive JBS attention, and not all "conservative" groups should be welcomed under the JBS umbrella. He pointed to our nation's World War II generals who won that horrendous war with a unified strategy and a single command structure. If members in the Northeast work on a JBS program, they should be able to count on members in the Southwest, Northwest, and throughout the nation working on the same program. Coordinated effort strengthens the work of all. In short, Thompson's message said, "Don't go off on tangents."

CHAPTER 68
2008: EU WANTS A NEW TOWER OF BABEL

CEO Art Thompson started the year 2008 with a short essay in the *Bulletin* about the need to retain our nation's political and moral pillars. He summed up his thoughts about our country's praiseworthy underpinnings with:

> Our entire system is built and sustained on a platform of the basic Judeo-Christian heritage brought to us from Western Europe. Attack this base and you are eroding the foundations of Americanism.

Appropriately added to what Thompson offered is the famous assertion of John Adams, our nation's second president. His comment given more than 200 years ago provided important perspective about our nation's structure and is as pertinent in these times as it was when he uttered it. He wanted Americans to understand that our country would endure only if the people governed themselves while the government was held in check by the restraints in the Constitution. The John Birch Society has always believed precisely what our nation's second president stated:

> Our Constitution was made only for a moral and religious people. It is wholly inadequate to the government of any other.

In the January *Bulletin*, *The New American* Editor Gary Benoit noted that 480,000 copies of the special issue targeting creation of the North American Union had already been distributed. He looked forward to reaching the one million goal. Early notice appeared in the *Bulletin* about the celebration to be held in October marking the 50th Anniversary of the founding of the Society. Many members throughout the country began planning trips to Wisconsin for the gala affair.

Members were reminded via the *Bulletin* of the 2002 attempt by Congressman Ron

Paul to have his colleagues consider a formal declaration of war before launching another attack on Iraq. The response he received from Committee Chairman Henry Hyde (R-Ill.) in that 2002 session of the House International Relations Committee consisted of downright disdain for the Constitution. Dr. Paul openly stated his intention to vote against his resolution because he didn't think the U.S. should go to war against Iraq. But Hyde told him that relying on the Constitution's requirement for a declaration war before sending troops into battle was "anachronistic and not done anymore." Society members who learned of Hyde's disgraceful attitude wondered if the portion of the Constitution's mandate that "Senators and Representatives shall receive a compensation for their services" was also anachronistic.

The *Bulletin* reported the welcome news that a successful event in Boston had celebrated the 234th anniversary of the Boston Tea Party. Boston-based Regional Field Director Hal Shurtleff and I were among the speakers at Boston's historic Faneuil Hall. The *Boston Globe*, one of the nation's most liberal newspapers, managed to congratulate the 700 attendees who braved a substantial snowstorm to attend. I chided fellow Americans who have forgotten – or had never been taught – that our nation "didn't become the greatest nation on earth because of what government did. It became the envy of the world because of what government was prohibited from doing by the Constitution." This entire program was broadcast simultaneously to groups throughout the nation, and then posted on the YouTube network where many more were able to appreciate the celebration and were introduced to the Society.

Under the headline "Our Constitution Should Be Obeyed, Not Interpreted," I countered the widespread notion that the main task of the Supreme Court is "interpret the Constitution." Not so, I insisted in an article appearing in the *Bulletin*. "Swearing an oath to the Constitution is akin to signing a contract and after a contract is signed, does anyone think that either party to it immediately possesses power to interpret it beyond its clear meaning?" I stressed, "If there is a need to fix something in the Constitution, the amendment process is the proper way to proceed. A reminder about the worth of Welch's 1961 "Republics and Democracies" speech appeared in the *Bulletin*. All were urged to re-read what he said – or read it for the first time.

An audience of more than 500 at a New Hampshire "Liberty Forum" heard my speech entitled "What About the Constitution?" In those remarks, I offered, "If the Constitution were honored by those who swear an oath to it, there would be no undeclared wars and no policing the planet by America's forces." I proceeded to list several government agencies and bureaus (Departments of Education, Energy and Transportation plus the monstrous EPA and more) whose very existence has no constitutional foundation and certainly clashes with the limitations in the Constitution.

Declining attendance over recent years forced the Society to reduce the number of Summer Camps for teenagers from ten to seven. Reasons for the cutback included families having fewer children and the rising cost to attend. Without doubt, the shrinking value of the dollar brought on by inflation had claimed another victim.

Americans from coast to coast were rightly angered when hundreds of thousands of demonstrators clogged the streets of major cities, waved Mexican flags, demanded favors from government, and trashed the Stars and Stripes. President Bush responded to these outrages by pledging in a televised speech that he would 1) fix the illegal immigration problem, 2) control the border, 3) create technological border security, 4) confront drug trafficking and other crimes resulting from illegal immigration, and 5) oppose amnesty for all illegal border crossers. None of these pledges was realized. Instead, Mr. Bush expressed strong support for the McCain-Kennedy "comprehensive" immigration measure when all realistic students of the immigration problem knew that any "comprehensive" measure to deal with immigration problems meant amnesty for millions of illegal entrants.

Public Affairs Director Bill Hahn reported that a flurry of media attention had focused attention on the Society-created "Constitution Quiz," the query sent to many newspapers. The successful use of this quiz encouraged a follow-up "Presidents Day Quiz" which was also sent to daily newspapers and radio talk show hosts.

CEO Thompson discussed in detail the relevance of a poster produced by the European Union depicting a modern rebuilding of the Tower of Babel. Pointing to the biblical account of the Babel incident in Genesis, Thompson insisted that God Himself had dealt with world government planners by confounding the tongues and dispersing the people. And he further noted that a portion of the EU's poster contained stars that were actually satanic pentagrams. The poster had been brought back to the JBS from Europe by Bill Jasper who acquired it during one of his fact-finding trips to Brussels.

I managed to attend a meeting at the U.S. State Department where foreign policy experts discussed plans to expand the role of the Security and Prosperity Partnership and further the plan to have the U.S. "integrate" with the European Union. After two hours of listening, I rose to ask why there were no members of Congress at this gathering and, further, did the 30 participants intend to cancel U.S. sovereignty as had already been accomplished in Europe via the European Union. The moderator, a CFR member from a prestigious DC law firm, quickly stated that those questions could be asked after the meeting adjourned. A burly individual who made sure I understood I was no longer welcome at the meeting then escorted me out of the gathering all the way to the front door of the State Department building.

Congressman Ron Paul sent a most welcome endorsement of the JBS along with his acceptance of the invitation to participate in the forthcoming 50th Anniversary celebration. He stated:

> The John Birch Society is a great patriotic organization featuring an educational program solidly based on constitutional principles. I congratulate the Society in this, its 50th year. I wish them continued success and endorse their untiring efforts to foster "less government, more responsibility – and with God's help – a better world."

In a *Bulletin* column, Jim Fitzgerald reminded everyone of the subversive goals uttered by prominent CFR members such as:

> 1) Ford Foundation President H. Rowan Gaither in 1953 admitted that he and his colleagues were busily working "to so alter life in the United States that we can be comfortably merged with the Soviet Union;"
> 2) Walt W. Rostow in 1960 advocated casting independence aside in favor of "creation of world law and some form of world government;"
> 3) State Department official Richard N. Gardner urged performing "an end run around national sovereignty, eroding it piece by piece" in 1974; and
> 4) David Rockefeller who stated in his own 2002 book *Memoirs*, "Some even believe we are part of a secret cabal working against the best interests of the United States, characterizing my family and me as 'internationalists' and of conspiring with others around the world to build a more integrated global and political economic structure – one world, if you will. If that's the charge, I stand guilty, and I am proud of it."

Many similar un-American comments expressing conspiratorial intent given by highly placed individuals could have been added to these few.

As the year wound down, Art Thompson joyfully announced that 1,100,000 copies of the "Merger In The Making" issue of *The New American* were now in the hands of Americans. The goal of distributing one million had been reached, and even exceeded. The project calling for a merger of the three North American nations and the formation of the North American Union had likewise been rejected in 21 state legislatures. His claim that the JBS effort "slowed down the NAU initiative" was actually understated because, without JBS efforts, President Bush's plan to merge Canada, the U.S., and Mexico by 2010 may well have been a success. No announcement of this significant defeat was ever stated by the U.S. President or the similarly internationalist-minded leaders of Canada and Mexico.

Members were urged to remind (or inform) leaders of secondary government schools that an actual law passed by Congress in 2004 required that students be given an hour of instruction about the Constitution in any school receiving federal funding. The law's requirement called for carrying out this mandate on or about September 17 as a way to commemorate the 1787 anniversary when the Constitution first saw publication. The *Bulletin* encouraged members to provide a copy of the "Overview Of America" DVD to teachers and school administrators for use in fulfilling the law's requirement.

Many champions of the Second Amendment were cheered by the Supreme Court's decision in *District of Columbia v. Heller*. It affirmed that the Amendment protects an individual's right to possess firearms, a position regularly attacked by liberals and others. But, as much as applause for that portion of the decision was given, the claim within the ruling that the Second Amendment "confers" the right was deemed "totally and dangerously false" by the *Bulletin*.

Further analysis of the Heller decision noted that the Second Amendment never conferred a right to be armed. Instead, its wording clearly indicated that the right already existed (see "endowed by their Creator" in the Declaration of Independence) and cannot be taken away by legislation, court rulings, or some other government action short of an amendment. The constitutions of Mexico and the former Soviet Union claimed that the people possess a lengthy listing of basic rights given them by government instead of attributing the granting of important rights to God Almighty. Under this wording, government supplied rights can be restricted or even canceled by law in these other countries. Laws surely did block the exercise of the right to be armed in the USSR and continue to do so in Mexico. So, too, does the UN's Universal Declaration of Human Rights follow the patterns set by the former USSR, Mexico and many other nations.

Though the first part of the Heller decision was most welcome, the concluding thought in the ruling contained a potential for serious future mischief based on its claim that gun rights are granted by government. If government grants the right, then government has sufficient power to cancel it. As one observant commentator stated, "The Supreme Court has done freedom-loving Americans no enduring favor with this ruling."

An unusual demonstration of teamwork occurred on September 16 when alert citizens in Canada and counterparts in the U.S. created a massive phone protest aimed at creation of the North American Union. The Canadians contacted their members of Parliament and U.S. citizens called members of Congress to express opposition to the planned merger.

The *Bulletin* issued a warning about the repeated misuse by members of Congress of the Constitution's "necessary and proper" clause appearing in Article I, Section 8. After listing powers given to Congress in this Article's previous 17 clauses, the Constitution grants power to Congress "To make all laws which shall be necessary and proper for carrying into execution the **foregoing** [emphasis supplied] powers, and all other powers vested by this Constitution in the Government of the United States, or in any department or officer thereof." The mention of "foregoing powers," a limiting phrase that is regularly ignored by current elected officials, explains the intent of the Founders. They clearly meant that the clause should be cited only to enable Congress to enact laws to carry out the powers noted in the earlier portions of Article I, Section 8 and elsewhere in the Constitution. It was never meant to be a granting of permission to make laws about any matter whatsoever.

Because 2008 was a presidential election year, there were plenty of candidates for Americans to choose from, but Congressman Ron Paul (R-Texas) gained the greatest support from JBS members. More a Libertarian and hard-money advocate than a committed member of the GOP, Paul's belief that the U.S. Constitution should be faithfully honored set him apart. A highlight of the Paul campaign came when 12,000 joyous followers assembled in Minneapolis on September 2, 2008, for the "Ron Paul Rally for the Republic." Across the Mississippi River in St. Paul on that same date, the Republican Party staged its quadrennial convention and attracted approximately half the number that cheered for Ron Paul at his event in Minneapolis.

As JBS President, I was pleased to be one of the speakers at the Ron Paul Rally. But I had to overcome a minor slur even on this occasion. Somehow, an ambitious individual considered by the Establishment to be its type of "conservative," Tucker Carlson by name, had been tapped to be the emcee. He had already welcomed several others to the podium for their talks, even messing up his assignment by reading the introduction of one participant when the next speaker was someone else. When it came time for him to introduce me as the President of The John Birch Society, he refused and walked off the stage. So I had to introduce myself and I did so with, "My name is John McManus and I approve this message."

Carlson's performance on that occasion surely indicated his willingness to bow to the Establishment. He operated under the assumption that any seeming acceptance of the worth of The John Birch Society, however minor, could be held against him by those he had to please in order to climb his profession's ladder. Before too long, he issued his unqualified endorsement of same-sex marriage. My attitude, and that of The John Birch Society, is that same-sex marriage is an abomination.

As reported in the October 2008 *Bulletin*, MSNBC's Carlson had previously invited a brothel owner and two of its prostitute employees to a Ron Paul event in Nevada. The local left-wing media enjoyed having the opportunity to report that a brothel owner had endorsed Ron Paul. Nice work Carlson!

During my 20-minute speech, my mention of the Federal Reserve stimulated the audience to begin chanting, "End the Fed." Good for those 12,000 people! I then told of Ron Paul's enthusiastic endorsement of the Society, held up a copy of the Constitution to remind all that its very existence was being threatened by the proposed Con-Con, and pointed out several features of the Constitution that are regularly ignored by Congress – such as Article I, Section 1, Sentence 1. My time at the podium ended with a call for all to learn about the Society because "If you like Ron Paul, you'll love The John Birch Society." The JBS booth at the rear of the hall was quickly overwhelmed by enthusiastic rally attendees seeking further information. A sizable number joyfully joined the Society right on the spot.

The November *Bulletin* displayed more than a dozen photos taken during the well-attended JBS 50th Anniversary party. Robert Welch's two sons were shown enjoying the proceedings. Photos of Ron Paul, Chuck Baldwin (who interrupted his American Party presidential run to be there), several Council Members, and veteran JBS staff personnel filled several pages.

Precisely while the 50th Anniversary celebration was underway, Congress was in the midst of creating the great bailout of Wall Street. Originally, a three-page measure calling for $700 billion to rescue several banking institutions went down to defeat in the House. A New Jersey congressman commented that his constituents were split 50-50 regarding the measure. He clarified: "50 said 'No' and 50 said 'Hell No!'" But the Senate then approved a more expensive measure filling 400 pages. It went back to the House as an addendum to another measure and 58 members who had voted No on the first proposal switched their votes and approved a call for more than $800 billion to rescue the megabanks. Most lamely said they were opposed to a "bailout" but favored the latest measure because it was a "rescue." Obviously, the nation needed more John Birch Society-style education.

In December, CEO Thompson referred to Carroll Quigley's summation of the nation's rigged political process. In his *Tragedy and Hope* book, the Georgetown professor explained that "the two parties should be almost identical, so the American people can throw the rascals out at any election without leading to any profound or extensive shifts in policy." When John McCain ran against Barack Obama, Quigley's wish supplied a dose of reality. Obama won, but a McCain presidency would differed little had he been elected.

The year ended with an announcement that DVDs of my speech "Dollars and $ense" were now available. Dealing with the nature of money, the Federal Reserve, the truth about inflation, and the Founders attitude regarding money, the presentation offered a "What must be done!" section listing needed steps to keep the nation from losing independence as a result of enormous indebtedness.

Chapter 69
2009: Obama Adds Revolutionary To Court

In addition to publishing *The New American* every two weeks, the amazingly capable staff of the magazine also posts numerous short articles every day on www.thenewamerican.com. Editor Gary Benoit noted in the January 2009 JBS *Bulletin* that 166,073 individuals had visited the site during the first three months after its redesign. Impressive? Yes indeed. Anyone who has not taken a look at this adjunct of the Society's work is hereby encouraged to do so.

Calls for abolishing the Federal Reserve received deserved attention in the *Bulletin*. Creating awareness about the need to do so arrived in a letter from Zimbabwe telling of the horrors that printing press money and inflation had brought to a once-thriving economy. Sent by a native Zimbabwean who remembered when his country (previously known as Rhodesia) had been exporting food and other items to neighboring countries, it stated in part:

> We are locked in a death grip and things are falling apart at a rapid pace.... On the shelves of the local supermarket, they had: light bulbs, cayenne pepper, a few vegetables which were distinctly past their best, and a few packets of meat which didn't look too safe. More than half of the supermarket is completely empty and closed off with strings of white plastic tape.

Could such a horror be in America's future? The answer is that it certainly could and the sure way to keep that bleak scene from occurring here is to phase out the Federal Reserve and get back to commodity money – preferably gold or silver.

Announcements of several ways to combat looming economic disaster appeared in the *Bulletin*. These were the new "Dollars and $ense" DVD, a companion 38-page booklet carrying the same title, and my forthcoming speech tour dealing with the threat.

Journalist Kristof Berking from Germany contacted the Society after attending last October's Ron Paul Rally for the Republic. He visited the Society's Wisconsin headquarters and wrote about the Ron Paul event and the Society for his newspaper in Germany. But he additionally wanted to interview "President McManus." Unfortunately, I was traveling and not at the Society's headquarters. Berking eventually interviewed me by telephone and his subsequent lengthy article appeared in *Junge Freiheit* under the headline "Weder Obama Noch McCain" (Neither Obama nor McCain). He then shared his taped recording of the interview with another German journalist who carried the JBS message to additional readers.

The *Bulletin* reported that Pepperdine University Professor of Economics George Reisman issued a definition of "laissez-faire capitalism" to counter numerous liberal commentators who were wrongfully blaming sound economics for the nation's difficulties. Reisman wrote that a correct definition of "laissez-faire economics" would state that it includes…

> …private ownership of the means of production with government limited to the protection of the individual's rights against the initiation of physical force. There are presently 15 federal cabinet departments, nine of which exist for the very purpose of respectively interfering with housing, transportation, healthcare, education, energy, mining, agriculture, labor and commerce. Under laissez-faire capitalism, 11 of the 15 cabinet departments would cease to exist and only the departments of justice, defense, state and treasury would remain.

Birch Society members cheered the good professor's most welcome statement.

As a unique way of publicizing my forthcoming "Restore Our Freedom and Prosperity by Restoring Sound Money" speech, Utah Section Leader Robin Smith started the "Good as Gold Committee" in his state. This local group sent copies of the "Dollars and $ense" DVD to 104 Utah state legislators. One recipient responded immediately saying, "This is very sobering. I'm going to share it with others." Society members were pleased to learn that the Washington-based CATO Institute had gathered approval from 200 educators, mostly economists, for a statement telling President Obama that his plan to rescue the nation from its huge indebtedness and economic slowdown would not work and would produce more harm. The CATO statement appeared in numerous large circulation newspapers as a full-page ad.

The Society's campaign to block ratification of the Law of the Sea Treaty (LOST) gained traction with the publication of Bill Jasper's article telling of its danger. In short, the treaty would give the UN control over the world's oceans and major waterways. The campaign has proven to be successful as ratification of LOST has not been accomplished.

A photo reproduction of the cover of the February 16, 2009, issue of *Newsweek* magazine showed its headline, "We Are All Socialists Now." The accompanying article noted that President Obama, identified by the magazine as a socialist, had won the election while promoting socialism and was now leading even more Americans into the socialist camp. *Newsweek* wasn't unhappy about the development.

In the midst of an economic slowdown and ascending national indebtedness, the Obama administration announced a $51 billion foreign aid program. Foreign aid, of course, has always been totally unconstitutional. Most of the supporters of this federal government program have no idea that the funds given away are always provided to foreign governments whose leaders use the grants to cement control over their nations. The $51 billion about to be dispensed was tacked on to the soaring national debt. The *Bulletin* reported that more than 1,100 people had already attended my "America's Economic Meltdown" speech.

The passing of former highly placed CIA official Tom Braden stimulated publication in the April *Bulletin* of a brief review of his career. An early disciple of CFR Founder Edward Mandell House and a veteran of both the CIA and its OSS predecessor, Braden served for a time as a journalist. He distinguished himself in 1967 when he wrote an article entitled "I'm Glad the CIA is Immoral." He boasted that he had helped the Agency funnel taxpayer dollars to the leftist National Student's Association, the left-wing United Auto Workers, socialist labor leaders in Europe, and even U.S. Communist Party founder Jay Lovestone. During a television program he co-hosted with Pat Buchanan, he casually remarked that CIA funding had helped keep the Communist Party's *Daily Worker* afloat.

While there have been some patriotic individuals in the CIA's employ, the Agency's history – only a portion of which we mention here – shows that it uses the billions at its disposal to fund America's domestic and foreign foes, with little or no congressional oversight. The JBS position continued to call for terminating the existence of this secretive and frequently subversive agency.

A full page of the May *Bulletin* contained suggestions for members under the headline "Action for Activists." It listed 20 activities members have employed over the Society's 50 years. Such efforts as writing letters, sponsoring speakers, manning tables and booths at various events, sponsoring speakers, challenging or congratulating elected officials, distributing pamphlets and DVDs, and more were mentioned.

My travels also brought me to New York City where I delivered a speech to a local branch of the MENSA organization. This group's members pride themselves on being highly intelligent. A respectable turnout of 75 persons listened intently to my "America's Economic Meltdown" presentation. A MENSA official later informed the Society that the member of the group assigned to send notification of the meeting to area MENSA members had done so one day **after** the event. Either that particular member of MENSA isn't as intelligent as advertised or he was wise enough, and leftist-leaning enough, to keep others from attending. No one ever told the JBS the reason for this failure to send the notice prior to the event.

With former House Speaker Newt Gingrich seemingly set to become the next GOP candidate for President, Society members showed "The Real Newt Gingrich" to fellow Americans. A presentation given by me, it supplied details about Gingrich's membership in the CFR, his successful leading of the GOP majority into backing the inconsequential "Contract with America," his pivotal role in gaining congressional approval of NAFTA, his repeated votes for big government and more spending, and more. CEO Thompson claimed that this DVD presentation would keep Gingrich from being the GOP nominee for president. The program was indeed shown widely and Art Thompson was likely correct in his assessment of its impact.

Encouraged by staff personnel, members succeeded in finding good prospects for the JBS in the many Tea Party groups springing up nationwide. Regional Field Director Bliss Tew urged JBS members to seek out and enlist Tea Party adherents – not to have them quit the Tea Party, but to avail themselves of the opportunity to become members of the Society as well.

Editor Gary Benoit expressed sheer delight when the site he oversees, thenewamerican.com, attracted more than 100,000 viewers in the single month of April. I reminded JBS members that the best solution to the nation's economic doldrums would not include having the federal government DO something like creating another layer of government regulation but to UNDO numerous government programs and agencies already functioning. The *Bulletin* noted that, at the halfway point in my speech tour, I had already delivered the "America's Economic Meltdown" speech to audiences totaling 3,100 persons. That number would climb to more than 6,000 before the tour ended.

Jim Fitzgerald provided a short review of Welch's 1966 speech "The Truth in Time." An outline of conspiratorial designs beginning with Weishaupt's Illuminati in 1776 and leading up to the "insiders" of our day, Welch had admitted that there was a need for "a hundred volumes of a thousand pages each" to make the history of the plot "clear and convincing." While urging all to engage in activity to expose the plot, Fitzgerald noted that "The conspirators do not care so much about what you know if you do nothing about it." The Society, unlike numerous patriotic organization, not only dispenses sound information, it offers numerous action programs to right the ship of state. Education without action leads to frustration, even despair.

In the constant battle to protect the Constitution from wholesale revision via a Con-Con, the comments of James Madison have always been very useful. Our nation's fourth president performed the great service of taking notes at the 1787 Convention and has justifiably been named the "Father of the Constitution." He then wrote several of the essays in the 1788 collection known as *The Federalist Papers*. In one of his essays, he commented about participating in the 1787 convention:

> Having witnessed the difficulties and dangers experienced by the first convention, which assembled under every propitious circumstance, I should tremble for the result of a second....

Larry Greenley told of new strategies and "the biggest onslaught" of moves ever taken to boost acceptance of the call for a Con-Con. To generate support for the ill-advised use of the Constitution's Article V, Con-Con promoters were relying on the internet to spread their misleading and dangerous proposal.

Readers of *The New American* were reminded to use its semi-annual "Freedom Index" to inform fellow Americans about the voting records of their congressman and senators. Reports about the performances by all 435 members of the House and all 100 senators are shown in the Index. Reprints made available each time a new Index is published have become a popular educational tool and a valuable source of facts about an elected official's performance.

President Obama tapped Judge Sonia Sotomayor to fill the Supreme Court seat vacated by the retirement of Justice David Souter. A graduate of Yale University Law School, Sotomayor's membership in the National Council of La Raza received scant notice when it should have disqualified her. La Raza ("The Race") is the revolutionary Mexican-American organization calling for cancellation of U.S. immigration laws and the granting of amnesty for millions who have entered our country illegally. The group's long-range plan even called for returning four southwestern states and parts of two others to Mexico. In saner times, the choice of Sotomayor for a place on the high court would have been as likely as seeing the sun rise in the West and set in the East.

CEO Art Thompson and Director of Field Activities Jim Fitzgerald saw fit to refer to Thomas Jefferson's sage advice about correcting apathy and ignorance. In his 1820 letter to a fellow Virginian, the man who had served as our nation's third president wrote:

> I know of no safe depository of the ultimate powers of the society but the people themselves; and if we think them not enlightened enough to exercise their control with a wholesome discretion, the remedy is not to take it from them but to inform their discretion by education. This is the true corrective of the abuses of constitutional power.

Relying on education, as urged by Jefferson, has always been the solution recommended by The John Birch Society.

I journeyed to New York City to appear as a guest on Judge Andrew Napolitano's "Freedom Watch" television program. The popular show provided me with an hour to present JBS views about the nation's economic travails and related concerns. The invitation actually resulted from an earlier Napolitano request that his viewers tell him who would be a good guest to appear on the show. JBS members sent a flood of recommendations and their effort paid off. The program was shown and then made available on the Freedom Watch web site. Soon afterward, Fox News canceled Napolitano's show.

A welcome surprise greeted two Society officials when they slipped into a regular meeting of the Hamilton Tea Party in Montana. Robert Brown and Lionel Terzi were thrilled to find "Overview Of America" being shown to the 500 attendees. The two made themselves known when the DVD ended and they were immediately swamped by eager Montanans seeking to purchase copies of the popular DVD. Many also purchased books, magazines and other DVDs. The two JBS staff members then arranged for me to deliver a speech to that Tea Party group during my upcoming tour. Lionel Terzi happily reported that many prospects for membership eagerly provided their contact information.

Northeast Regional Field Director Hal Shurtleff reported for the third year in a row that the Society had set up a booth at the National Convention of State Legislators, this time at the group's gathering in Philadelphia. Local members Al Zeller, Mill Affleck, Donna and Charlie Ward, Chuck Baker and others greeted the legislators at the JBS table and found solid agreement among the many attendees that there should be no Con-Con.

Pointing out that "terrorism is the most certain tactic to propel people into accepting more controls from their own government," CEO Thompson announced his upcoming 17-engagement speaking tour in which he would deliver "Exposing Terrorism." The *Bulletin* told of the availability of his analysis of terrorism in a DVD and a booklet. Bill Jasper's "Terrorist Targeting of Police," a reprinted article from *The New American*, had also become available.

For one indication of how far many U.S. leaders have strayed from the Constitution, the *Bulletin* pointed out the response given by House Speaker Nancy Pelosi to a simple question posed by a Cable News Service reporter. He asked the California Democrat where in the Constitution Congress had been granted authority to enact healthcare legislation. Her total answer was a sassy "Are you serious?" Obviously, Pelosi believed that the American people should accept without question everything presented by Congress. Whether any measure had constitutional authorization wasn't her concern. Pelosi and too many others like her believe they can enact any law the Constitution does not specifically prohibit. That, of course, is completely wrong. Anyone who reads the Constitution finds that the federal government is permitted only to enact legislation authorized by the document – quite a difference from the attitude employed by so many elected officials.

As did Welch upon numerous end-of-the-year occasions, CEO Thompson composed a message stressing hope for the future and had it published in the December 2009 *Bulletin*. Among the many developments that gave him hope – and likewise supplied hope to others – were 1) the sale of 100,000 copies of the Society's DVD "Overview Of America." He added, "This does not count two other means of dissemination of its powerful message: the 'pirating' of copies which is substantial and the placement of all or parts of 'Overview of America' on some 12,400 websites; 2) the distribution of the 'Dollars and $ense' DVD that might surpass 'Overview' in copies sold because it has taken half the time to reach the 50,000 plateau; and 3) the reaching out to huge numbers of people almost instantly via *The New American* website which had become an increasingly important avenue for communication." Thompson concluded his look ahead with, "Yes indeed there is reason for hope."

Adding his own comment about hope, a Chapter Leader named Bob McCune said: "Be positive. Things look grim, but there's still hope. I don't do my Birch work for fun. However, I try to have fun doing it. My goal is to lay a firm foundation for my children and others, that they might have the knowledge and the tools to retain liberty and pass it on."

CHAPTER 70
2010: FIDEL PRAISES OBAMACARE

During 2009, members in New Jersey, New York and Connecticut set up tables or booths at 72 street fairs. Each of these events enabled members to greet the public, distribute literature, sign up new members, acquire prospects, and let the area's liberals know that their dominance was waning. Area Coordinator Kip Webster confirmed that the exposure of the Society at these fairs "pays immediate and long-term dividends." He provided guidelines showing others how they could achieve similar success.

In his initial essay for the year 2010, Art Thompson repeated what Founder Welch had always contended: "Nothing can replace an informed electorate." For an example of what can happen when there is no solid information, he pointed to the plan known as "term limits." Calling it a "dead end" which, in most cases, would replace a left-leaning legislator with another left-leaning legislator, he maintained that it would also force decent upholders of the Constitution in elected positions to leave their hard-earned posts. It would be folly, suggested Thompson, to force out of office some constitutionally sound individuals by limiting the time they could serve. Promoters of "term limits" refuse to look upon Election Day as a turning point when the terms of politicians can be more than limited – they can be terminated.

A Washington-based organization entitled "The Hill" asked me to participate in providing a brief written answer to a daily "Big Question." Responses were then posted on the group's website, "thehill.com," for widespread viewing. Here are two samples of my participation in this unique forum:

Q. Will the December 3 Jobs Summit help President Obama politically or highlight a weakness?

A. Meaningful jobs are created by manufacturers, not by governments. In fact, wealth should be known as productivity, the creation of goods from the raw materials of the Earth. A nation is wealthy when its people are engaged in manufacturing, but America has lost close to half its manufacturing jobs during the past three decades. The chief impediment to wealth production is always government – with its taxation and regulatory burdens. If Mr. Obama does not lead an effort to reverse government's job-destroying policies, he should certainly be hurt politically. But, sadly, few Americans realize that government is the real reason why jobs are disappearing here at home.

Q. Will the effort to fund a troop surge in Afghanistan divide the Democratic Party?

A. Anything that will divide the Democratic Party would be helpful to America. The party has, in general, become the socialist party of America and many of its members have linked with the organization known as the Democratic Socialists of America. Socialism is, of course, the antithesis of Americanism. It was practiced in the Union of Soviet Socialist Republics (USSR) and by the National Socialist (NAZI) Party in Germany. It would be wonderful for America if many of the Democrats in Congress would begin to honor their oath to the U.S. Constitution and work for less government, not more. The solution to the conflict in Afghanistan is either to declare war and win, or decide in the absence of a constitutionally required formal declaration of war, to leave and let the Afghans decide who will lead their nation.

After several months of Society participation in this program, someone from "The Hill" contacted me to extend thanks for my "very different but very welcome" contributions. Later, I visited the Washington-based office of "The Hill" to say hello and thank the program's personnel for having the JBS as a participant. Soon afterward, with no warning, I ceased receiving any more questions. Telephone calls seeking to learn what had happened got me no explanation about no longer being contacted. Had someone decided that JBS thoughts were no longer welcome? JBS personnel were never able to get any answers.

When the UN sponsored an important "Global Warming" Summit Meeting in Copenhagen, Denmark, *New American* stalwarts Bill Jasper and Alex Newman attended and reported for the Society's affiliated magazine what they discovered. The conference turned out to be a dud in many ways. But at least one participant figured out what was intended. Lord Christopher Monckton, former science adviser to British Prime Minister Margaret Thatcher, said the real objective of the gathering was to "impose a world government on the world." He was delighted to meet two Americans who shared his views.

In his remarks about the threat of terrorism, CEO Thompson always pointed to Russian hands in spreading the deadly process throughout the world. As one dramatic example, he focused on the second in command of Al Qaeda, the "trained KGB asset" whose name is Ayman al-Zawahiri. For an understanding of the role in this and other moves being played by the Russian hierarchy, he urged obtaining and reading Golitsyn's *New Lies For Old*. Like other Society leaders, Thompson believed that the works of this high-ranking Soviet defector were worthy of serious study.

After my very successful speaking tour discussing "America's Economic Meltdown," the Speakers Bureau announced a new tour for me beginning in April (2010). The subject: "Stealing the American Dream: How Illegal Immigration Affects You." I planned to dwell on the proposed congressional legislation leading to amnesty for millions.

A review of the attack on basic morality appeared in the *Bulletin's* mentioning of President Clinton's imposition of the "Don't Ask, Don't Tell" policy within the military. It then warned of President Obama's plan to cancel all bans on homosexuals serving in the military, a goal soon achieved during his first term in office. Instead, the Society recommended dusting off and reestablishing Department of Defense Directive 1332.14 that, for 215 years, had stated, "Homosexuality is incompatible with military service."

After the Federal Reserve added $1 trillion to the national debt during the past two years, Congress raised the debt ceiling by $1.9 trillion. Asked about the enormous $1.6 trillion shortfall forecast for the current fiscal year, Mr. Obama offhandedly responded, "It keeps me awake at night." The *Bulletin* commented: "Yet he is still trying to ram a costly healthcare program through Congress, he hasn't proposed any real cuts in government spending, and he shows no sign of any lack of sleep." The National Debt rose to just short of $20 trillion as Obama continued the pattern of doubling the debt every eight years.

CEO Thompson wrote about "The Effectiveness of The John Birch Society." He reminded older members and informed newer Birchers that the Society could claim complete or partial victories in such campaigns as:

- "Support Your Local Police"
- opposition to abortion via creation of one of the first film programs dealing with the topic that carried the title "Innocents Defiled"

- defusing planned Civil Rights rioting and destruction
- blocking passage of the Equal Rights Amendment
- exposing the records of numerous congressmen and senators who were then rejected by voters
- protecting the God-given right to be armed
- combating and explaining terrorism
- impeding adoption of the pagan Earth Charter promoted by the UN
- refusing to bow to widespread fears that the nation would grind to a halt because of Y2K
- having a hand in the impeachment of President Clinton (as reported by the *Washington Post*)
- blocking the creation of the Free Trade Area of the Americas (FTAA) and the North American Union (NAU)
- exposing the United Nations
- stressing the Constitution instead of Conservatism or Neoconservatism
- blocking the plans of misguided Americans who were seeking creation of a Con-Con
- distributing enormous amounts of literature along with internet exposure, speech programs, and more.

Thompson claimed that no other organization could even come close to matching such a positive record. But, he indicated, there remained plenty of work still needed to reach the Society's goals.

For an example of conspiratorial creation of a crisis followed by federal creation of more centralized power to deal with it, I reviewed the Soviet Union's launch of Sputnik in 1957. Because of that success, U.S. leaders went along with the claim that our nation was second-rate in scientific and military capability. The U.S. federal government quickly increased its takeover of America's education system, and also raised taxes, engaged in more inflationary spending, and centralized more power in Washington. All of this and more had to be done because, as a wave of propaganda insisted that Sputnik had demonstrated, the Soviets were now ahead of the U.S. in science, technology and military capability. Years later, Government officials stated that they had the capability of putting a satellite in orbit but were ordered not to do so by high-ranking U.S. officials.

The *Bulletin* carried Bill Hahn's enthusiastic report about the warm reception the Society received at the three-day CPAC convention held in Washington. All 5,500 attendees received a copy of "Overview Of America" and several other JBS-produced items. Literature sales were brisk and the exposure of the Society at a "conservative" gathering proved to be a superb opportunity for many to learn about the Society when they previously knew little or nothing about the organization.

When President Obama signed the healthcare measure to which his name had been attached, the *Bulletin* noted the applause registered by Fidel Castro. The long-reigning Cuban dictator wrote of Mr. Obama's success in saddling America with a government healthcare program. He stated in a message about our nation's president, "We consider health reform to have been an important battle and a success of his government." Students of history weren't surprised because Russia's Vladimir Lenin, one of Castro's important heroes, had frequently stated, "Socialized medicine is the keystone in the arch of the socialist state." The long-reigning Cuban dictator also suggested that Obama should move ahead on climate change and immigration reform. Obama did both.

The escalating attack on America's religious-based culture gained another victory when a group of award-winning high school musicians in the state of Washington were denied the opportunity to play their choice of music at graduation. Tradition at their school had long granted the award winners the right to select whatever piece of music they wished to perform. They immediately chose "Ave Maria" and the school's nervous superintendent then cited "separation of church and state" (a mandate nowhere found in the U.S. Constitution) in disallowing such a performance. The youngsters sued, were rebuffed at lower courts, and their appeals went all the way to the Supreme Court. When the high court declined to hear their plea, the lower court's ruling against the students prevailed. Although many considered this outrage a small matter, it nevertheless constituted a significant indicator of which way America was heading. The *Bulletin* reported it for that reason.

After warning about the consequences of ObamaCare, *The New American* published a comprehensive analysis of its intrusion into the private healthcare sector in the May 10, 2010 issue.

The July *Bulletin* listed several key features of the work of the Society setting it apart from other groups and organizations. For instance, JBS is a nationwide organization, has a moral base, opposes and exposes conspiracy, possesses the benefit of experience, and has a proven track record. Also, as an example of action suggested by no other group or organization, the Society continued its campaign to have the nation's government-funded schools obey the federal law requiring instruction about the Constitution on or near Constitution Day (September 17th). The law, passed as part of an appropriations bill, can be found in Public Law 108-447, Section 111.

Reminders were issued about the availability of Welch's "John Birch Society's Resolutions." First issued in 1970, many new members had never read the contents of this 20-page booklet. The Intercollegiate Studies Institute published the findings of its civic literacy test and discovered that college graduates knew little about Lincoln's Gettysburg Address, Washington's Farewell Address, and Thomas Jefferson's authorship of the Declaration of Independence. In addition, the Institute found that 32 percent of the college graduates it surveyed believe that a president has power to declare war. The *Bulletin* concluded that "a college degree moves a person toward the Democrat/liberal side of the political spectrum."

Countering the many fellow Americans who have been led to believe that the U.S. Constitution was created for a horse-and-buggy age and no longer possesses any meaning for the highly advanced society our nation had become, CEO Thompson stressed an important truism:

> Let us make the point that the Constitution was written neither for an agrarian nor an industrial country. It was written based on human nature, the nature of government, and the need to limit government and its power.... It is relevant to any community provided there is a base of morality and awareness that rights are God-given.

Combating ObamaCare led to sponsorship by the Society's Speakers Bureau of several doctors who took time away from their practices to present hard truths about this latest federal intrusion into the private sector. Members were encouraged to distribute some or all of the various pamphlets, handouts, and reprints dealing with ObamaCare. The *Bulletin* acknowledged the work of 14-year-old JBS member Colleen Ward who had received an "A" grade in her school for an essay she wrote criticizing the federal government's No Child Left Behind Act. Her teachers were so impressed with her critique that they distributed copies throughout her home state of New Jersey. Her parents, Donna and Charles, who were JBS leaders in southern New Jersey, were very proud of their daughter's effort.

CEO Art Thompson appointed veteran Oklahoma member Clark Curry to the post of Chief Operations Officer. Curry had demonstrated excellent leadership capabilities while serving as a chapter and section leader for many years, and while running the successful insurance agency bearing his name. His knowledge of all aspects of the Society's work had earlier led to his appointment as a Council Member and a member of its Executive Committee. He then rose to become Chairman of the Society's Executive Committee.

Along with Curry's appointment, veteran staff member Martin Ohlson was then named Vice President for Development. Marty had earlier served as a Coordinator and had become the Society's chief fundraiser replacing longtime veteran Larry Waters. Also, after several years of manning the Society's Public Affairs desk, Bill Hahn earned appointment as Vice President of Communications.

Summer intern Christian Gomez debuted as a writer for the Society with his stirring tribute to the late Dr. Larry McDonald. Recounting the story of KAL Flight 007, Gomez noted, "McDonald was the only sitting congressman ever killed [or captured] by Communists during the Cold War."

Previous alerts about the dangerous unreliability of Newt Gingrich and his proposals impelled me to be wary of the former House Speaker's formation of his "American Solutions" organization. It featured a call for a Balanced Budget Amendment to the Constitution, something not needed if reliance on the Constitution's Article I, Section 7 was employed. Budget-busting measures can be eliminated by a majority of House members. There is no need for relying on the arduous process of gaining two-thirds approval from both Houses of Congress and three-quarters approval from the states in order to balance the budget. A former history teacher and high-ranking member of Congress, Gingrich should have been aware that his new organization was proposing something that was not only unnecessary, it ignored the Constitution's clear intent. I then suggested that he may have been slyly providing a boost for the promoters of a Con-Con with his expression of support for an amendment to balance the budget.

The October 2010 *Bulletin* pointed out that 150 new government agencies would result from the creation of ObamaCare. State legislatures were encouraged to pass measures nullifying the new law, not partially but fully. CEO Thompson issued a warning about the work of the "Socialist International." Drawing from a February 2010 thenewamerican.com article written by Bill Jasper, he discussed the acquisition by hard-core socialists of more than 70 seats in the U.S. Congress. Nevertheless, the Society's CEO cautioned against deciding that this organization, or the CFR, or some other hard left group constituted the core of the plot against civilization. The JBS position had always been that these were only outer rings of the overall Conspiracy seeking control over mankind.

Deserved accolades were again published about Frederic Bastiat's small 1850 book entitled *The Law*. A brief sample of the enduring wisdom penned by the 19th Century French legislator in his must-read book claimed: "Life, liberty and property do not exist because men have made laws. On the contrary, it was the fact that life, liberty and property existed beforehand that caused men to make laws in the first place."

Society cooperation with other patriotic groups reached a new level of success when 2,000 persons gathered at a Tea Party in California's Bay area. Members who staffed the JBS booth at this event reported that "people were four deep" waiting to purchase copies of "The New World of ObamaCare," plus DVDs, books, pamphlets, and magazines. Pointing to President Obama's description of the results of the 2010 congressional elections as "a shellacking," I enthusiastically noted that an increasing number of Americans were referring to the Constitution as America's standard, replacing the undefined and shifting reliance on "conservatism."

Chapter 71
2011: JBS Exhibits at CPAC

In his initial essay for 2011, Art Thompson discussed three aspects of the society that set it apart from other groups and organizations. These are: 1) reliance on the Constitution and, especially, on its original meaning; 2) strategy and tactics based on a firm commitment to morality in every undertaking; and 3) understanding that the battle is essentially with evil men, not with their deceptive ideas and destructive plans. In other words, there are evildoers who know as well as anyone that what they seek is unquestionably evil. In his comments about this matter, Robert Welch frequently described the foe as a "satanic and diabolically driven conspiracy."

Distribution of a pro-Con-Con tract promoted by a group labeling itself *The Founders Alliance* prompted a response from the Society. Although correcting much of what it stated had to be done, this new group surprisingly admitted in its "Time For a Change" that the 1787 Convention "was a runaway." This, of course, had long been one of the major JBS arguments against creating a new Con-Con. *The Founders Alliance* then claimed that any recklessness produced by a Con-Con could be blocked during the state ratification process. But the 1787 Convention actually altered the state ratification process and any new Con-Con could do likewise, even abolish any role for state legislatures. Numerous other weaknesses in the arguments presented in this tract entitled "Time For a Change" were shown.

Looking back over the years of JBS effort showed that much of its growth and effectiveness resulted from meetings in the homes of members. Yes, prospects for membership can be discovered in public settings, but enlisting new members and generating activity most often results from small gatherings in homes. Continuing this practice was highly recommended.

The Society announced the creation of a "State Legislator Packet" containing the "Overview of America" DVD, several pamphlets and booklets, and a copy of *The Law*. Members were asked to share this small storehouse of information promoting good government with each of their state's elected officials. The request was prompted in part because at a Town Meeting held in Democrat Congressman Pete Stark's California district, a constituent asked the veteran legislator where the federal government obtained authority to enact a particular law. The congressman responded, "In this country, the federal government can do pretty much whatever it wants to." The angry citizen who asked the question reported Stark's response to the Society. No clearer statement about the willingness of some in Congress to ignore the Constitution's limitations on government power has ever been uttered by a sitting congressman.

Addressing the subject of "conspiracy," I stressed that there were relatively few deeply committed conspirators. And I explained further that there were many who were willingly carrying out the designs of the plotters for the rewards – fine jobs, promotions, and other favors – that were regularly bestowed. The *Bulletin* then pointed to the plan to cut UN funding promoted by House Foreign Affairs Committee Chairman Ileana Ros-Lehtinen (R-Fla.). That might sound good, I contended, but what was needed is complete withdrawal from the world body, not just a reduction in funding.

After Society Member Jackye Powell paid for placement of a "STOP ObamaCare" billboard along a busy highway in Arizona, the owner of the billboard company took it down because it was "controversial." So the determined JBS member sought another billboard company whose leader welcomed her business.

For a time, JBS conducted outreach programs under the name of Campus Liberty Alliance. Its Coordinator, Sam Antonio, thought so highly of advice Welch had given me in a hand-written note that he sought space in the *Bulletin* to cite it. Welch stated the following:

> A man who knows not, and knows not that he knows not, is a fool. Shun him!
> A man who knows not, and knows that he knows not is in need. Help him!
> A man who knows, and knows not that he knows, is asleep. Awaken him!
> A man who knows, and knows that he knows, is wise. Follow him!

Commenting on the controversy in Wisconsin that impelled mobs to shut the state government down for days, Art Thompson suggested that the demonstrators who had stormed the Wisconsin State House were employing tactics recommended by the National Education Association, the powerful teachers' labor union. He further noted that the NEA had recommended books authored by Chicago revolutionary Saul Alinsky. In his increasingly famous work entitled *Rules for Radicals*, Alinsky had written a tribute to "the first radical – Lucifer."

The *Bulletin* announced publication of a new paperback edition of my book about William F. Buckley, Jr. Before he passed away, Buckley surprisingly acknowledged the book's existence when he told an interviewer, "It's about 300 pages…. It's mostly about how I became a member of the Council on Foreign Relations." Of course, the book provided a great deal more about the "conservative" most loved by liberals and leftists. The late Joe Sobran, who worked side-by-side with Buckley for 21 years before being betrayed by the man he thought was a friend, commented enthusiastically after reading what I had written, "I wish I'd known about all of this when I was working for him."

The Society began targeting the UN's *Agenda 21*, the massive program for social engineering that would, if fully implemented, accomplish regimentation of all life on Earth before the end of the 21st Century. Hence the name "Agenda 21." Announced to the world at the 1992 Earth Summit held in Brazil, its 1,100- page plan contained a beginning summary of its full intent written by one of its editors, Daniel Sitarz. With gushing enthusiasm for the entire plan, Sitarz wrote:

> *Agenda 21* proposes an array of actions which are intended to be implemented by every person on earth…. It calls for specific changes in the activities of all people. Effective execution will require a profound reorientation of all human society, unlike anything the world has ever experienced…. This shift will demand that a concern for the environmental consequences of every human action be integrated into individual and collective decision-making at every level.

Tom DeWeese, the veteran opponent of *Agenda 21* and its designs on mankind's freedom, had led the campaign to expose this totalitarian scheme. He welcomed The John Birch Society's involvement knowing that Society members across the nation would slow down, even cripple, any enforcement of the huge plot. He was correct. Society members immediately began distributing flyers and articles prepared for the purpose of exposing the UN's role behind the scheme, identifying the various names under which it was operating, and blocking further implementation of *Agenda 21's* designs.

A new proposal to alter the process for electing the nation's President arose. Called "National Popular Vote," it sought to do away with the Electoral College method for choosing a president. Instead, the candidate receiving the most popular votes would be declared the victor. The role of the smaller states would essentially be diminished, if not completely wiped out. Viewed as another step toward pure democracy, the proposal merited opposition and members began registering their disagreement with state and national leaders.

With another call for increasing the national debt ceiling on the horizon, I suggested that huge national indebtedness could lead to default and loss of national sovereignty before too long. As the admitted National Debt climbed past $14 trillion and all indications were that it would grow, I urged JBS members to contact their elected congressional representatives to ask for abolition of such unconstitutional federal programs as Foreign Aid, the Departments of Education, Energy, Housing and Urban Development, and more.

CEO Thompson explained that devious changes in the meanings of words have led to serious consequences for the American people. He termed these changes "semantic warfare." For an example, he pointed to the change in the meaning of **Inflation** from something that should be blamed on government and the Federal Reserve to now being blamed on merchants and businessmen. Inflation is an increase in the quantity of money that causes existing money to lose value. It results in a rise in the prices for goods and services. Merchants and businessmen are not the culprits. Surprisingly, the *Wall Street Journal* correctly noted in an article that even some dictionaries have defined inflation wrongly, claiming that it is the condition of rising prices, not the scourge of flooding the nation with unbacked currency.

Other changes deserving of mention in the semantic warfare arena included **Choice**, a word customarily used where there are legal and moral options. But a newer use employs the word to hide the deliberate murder of unborn babies. **Healthcare** is far from addressing health as the program bearing that name should be known as "people control." And **Democracy** that was so soundly rejected by America's Founders as unquestionable evil has been transformed into something everyone is encouraged to praise.

Regional Field Director Robert Brown cautioned members not to shock others with too much information too soon. Rather, he suggested sharing a DVD or an article and asking a recipient to provide an opinion about it. Countering President Obama's claim that America's current wars (Iraq, Afghanistan and Pakistan) have cost $1 trillion, Brown University's Watson Institute for International Studies reported and the JBS agreed, that the cost of these wars was at least $3.7 trillion, and maybe as high as $4.4 trillion.

I reported about formally debating the merits of the Federal Reserve with an economics professor during the July 4th "We the People Convention" in Columbus, Ohio. During the encounter, the professor never responded to my claims that 1) honest money has to be a tangible commodity such as gold or silver; 2) the Constitution grants power to Congress to "coin money," not to issue it or to transfer its assumed power to the privately owned Fed; 3) the Fed is the engine of inflation that continues to rob the people of their wealth. No amount of factual information, common sense, or historical evidence about Karl Marx and CFR founder Edward Mandell House calling for the Federal Reserve swayed the man. However, the audience responded positively to the arguments I presented.

Later discussion about this debate with several who had attended the event brought to mind a limerick that seemed to have been written to describe the bobbing and weaving professor.

> There once was a man named Gesser
> Whose knowledge grew lesser and lesser.
> It soon grew so small,
> He knew nothing at all,
> And now he's a college professor!

Success at the CPAC Convention in the nation's capital encouraged Society leaders to exhibit at the Liberty Political Action Conference (LPAC) in Reno, Nevada. Close to 600 attended this inaugural event where plenty of JBS books, magazines, DVDs, and reprints of articles from *The New American* ended up in eager hands. CEO Thompson spoke to the throng about reasons why ObamaCare should be repealed.

Congressman Ron Paul introduced the Free Competition in Currency Act (H.R. 1098). Immediately endorsed by the Society, the measure called for terminating the legal tender law that forces acceptance of Federal Reserve currency, for abolishing several unnecessary laws against counterfeiting that have been used to bar competing currencies, and for overturning tax laws that penalize the use of gold and silver coins as money. A significant step toward honest money, the measure received little backing in Congress where most members haven't any knowledge about sound money and the Constitution's provisions dealing with money.

Members and staff enthusiastically welcomed the Society's publication of "Reality Versus Myth," my 38-page booklet that addressed – and in many instances corrected – the many myths spread about the Society over several decades. Veterans as well as newer members were pleased to have its information to use in responding to foolish or malicious charges hurled at them and the Society.

The *Bulletin* presented some needed perspective about polling to keep members from relying on this frequently fraudulent shaping of opinion. I told of the George H. W. Bush administration's consideration of publishing "results" of a poll that the Bush team never conducted. Early in the 1992 presidential campaign, GOP leaders were considering dumping Vice President Dan Quayle from the ticket. Former Bush press secretary Marlin Fitzwater provided details in his 1995 book entitled *Call the Briefing*. The plan called for using made-up poll results and attributing them to Secretary of State James Baker and campaign manager Robert Teeter. Fitzwater even told of President Bush being in on the scheme. But the dump-Quayle plan fizzled and the former Indiana senator remained on the GOP's slate for the 1992 contest that ended in their defeat by the Clinton-Gore Democratic slate. Are many other never-taken poll results announced to sway public opinion? No one knows for sure. But, based on Marlin Fitzwater's frank report about the potential to use a never-taken poll, it is known that the tactic can be employed. And for Fitzwater to discuss the fakery so openly surely suggests that the process had often been employed.

Add to this little known aspect of polling the certainty that questions asked by a clever polltaker can easily gain a desired result. Further, George Gallup and Elmo Roper, both members of the Council on Foreign Relations, began the process of polling in America. Also, modern polling doesn't as much measure opinion as it shapes the public's thinking. Finally, when one realizes that the first modern polltaker was Russia's Vladimir Lenin, one can begin to understand how such an inexact measuring of public opinion has become a useful weapon used by unscrupulous political figures.

The JBS argument claiming that heavy indebtedness can eventually lead to loss of sovereignty became more easily understood when economic woes in Greece threatened to bring down the entire European Union's monetary system. Because of Greece's profligacy, the European Union moved in and took over management of Greece's affairs. There is a lesson associated with what happened in faraway Greece but U.S. leaders don't want to learn from it or have the public made aware of what can happen. Enormous American indebtedness, with no sign of reversing the suicidal course presently being taken, could very soon see a scrapping of the dollar and the insertion of currency issued by the UN's International Monetary Fund or World Bank. The lesson given in the Greek situation seems not to have been learned by U.S. leaders. Or maybe it has been learned and what happened in that relatively small country could easily happen here where the nation's debt is enormously higher. Addressing it the way the EU has addressed Greek indebtedness could lead to cancellation of independence in the "land of the free and the home of the brave."

Chapter 72
2012: Exposing the SPLC

In the face of new Conspiracy-created attacks on national independence and on the Society itself, recommendations about dealing with them appeared regularly in the monthly *Bulletin*. As a result of the number and variety of matters needing attention, the Society's monthly message sent to members (and non-member subscribers) had become somewhat cluttered. Therefore, CEO Thompson decided that members needed a new roadmap to help them know what was most important, where they should devote their time and energy, and which current activity or individual should receive appropriate expressions of displeasure or gratitude for their work. "It is time for a revised John Birch Society Agenda," he concluded. And the January 2012 *Bulletin* is where a new Agenda first appeared.

The ten most important topics pointed to by Thompson at the start of 2012 were: 1) Recruiting, 2) Stop the New World Order, 3) Preserve the U.S. Constitution, 4) Support Your Local Police, and 5) Rebuild America's Cultural Base. Following those significant concerns were 6) Promote *The New American* magazine and its Web Site; 7) Recommend JBS.org as the Entry Point for the various JBS Divisions; 8) Self-Education, 9) Pending Legislation, and 10) Temporary Matters.

The Society's unquestioned effectiveness had been demonstrated when President George W. Bush's brazen determination to place America in a North America Union by 2010 had to be postponed. JBS-led opposition to that scheme had won the battle – but perhaps only temporarily. The President announced 2020 as the new date for merging the three nations. But while a celebration was in order, all were cautioned to keep spreading information about this significant threat to national independence. The plot had not been scrapped; it had been put off for another day.

The Society came into possession of the material given by government to prospective U.S. citizens. One handout immediately referred to "Principles of American Democracy" and nowhere was the Founding Fathers' clear intention to create a Republic mentioned.

One of the questions given a citizenship candidate asked: "What are two ways that Americans can participate in their democracy?" Passing this test to become a citizen in no way led a person to the fundamental understanding that our nation's system of government is a republic. The "test" leading prospects to citizenship actually contributed to making these eager people less aware of the fundamentals that made our country the envy of mankind.

The *Bulletin* reported a new high in the number (more than half a million) who turned to thenewamerican.com in a single month for information and perspective. The popularity of the JBS-related site continued to grow.

Early in 2012, President Obama requested Congress to raise the debt ceiling – already at $15.2 trillion and Congress dutifully complied. Interest paid to debt holders during the single fiscal year of 2011 soared to $454 billion. This is money extracted from U.S. taxpayers or created out of thin air by the Federal Reserve.

Thompson listed some of the subversive goals of the large tax-exempt foundations (Rockefeller, Carnegie, Ford, etc.). These were uncovered decades ago during congressional investigations chaired by Congressman Carroll Reece (R-Tenn.). The goals of these wealthy dispensers of funds to left-wing groups were then, and still are:

- Use war to change society.
- Control public education in order to stifle the nation's return to life as it existed prior to any war.
- Seize control of the teaching of history.
- Move key aspects of American life toward acceptance of entry with other nations into a one-world government.

When the Hungarian government replaced its communist-favoring constitution after the implosion of the Soviet Union, its new constitution proclaimed that parents are the primary guardians of their children, and life must be protected from conception. Fearing that abortion, same-sex marriage, and homosexual "rights" would be banned in Hungary, Amnesty International and Human Rights Watch cited several UN Conventions in their protest about this small country's action. This matter, prominently noted in the *Bulletin*, supplied another excellent reason why the U.S. should withdraw from the world body.

The new Constitutional Sheriffs and Police Officers Association held its inaugural meeting in Las Vegas. The brainchild of former Sheriff Richard Mack, the gathering attracted 110 elected sheriffs, deputies, and other law-enforcement officials. Senior JBS staff official Jim Fitzgerald, who years ago had served as a policemen in New Jersey, told the attendees about the subversive efforts of the Southern Poverty Law Center, and issued a warning about President Obama's call for creation of a Civilian National Security Force, an obvious first step toward creation of a national police organization.

The 30th printing of the Society's *Blue Book* assured it a place as one of America's most popular books. Approximately half a million copies had already been distributed.

Members were advised that they had a notable ally in the labeling of our nation's enemy "a Conspiracy." In the August 1956 issue of *The Elks Magazine*, then-FBI Director J. Edgar Hoover wrote:

> We must now face the harsh truth that the objectives of communism are being steadily advanced because many of us do not readily recognize the means used to advance them. Yet the individual is handicapped by coming face to face with a conspiracy so monstrous he cannot believe it exists. The American mind simply has not come to a realization of the evil which has been introduced into our midst. It rejects even the assumption that human creatures could espouse a philosophy which must ultimately destroy all that is good and decent.

Thompson expressed his concern about FOX News dismissing Judge Napolitano and Glenn Beck. And he noted that Pat Buchanan had been axed by MSNBC. Each of these television personalities had welcomed Society representatives on their shows. The Society's CEO wondered if the long arm of the Conspiracy had a hand in removing those popular television personalities and their guests from being seen and heard.

The *Bulletin* provided a reminder of one of Robert Welch's favorite guiding principles: "Morality sees farther than intellect." Written by 19th Century historian James Anthony Froude, its meaning in modern parlance could be, "No matter how smart you are, or how smart you think you are, your commitment to morality is a more important measure of your worth." To further mankind's reliance on morality, Welch had published the aforementioned *John Birch Resolutions*. In the Introduction to this valuable treatise, he wrote:

> So the time has come – in fact it is long overdue – when many of the moral uncertainties of today, most of which have been introduced into our contemporary world by this satanic Conspiracy for its own evil purposes, ought to be swept away. This guidance should be provided, of course, by our great religious bodies. But too many of them are now merely adding to the confusion, or fighting with each other (or even within themselves) over matters of dogma

and doctrine. And it is imperative under present circumstances that somebody should put down in unmistakable language the primary features of a moral code to which all good people can readily subscribe.

More than the brief JBS motto "Less government, more responsibility, and ... with God's help ... a better world," *The John Birch Resolutions* provides an excellent guide for anyone at a time when virtually every formerly God-established and rock-solid standard is under attack.

The *Bulletin* warned of a new campaign against freedom that must to be watched and dealt with. It involved a specialized arm of the United Nations known as the International Telecommunications Union, an agency designed to gain control over various aspects of Internet use. Advances toward such a goal had been unsuccessful to date but could return at any time. Letters to Congress alerting its members to guard against any UN control were urged.

The understanding contained in the summary statement, "One seeks authorization to act from a superior, not an inferior," explained in a few words why the efforts of the U.S. military since 1945 have been so spotty. As noted in the May 2012 JBS *Bulletin*, all U.S. military activity once the U.S. joined the UN, had to be authorized, and therefore controlled, by the world body. The Korean War began in 1950 under UN authorization (UN flags were even flying over the U.S. forces). Three years of combat in that struggle led to a stalemate that has never been settled. Authorization from the UN "Regional Arrangement" known as SEATO led to actual defeat in Vietnam where a victory could have been achieved. A UN Security Council Resolution authorized the Desert Storm attack against Iraq in 1991. The second war against Iraq, begun in 2003, derived its authorization from a UN resolution. And the struggle in Afghanistan could be traced to its launch via UN authorization and its continuation as a NATO operation. Society members were urged to call attention to this serious betrayal of our nation's independence.

Each of these conflicts gained approval from docile – even unaware – members of Congress all of whom had sworn an oath to abide by the U.S. Constitution. And Article I, Section 8 of our nation's "supreme law of the land" states that Congress alone – not the UN or one of its subsidiaries – can authorize sending our military forces into war. No better way exists to demonstrate that our nation already submits to a superior known as the United Nations. No better reason exists for withdrawing the U.S. from the world body.

Beginning in 2010, the Society started honoring an annual "Exemplary Americanist" by presenting an honoree with a suitable plaque bearing the inscription, "The John Birch

Society honors [this recipient] for commitment to family, character, morality, and responsibility – the foundation of a free society." In 2010, Reverend Jesse Lee Peterson, the founder and president of Southern California's Brotherhood Organization for a New Destiny (BOND), was the first recipient. In 2011, Katie Wasem accepted the award for her late parents who were killed in a tragic auto accident in 2009. Cliff and Dorothy Wasem were exemplary JBS members and Cliff had been a member of the Executive Committee of the Society's Council. The 2012 recipient(s) were Oklahomans Tom and Kay Hill. While leading the Kimray Corporation, Tom also spent a great deal of time and resources to promote the Character First program and the Character Training Institute that started among Kimray employees and has spread far and wide to thousands of businesses in the U.S. and foreign countries.

In addition to the Special Issue of *The New American* explaining the attacks on police and countering the drive to create a national police force, the Society produced a brief DVD message exposing the Southern Poverty Law Center. The SPLC had frequently made its presence known as an opponent of police attempts to restore order in the streets of America. Supposedly an opponent of hate groups and individuals, the SPLC even named me on its listing of the more dangerous individuals in America. Others so named included Congressman Steve King (R-Iowa), film producer and writer Dinesh D'Souza, even African-American law professor Carol Swain. I was designated "dangerous" by the SPLC for having accused the U.S. government and the Federal Reserve of "destroying the dollar and setting us up for world currency, world control, and world government." When I learned of this designation by the SPLC, I announced that being included constituted "a badge of honor."

A new DVD entitled "Agenda 21: How Will It Affect You?" was added to the lengthening list of JBS-produced programs. Immediately available via YouTube, it promised to be of great help for members seeking to introduce and expose the latest UN attempt to destroy freedom.

Members were again asked to contact each of their two senators and ask for rejection of the Law Of the Sea Treaty (LOST). One of this pact's strongest Senate promoters, Senator Richard Lugar (R-Ind.), had just been beaten in a primary and his defeat was blamed in part because of his support for LOST. The main architect of this UN treaty, recently deceased Canadian Elisabeth Mann Borgese, just happened to be an openly proud Marxist who led the subversive World Federalist organization in her nation. The treaty would cede control over the world's oceans and undersea assets to the UN and world government.

The New American published Alex Newman's explosive report about the many massacres of Christians in the Middle East. He wrote that it is "likely true" that U.S. foreign policy led to weapons reaching Islamist militants who were then responsible for the deaths of an ascending number of peaceful Christian people.

With financial help supplied by generous donors, the American Opinion Foundation, the parent of the Society affiliated Freedom Project Academy, purchased its own 15,000 square foot building located about a mile from JBS headquarters. FPA's on-line home schooling program continued to attract students from all over the nation, and even some from other nations. This sorely needed venture would henceforth be led by Dr. Duke Pesta, a college professor whose vibrant exposure of the destructiveness contained in the federal government's Common Core Standards had already earned him national praise.

CEO Thompson pointed to the various dangers in ObamaCare, not only because of what it means to the health care industry, but because it is a major step in leading the United States into merger with other nations in a one-world system led by the United Nations. He repeated Vladimir Lenin's claim that "Socialized medicine is the keystone in the arch of the socialist state." ObamaCare was never so much about health as it is about people control.

Most Americans are aware of the period known as a "Lame Duck Session" that occurs after a November election but before newly elected officials take office the following January. Serious mischief frequently occurs during the month of December after a national election. So the Society issued a warning to be on guard against moves to have the Senate ratify a UN Small Arms Trade Treaty, the Law Of The Sea (LOST) treaty, and the UN Convention on the Rights of Persons with Disabilities, a measure designed more for additional UN power than for concern about people in wheelchairs.

One excellent way to counter the widespread notion that the UN is a do-nothing organization and never accomplishes anything became available with *The New American's* excellent survey of little-known but widespread UN global bureaucracy activity. Bill Jasper supplied the needed awareness in his "The United Nations: On the Brink of Becoming a World Government." He showed that the UN has a commission, an agency, an organization, a bank, or an office for gaining control over people in every corner of the globe. Reprints of this article were immediately made available.

The *Bulletin* did a bit of boasting about the Society's success in blocking some major moves by the enemies of national independence. While urging continued opposition to several sovereignty-compromising initiatives, the *Bulletin* noted that, among the promoters of the merger of nations and the creation of world government, there were some who recognized that their main enemy had been – and continued to be – The John Birch Society. Actual confirmation from the Left that this was the case came in a book containing some grudging admission of JBS effectiveness written by Robert Pastor, the aptly named "Father of the North American Union." In his *The North American Idea: A Vision of a Continental Future*, Pastor wrote that his plan had been scuttled by the combined efforts of author Jerome Corsi, Eagle Forum's Phyllis Schlafly, and "a resurgent John Birch Society." He nevertheless announced plans to continue creating his dream of a "community" of nations and denied ever wanting to have them form a "union." Another semantic ruse? Yes, indeed. Robert Pastor died from cancer in January 2014 at 66 years of age.

Chapter 73
2013: Internet Traffic Soars

Gary Benoit led off 2013 with an "encouraging" report from Google Analytics showing that during the previous year, 6.3 million "unique visitors" had turned to thenewamerican.com for its news and commentaries – up from 4.7 million the previous year.

Failure to succeed in their plan to establish a North American Union by 2010 led its promoters to shift their emphasis toward the Trans-Pacific Partnership (TPP). A welcome form of opposition to this scheme saw several members of Congress send their justifiable concerns in a letter to U.S. Trade Representative Ron Kirk. It warned that the TPP…

> will create binding policies on future Congresses in numerous areas [including] those related to labor, patent and copyright law, land use, food, agriculture and product standards, natural resources, the environment, professional licensing, state-owned enterprises and government procurement policies, as well as financial, healthcare, energy, telecommunications, and other service sector regulations.

The full truth about the Trans-Pacific Partnership is that it would cost jobs, dilute sovereignty, and seriously entangle our nation with many others. But its most disturbing feature is that it would make transition to the New World Order more easily accomplished, probably with little more than a few phone calls. JBS members were urged to contact their congressman and two senators to register opposition to U.S. entry into the TPP. In addition, all were asked to oppose giving President Obama Trade Promotion Authority (TPA). This form of completely unconstitutional power-transfer from Congress to the president would result in giving the Executive Branch sole negotiation authority on any trade measure plus allowing Congress only an up or down vote for passage – with no amendments allowed. It would confirm that the President had become close to being an emperor, not a president with limited powers.

The *Bulletin* also attacked the false argument claiming that, because free trade among the Nation's states led to beneficial movement of goods state-to-state, a similar arrangement among countries would produce similar benefits. But free trade worked well within our country because there was a national government possessed with constitutional power to "regulate commerce ... among the several States." If free trade were to be established among nations via the TPP or some similar pact, there would have to be an equivalent overseer of rules and rulers possessed with unquestioned power. That, of course, would dilute national sovereignty and create a bureaucracy that would surely gobble up freedom. Would that setter of rules be the United Nations? Of course!

So, claiming that the success within our nation should be duplicated by nations submitting to an international overseer would mean turning over sovereignty to a regional governing body. This would mean creating a super government that would rule those nations. The argument favoring such a plan is misleading at best and deceptively dangerous at worst.

Frustrated partisans hoping to force creation of a Con-Con came up with a new wrinkle to promote their plan. They would now term their goal a "Compact For America" seeking only a "limited" Con-Con. These enemies of the Constitution unsurprisingly ignored the possibility that a runaway convention would result, which is precisely what occurred in 1787. The haughty casting aside of the Articles of Confederation in 1787 demonstrated the power inherent in any Con-Con – which is why there has never been another in the history of our nation. JBS members continued to inform fellow Americans about the potential loss of the current U.S. Constitution should there be a new Con-Con.

CEO Thompson suggested using some pertinent questions when confronting someone favoring a Con-Con. Honest consideration of these should awaken anyone to the danger and folly of opening up the Constitution for change. Some of his questions were:

1. Do congressional or administration leaders adhere to the Constitution?
2. If they do not follow the law they have sworn to uphold, do you think they would abide by a good amendment or a revised Constitution if one were created?
3. If you are not currently electing constitutionally-minded politicians, can you expect to elect or have constitutionally-minded delegates appointed as delegates to any Con-Con?

Additional exposure of the Southern Poverty Law Center (SPLC) appeared in the "To Protect and Serve" special report published in *The New American*. The JBS-created DVD entitled "Protecting Rights: Loyal Americans Targeted by the SPLC" supplied additional condemnations of the SPLC. JBS members were encouraged to obtain these items for their use and for providing copies to their local police chief.

JBS members shed no tears when *Newsweek* magazine ceased publishing its print version. During the previous eight years, *Newsweek's* circulation fell by half to 1.5 million and its advertising revenue declined by 80 percent. Owners indicated that they would continue operations via the internet. Other print publications were likewise suffering similar losses in both readership and advertising.

Larry Greenly delightedly reported that Harvard law professor Laurence Tribe's 15-minute speech at the September 25, 2011, Harvard Conference on the Constitutional Convention contained arguments against holding a convention that were surprisingly similar to what the Society has always maintained. Members were urged to obtain a copy of the professor's remarks via YouTube.

When Alex Newman's report in *The New American* about an enormous government land grab in Brazil appeared, his goal was to alert Americans to any similar program here in America. Newman had lived in Brazil for four years and was still fluent in the Portuguese language. Once the article reached Brazil, it became an instant sensation and it received wide coverage in newspapers and television broadcasts.

Agenda 21 had already been adopted in many communities without their leaders knowing they had become members of a freedom-destroying UN program. After receiving funds and assurances about the need to save the planet, community after community had signed on to Agenda 21's "ICLEI," the International Council for Local Environmental Initiatives. But a simple computer search of the ICLEI website showed unquestionably that ICLEI was a UN program tied to the UN's Agenda 21. JBS members were encouraged to demonstrate this pertinent fact when discussing ICLEI with their local governmental leaders, most of whom had no awareness about this organization's UN parentage. Wherever they were able to do so, local leaders were surprised, some even angered, about having been lured into something they surely didn't want.

Soon, the indisputable evidence of ICLEI's ties to the UN and Agenda 21 was no longer so easily shown via the Internet. The ICLEI website had been drastically altered. Henceforth, it took a great deal more effort to convince local government leaders to reject the rosy promises of the government personnel who were promoting ICLEI and not identifying it as a UN program.

Senior staff official Jim Fitzgerald reported that mailings of pertinent information to more than 16,000 police chiefs about the dangerous plan to create a national police force and about the Southern Poverty Law Center's smear attacks aimed at solid Americans had created substantial impact. The SPLC even hired a journalist to travel the nation and write a smear piece about the Society. His subsequent article turned out to be "a feeble attempt to discredit JBS" according to Fitzgerald.

Members were encouraged to obtain extra copies of the March 18, 2013, issue of *The New American* and share them with gun owners. In this particular issue, Rebecca Terrell discussed the link between psychiatric medications taken by deranged shooters and the carnage they caused in school shootings and theaters. Special attention was also given to Joe Wolverton's article tracing Nazi era moves from gun registration to gun confiscation. The lesson he provided was clear: Don't allow gun registration because it will be followed by confiscation.

When the UN sought signatories to its Arms Trade Treaty, they found a willing accomplice in the Obama administration whose officials applauded the UN's "Final United Nations Conference on the Arms Trade Treaty." But U.S. entry into this frightful treaty still required approval by two-thirds in the Senate. As speedily as he could, Senator James Inhofe (R-Okla.) introduced an amendment to a budget measure that boldly called for "upholding Second Amendment rights and preventing the United States from entering into the United Nations Arms Trade Treaty." His measure won Senate approval by a 53 to 46 margin. The *Bulletin* then listed the names of the 46 senators whose negative vote indicated a desire to diminish the rights of gun owners. Calls to the offices of senators (pro or con regarding the Inhofe measure) were recommended.

The states of Alabama and Tennessee had already enacted legislation prohibiting implementation of Agenda 21 within their boundaries. State legislatures in Oklahoma and Arizona started the process of passing similar measures. In Utah and South Dakota, attention was drawn to Agenda 21 but legislation in those states didn't bar participation in the UN program. Writing in the *Bulletin*, Christian Gomez recommended that state legislatures should follow the lead set by Alabama to keep the UN program from being adopted in their state.

A new 46-page booklet entitled *America and the United Nations* became available. Written by me, it immediately proved helpful in combating UN campaigns such as Agenda 21, restricting gun ownership, domination of our nation's military, and more. The booklet cited the anti-UN warning given by former State Department official J. Reuben Clark who had read the *UN Charter* soon after its 1945 publication. His immediate and emphatic assessment stated: "The Charter is a war document, not a peace document [that] makes it practically certain that we shall have future wars." In 1919, Clark had capably alerted some key senators to oppose U.S. entry into the League of Nations. His effort led to Senate rejection of the League of Nations.

Combating amnesty for illegal immigrants continued to be a Society project. In the *Bulletin*, Larry Greenley pointed out that the 1986 law dealing with immigration gave amnesty to three million illegal entrants while promising there would never again be an amnesty proposal. But in 2013, a new comprehensive amnesty proposal, "The Border Security, Economic Opportunity, and Immigration Modernization Act" (S. 744), arrived for Senate approval. JBS members were urged to contact their senators to register opposition to this measure but the senators had already voted against passage.

While the proposal to have the U.S. join with Canada and Mexico in a North American Union (NAU) was still being discussed, similar action that would have had the United States merge with the European Union by 2015 constituted an additional threat. Labeled the Transatlantic Trade and Investment Partnership (TTIP), it too would compromise national sovereignty. Art Thompson recommended that opposition to these supposed "free trade" agreements should include a statement issued by Karl Marx in January 1848. Long ago, the father of modern Communism stated: "Free trade breaks up old nationalities … in a word, the free trade system hastens social revolution."

In the wake of the bombings at the Boston Marathon, CEO Thompson reviewed some past discussion about the history of terrorism. His brief lesson provided valuable insight about revolutionary employment of this tactic in order to topple governments.

Larry Greenley urged members to contact state officials to have them stop or repeal Common Core educational standards. Reprints of *The New American* article "Common Core: A Scheme To Rewrite Education" were offered. In addition, the *Bulletin* recommended the 70-minute DVD "Dangers and Threats To American Liberty and Education: Common Core." Greenley summarized one additional aspect of this new federal intrusion into the field of education:

> These standards represent an acceleration of the dumbing down and nationalization processes in effect in our public schools. Since the main national standard tests, SAT and ACT, would be based on Common Core standards, private and home schools would also be forced to teach according to Common Core curricula.

A message sent by Oklahoma Section Leader Bob Donohoo to members in his area provided insight into the danger of creating a new Con-Con. Citing a passage from the Articles of Confederation dealing with a possible future Con-Con, he pointed out that the then "law of the land" (the Articles of Confederation) allowed no amendments unless they were "confirmed by the legislatures of <u>every</u> state (Emphasis supplied)." Donohoo wrote:

> As history shows, the Articles were discarded and the new Constitution was offered in its place. But the delegates to the 1787 convention hadn't been given power to abolish the Articles of Confederation. They simply cast the Articles aside and wrote an entirely new document. In part, the new Constitution stated that the ratification of "nine States," not every state, "shall be sufficient for the Establishment of this Constitution." If such a change, even a total discarding of the Articles, could be accomplished in that convention, the precedent set could be cited as authorization for other changes during any new convention. A change to having a mere majority (not nine or unanimous) state approvals of the ratification process could be inserted. In other words, the precedent set by the actions of the delegates at the 1787 convention invites what is called a "runaway" in any new convention. And this is precisely why there has never been another constitutional convention in the history of our nation, and additionally why there should be none in these years.

President Obama and Secretary of State John Kerry announced their support for the UN's "Arms Trade Treaty." Already accepted by 113 of the UN's member nations (there are 193), the measure would severely impact the God-given right of individual citizens to be armed. Chances of gaining the required two-thirds of the Senate for approval of this UN grab for power were slim. But, as a precaution, JBS members were advised to contact their two U.S. senators to register disapproval of the UN proposal.

I provided a brief look at some of the dangerous UN Charter provisions while noting that only two senators voted against entry into the world body on July 28, 1945. The two, Republicans William Langer of North Dakota and Henrik Shipstead of Minnesota, gave sound reasons for their refusal to go along with the majority in their speeches prior to the Senate's 89-2 vote of approval. Then, in December 1945, after previous Senate action had already placed our nation in the world body, Congress passed the United Nations Participation Act giving the president power to send U.S. military forces into any action he deems necessary <u>without</u> prior congressional approval. In the House, this measure effectively overrode the constitutional requirement for a congressional declaration of war before sending forces into battle. Yet it won approval by a vote of 355 to 15. After achieving victory in World War II, our nation's forces have not won any conflict into which they have been sent. From the date of entry into the UN, they have always been under some form of UN control.

Congressman Ron Paul (R-Texas) regularly authored a measure calling for the U.S. to withdraw from the UN. After he retired, Congressman Paul Broun (R-Ga.) reinserted the measure. After Broun left his place in the House for a Senate run, Congressman Mike Rogers (R-Ala.) introduced the bill. JBS members are regularly reminded of the need to gain more co-sponsors for H.R. 193, the measure calling for the U.S. to reassert its full independence by withdrawing from the United Nations.

CHAPTER 74
2014: BEWARE ENTANGLING ALLIANCES

CEO Thompson looked back over the Society's years of effort and reminded members of four "ingredients that make JBS so dangerous" to the enemies of our country. These are the Society's focus, monolithic structure, national field staff, and nationwide network of chapters. He noted that no other organization can claim such organizational strength.

As to what holds the Society back from achieving its goals, he pointed to two significant "roadblocks." These are: 1) the necessary numbers of people engaged in the work of the Society; and 2) the necessary funds to carry out our mission. Both of these yet-to-be-conquered hurdles have always been a concern. Triumphing over each would lead to gaining the overall victory of defeating the Conspiracy.

Regarding the need for funding, I have often thought of Robert Welch's attitude as he expressed it in the mid-1960s. Always bedeviled by the need to raise funds, he said, "If I had available for the Society the amount of money dispensed during a single week for welfare of various kinds in New York City alone, the Society could defeat the Conspiracy in approximately two years." Simply saying that – and backing it up with some figures – impelled a few well-to-do supporters to dig more deeply and help more.

The *Bulletin* pointed to a recently issued State Department publication listing 37 treaties that had been submitted to the Senate for confirmation. In addition to the TPP and TTIP, the list included the dangerous UN Arms Trade Treaty (ATT), the UN's Convention on the Rights of Persons with Disabilities (CRPD), and numerous smaller pacts that would eat into national independence.

Ratification of ATT would deny citizens the "right to sell, trade, or transfer all means of armed resistance." It even required signatory nations to "establish and maintain a national control system, including a national control list." These ominous features of the UN's attempt to grab additional power didn't disturb Secretary of State John Kerry who eagerly signed the pact "on behalf of President Obama." Resistance to the ATT had already been demonstrated when 53 senators indicated their intention to block its ratification.

Opposition to the UN's Disabilities Convention arose from home-school advocates who saw several new layers of government regulations – some international – overriding parental authority in the care of children with disabilities. In addition, a careful reading of the treaty showed that it guaranteed access to "reproductive health." This would give the UN authority to meddle more deeply than ever in such areas as abortion, contraception, sterilization and sex education. Already second to no other nation in dealing with the rights of the disabled, the U.S. had no reason to worry about "looking bad" for not approving the Disabilities Convention. Clearly, this treaty's goal sought establishment of more international power over the laws of many nations, especially those in the U.S.

Art Thompson's new book, *International Merger by Foreign Entanglements*, became available. In 145 pages, it showed the danger to independence of various pacts and treaties in addition to issuing a warning about the U.S. duplicating or joining the European Union. The EU had already severely compromised independence for its member nations.

While the U.S. government, mass media, educators, and even clergy continued to inform the American people that China poses no threat to freedom, the Society issued a completely different attitude in a warning about a growing threat from China. If others wished to close their eyes to China's never-renounced intention to conquer the United States, the Society would not ignore what it deemed to be a planned calamity. Aided by some in America, Chinese leaders have beguiled many into believing that the Beijing brand of Communism is different, even worthy of praise. But population control and forced relocation of masses continue in China as government policies, along with suppression of unapproved religions, silencing of educators, control of the press, monitoring the Internet, and more.

Protecting the Constitution from being discarded during a Con-Con continued to be a member assignment. Attorney Joe Wolverton supplied a new weapon for this campaign in his *New American* article "Nullification vs. Constitutional Convention." He urged, "A string of state nullification victories would not only create a bandwagon effect encouraging other states to join the nullification movement, it would contribute to overall awakening – shortening the time it would otherwise take to create a constitutionalist U.S. Congress."

As noted previously, several state legislatures had rescinded their prior calls for a Con-Con. Some proponents of a Con-Con erroneously claimed that rescissions are invalid, that once a state legislature issues a call for a Con-Con, it can never change its mind. As of May 2014, the required 34 states had issued Con-Con calls but 12 states had formally rescinded theirs. Congressman Duncan Hunter (R-Calif.) asked Congress to check whether the two-thirds threshold for creating a Con-Con had been reached. Members were urged to contact representatives in Congress informing them that any state can change its mind and that the required 34 calls for a Con-Con had not been reached.

For those who have never read the "Charter of the United Nations," two of its articles among many others were shown in the pages of the *Bulletin* to be reasons why anyone desirous of maintaining freedom and national independence should want to Get US out! The Charter's Article 25 states: "The Members of the United Nations agree to accept and carry out the decisions of the Security Council...." Our own nation's leaders at the presidential and congressional levels frequently bow to the requirement stated in Article 25. Doing so makes meaningless their solemn oath to uphold the U.S. Constitution. "But we have a veto," say UN partisans. A proper response to that should be, "But when have our representatives at the UN ever used it properly?"

The other highly ignored but dangerous portion of the Charter appears in Article 2 where there is assurance that "nothing in the present Charter shall authorize the United Nations to intervene in matters which are essentially within the jurisdiction of any state [i.e. country]." But ignoring restrictions clearly spelled out in its own Charter, the UN stopped a gold mining operation in Montana; sought to block the execution of a brutal murderer in Virginia; claimed U.S. use of capital punishment to be a violation of international standards; criticized existing bans on abortion; condemned U.S. Border Patrol activity; and more. In short, the UN violates its own Charter's limitations, is a lawless entity, and continues its efforts to gain total control of the planet.

Years before he passed away, Welch stated, "Withdraw the United States from the United Nations and you will have broken the back of the Conspiracy!" He was correct 50 years ago, and his assessment is no less correct today.

Members were reminded that reliance on any element of the mass media, even those outlets thought to be sound providers of what's needed to preserve freedom, is a dangerous route to follow. No JBS official is advocating a refusal to read or listen to newspapers, radio/television news, popular magazines, etc. But all Americans are encouraged to supplement the popular purveyors of news and perspective with information supplied by the *Bulletin*, *The New American* and the magazine's web site. As many have discovered, JBS offers hidden facts and remarkably different perspective, the kind of understanding every American truly needs.

CEO Thompson suggested that imposition of Common Core standards on America's schools is the logical consequence of following a strategy proposed in 1848 by Karl Marx in *The Communist Manifesto*. The little-known portion of this revolutionary document discusses the creation of "despotic inroads on the rights of property, and on the conditions of bourgeois production." These, wrote Marx, would prove to be "economically insufficient and untenable." But the Marxists who created them knew they wouldn't satisfy the needs of the people. The criminals creating such failures would, therefore, have an opportunity to implement "further inroads upon the old social order." The Marxist plan, according to the *Manifesto* itself, actually sought initial failure followed by corrective measures that would make matters worse – all designed to inflict harm on the people and bring them into total submission. Diabolical cleverness? Absolutely!

In recent years, America's schools have been saddled with a parade of federal education programs that haven't even come close to reversing the downward slide of student performance. These were Outcome Based Education, Goals 2000, No Child Left Behind, and Race To the Top. The results produced by these highly touted programs led to declining world rankings of America's teens – such as 31st in math, 24th in science, and 21st in reading. Quoting Marx, these results were "insufficient and untenable." So, as the *Manifesto* boldly urged, "further inroads upon the old social order" were called for. The schools, already operating under failing federal mandates, are required to teach according to Common Core standards which competent educational experts have claimed are the worst yet. The standards set by Common Core may have been the goal in the first place.

Although it first appeared in 1961, a State Department Document 7277 entitled "Freedom From War: The U.S. Program For General and Complete Disarmament in a Peaceful World" has never been withdrawn as our nation's policy. It has, however, received plenty of attention from the Society because of 50 years of publicizing its goals. One of its more infuriating passages contains the following direct attack on the private ownership of weapons:

> The manufacture of armaments would be prohibited except for those of agreed types and quantities to be used by the U.N. Peace Force and those required to maintain internal order. All other armaments would be destroyed or converted to peace purposes.

In other words, no one but members of the U.N. Peace Force would be allowed to possess a weapon. The title given this subversive document even contains a lie. It claims to want "Complete" disarmament. But careful reading shows that it calls instead for <u>selective</u> disarmament, leaving weapons in the hands of UN personnel and no one else.

Withdrawing from membership in the UN is the only sane course for America.

The August *Bulletin* announced that congressional action toward passage of the Trade Promotion Authority (TPA) had been "stalled." TPA awards the president completely unconstitutional power over treaty matters. If Congress should pass TPA, it would lose its rightful power to add amendments and would have only a Yes or No vote with no discussion allowed. Previous presidents have sought and gained such power and President Obama wanted it as well. But mounting congressional opposition to such a cave-in seemed to be winning the battle.

The American Opinion Foundation's educational arm produced a 42-minute DVD entitled *Who Owns Your Children? – The Dangers of Government as a Parent*. Much of the program describes the capture of American education by collectivists and humanists. It quickly attracted great attention at numerous homeschool conferences.

A new recruiting tool entitled *Restoring America: The Heartbeat of the Americanist Cause* became available. A colorful pictorial display of Society programs and goals, it was designed for use in recruiting on an individual basis and it promised to aid members who have never had much success in the important work of numerically building the organization.

After China's Houlin Zhou won appointment as the leader of the UN's International Telecommunications Union (ITU), fears rose that the UN might be seeking to control the Internet. There isn't any doubt that totalitarians want such power. That kind of domination over internet usage already exists in China, but it can also be found in Cuba, Iran and Saudi Arabia. Society members were encouraged to spread awareness that protecting the free flow of information via the internet should be everyone's task.

CHAPTER 75
2015: *Overview* In Spanish

The January 2015 *Bulletin* contained photographs of four separate trifold flyers produced to combat the so-called "free trade" agenda. Members readily increased distribution of each. In this same *Bulletin*, numerous other trifolds, reprinted articles, and DVDs for use in the campaign to block creation of a Con-Con were shown. Members had plenty of ammunition to help legislators and the public understand the threats posed by the Trans-Pacific Partnership (TPP) and the Transatlantic Trade and Investment Partnership (TTIP). Likewise, trifolds were available to show the different but real threat emanating from a possible Con-Con.

CEO Thompson urged all to refer to "Union" rather than Partnership when discussing the TTP and TTIP. "Let's call them what they are," he advised. "They are designed to bring about unions with other nations and groups of nations." He pointed to George Washington's counsel that America should have commercial relationships with other nations, not political connections.

Larry Greenley happily announced the availability of Bill Jasper's article exposing the role of the American Legislative Exchange Council (ALEC) in promoting both the dangerous trade agreements and the Con-Con. Entitled, "Not So Smart ALEC," the article noted ALEC's 300 corporate and foundation associates and 2,000 state legislator members.

Jim Fitzgerald pointed to the funding by leftist billionaire George Soros of various groups protesting police work that resulted in the deaths of two black citizens. He referred to an important article by the *Washington Post's* Kelly Riddell naming the groups that received a total of $33 million per year from the Soros-led Open Society Foundation.

Promotion of S. 264, the "Audit the Fed" bill, received needed attention. Over recent years, the House had twice passed measures calling for such an audit, but each died in the absence of Senate action. But Senator Rand Paul (R-Ky.) backed a move in the Senate that quickly gained 30 co-sponsors. Now over 100 years old, the Federal Reserve has never been audited and its owners have never been officially identified.

CNN anchor Chris Cuomo received a deserved rebuke in the *Bulletin* and elsewhere after his on-air statement that "Our rights do not come from God...They come from man ... from collective agreement and compromise." His guest at the time was Alabama Supreme Court Justice Roy Moore who calmly but emphatically assured the liberal television personality that our rights "come from God, as clearly stated in the Declaration of Independence." Sadly, Chris Cuomo is not alone in never having learned this fundamental truth. Many Americans aren't aware of it either and are therefore vulnerable to seeing cancellation of everyone's God-given rights.

A newly reprinted article from *The New American* contained the headline: "The Solution is the Constitution, Not Article V." Several books published by other patriotic groups but dealing with Society issues became instant favorites. These included:

> *Common Ground on Common Core*, a 436-page book full of arguments from across the political spectrum targeting the imposition of the Common Core State Standards on the nation's schools.
>
> *World Federalism* containing important facts about the history of groups touting "federalism" while paving the way for the New World Order.
>
> *Licensed To Lie* presents a riveting account of a former Federal Appeals attorney who, after 30 years of working within the system, decided to expose what she now refers to as the Department of "Injustice."
>
> *Crimes of the Educators* providing a history of the architects of America's public school disaster. One of the co-authors of this latest book was veteran JBS member Samuel Blumenfeld, the creator of a very successful program that taught old and young how to read using phonics.

The Society mourned the loss of Council member David Eisenberg. A career aeronautical engineer, Dave examined the claims of the Society on his own and concluded that there was no basis for the charge that the organization was dangerous, un-American, even anti-Semitic. Finding no evidence to support those slurs, he examined the Society more deeply, joined in 1964, and remained a faithful member with wife Natalie for more than 50 years. He frequently made himself available to counter the anti-Semitic label placed on the Society by its enemies.

As a way of reaching out to Spanish speakers in America, the Society produced a Spanish-language version of *Overview of America*. Immediately popular in areas populated by Hispanic Americans, the half-hour program led to a new source of members and prospects.

Senator Jeff Sessions (R-Ala.) received well-deserved congratulations for his opposition to the Trans-Pacific Partnership (TPP). In a letter sent to President Obama, he pointed out that the TPP has "all the hallmarks of a nascent European Union." One of the objections raised by Sessions noted that the "secret text" (he had managed to view it despite Obama administration impediments) creates a Commission with authority "to amend the agreement after its adoption, add new members, and issue regulations" dealing with labor, immigration, environmental and commercial policy. Bill Jasper wrote an excellent analysis of the matters raised by Sessions for *The New American*.

Most Americans in 2015 had never heard of William Z. Foster. The top leader of the Communist Party USA for 25 years beginning in 1933 (except for a single year during World War II) Foster authored the 1932 book *Toward Soviet America* containing his recommendations for converting our nation into a Communist tyranny. Among many seemingly outrageous proposals at the time, Foster called for creation of a national Department of Education that would see to it that educational studies "will be revolutionized, being cleansed of religious, patriotic, and other features of the bourgeois ideology." Sadly, many of the steps urged by Communist Foster in 1932 have been implemented.

On May 4, 1980, with heavy backing from President Jimmy Carter, the National Education Association and the Democratic Party leadership, Congress created the Cabinet-level Department of Education. Helped by revolutionary decisions of the courts, the schools were subsequently "cleansed" of all mentions of religion; patriotism is no longer encouraged; and the teaching of morals has been replaced by "do your own thing" morality – which is no morality. The Birch Log for June 5, 1980 reported this huge victory for communism. Reminding JBS veterans, and informing newer members, about this significant communist victory stimulated renewed campaigns to warn fellow Americans of the enemy's progress. The-hard-to-find 1932 Foster book is well worth reading today.

In the wake of the Supreme Court's bizarre ruling in *Obergefell v. Hodges* that the U.S. Constitution contains a right to same-sex "marriage," Gary Benoit insisted that "the Supreme Court cannot alter reality. Just as it cannot change the composition of water by declaring it now to be comprised of elements other than hydrogen and oxygen, the Court cannot change the nature of marriage by calling same-sex unions "marriage." Marriage, he insisted, is the "union of one man and one woman."

Art Thompson delightedly pointed out that "at least a million viewers come to our Internet sites and affiliates every month." The *Bulletin* showed screenshots of the JBS YouTube Channel, the Facebook Page, the Support Your Local Police page, and the Choose

Freedom – STOP the Free Trade Agenda page, all of which can be found at JBS.org.

Under a headline asking, "Are Anchor Babies Full Citizens?", the *Bulletin* traced the tortured history of the Supreme Court's 1982 decision sanctioning the designation of automatic citizenship for infants born within the United States. While other nations were repealing "birthright citizenship" (Australia, Ireland, New Zealand, Dominican Republic for instance), the U.S. and Canada continued to confer this precious status on an infant, and that status enables the entry of parents, siblings, aunts, uncles and others to reside legally, all relying on the so-called "choice" of the newborn infant. Because this practice had been made legitimate by a Supreme Court decision, the Society recommended that it be undone by another ruling of the high court.

The Society revived its Support Your Local Police – And Keep Them Independent ad hoc program. Supporting items included *The New American* for September 21, 2015 headlined "Police Under Fire," a 21-page booklet explaining the wisdom of keeping control of police at the local level, and an assortment of pamphlets and other related items.

Afterword
Becoming President Emeritus

In January 2016, I stepped down from my "inside" position as President of The John Birch Society. From then onward, I would be known as "President Emeritus." Thus, I will leave it to others to add to this chronicling of the history of the organization to which I have given so many of my years. I am hugely grateful for the confidence placed in me by others and for the love expressed to me by thousands upon thousands of members.

For many years, liberal politicians, pundits, professors and others have dispensed conflicting attitudes about The John Birch Society. They sought to have the public believe Robert Welch's creation posed a worrisome threat to freedom and, before too long, that it had become a past phenomenon no longer worthy of concern. But at the same time, these enemies of the Society were forced to deal with awareness that the organization had flexed its muscles and slowed or even blocked movement toward a variety of liberal ("progressive") goals or had sidetracked the intent to compromise, even destroy, national independence in favor of an all-powerful "new world order." Such awareness on the part of those who seek to discount the Society's limited but real successes has rarely been publicly acknowledged. But, in the midst of many who know but won't admit that the Society's work has produced numerous successes, I have sought to provide indisputable evidence that the organization's educational strategy and morality-based tactics have won a goodly share of battles.

Promoters of a North America Union, for example, found a formidable foe in JBS. Enthusiasts for a Con-Con made a similar discovery. Seekers of disarmament of both our nation's military and private citizens found the Society to be a well-constructed brick wall. So, too, have many liberals, progressives, ladder climbers, and worker bees for a Conspiracy discovered substantial society-generated resistance as they …

- seek UN supremacy over mankind,
- labor to ban private gun ownership,
- insist dishonestly or ignorantly that our nation's governing system has al-

ways been "democracy,"
- propose that the untouchable Federal Reserve manages our nation's economy properly and well,
- consider the U.S. Constitution a hoary relic of the past in need of reform or replacement,
- arrange to have the U.S. military serve as the policemen of the world under United Nations authorization,
- call for open borders and welfare for those who arrive in the U.S. illegally,
- find little or no reason to object to staggering national indebtedness,
- wink at abysmal educational rankings while claiming that another federally mandated program will reverse decades of dismal student performance.

The John Birch Society is actually known well by its enemies. The greatest fear of these foes remains the organization's potential. They know that its roadmap to success based on creation of citizen awareness cannot be ignored or dismissed with persistent scoffing. From its initial burst of enlistees, the Society has continued to gain new adherents, not in the numbers gathered during the organization's early days, but with enough new enlistees to reach out and awaken many more Americans.

Robert Welch predicted attracting large numbers in the Society's early years. This would be followed, he believed, by slower growth but increasing effectiveness. Then, he believed, a massive awakening among Americans would occur. It would be an honest seeking of JBS leadership to combat ever-growing government power, a development that would rout the conspiratorial force that had gained near total control of our country and mankind itself.

His prediction was given, never in so many words, but pictorially in the original logo he created for the Society. Called a "swoosh" by some and a "dog ear" by others, the logo remained in use while Robert Welch lived. It portrayed his assessment of growth and effectiveness in a mathematical-like curve that rises slowly at first, ascends rapidly, flattens out for a good while, and then takes off surging toward overall victory. The Society started with the small gathering in Indianapolis, grew dramatically during its early years, endured a long period of slower growth while building effectiveness, and seems ready to enjoy the sharp increase in numbers and successes depicted in the logo.

On the very few occasions when he was asked about the logo he had devised, Welch would explain that it showed past history and yet-to-be-achieved success. He would always add that the success he foresaw wasn't up to him but to the increased numbers and effectiveness of those who would join the Society. While he was the creator of this unique organization, he always paid deserved credit to the many tens of thousands who joined it and put their talents, reputation and resources into the effort. And he frequently thanked the men who served as field staff coordinators, many of whom had given up better-paying jobs to take on the task of building and assisting the Society's chapters. Likewise, he expressed his gratitude to the men and women who filled office positions in Belmont, Massachusetts and San Marino, California.

Welch made a habit of reminding audiences and visitors that his goal never included acquisition of power. He sought "less government." He wanted "more responsibility" among people, organizations, businesses, and governments. He believed that such a combination would, with God's – only when it was deserved – lead to the "better world" he believed could be established.

Successful implementation of The John Birch Society's program based on "education is our total strategy and truth our only weapon" will continue. It is hoped that this book, recounting the many successes and history of what is truly a unique but much needed organization, will help in a campaign culminating in triumph over the satanic and diabolical enemy of our nation and all of mankind.

APPENDIX
WHO WAS JOHN BIRCH?

With his death and in his death, the battle lines were drawn in a struggle from which either Communist or Christian-style civilization must emerge with one completely triumphant and the other completely destroyed.

— Robert Welch, 1954

In 1953, a full five years before he launched the Society, Robert Welch stumbled across the name of John Birch while "reading the dry typewritten pages in an unpublished report of an almost forgotten congressional committee hearing." He found in those pages the words of U.S. Army Captain John Birch who, while following orders to discover the intentions of Mao Tse-tung's Communist forces in China, was murdered by the supposed U.S. allies in the war against Japan. The grisly event occurred on August 25, 1945, a mere ten days after the final shots of World War II had been fired.

Prior to U.S. entry into World War II in the wake of the Pearl Harbor attack, four different military groups were actively fighting for control of China. These were the Japanese invaders, Chinese Communist forces led by Mao, Nationalist Chinese forces led by Generalissimo Chiang Kai-shek, and a fairly sizable American-led military detachment working as allies of the Nationalist Chinese. It was this latter group that eventually enlisted John Birch who had been in China since 1940 serving as a Baptist missionary. All sides knew that once the war ended and the Japanese forces went back to their homeland, the two Chinese factions would contend for control of the huge nation.

On the fateful day of August 25, 1945, ten days after Japan had surrendered, Captain Birch and several Nationalist Chinese comrades were dutifully following orders to meet with and learn the intentions of a group of Chinese soldiers thought to be affiliated with Mao's forces. While Birch and the dozen who set out with him were following the directives they had been given, circumstances developed which led Birch and Lieutenant Tung of the friendly Chinese forces to continue the assignment alone. Other members of the team cautioned Birch that he might be placing himself and Tung in danger, but John responded, "It doesn't make much difference what happens to me, but it is of utmost importance that my country learn now whether these people are friend or foe." It was these words on one of those "dry typewritten pages" that so intensely intrigued Welch. He promptly decided to dig more deeply into the life and death of this unusual soldier.

What befell Birch had already been the fate of many who confronted Communist forces in China – and in numerous other lands. After meeting with a contingent of very belligerent Communist soldiers, Birch and his companion were forcibly disarmed. John protested and both men were promptly shot and bayoneted. John shouted to Tung, "I can't walk any more." With a substantial wound in his own leg, the Chinese soldier watched as John, helpless to defend himself, was repeatedly bayoneted. He died almost instantly. Believing they had killed both men, the Communist soldiers left the scene of their atrocity. Later in that fateful day, a Chinese woman happened upon the scene. She found Birch dead and Tung alive but in need of medical attention. Brought to safety where he provided the grim details about what had occurred, Tung eventually recovered from his wounds.

Welch proceeded to learn a great deal more about John Birch's life and death from sketchy government files, information supplied by then-Senator William Knowland of California, and visits with John's parents at their modest home in Macon, Georgia. He gathered every related fact in order to write, in 1954, the small book of slightly more than 100 pages entitled *The Life of John Birch*. Welch discovered during his research that government officials had suppressed information about Birch's murder. And he learned further that Birch's parents, while they had been notified of their son's death, were never given details about what had actually occurred until after Chinese Communist forces had seized control of the entire nation in 1949.

Soon after the Henry Regnery Company released the book, the *Saturday Evening Post* published a long editorial based on information Welch had supplied. The magazine stated in its January 22, 1955, edition that, had the information in the book about John Birch's life and death been known, the Korean War (1950-1953) might well have been prevented.

Rescuing the Doolittle Crew, Becoming a U.S. Soldier

Welch recounted many of Birch's amazing exploits as a newly commissioned U.S. Army officer. Arriving in China as a Baptist missionary in 1940, he had quickly mastered the language, developed an ability to live amongst the Chinese people, and became a well-loved leader in numerous parts of the nation. While conducting his missionary work early in 1942, a Chinese acquaintance steered Birch to Colonel Jimmy Doolittle and his crew who had dropped their bombs on Tokyo in a daring April 1942 raid. Their mission was the first retaliation visited upon the Japanese homeland after the December 7, 1941, attack at Pearl Harbor. Japanese forces would harshly deal with any Americans who participated in that raid over Tokyo.

The American airmen had followed orders to fly their planes to China after dropping their bombs and then bail out when they ran out of fuel letting their planes crash. Which is precisely what they did. Had the Japanese caught any, they would likely have been executed.

Crews from some of the planes that participated in the Doolittle-led mission were never heard from again. Others were captured and sent to prison camps in Japan. Doolittle and his men, however, were fortunate to have been brought to safety from interior China by John Birch.

It was because of the help he supplied to Colonel Doolittle that the American forces led by General Claire Chennault, the U.S. commander of the famous "Flying Tigers," first learned of John's very existence. Once made aware of his work among the Chinese, Chennault sent for him and asked him to join the American forces. John stated he would be most happy to be their chaplain but Chennault explained that he already had a chaplain and needed someone like John who spoke the Chinese language, could live amongst the Chinese people, and serve the important role of gathering intelligence for the war effort. John accepted that assignment.

Commissioned as an army lieutenant on July 4, 1942, John immediately began his dangerous work tracking Japanese military forces and reporting on their whereabouts and likely plans. Details about his many exploits over three full years could fill many pages. Every American who served in China during the war knew of the critically important and dangerous work being performed by John Birch. He was highly decorated for what he accomplished and probably should have been awarded the Congressional Medal of Honor.

Why, then, did forces that were supposed to be allies in the war against the Japanese invaders murder him? The answer, according to Welch and backed up by subsequent history, is that Birch's leadership, obvious opposition to the Chinese Communists, and love for the Chinese people – a love enthusiastically shared by them – would have posed a formidable obstacle to Communist plans to seize control of an important sector of the Chinese nation. John had to die if the Red Chinese were to succeed in taking over the country.

We of course don't know whether John, had he lived, would have eventually returned to the United States. Had he done so, the attitude he expressed in one of his letters would have fit squarely into the organization formed by Robert Welch. Before his exemplary life was brutally snuffed out by Chinese Communist forces, he wrote: "I want of government only protection against the violence and injustices of evil or selfish men."

Of John Birch, Robert Welch would write that "he was the first, or very nearly the first, casualty in an American uniform" in the war between freedom and communist slavery that ravaged China. Only 27 years old when brutally slain, John Birch is a fitting symbol for the organization that bears his name. George and Ethel Birch, his parents, were always extremely grateful to Robert Welch for the book honoring their son's life and exploits. They eagerly gave permission for the use of John's name as a symbol for the Society. The two became early and enthusiastic Society members and never wavered in their appreciation for the organization and in their admiration for the man who had so greatly honored their son.

While engaged in Birch Society business in the early 1970s, I had the pleasure of visiting Mr. and Mrs. Birch at their home in Macon, Georgia. Delighted to have a Society official as a visitor, they showed some photos of their son as he grew into manhood and they talked freely about John and his love for the country whose uniform he was wearing when he was slain. Mrs. Birch expressed her earnest belief that her son, had he lived, would have received the Congressional Medal of Honor. She added that he should have been given the award even if posthumously. She received no disagreement from me.

Years later, one of John Birch's relatives, obviously prodded by an ambitious reporter aiming to inflict harm on the Society, allowed herself to be quoted in print that John, had he lived, would never have belonged to such an organization as the one named after him. When I responded to her in a letter that John's parents obviously disagreed and were, in fact, far more able than she to register an opinion about John's attitude, she never publicly addressed the issue again.

After the Society had been formed, Mr. and Mrs. Birch traveled to California and elsewhere on numerous occasions to speak at Society events honoring Robert Welch and building the Society. The two always expressed delight in having their son's name as the organization's symbol. In later years after Mrs. Birch had passed away, George Birch continued to travel to JBS events to offer an opening prayer.

Index Of Persons

Abernathy, Ralph, 193
Acheson, Dean, 31
Adams, John, 14, 351, 403
Adamson, N.E., 54-55, 66, 99, 137
Adelmann, Robert, 267
Adenauer, Konrad, 33, 35
Affleck, Mill, 416
Agnew, Spiro, 228
al-Zawahiri, Ayman, 421
Alibek, Ken, 311
Alibekov, Kanatjan, 311
Alinsky, Saul, 186, 202, 428
Allen, Gary, 6, 170, 190, 199-200, 210, 213, 217, 227, 237-239, 241, 248, 251-252, 268, 287, 298, 376
Allen, James S., 160
Allen, Walter, 5
Ambro, Jerome, 243-244
Anderson, Jack 234
Anderson, Tom, 62, 66, 125, 254
Andrews, T. Coleman, 39, 106, 109, 170, 200
Annan, Kofi, 352, 399
Antonio, Sam, 401, 428
Armstrong, Mike, 359
Armstrong, William, 280
Ashbrook, John, 288, 375
AuCoin, Les, 244
Avery, Dave, 211
Baehr, Ted, 400
Baker, Chuck, 416
Baker, James A. 317
Baldridge, Malcolm, 273
Baldwin, Chuck, 409
Bang-Jensen, Povl, 63
Barker, A. Clifford, 258-259, 296
Barlow, Bill, 218
Barr, Bob, 362
Barruel, Augustin, 181, 387
Bartley, Robert, 315
Bastiat, Frederic, 231, 425
Bayh, Birch, 271, 295
Beatty, John, 66
Beck, Glenn, 401, 435
Beckman, Petr, 254
Beebe, Marion, 88
Beebe, Murray, 88
Behreandt, Dennis, 366
Bell, Robert "Bob", 320, 388
Bellmon, Henry, 272
Benoit, Gary, 258, 267, 281, 287, 314, 318, 321, 340, 342, 362, 368, 371, 381, 403, 411, 414, 441, 457
Benson, Ezra Taft, 123, 125, 130, 172, 255, 336, 369
Benson, George, 97
Benson, Reed, 161, 183-184, 186, 199
Berking, Kristof, 412
Bernanke, Ben, 379
Bernhard (Prince), 148
Betancourt, Romulo, 110
Bethell, Tom, 393
Billington, James H., 280
Birch, Ethel, 139, 194, 255

Birch, George, 130, 194, 255, 293
Birch, John, 1-8, 12-15, 17-19, 23-24, 31, 33, 36, 39-40, 45-47, 50-51, 53, 58-60, 62-63, 66, 69, 71-72, 77, 82, 85-87, 89, 97-101, 103, 105-106, 108-109, 120-122, 125-127, 130-137, 140-141, 145-146, 151, 153-156, 162-163, 165-167, 169, 171-173, 175-177, 190, 192, 194-195, 198, 200-201, 205-209, 211, 214, 221-222, 226, 234, 237, 241, 244-245, 248, 251-252, 255-257, 259, 263, 265-267, 269, 279, 290, 293, 297, 299, 303-305, 310, 314-315, 328-329, 334, 336, 340-341, 345, 350-351, 355, 359, 366, 369, 372-373, 376, 390-391, 394, 401, 403, 406, 408-409, 416, 421, 424, 429, 433, 435-436, 438-439, 459-461, 463-466
Blackstone, William, 346
Blake, Gene, 105
Bloomfield, Lincoln P., 373
Blumenfeld, Samuel, 129, 456
Boettiger, Anna R., 75
Bogensberger, Bob, 214
Bolton, John, 388
Bonaparte, Napoleon, 11
Bonta, Steve, 380
Borgese, Elisabeth M., 437
Boutros-Ghali, Boutros, 330
Bowen, Catherine Drinker, 380
Bowers, Sam, 152
Bozell, L. Brent, 147
Braden, Spruille, 66, 106, 110
Braden, Tom, 66, 413
Bradley, Tom, 331
Brazenas, Vilius, 267, 373
Bremer, Arthur, 219
Bridges, Harry 126
Bridges, Styles, 61
Brinkley, David, 154
Brock, Bill, 193
Broder, David, 320
Brooke, Edward, 271
Broun, Paul, 447
Brown, Julia, 128, 161-163, 192, 209, 211, 266, 293
Brown, Leland, 211
Brown, Pat, 100
Brown, Robert, 416, 430
Bryant, William Cullen, 116
Brzezinski, Zbigniew, 202, 239
Bubolz, G. Allen, 313, 322
Buchanan, Patrick, 186, 368, 413, 435
Bulganin, Nikolai, 47
Bunche, Ralph, 111, 202
Bunker, Laurence E., 39, 138
Burke, Edmund, 301
Burnham, James 113, 165
Burns, James M., 307
Burns, John, 357
Bush, George H. W. , 4, 254, 273, 314, 317, 320-321, 324, 329-330, 431
Bush, George W., 14, 262, 367, 372, 376, 380, 383-384, 390, 395, 433

Butko, Greg, 393
Byrd, Robert, 362
Calderone, Mary, 197
Caldwell, Taylor, 111, 169, 210, 232, 369
Canwell, Frank, 111
Carnegie, Andrew, 273, 434
Carter, Jimmy, 239, 287, 457
Carto, Willis, 202
Caruth, William, 267, 314
Casteneda, Jorge, 390
Castle, Eugene, 61
Castro, Fidel, 37-38, 47, 103, 255, 323, 423
Chandler, Otis, 105
Chavez, Cesar, 200, 223
Cheney, Dick, 372
Chennault, Claire, 133, 465
Chenoweth, Helen 359, 365
Cherry, Bill, 221, 292
Chesterton, G. K., 369
Childs, Marquis, 251
Chung, Johnny, 354
Churchill, Winston, 232
Cicero, M. Tullius, 169
Clark, J. Reuben 444
Clements, Ed, 401
Clinton, Hillary 186
Clinton, Bill, 3, 260, 329, 331, 350, 355, 357, 362, 369, 371, 421-422
Collins, James 245
Compean, Jose, 399
Conner, S. J., 154
Conte, Silvio, 82
Coolidge, Calvin, 389
Corsi, Jerome, 397, 439
Corti, Egon C., 218
Courtney, Phoebe, 274, 324
Cox, Jack 270, 309
Cozzette, Ed, 244
Crino, Art, 388
Cronkite, Walter, 172, 147
Crow, Joe, 199, 209, 211
Culbert, Mike, 43, 143
Cuomo, Chris, 456
Currie, Lauchlin, 32
Curry, Clark, 424
Cushing, Richard Cardinal, 106, 148
Custer, George, 298
Daly, Arthur, 125
Daugherty, Harry 205
Davidson, Alan, 211
Davis, Forest, 113
Davis, Ralph, 66
Davis, Tom, 348
de Toledano, Ralph, 115
DeBorchgrave, Arnaud, 315
DeGaulle, Charles, 116
Dennis, Delmar, 152-153, 218, 256
Detweiler, George, 380-381, 385, 399
DeWeese, Tom, 397, 429
Dewey, John, 253
Dice, Marguerite, 51-52, 136
Diem, Ngo Dinh, 37, 111
Dies, Martin, 104, 170

INDEX OF PERSONS

Dillon, C. Douglas, 179
Dinsmore, Herman 206, 209, 211
Disraeli, Benjamin, 380
Dodd, Norman, 231
Dong, Pham Van, 182
Donohoo, Bob, 445
Doolittle, Jimmy, 133, 376, 464
Douglass, Joseph, 372
Draskovich, Slobodan, 176
Dravecky, Dave, 298
Drummey, James 321
du Berrier, Hilaire, 31, 58, 111, 126, 173-174
Dulles, Allen, 179
Dulles, John Foster, 76, 253
Dunham, Bill, 233, 252, 273
Durham, Douglas, 222
Eastland, James 100
Echohawk, Vangie, 222
Edwards, John, 187
Einstein, Albert, 252
Eisenberg, David, 137, 456
Eisenhower, Dwight, 71, 73, 77, 80-81, 98-99, 183, 231, 253
Epstein, Julius, 63
Ervin, Sam, 207
Evans, M. Stanton, 104, 350
Evans, Medford, 35, 46, 210
Everett, Charlie, 309, 314
Exner, F. B., 110
Fall, John, 222, 297
Fall, William P., 226
Fannin, Paul, 233
Fazio, Vic, 357
Feinstein, Diane, 278
Fels Barnes, Joseph, 77
Fenton, Francis, 137, 198, 210-211, 273
Field, Frederick Vanderbilt 32
Fitzgerald, Jim, 359, 400, 406, 414-415, 434, 443, 455
Fitzwater, Marlin, 432
Flynn, Elizabeth Gurley, 202
Flynn, John T., 113, 115
Fonda, Jane, 226, 278
Ford, Gerald, 228
Foreman, Al, 377
Forrestal, James, 63
Forster, Arnold, 175
Fortas, Abe, 193-194, 202
Fortkamp, Frank, 268
Foster, Ezola, 368
Foster, William Z., 110, 202, 253, 457
Fotheringham, Don, 260, 319, 333, 335, 340, 367, 371, 377
Fox, J. Edward 313
Fox, Vicente, 383
Francis, Sam, 342
Franco, Francisco, 205, 33
Frankfurter, Felix, 21, 253
Froude, J. A. 36
Futrell, Mary Hatwood, 314
Gaddafi, Muammar, 275
Gaither, Rowan, 231, 406
Gallup, George, 432

Gannon, Francis X., 202
Gardner, Richard N., 406
Garrett, Garet, 114
Gatsis, Andrew, 218, 293, 296, 333
Gertz, Elmer, 200-201
Gibson, Mel, 347
Giddings, Douglas, 400
Ginder, Richard, 123
Gingrich, Newt, 339, 347, 361, 387, 414, 425
Goehring, Cliff, 351, 357
Goldstein, Bernard, 223
Goldwater, Barry, 61, 66, 68, 109, 119, 147, 157, 174, 245
Golitsyn, Anatoliy, 291, 318
Gomez, Christian, 425, 444
Goode, Virgil, 362
Goodling, Bill, 245
Gorbachev, Mikhail, 291, 314, 323-324, 376-377
Gordon, Rosalie, 94, 115
Gore, Al, 358, 371, 389, 397
Gow, Tom, 314, 322, 351, 362, 372, 385
Graham, Katharine, 315
Gramsci, Antonio, 362, 367
Gravel, Mike, 271
Greaves, Percy, 224
Grede, Wm. J., 39, 136, 195, 292-293, 296
Greenley, Larry, 362, 394, 415, 445, 455
Griffin, G. Edward, 19, 96, 153, 161, 163, 233
Grigg, William Norman, 340
Guidry, Bill, 278, 287, 298
Gumaer, David, 162, 207, 209-211
Gurney, Edward, 200
Gutierrez, Alberto Ostria, 115
Haass, Richard N., 394
Hahn, Bill, 405, 423, 425
Haig, Alexander, 314
Haley, J. Evetts 126, 147
Hall, Gus, 163
Halperin, Morton, 335
Hamilton, Grace, 225
Hammarskjold, Dag, 63
Handy, Gary, 252, 277
Harrington, John, 147
Harrington, Michael, 372
Harvey, Paul, 110
Harwood, Richard, 8, 12
Hastert, Dennis, 361
Hatfield, Mark, 82
Hayes, Lee, 190, 209, 211
Healey, Dorothy, 94
Hecke, Randy Van, 244
Hefley, James, 269, 341
Hefley, Marti, 269, 341
Heinsohn, A. G., 66, 108
Helm, Mary, 218
Helms, Jesse, 310, 347
Hempstone, Smith, 331
Herger, Wally, 245
Herter, Christian, 97
Hesburgh, Theodore, 315
Hiestand, Edgar, 99
Highsmith, William, 194

Hightower, 267
Hill, Tom and Kay, 437
Hill, Thomas, N. 59, 284, 290
Hills, Carla, 398
Hiss, Alger, 32, 115, 258, 329
Hitler, Adolph, 121, 226, 288, 377
Hoar, Bill, 274, 299
Hogan, Jim, 243-244
Holmes, Lola Belle, 161
Hoover, J. Edgar 88, 107, 123, 177, 203, 218, 336, 435
Horner, Christopher, 401
House, Edward Mandell, 361, 413, 431
Hoyer, Steny, 328
Huang, John, 354
Huck, Susan, 219
Huddleston, Sisley, 115
Humphries, Sally, 280
Hunt, Nelson Bunker, 275, 293
Hunter, Edward, 86, 125, 241
Huntley, Chet, 154
Hurley, Patricia, 267
Hurtig, Mel, 397-398
Hussein, Saddam, 4, 321, 378
Hyde, Douglas, 311
Hyde, Henry 404
Ingraham, Jane, 323, 351
Inhofe, James, 333, 444
Jackson, Jesse, 293
Jasper, William F., 305, 308, 311, 314, 328-332, 337, 339, 342, 345-346, 350-353, 356, 368, 372-376, 384, 388, 396, 400, 405, 412, 426, 420, 425, 438, 455, 457
Javits, Jacob 82
Johnson, Manning, 63, 126
Johnson, Lyndon B., 129, 157, 193
Jordan, George Racey, 114, 349
Kai-shek, Chiang, 32, 35, 205, 369, 463
Katshick, Madame Chang, 32
Kaufman, Irving 245
Keller, James, 113
Kelly, Clarence, 226
Kennedy, John F., 7, 69, 111, 118, 129, 141, 145, 148, 179, 233
Kennedy, Robert, 288
Kennedy, Ted, 254, 268
Kent, William, R. 40
Kerry, John, 384, 446, 449
Ketchel, Melvin, 194
Keynes, John Maynard, 222
Khrushchev, Nikita, 37, 47, 58, 255
Ki-moon, Ban, 399
Kimmel, Husband, 351
King, Larry, 3
King, Martin Luther, 111, 127, 146, 160-162, 164, 177, 192, 202, 218, 266, 268, 287, 293
King, Steve, 437
Kirk, Gerald, 161, 209, 211
Kirk, Ron, 441
Kirk, Russell, 110, 119
Kissinger, Henry 228, 238, 253, 269, 314
Knight, Granville, 66

Index Of Persons

Knowland, William, 35, 464
Koch, Charles, 191
Koch, Fred, 40, 136, 191
Kohlberg, Alfred, 61, 66, 68
Kolbe, Jim, 327
Kopechne, Mary Jo, 268
Krock, Arthur, 157
Krupsak, Mary Anne, 234
Kubek, Anthony, 110
Kuchel, Thomas, 82
Lacy, Sterling, 309
Laden, Osama bin, 353
LaHaye, Tim, 60
Lake, Anthony, 350
Lambro, Donald, 273
Land, Richard D., 400
Lane, Arthur Bliss, 46, 114, 350
Langer, William, 446
Langguth, Jack 130
Lanz, Pedro Diaz, 126
LaPierre, Wayne, 384
Larson, Arthur, 155-156, 175
Lattimore, Owen, 32
Lausche, Frank, 35
Leavitt, Mike, 345
Lee, Robert W., 183, 290
Lehman, John, 291
LeMay, Curtis, 213
Lenin, Vladimir, 46, 227, 423, 432, 438
Lewinsky, Monica, 354
Lewis Jr., Fulton, 119
Lewis, Clyde, 138, 268, 293
Lincoln Rockwell, George, 226
Lincoln, Abraham, 11-12
Linda, Tomsanqa, 319
Lindsay, John, 173
Lindzen, Richard, 397
Linowitz, Sol, 154
Lippmann, Walter, 202, 253
Littell, Franklin, 176, 184
Livingston, Robert, 361
Lodge, Henry Cabot 148
Loeffler, Jim, 195
Lord, Winston, 278
Love, Robert, 190-191
Lovestone, Jay, 413
Lowman, Myers, 125
Lucier, James, 111, 185, 350
Luers, William, 396
Lugar, Richard, 320, 437
Lumumba, Patrice, 117
Mabley, Jack 72, 83, 85, 231
Mack, Richard, 434
Maddox, Lester, 194
Madison, James, 90, 415
Mahoney, Patrick, 267
Mandela, Nelson, 319
Manion, Clarence, 66, 110, 138, 176
Mann, C.O. "Buck", 207
Mansfield, Mike, 82
Marshall, George C., 113
Marshall, Thurgood, 202
Martin, Joseph, 31

Martin, Malachi, 353
Martin, Rose L., 177
Marx, Karl, 231, 431, 445, 452
Masland, Frank, 66
Mass, Warren, 233, 368, 373, 376, 380, 390
Matthews, J. B. 66, 114
Mauney, Mal, 219
Maynes, William, 320
McCain, John, 410
McCarthy, Joseph, 63, 104, 113, 133, 181, 205, 350, 369
McDonald, Harold 263, 289
McDonald, Kathryn, 296
McDonald, Larry, 137-138, 193-194, 203, 229, 238, 254, 259, 263, 266, 268-270, 289-293, 296, 304, 308, 322-323, 333, 341, 375-376, 380, 400, 425
McGee, Gale, 251
McGehee, Frank, 125
McGovern, George, 219
McGovern, James, 367
McGrath, H. Read, 324
McHugh, James, 198
McIlhany, William, 153, 267, 273
McKesson, Roy, 296
McKesson, Sandy, 296
McKinney, Harold 125
McManus, John, 135, 258, 260, 408
McMillan, W. B., 39, 51
McNamara, Robert, 111, 148, 179
McVeigh, Timothy, 342
Mehrten, Joe, 279, 286, 291-292, 299
Mencken, H. L., 233
Menjou, Adolphe, 66, 87
Meyer, Frank, 165, 167
Meyner, Helen 243
Michaels, Patrick, 332, 389
Mikolajczyk, Stanislaw, 35
Miller, William, 334
Millett, Lewis, 267
Mindszenty, József Cardinal, 369
Mitchell, John, 223
Monckton, Christopher, 421
Mondale, Walter, 254
Moore, Roy, 456
Moore, Thomas Gale, 321
Moorer, Thomas, 362
Morgan, William, 181
Morrison, Chester, 105
Mosk, Stanley, 99
Mugabe, Robert, 269
Murphy, Patrick, 233
Mustapha, Si, 62
Mustin, Lloyd, 243
Myrdal, Gunnar, 94
Napolitano, Andrew, 416
Nary, William, 322
Nehru, Jawaharlal, 110
Nelson, Steve, 94
New, Michael, 342
Newman, Alex, 420, 437, 443
Nixon, Richard, 69, 97, 206, 217, 219, 223-224, 226, 228, 323

Nocera, Joseph, 366
Nolte, Cliff, 267
Norman, Jose, 126
North, Oliver, 308
Nutter, John, 346
O'Connor, Sandra Day, 367, 381
O'Neill, Thomas "Tip", 270
Obama, Barack, 186, 410
Ober, Richard, 81
Ohlson, Martin, 425
Oliver, Revilo, P. 40, 176
Ondre, Mike, 227
Orwell, George, 288
Oswald, Lee Harvey, 129, 141, 145
Paar, Jack 89
Parker, Cola, 66
Pastor, Robert, 390, 398, 439
Patterson, Leonard, 67-68, 161, 163
Patton Jr., George, 287
Paul, Rand, 455
Paul, Ron, 42, 351, 359, 361, 373, 396, 403, 406, 408-409, 412, 431, 447
Paxton, Floyd, 184
Pearson, Drew, 146, 177
Pegler, Westbrook, 111
Pelosi, Nancy, 417
Pence, Mike, 381
Pepper, John, 160
Perkins, Fred, 125
Perloff, James, 310
Perot, H. Ross, 329
Pesta, Duke, 438
Peterson, Jesse Lee, 437
Petro, Sylvester, 115
Pettengill, Samuel, 61
Pew, J. Howard, 275
Phelps, M. T., 68
Philbrick, Herbert 66
Phillips, Howard 258, 396
Pius XI, 198
Pogany-Pepper, Joseph, 160
Poole, Elisha, 293
Potter, Harry 368
Powell, Colin, 14, 372
Powell, Jackye 428
Powers, Gary, 67
Probert (Welch), Marian, 21, 133
Purdy, Darvin, 278
Putnam, George, 185
Quayle, Dan, 432
Quigley, Carroll, 7, 12, 241, 330, 410
Quinn, LaRita, 125
Rafferty, Max, 248
Ramos, Ignacio 399
Rarick, John, 184
Ray, Dixy Lee, 333
Reagan, Ronald, 271, 277, 302, 309, 367
Reece, Carroll, 434
Reeder, Bob, 237
Regan, Donald, 273
Reisman, George, 412
Reno, Janet, 358
Reuther, Walter, 175, 202

469

INDEX OF PERSONS

Rhee, Syngman, 32, 35
Ribicoff, Abraham, 272
Rice, Charles, 248
Rice, Condoleezza, 372, 388
Richardson, Bill, 328
Richstein, Richard, 322
Riddell, Kelly, 455
Rivers, Mendel, 95
Robertson, Pat, 285
Robison, John, 181, 201, 387
Rock, Johnson Holy, 222
Rockefeller, David, 148, 228, 239, 254, 263, 269, 333, 376-377, 406
Rockefeller, Nelson, 127, 151, 153, 224, 227-228, 231, 234, 323
Rodriquez, Michael, 347
Roemer, David, 59
Rogers, Mike, 447
Romney, George, 123
Rooks, Eugene, 222
Roosevelt, Edith Kermit, 7, 12
Roosevelt, Theodore, 7
Root, E. Merrill, 110, 125, 198
Roper, Elmo, 432
Ros-Lehtinen, Ileana 428
Rostow, Walt W., 406
Rousseau, John Jacques, 185
Rousselot, John, 99, 122, 125, 155, 168, 183, 208
Rubin, Isadore 198
Ruby, Jack 129
Ruckel, Walter, 293
Rueda, Enrique, 284
Rumsfeld, Donald, 372
Rusk, Dean, 148, 179
Rust, Zad, 214
Ruthenburg, Louis, 40
Safire, William, 292
Salazar, Antonio, 33
Schlafly, Phyllis, 147, 218, 397, 439
Schmitz, Glenn, 293
Schmitz, John, 195, 208, 219
Schneider, James J., 346
Schuyler, George, 161, 170
Schwartz, Bernard, 354
Schwarz, Fred, 69
Schwarzenegger, Arnold, 387
Scott, Fitzhugh, 40
Scott, Robert E. Lee, 209, 211
Seko, Mobutu Sese, 118
Sennholz, Hans 110, 170
Sessions, Jeff, 457
Sevier, Nelson, 194
Shaack, Michael, 201
Shams, Abdul, 309
Shannon, Thomas, 398
Shifrin, Avraham, 285
Shippers, David, 369
Shipstead, Henrik 446
Short, Walter, 351
Show, Eric, 293, 298-299
Shultz, George, 273, 295, 398

Shurtleff, Hal, 401, 404, 416
Simpson, Colin, 232
Simpson, James, 66
Sitarz, Daniel, 429
Skousen, Cleon, 126, 172, 241
Smedley, Agnes, 32
Smith, Charlie, 209, 211, 213
Smith, G. Vance, 260, 314, 390
Smith, Robin, 412
Smoot, Dan, 57, 63, 95, 106, 116, 125, 179, 214-215, 224, 226, 239, 273, 293
Snyder, Kent, 396
Sobran, Joseph, 360, 429
Solis, Willy, 296
Solomon, John, 317
Somoza, Anastasio, 270, 309
Sorge, Richard, 114
Soros, George, 347, 455
Sotomayor, Sonia, 415
Soustelle, Jacques 58
Souter, David, 415
Stang, Alan, 111, 160-161, 163, 170, 186, 200, 208-211, 219, 221, 223, 232, 237, 268, 273-274, 281, 292, 369
Stanley, Scott, 110, 170, 258, 290, 293
Stanmeyer, William, 249
Stark, Pete, 428
Steiger, 186
Stennis, John, 122, 221
Stewart, David, 129, 141
Stewart, Maxwell, 32
Stockman, David, 273
Stoddard, Robert, 40, 135, 138, 293
Stone, Charles, B. 66
Stone, Willis, 128
Stormer, John, 147, 170
Strong, Maurice, 377
Sturdza, Michel, 214, 268
Sukarno, Achmed, 166
Sutton, Antony, 225, 234, 239, 308
Swain, Carol, 437
Sweezy, Paul, 94
Swigert, Ernest G., 39
Symms, Steve, 269
Taft, Robert, 31, 63, 205, 368
Talbott, Strobe, 368
Tansill, Charles T., 170
Taylor, Gene, 362
Teeter, Robert, 432
Templeton, Garry, 298
Terrell, Rebecca, 444
Terzi, Lionel, 416
Tew, Bliss, 414
Thant, U, 111, 399
Tharoor, Shashi, 396
Thatcher, Margaret, 421
Thomas, Clarence, 323
Thompson, Arthur R., ii, 265, 390
Thomson, Meldrim, 224, 234, 242, 252, 293
Thurmond, Mark, 298
Tijerina, Reies, 186, 223, 272
Tito, Josip Broz, 110, 119

Todt, George, 130
Toft, Jim, 357, 376-377, 379-380
Tribe, Lawrence, 443
Trie, Charlie, 354
Trotsky, Leon, 177
Truman, Harry S., 7, 31, 138
Tse-tung, Mao, 32, 37, 69, 463
Tshombe, Moise, 117
Tung, Lieutenant, 463
Utt, James, 105, 154, 174
Van Gorder, Dan P., 177
Vandel Heuvel, Williams, 396
Vanderbilt, Frederick, 32
Vincent, John Carter, 32
Voltaire (Arouet), 185
Voroshilov, Klimenti, 47
Wallace, George, 69, 213, 219
Ward, Charlie, 416
Ward, Harry 176, 202, 253
Warren, Earl, 93, 95-96, 107-108, 122, 126, 129, 139, 146-147, 189, 193-194, 228
Wasem, Cliff, 437
Wasem, Dorothy, 437
Wasem, Katie, 437
Washington, George, 38, 455
Waters, Larry O., 390
Webster, Kip, 419
Wedemeyer, Albert C., 35
Weinberger, Caspar, 273
Weishaupt, Adam, 185, 207
Welch III, Robert H., 390
Welch, Hillard W. 390
Welch, James O., 21, 23, 89, 134
Welch, Robert, 1-3, 8, 11, 13-21, 25, 37-40, 46, 51, 54, 59, 86, 89, 91, 93, 99, 103, 106, 113, 120-121, 125, 130, 132-138, 140, 153, 156, 165, 167, 177, 184-186, 198, 200, 213, 233, 238, 255-257, 259, 268, 283-284, 289, 291-293, 297, 299, 301, 304, 309, 334, 336, 341, 345, 349, 359, 365, 369, 377, 390, 396, 409, 427, 435, 449, 459-460, 463, 466
Wells, Betty, 225
Werdel, Thomas, 100
Westerfield, Rex, 162, 184, 194, 200, 221
Wiggins, Alan, 298
Williams, Hosea 162
Williams, Walter, 284
Willoughby, Charles, 114
Wilson, Woodrow, 90, 362
Wirt, William, 181, 349
Wirth, Tim, 318
Wolfowitz, Paul, 372
Wolverton, Joe, 444, 450
Wood, Wallis "Chip", 1
Woodbury, David, 194
Woods, Tom, 389, 393
Yearling, Freeman, 161
Young, Stephen, 82, 104
Zeller, Al, 416
Zhou, Houlin 453
Ziyang, Zhao, 296

Books

by John F. McManus

An Overview of Our World (1971). The text of the soundtrack for a lengthy filmstrip program of that same name, it provides commentary about political and economics systems, an analysis of the 200-year-old Conspiracy seeking world domination, and how to combat it while preserving freedom. (60 pages)

The Insiders, Architects of the New World Order (Five editions, 1979 to 2004). Separate analyses of the Carter, Reagan, Bush I, Clinton, and Bush II administrations, each of which was dominated by members of the Council on Foreign Relations, the Trilateral Commission, Rhodes Scholar program, Bilderberger Movement, and related Insider groups. Each administration is shown to have worked to build a tyrannical New World Order. (Fifth Edition 205 pages)

Financial Terrorism: Hijacking America Under the Threat of Bankruptcy (1993). A current and historical discussion of economics and the threat to our nation's independence caused by turning away from sound principles and allowing Marxism and the Federal Reserve to direct American policy. Supplies definitions of money and inflation including what America's founders thought about fiat money and debt. (278 pages)

Changing Commands: The Betrayal of America's Military (1995). An exposure of plans to convert America's military from a defender of the nation to an enforcer of a New World Order under the United Nations. Contains opposition to internal changes in the makeup of our nation's armed forces. (233 pages)

William F. Buckley, Jr.: Pied Piper for the Establishment. (2002) Shows that Mr. Buckley, far from being a leader of principled conservative values, spent his long career undermining fellow conservatives, adopting liberal causes, and betraying the nation he served during his five-plus decades of notoriety. (259 pages)

AN INVITATION!

Over the years, many individuals have contacted The John Birch Society to ask for introductory information about the organization and its work. Society staff personnel are always pleased to hear from anyone.

Perhaps you are one who, after reading this book, would like to know more about the organization than has been provided. Or, you might have questions about what you have read.

If so, you will be pleased to know that additional information about the Society and its affiliated magazine, The New American, is available for the asking. Contact any one of the addresses given below and ask for free information.

Should you find the contents of this book more than just a compilation of interesting information and, instead, an urging to become involved in the Society's work, ask for information about how to become a member.

The Society can be reached as follows:

Via Mail: 770 Westhill Blvd., Appleton, WI 54912

Via Telephone: 920-749-3780 or 1-800-JBS- USA1

Via Internet: JBS.org